# OpenShift Cookbook

Over 100 hands-on recipes that will help you create,
deploy, manage, and scale OpenShift applications

**Shekhar Gulati**

[PACKT] open source*
PUBLISHING   community experience distilled

BIRMINGHAM - MUMBAI

# OpenShift Cookbook

First published: October 2014

Production reference: 1221014

Published by Packt Publishing Ltd.
Livery Place
35 Livery Street
Birmingham B3 2PB, UK.

ISBN 978-1-78398-120-5

www.packtpub.com

Cover image by Gagandeep Sharma (er.gagansharma@gmail.com)

# Credits

**Author**

Shekhar Gulati

**Reviewers**

Troy Dawson

Andrea Mostosi

Rahul Sharma

**Acquisition Editor**

Richard Harvey

**Content Development Editor**

Neil Alexander

**Technical Editors**

Sebastian Rodrigues

Gaurav Thingalaya

**Copy Editors**

Sarang Chari

Deepa Nambiar

Adithi Shetty

**Project Coordinator**

Sageer Parkar

**Proofreaders**

Maria Gould

Lauren E. Harkins

Jonathan Todd

**Indexer**

Tejal Soni

**Production Coordinators**

Aparna Bhagat

Shantanu N. Zagade

**Cover Work**

Aparna Bhagat

# About the Author

**Shekhar Gulati** is a developer and OpenShift evangelist working with Red Hat. He has been evangelizing about OpenShift for the last 2 years. He regularly speaks at various conferences and user groups around the world to spread the goodness of OpenShift. He regularly blogs on the OpenShift official blog and has written more than 50 blogs on OpenShift. Shekhar has also written many technical articles for IBM developerWorks, Developer.com, and Javalobby.

# About the Reviewers

**Troy Dawson** is most famous as one of the two original developers of Scientific Linux. His work on Scientific Linux first began during his 18 years at Fermilab. He started out at Fermilab running and operating the Tevatron accelerator, but has shifted to computers for the last 12 years. Troy not only worked as a system administrator, but also helped create the operating systems he administered. He was half of the team that built and maintained Fermi Linux. That same team later created Scientific Linux for labs and universities outside of Fermilab.

In 2011, Troy stepped out of the Scientific Linux spotlight and started working behind the scenes on the OpenShift project. He began work on OpenShift during the first year of its creation. Troy is currently on the OpenShift Online Operations team, but his packaging and debugging work spans the entire project.

**Andrea Mostosi** is a technology enthusiast. He has been an innovation lover since he was a child. He began his professional career in 2003 and worked on several projects, playing almost every role in the computer science environment. He is currently the CTO of The Fool, a company that tries to make sense of web and social data.

I would like to thank my geek friends: Simone M., Daniele V., Luca T., Luigi P., Michele N., Luca O., Luca B., Diego C., and Fabio B. They are the smartest people I know, and comparing myself to them has always pushed me to do better.

**Rahul Sharma** is a senior developer with Mettl. He has 9 years of experience in building and designing applications on Java/J2EE platforms. He loves to develop open source projects, and has contributed to a variety of them, such as HDT, Crunch, Provisionr, and so on. He often shares his knowledge at http://devlearnings.wordpress.com/.

# www.PacktPub.com

## Support files, eBooks, discount offers, and more

You might want to visit www.PacktPub.com for support files and downloads related to your book.

Did you know that Packt offers eBook versions of every book published, with PDF and ePub files available? You can upgrade to the eBook version at www.PacktPub.com and as a print book customer, you are entitled to a discount on the eBook copy. Get in touch with us at service@packtpub.com for more details.

At www.PacktPub.com, you can also read a collection of free technical articles, sign up for a range of free newsletters and receive exclusive discounts and offers on Packt books and eBooks.

![PACKTLIB logo]

http://PacktLib.PacktPub.com

Do you need instant solutions to your IT questions? PacktLib is Packt's online digital book library. Here, you can access, read and search across Packt's entire library of books.

## Why Subscribe?

- Fully searchable across every book published by Packt
- Copy and paste, print and bookmark content
- On demand and accessible via web browser

## Free Access for Packt account holders

If you have an account with Packt at www.PacktPub.com, you can use this to access PacktLib today and view nine entirely free books. Simply use your login credentials for immediate access.

# Table of Contents

# Preface

OpenShift is an open source, polyglot, and scalable Platform as a Service (PaaS) from Red Hat. At the time of writing this, OpenShift officially supports the Java, Ruby, Python, Node.js, PHP, and Perl programming language runtimes, along with the MySQL, PostgreSQL, and MongoDB databases. It also offers Jenkins CI, RockMongo, Mongo Monitoring Service agent, phpMyAdmin, and a lot of other features. OpenShift, being extensible in nature, allows developers to extend it by adding support for runtimes, databases, and other services, which OpenShift currently does not support. Developers can work with OpenShift using command-line tools, IDE integrations, or a web console. OpenShift manages application deployment using a popular version control system named Git. The OpenShift PaaS has made cloud-enabled web application development an easy process. It is straightforward to deploy existing or new applications on OpenShift. Many developers around the world are making use of the OpenShift capabilities to develop and deploy faster.

Getting started with OpenShift is easy, but as is the case with many of the tools we use to develop web applications, it can take time to appreciate all the capabilities of OpenShift. The OpenShift platform and its client tools are full of features you might never have known to wish for. Once you know about them, they can make you more productive and help in writing scalable web applications.

*OpenShift Cookbook* presents over 100 recipes written in a simple and easy-to-understand manner. It will walk you through a number of recipes, showcasing the OpenShift features and demonstrating how to deploy a particular technology or framework on it. You can quickly learn and start deploying applications on OpenShift immediately. The cookbook also covers topics such as horizontal scaling and application logging and monitoring. The recipes covered address the common, everyday problems required to effectively run applications on OpenShift. The reader is assumed to be familiar with the PaaS and cloud computing concepts. The book does not need to be read from cover to cover, which enables the reader to choose chapters and recipes that are of interest. *OpenShift Cookbook* is an easy read and is packed with practical recipes and helpful screenshots.

# What this book covers

*Chapter 1, Getting Started with OpenShift*, begins with an introduction to OpenShift and creating an OpenShift Online account. You will create your first OpenShift application using the web console and understand common OpenShift terminology, such as gears and cartridges. The web console is often the primary interface to OpenShift that developers use. It also discusses how to install the rhc OpenShift command-line tool and how to perform basic operations with it.

*Chapter 2, Managing Domains*, discusses the concept of domains and namespaces. You will learn how to perform operations, such as creating, renaming, viewing, and deleting on a domain. In addition, the chapter also covers the concept of membership, which enables team collaboration.

*Chapter 3, Creating and Managing Applications*, covers how to create applications using the rhc OpenShift command-line tool. The rhc command-line client is the most powerful way to interact with OpenShift. You will learn how to perform various application management operations, such as starting, stopping, cleaning, and deleting the application using rhc. It also discusses advanced OpenShift features, such as deployment tracking, rollback, configuring the binary file, and source code deployment. In addition, you will also learn how to use your own domain name for OpenShift applications.

*Chapter 4, Using MySQL with OpenShift Applications*, teaches readers how to use a MySQL database with their applications. It will also cover how to update the default MySQL configuration to meet the application needs.

*Chapter 5, Using PostgreSQL with OpenShift Applications*, presents a number of recipes that show you how to get started with the OpenShift PostgreSQL database cartridge. You will learn how to add and manage the PostgreSQL cartridge, take backups of a PostgreSQL database, list and install the PostgreSQL extensions, and use the EnterpriseDB PostgreSQL Cloud Database service with OpenShift applications.

*Chapter 6, Using MongoDB and Third-party Database Cartridges with OpenShift Applications*, presents a number of recipes that show you how to get started with the OpenShift MongoDB cartridge. You will also learn how to use downloadable cartridges for MariaDB and Remote Dictionary Server (Redis).

*Chapter 7, OpenShift for Java Developers*, covers how Java developers can effectively use OpenShift to develop and deploy Java applications. You will learn how to deploy Java EE 6 and Spring applications on OpenShift. OpenShift has first-class integration with various IDEs, so you will learn how to use Eclipse to develop and debug OpenShift applications.

*Chapter 8, OpenShift for Python Developers*, covers how Python developers can effectively use OpenShift to develop and deploy Python applications. This chapter will teach you how to develop Flask framework web applications on OpenShift. You will also learn how to manage application dependencies, access your application virtualenv, and use standalone WSGI servers, such as Gunicorn or Gevent.

*Chapter 9, OpenShift for Node.js Developers*, covers how to build Node.js applications with OpenShift. You will learn how to use the Express framework to build web applications. This chapter will also cover how to manage application dependencies using npm, working with web sockets, and using CoffeeScript with OpenShift Node.js applications.

*Chapter 10, Continuous Integration for OpenShift Applications*, teaches readers how to use continuous integration with their OpenShift applications. You will learn how to add the Jenkins cartridge to your application and customize a Jenkins job to meet your requirements. Also, this chapter covers how to install the Jenkins plugins, build projects hosted on GitHub, and define a custom Jenkins workflow for OpenShift applications.

*Chapter 11, Logging and Scaling Your OpenShift Applications*, consists of recipes that will help you work with application logs. You will learn how to create autoscalable applications. You will learn how to disable autoscaling and manually scale OpenShift applications using the rhc command-line tool.

*Appendix, Running OpenShift on a Virtual Machine*, explains how to run an instance of OpenShift in a virtualized environment.

# What you need for this book

All the recipes contain references to the required tools that are used in each recipe. It is expected that you are a web developer, well versed in your web framework. You should have working knowledge of Git and Bash. If you are a Java developer, you will need the latest version of Java and Eclipse. If you are a Python developer, you will need Python, virtualenv, and a text editor. If you are a Node.js developer, you will need Node.js and a text editor.

# Who this book is for

This book is aimed at readers interested in building their next big idea using OpenShift. The reader could be a web developer already using OpenShift or planning to use it in the future. The recipes provide the information you need to accomplish a broad range of tasks. It is expected that you are familiar with web development in a programming language that you wish to develop your web application in. For example, if you are a Java developer, then it is expected that you know the Java EE or Spring basics. This book will not cover the Java EE or Spring basics, but will cover how to deploy Java EE or Spring applications on OpenShift.

# Conventions

In this book, you will find a number of styles of text that distinguish between different kinds of information. Here are some examples of these styles, and an explanation of their meaning.

Code words in text, database table names, folder names, filenames, file extensions, pathnames, dummy URLs, user input, and Twitter handles are shown as follows: "Instead of `osbook`, the message would refer to your domain name."

A block of code is set as follows:

```
[remote "origin"]
  url = ssh://52bbf209e0b8cd707000018a@myapp-
osbook.rhcloud.com/~/git/blog.git/
  fetch = +refs/heads/*:refs/remotes/origin/*
```

Any command-line input or output is written as follows:

```
$ ssh 52b823b34382ec52670003f6@blog-osbook.rhcloud.com ls
app-deployments
app-root
git
mysql
php
phpmyadmin
```

**New terms** and **important words** are shown in bold. Words that you see on the screen, in menus or dialog boxes for example, appear in the text like this: "Click on the **I Accept** button and the browser will redirect to the getting started web page."

> Warnings or important notes appear in a box like this.

> Tips and tricks appear like this.

# Reader feedback

Feedback from our readers is always welcome. Let us know what you think about this book—what you liked or may have disliked. Reader feedback is important for us to develop titles that you really get the most out of.

To send us general feedback, simply send an e-mail to feedback@packtpub.com, and mention the book title through the subject of your message.

If there is a topic that you have expertise in and you are interested in either writing or contributing to a book, see our author guide on www.packtpub.com/authors.

# Customer support

Now that you are the proud owner of a Packt book, we have a number of things to help you to get the most from your purchase.

## Downloading the example code

You can download the example code files for all Packt books you have purchased from your account at `http://www.packtpub.com`. If you purchased this book elsewhere, you can visit `http://www.packtpub.com/support` and register to have the files e-mailed directly to you.

## Errata

Although we have taken every care to ensure the accuracy of our content, mistakes do happen. If you find a mistake in one of our books—maybe a mistake in the text or the code—we would be grateful if you would report this to us. By doing so, you can save other readers from frustration and help us improve subsequent versions of this book. If you find any errata, please report them by visiting `http://www.packtpub.com/support`, selecting your book, clicking on the **errata submission form** link, and entering the details of your errata. Once your errata are verified, your submission will be accepted and the errata will be uploaded to our website, or added to any list of existing errata, under the Errata section of that title.

## Piracy

Piracy of copyright material on the Internet is an ongoing problem across all media. At Packt, we take the protection of our copyright and licenses very seriously. If you come across any illegal copies of our works, in any form, on the Internet, please provide us with the location address or website name immediately so that we can pursue a remedy.

Please contact us at `copyright@packtpub.com` with a link to the suspected pirated material.

We appreciate your help in protecting our authors, and our ability to bring you valuable content.

## Questions

You can contact us at `questions@packtpub.com` if you are having a problem with any aspect of the book, and we will do our best to address it.

# 1
# Getting Started with OpenShift

This chapter presents a number of recipes that show you how to get started with OpenShift using the web console and `rhc` command-line client. You will learn how to host your own WordPress blog with a button click, make source code changes and deploy them, and perform basic operations with the `rhc` command-line client. The specific recipes of this chapter are:

- ▸ Creating an OpenShift Online account
- ▸ Creating OpenShift domains using the web console
- ▸ Creating a WordPress application using the web console
- ▸ Uploading SSH keys using the web console
- ▸ Working with the SSH key passphrases
- ▸ Cloning the application to the local machine
- ▸ Deploying your first change
- ▸ Checking the application's gear quota and limits
- ▸ Installing the OpenShift rhc command-line client
- ▸ Setting up an OpenShift account using rhc
- ▸ Enabling the autocomplete feature in an rhc command-line client
- ▸ Viewing the account details using rhc
- ▸ Specifying a different OpenShift server hostname
- ▸ Updating rhc

# A brief introduction into OpenShift

A few years ago, I wanted to write a web application that would process a stream of tweets about a movie and then output the overall sentiment about it. This would help me decide whether I should watch a movie or not. So, I researched for a hosting provider and found out that I could rent a few virtual machines from Amazon to host my web application. This was my entry into the world of cloud computing. Cloud computing allows access to a shared pool of computing (both hardware and software) resources available as a service over the network, which is pay per use, has an elastic nature (that is, can be scaled up and down), and is available on demand. It has three delivery models:

> ▸ **Infrastructure as a Service (IaaS)**: This is the most fundamental delivery model where a user can provision compute, storage, and other resources such as network to run an application, but the user has to install and manage the application stack required to run the application. Examples of IaaS include Amazon EC2, Google Compute Engine, and Rackspace.

> ▸ **Platform as a Service (PaaS)**: PaaS provides an application development platform to help developers build their applications using the runtimes, tools, libraries, and services provided by the platform provider. Examples of PaaS include OpenShift, Cloud Foundry, and Heroku.

> ▸ **Software as a Service (SaaS)**: SaaS is a set of applications (or software) that run on the cloud and are available as a service. Examples of SaaS include Google Apps and Microsoft Office 365.

As a developer, I liked the concept of PaaS, as it enabled me to use my skillset to focus only on the application code and let someone else worry about managing the application stack and infrastructure for me.

OpenShift is an open source, a polyglot, and a scalable PaaS from Red Hat. At the time of writing this book, OpenShift officially supports the Java, Ruby, Python, Node.js, PHP, and Perl programming language runtimes, along with MySQL, PostgreSQL, and MongoDB databases, and a lot of other features. Along with all the supported services, OpenShift users can also leverage marketplace (`https://marketplace.openshift.com/home`) to try and use other cloud services managed by various partners. The services supported by the partners vary from databases such as ElephantSQL scalable PostgreSQL as a Service to SendGrid's Email as a Service.

OpenShift is an umbrella under which three subprojects coexist. These three subprojects differ in the way they deliver the OpenShift technology to the users, developers, and community members. Each of the subprojects is described as follows:

- **OpenShift Origin**: OpenShift Origin is the open sourced, Apache License 2.0, community-supported version of OpenShift. It is the upstream feeder project to both OpenShift Online and OpenShift Enterprise. The project is available on GitHub at `https://github.com/openshift`.

- **OpenShift Online**: OpenShift Online is the public-managed version of OpenShift. It runs on top of Amazon EC2 and uses a hardened and stabilized version of OpenShift Origin. Every OpenShift Online user is entitled to a free plan. The free plan gives users access to three small instances with 512 MB RAM and 1 GB of disk space. OpenShift Online is also available as commercial offering via Bronze and Silver plans. The commercial plans allow users to get more resources, storage, and Red Hat professional support. You can learn about the OpenShift Online pricing at `https://www.openshift.com/products/pricing`.

- **OpenShift Enterprise**: OpenShift Enterprise is a Red Hat fully supported, private PaaS solution, which can run on enterprise hardware. OpenShift Enterprise can help make enterprises more agile and meet their business application demands.

This book will focus mainly on OpenShift Online, but the recipes apply to all three.

As a developer, you can interact with OpenShift in the following four ways:

- **Web console**: This is the easiest way to get started with OpenShift, as it does not require you to install any software on your machine. You can log in to the web console and start creating applications. At the time of writing this book, the web console lacks all the features available in the command-line tool.

- **The rhc command line**: This is a command-line tool that interacts with OpenShift. It is available as a Ruby gem. It is the most powerful way to interact with OpenShift because it exposes all the OpenShift functionalities.

- **IDE Integration**: If you are a developer who likes to do most of the coding from within an IDE, then you will be happy to know that OpenShift has first class integration with various IDEs such as Eclipse, IntelliJ IDEA, Zend Studio, and Titanium Studio.

- **The REST API**: You can write your own client using the OpenShift REST API. You can use this API to write plugins for IDEs such as NetBeans or write another command-line client. You can read the REST API documentation at `https://access.redhat.com/knowledge/docs/en-US/OpenShift/2.0/html-single/REST_API_Guide/index.html`.

The important OpenShift components are shown in the following diagram:

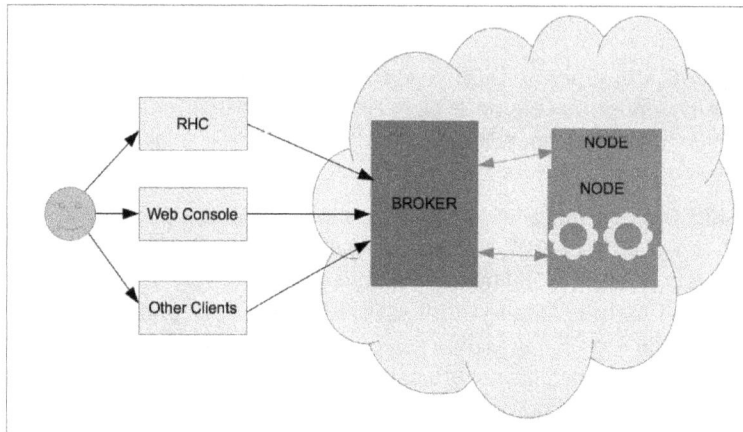

As shown in the preceding diagram, a developer interacts with OpenShift using one of the client interfaces, that is, the web console, `rhc` command-line client, or IDE support. OpenShift has the following three main components:

▸ **Broker**: All the clients interact with the broker using a well-defined REST interface exposed by the broker. The broker is responsible for all application management activities. It is a Ruby on Rails application that manages user logins, DNS management, and general application orchestration.

▸ **Node**: This is a set of RHEL instances that provides a multitenant environment for end user applications.

▸ **Gear**: A gear is a secure container that runs inside a node and host user applications. It is constrained by CPU, disk space, and memory.

> The broker and nodes use the ActiveMQ message queue to talk with each other. They both have the MCollective client installed on them to send instructions to each other.

Now that you know what OpenShift is and how you can work with it, let's kick off the first chapter. This chapter presents a number of recipes that gets you up to speed quickly by giving you information you need to create cloud applications using OpenShift. You will learn how to create your first OpenShift application using the web console, clone the application using Git, make your first source code change, and finally deploy that change to OpenShift. If this is the first time you are working with OpenShift, then you will be amazed by the speed at which you can create and deploy applications on OpenShift. This chapter will also cover how to install the `rhc` command-line client and perform some basic operations using it..

# Creating an OpenShift Online account

In this recipe, you will learn how to create an OpenShift Online account. You can sign up for an OpenShift Online account for free; all you need is a valid e-mail address.

## Getting ready

To create an OpenShift Online account, you need a web browser and a valid e-mail address.

## How to do it...

Follow these steps to create an OpenShift Online account:

1. Open a web browser and go to the sign-up page at `https://www.openshift.com/app/account/new`.

2. Enter the details required to create a new account and then submit the form.

3. After signing up, you will receive an e-mail in your inbox that contains the verification link. Click on the verification link to verify your e-mail address. This will redirect the browser to a web page, asking you to accept the legal terms to use OpenShift Online, as shown in the following screenshot:

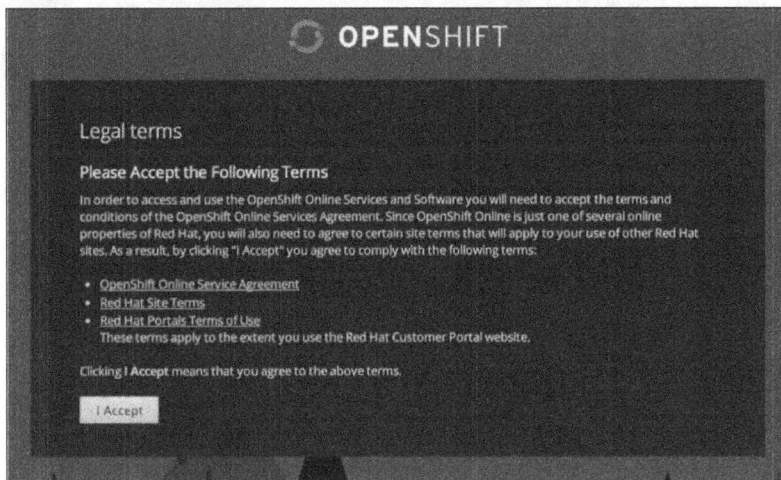

4. Click on the **I Accept** button and the browser will redirect to the getting started web page.

> If you do not receive a verification e-mail, make sure to check your Spam folder.

## How it works...

In this recipe, you learned how to create an OpenShift Online account. From a user's perspective, OpenShift Online is the easiest way to get started with OpenShift because you do not have to deploy and manage your own OpenShift installation.

When you sign up for OpenShift Online, you will be associated with a free plan. At the time of writing this, Red Hat gives every user three free gears on which to run their applications. A gear provides a resource-constrained container to run one or more cartridges. A cartridge provides the actual functionality required to run the application. OpenShift Online currently supports many cartridges such as JBoss, Tomcat, PHP, Ruby, Python, MongoDB, MySQL, and so on. Gear provides RAM and disk space to a cartridge. At the time of writing this book, each gear is 512 MB of RAM and 1 GB of disk space. A user can upgrade to the Bronze or Silver plan to get access to more and bigger resources. You can refer to the pricing web page at `https://www.openshift.com/products/pricing` for up to date information.

## See also

▶ The *Creating OpenShift domains using the web console* recipe
▶ The *Creating a WordPress application using the web console* recipe

# Creating OpenShift domains using the web console

After creating the OpenShift Online account, the first step is to create a domain. A domain or namespace is a logical container for applications. It forms parts of an application URL and is unique to an account. In this recipe, you will learn how to create a domain using the web console.

## Getting ready

Open the OpenShift Online login page at `https://openshift.redhat.com/app/login` in your favorite web browser and then sign in using your OpenShift Online credentials.

## How to do it...

1. To create a domain or namespace, go to the account settings web page at `https://openshift.redhat.com/app/console/settings` and enter a unique name. A domain or namespace should be unique across all the users. This means that you can't use `osbook` as a domain name because the OpenShift account associated with this book uses `osbook`.

Click on the **Save** button to create a new domain, as shown in the following screenshot:

Settings

ⓘ   You need to set a namespace before you can create applications

Namespace

Your namespace is unique to your account and is the suffix of the public URLs we assign to your applications. See the User Guide for information about adding your own domain names to an application.

http://applicationname-   | Domain name | .rhcloud.com

Your domain name must be letters or numbers with no spaces or symbols.

Save

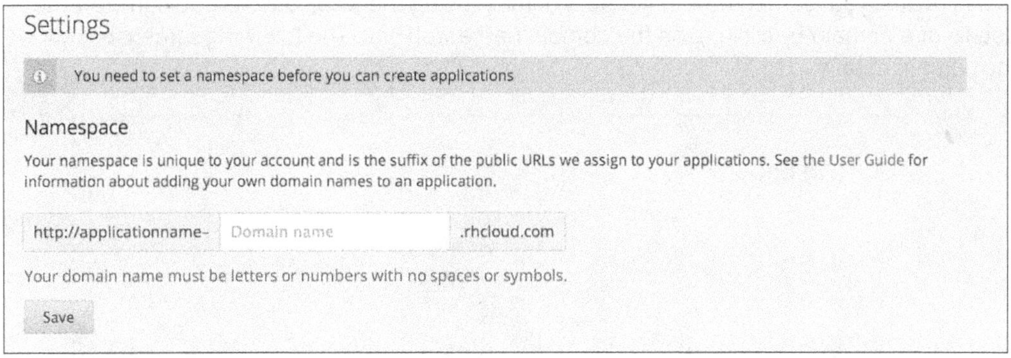

2.  After the domain is created, you will see a message, **The domain 'osbook' has been created**, on your screen. Instead of `osbook`, the message would refer to your domain name.

## How it works...

OpenShift requires you to have a domain before it can allow you to create applications. A domain represents a logical container for the applications under an OpenShift account. All the OpenShift applications must belong to a domain. It is unique across all OpenShift users and is a part of the application URL. For example, if your application name is `myapp` and your domain name is `osbook`, then your application URL will be `http://myapp-osbook.rhcloud.com`. A domain can contain as many as 16 alphanumeric characters and cannot have spaces or symbols. It is also sometimes called a namespace.

A user can join domains created by other OpenShift users. This allows users to work as a team. Depending on the OpenShift plan or configuration, a user will able to create more than one domain. The free plan does not allow a user to create more than one domain name, but you can still join other domains. We will discuss domains in detail in *Chapter 2, Managing Domains*.

You can see the created domains listed on the application settings web page at `https://openshift.redhat.com/app/console/settings`. This can be seen in the following screenshot:

Domains

See the User Guide for information about adding your own domain names to an application.

osbook                    0 applications              No other members

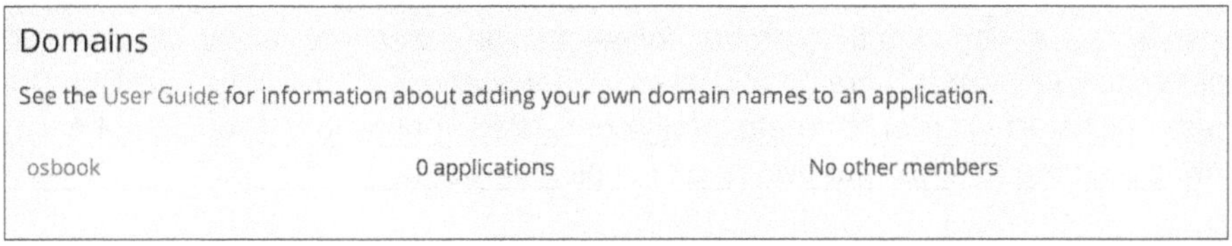

## There's more...

In this recipe, you learned how to create a domain using the web console. You can view the details of a domain by clicking on the domain name web link. The following screenshot shows the domain details:

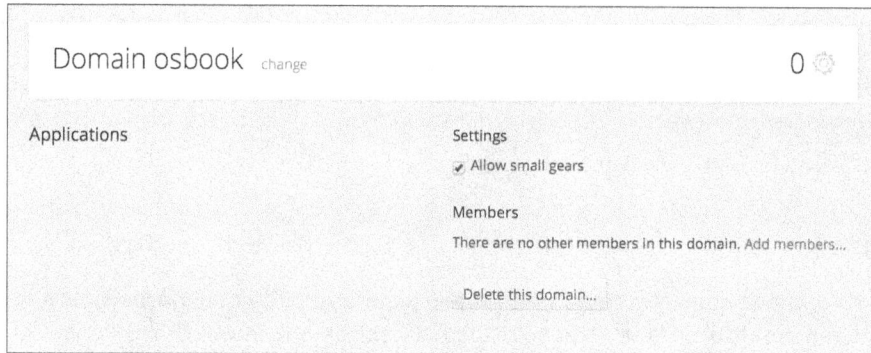

Domain osbook  *change*                                                    0 ⚙

Applications                          Settings
                                      ☑ Allow small gears

                                      Members
                                      There are no other members in this domain. Add members...

                                      Delete this domain...

In the preceding screenshot, you can see that there are no applications associated with this domain. As per the free plan configuration, you can only use small gears. If you uncheck the **Allow small gears** checkbox, then you will not be able to create any applications. You can also invite other users to join your domain by clicking on the **Add members...** web link. Team collaboration will be covered in detail in *Chapter 2, Managing Domains*. You can also delete a domain by clicking on the **Delete this domain...** button.

## See also

▶  The *Creating a domain using rhc* recipe in *Chapter 2, Managing Domains*

▶  The *Viewing domain details using rhc* recipe in *Chapter 2, Managing Domains*

▶  The *Adding an editor member to a domain using rhc* recipe in *Chapter 2, Managing Domains*

# Creating a WordPress application using the web console

In this recipe, you will create your first OpenShift application using the web console. The web console, as mentioned in the *Introduction* section, is a web interface to OpenShift that developers can use to quickly create and manage applications. You will use the OpenShift WordPress quickstart in order to create a fully configured application. If you do not have a blog, now is the time to have your own personal blog for free.

## Getting ready

Open the login web page at `https://openshift.redhat.com/app/login` in your favorite web browser and log in using your OpenShift credentials.

## How to do it...

Follow these steps to create a WordPress application using the web console:

1.  Go to the applications web page at `https://openshift.redhat.com/app/console/applications` and click on the **Create your first application now** web link.

2.  Under the **Instant App** section, click on the **WordPress 3.9** instant app. At the time of writing this book, the WordPress version is 3.9, as shown in the following screenshot:

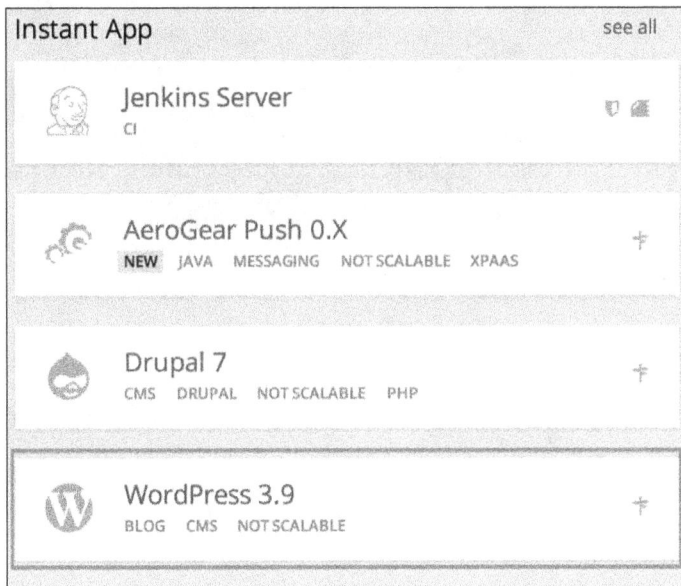

3. Enter a name for the blog and click on the **Create Application** button. I have used `blog` as the name of the WordPress application, as shown in the following screenshot:

| | |
|---|---|
| Based On | **WordPress 3.9 Quickstart** ✛ |
| | A semantic personal publishing platform written in PHP with a MySQL back end, focusing on aesthetics, web standards, and usability. Currently using version 3.9. |
| | The first time you access the app you'll be asked to set a username and password and give your blog a name. Be sure to track security updates from upstream. |
| | Learn more |
| | ☆ OpenShift maintained |
| | Does not receive automatic security updates |
| Public URL | http:// **blog** -osbook.rhcloud.com |
| | OpenShift will automatically register this domain name for your application. You can add your own domain name later. |
| Source Code | https://github.com/openshift    Branch/tag |
| | Your application will start with an exact copy of the code and configuration provided in this Git repository. OpenShift may expect certain files to exist in certain directories, which may require you to update your repository after creation. |
| Gears | **Small** |
| | Gears are the application containers running your code. For most applications, the small gear size provides plenty of resources. You can also upgrade your plan to get access to more gear sizes. |
| Cartridges | PHP 5.3 ⬍ and MySQL 5.1 ⬍ |
| | Applications are composed of cartridges - each of which exposes a service or capability to your code. All applications must have a web cartridge. |
| Scaling | No scaling ⬍ |
| | This application may require additional work to scale. Please see the application's documentation for more information. |
| | OpenShift automatically routes web requests to your web gear. If you allow your application to scale, we'll set up a load balancer and allocate more gears to handle traffic as you need it. |
| | Back    Create Application    +1 ⚙ |

4. After the application is created, you will be directed to a page that shows the MySQL connection details. You can view the newly created application details by clicking on **Continue to the application overview page**.

5. Your WordPress blog will now be running at `http://blog-{domain-name}.rhcloud.com/`. Replace `{domain-name}` with your OpenShift account domain name.

## How it works...

A quickstart is a preconfigured OpenShift application that provides a repeatable way to spin up an application with its source code and dependencies such as databases. You can view the list of actively maintained quickstarts at `https://www.openshift.com/quickstarts`. Note that the OpenShift team does not support these quickstarts. They are just to help you get your favorite project (mostly open source) running on OpenShift. In this recipe, you used WordPress quickstart to quickly scaffold a WordPress application. You selected the WordPress 3.x quickstart in the web console and gave it a name. An application name can contain 32 alphanumeric characters at most. The WordPress quickstart uses a public Git repository, which installs the WordPress application. It also defines the cartridges it will use. The WordPress quickstart uses the PHP 5.3 and MySQL 5.1 cartridges.

To create an application, click on the **Create Application** button. This will create an application container for us, called a gear, and set up all the required SELinux policies and cgroups configuration. OpenShift will also set up a private Git repository using the quickstart public Git repository. It will install the MySQL database on the application gear. The quickstart source code references the MySQL database using the environment variables. You will learn about OpenShift application details in *Chapter 3*, *Creating and Managing Applications*.

Finally, OpenShift will propagate the DNS to the outside world. The application will be accessible at `http://blog-{domain-name}.rhcloud.com/`. Replace the `{domain-name}` part with your own unique OpenShift domain name, sometimes called a namespace. Open the `http://blog-{domain-name}.rhcloud.com/` link in your favorite browser and set up your WordPress installation. After the setup, you will have your own WordPress blog and you can start blogging.

## There's more...

In this recipe, you learned how to create a WordPress application using the OpenShift web console. You can also view the application details by going to the **Applications** tab and then clicking on the application, as shown in the following screenshot:

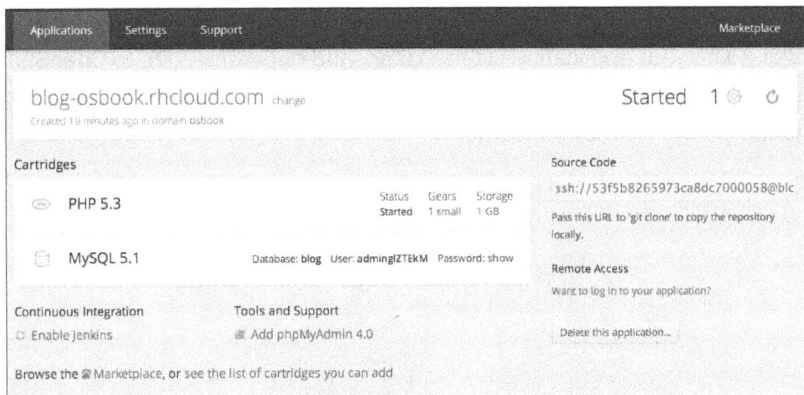

In the preceding screenshot, you can see the state of the application, that is, **Started**. You can restart the application by clicking on the restart button next to **Started**. The application uses the PHP 5.3 and MySQL 5.1 cartridges. To view the database password, you can click on the **show** web link. To add the phpMyAdmin 4.0 MySQL web client, click on the **Add phpMyAdmin 4.0** web link. Next, click on the **Add Cartridge** button to add the phpMyAdmin 4.0 cartridge.

The cartridge will be available at `https://blog-{domain-name}.rhcloud.com/phpmyadmin/`. The phpMyAdmin credentials are the same as the database credentials.

## See also

▸ The *Uploading SSH keys using the web console* recipe

▸ The *Cloning the application to the local machine* recipe

▸ The *Deploying your first change* recipe

# Uploading SSH keys using the web console

**Secure Shell** (**SSH**) is a network protocol that guarantees robust authentication, data encryption, and data integrity between two networked machines that connect over an insecure network. It uses the client-server architecture and transparently encrypts the data between the client and server. SSH clients communicate with SSH servers over encrypted network connections. There are plenty of free and commercial products available that implement the SSH protocol. SSH has various authentication mechanisms where OpenShift uses the public-private key pair authentication mechanism. Other SSH authentication methods such as password authentication and host-based authentication are beyond the scope of this book.

In this recipe, you will learn how to create a public-private key pair and upload the public key to your OpenShift account. OpenShift uses SSH for the following purposes:

▸ Providing a secure and encrypted connection between your machine and application gear

▸ Allowing remote access to your application gear

▸ Working with your application Git repository and deploying code to OpenShift

▸ Port forwarding, which allows users to connect to OpenShift services such as databases from their own machines

## Getting ready

To complete this recipe, you will need the OpenSSH SSH connectivity tools installed on your machine. These are very common as they come bundled with most Linux installations, Macintosh OS X, and almost all Unix-inspired operating systems. Microsoft Windows also has plenty of free and commercial SSH clients as mentioned at http://www.openssh.com/windows.html. Also, if you use PuTTy on your Windows machine, then you can refer to the official documentation at https://www.openshift.com/developers/install-and-setup-putty-ssh-client-for-windows.

To verify that the OpenSSH client tool is installed, run the following command:

```
$ ssh -V
OpenSSH_6.2p2, OpenSSL 1.0.1e-fips 11 Feb 2013
```

> The output of the preceding command will depend on your operating system and the OpenSSH version installed on your machine. If you get ssh: command not found, then the tools are not installed on your machine.
>
> This recipe will use the WordPress application created in the preceding recipe.

## How to do it...

Perform the following steps:

1. Run the ssh-keygen command to generate a new pair of SSH keys. The ssh-keygen command is one of the SSH tools installed by OpenSSH. This command will generate a key pair in the .ssh folder under the user's home directory:

   ```
   $ ssh-keygen -t rsa -b 2048 -C 'SSH keys to connect with
   OpenShift'
   ```

2. Go to the **Settings** web page at https://openshift.redhat.com/app/console/settings and paste the content of the public key. The public key is the key with the .pub extension. After pasting the public key content, click on the **save** button.

3. Go to the **Applications** web page at `https://openshift.redhat.com/app/console/applications` and click on the application for its details, as shown in the following screenshot:

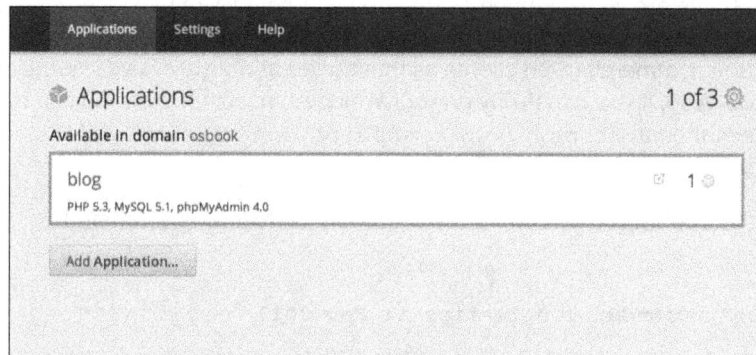

4. Next, view the application SSH details by clicking on **Want to log in to your application?**, as shown in the following screenshot:

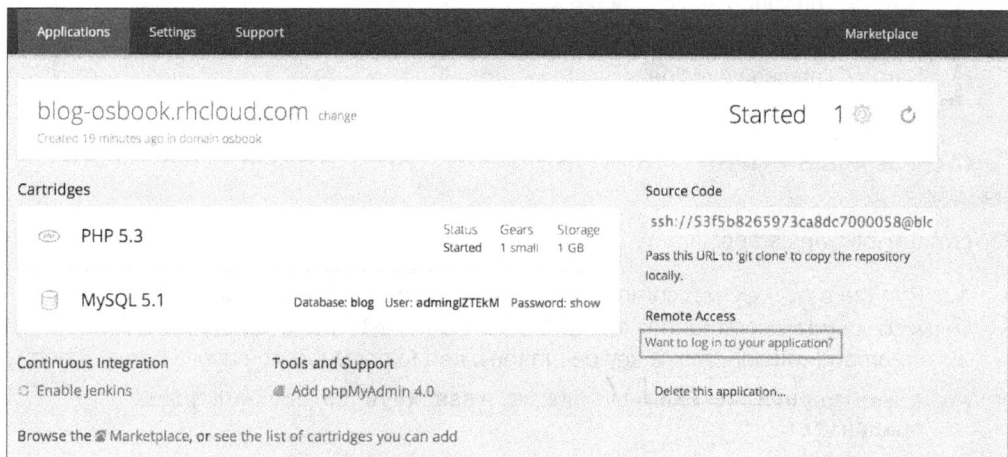

5. Copy the application SSH information shown in the following screenshot:

blog-osbook.rhcloud.com change

Created 19 minutes ago in domain osbook

Started 1 ⚙ ↻

**Cartridges**

| | | Status | Gears | Storage |
|---|---|---|---|---|
| 👁 | PHP 5.3 | Started | 1 small | 1 GB |

🗄 MySQL 5.1       Database: **blog**   User: **admingIZTEkM**   Password: show

**Continuous Integration**

↻ Enable Jenkins

**Tools and Support**

🔌 Add phpMyAdmin 4.0

Browse the 🛒 Marketplace, or see the list of cartridges you can add

**Source Code**

ssh://53f5b8265973ca8dc7000058@blc

Pass this URL to 'git clone' to copy the repository locally.

**Remote Access**

Want to log in to your application?
The command below will open a Secure Shell (SSH) session to your application on most operating systems. See our SSH help page for information about connecting with Windows, Mac, and Linux computers.

ssh 53f5b8265973ca8dc7000058@blog

Delete this application...

6. Open a new command-line terminal on your local machine and run the following command. Here, you will list the directories in the application's gear home folder. Replace the SSH information with your application SSH information.

```
$ ssh 52b823b34382ec52670003f6@blog-osbook.rhcloud.com ls
app-deployments
app-root
git
mysql
php
phpmyadmin
```

## How it works...

First, let's try to understand what you did in the preceding section. In the first step, you created a new pair of SSH keys. The `ssh-keygen` utility can take a number of options. Three of the many options used are as follows:

▸ The `-t` option is used to specify the type of the key. It can be either RSA or DSA, and in this case, the RSA key type is used. Note that OpenShift supports both the RSA and DSA key types.

- ▸ The -b option is used to specify the number of bits in the key. For RSA keys, the minimum size is 768 bits and the default is 2048 bits. Generally, 2048 bits is considered sufficient.

- ▸ The -C option is used to provide a comment, which can be useful to identify a key. This is appended to the public key.

The ssh-keygen command prompts the user with a few questions, as shown in the following command:

```
$ ssh-keygen -t rsa -b 2048 -C 'SSH keys to connect with OpenShift'
Generating public/private rsa key pair.
Enter file in which to save the key (/home/vagrant/.ssh/id_rsa):
Enter passphrase (empty for no passphrase):
Enter same passphrase again:
Your identification has been saved in /home/vagrant/.ssh/id_rsa.
Your public key has been saved in /home/vagrant/.ssh/id_rsa.pub.
The key fingerprint is:
ad:59:8a:02:e6:94:35:92:a3:b9:94:93:c8:9a:30:47 SSH keys to connect
with OpenShift
The key's randomart image is:
+--[ RSA 2048]----+
|                 |
|    .            |
|  E o            |
|o+o= .    .      |
|***       S o    |
|+0..      . =    |
|+ . . . +        |
|     .           |
|                 |
+-----------------+
```

Firstly, this command asks the user to provide the SSH key filename and its location. The default filename for RSA keys is id_rsa for a private key and id_rsa.pub for a public key. The default location to store these keys is the .ssh folder under the user's home directory.

Secondly, it asks the user to provide a passphrase. In order to not use a passphrase, just press *Enter* twice. The passphrase is used to secure the private key. If you enter a passphrase, you will be prompted to enter the passphrase every time you perform any operation that requires SSH. In the next recipe, you will learn how to use a passphrase without entering it each time.

When you run any SSH client, such as ssh, to connect with an SSH server, the client uses the private key to prove your identity to the server. The server uses the public key for authentication. If the authentication succeeds, then the connection proceeds. Otherwise, you will get an error message.

In the second step, you uploaded the public SSH key to the OpenShift account. OpenShift copies the public key into an authorization file on the application gear at ~/.ssh/ authorized_keys. Thereafter, when an SSH client requests a connection to the application gear, the SSH server running on the application gear consults the authorized_keys file to find the matching public key.

From step 3 to step 5, you learned how to find the SSH information for an application using the web console. In step 6, you tested the SSH connection by executing the ls command on the application gear. The first time you connect to an SSH server, you will be asked whether you want to connect to the server. This is because the client does not know about the server. The SSH client consults the known_hosts file at ~/.ssh/known_hosts for the server information. If there is no entry in ~/.ssh/known_hosts, then it will ask for confirmation, as shown in the following command:

```
$ ssh 52b823b34382ec52670003f6@blog-osbook.rhcloud.com ls


The authenticity of host 'blog-osbook.rhcloud.com (54.221.64.115)'
can't be established.

RSA key fingerprint is
cf:ee:77:cb:0e:fc:02:d7:72:7e:ae:80:c0:90:88:a7.

Are you sure you want to continue connecting (yes/no)? yes


Warning: Permanently added 'blog-osbook.rhcloud.com,54.221.64.115'
(RSA) to the list of known hosts.


app-deployments

app-root

git

mysql

php

phpmyadmin
```

After you enter yes, a new entry will be added to the known_hosts file at ~/.ssh/known_ hosts. The known_hosts file at ~/.ssh/known_hosts acts as a database, and the client will check this file for the server entry on every subsequent request.

> The OpenShift `rhc` command-line client also offers various commands to work with SSH keys. Once you have installed the `rhc` client, you can run the `rhc sshkey` command to view all the supported actions.

## There's more...

You can decide to use another name or location for the SSH key pair. You can create another SSH key using the `ssh-keygen` utility. This time, name the key `openshift_key`:

```
$ ssh-keygen
Generating public/private rsa key pair.
Enter file in which to save the key (/home/vagrant/.ssh/id_rsa):
/home/vagrant/.ssh/openshift_key
```

Go to the OpenShift account settings web page at `https://openshift.redhat.com/app/console/settings` and delete the existing key, as shown in the following screenshot:

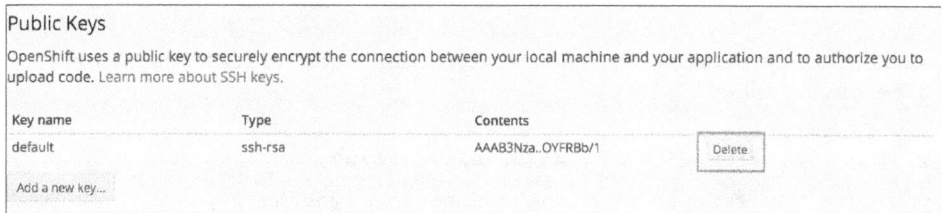

| Public Keys | | | |
|---|---|---|---|
| OpenShift uses a public key to securely encrypt the connection between your local machine and your application and to authorize you to upload code. Learn more about SSH keys. | | | |
| **Key name** | **Type** | **Contents** | |
| default | ssh-rsa | AAAB3Nza..OYFRBb/1 | Delete |
| Add a new key... | | | |

Now, upload the `openshift_key.pub` SSH key to your OpenShift account as discussed previously.

Run the `ssh` command again. This time, you will get an error, as the SSH client used the default key to connect with the SSH server. The default key name is `id_rsa`. Now, let's try to run the `ls` command on the application gear to confirm whether we get the `Permission denied` error:

```
$ ssh 52b823b34382ec52670003f6@blog-osbook.rhcloud.com ls
Permission denied (publickey,gssapi-keyex,gssapi-with-mic).
```

To get debug information, you should use the following command:

```
ssh -v 52b823b34382ec52670003f6@blog-osbook.rhcloud.com
ls
```

To get even more debug information, you should use the following command:

```
ssh -v -v -v 52b823b34382ec52670003f6@blog-
osbook.rhcloud.com ls
```

The number of −v options in the preceding command defines the verbosity.

To connect with the application gear, you have to connect using openshift_key. To use a different key, run the following command:

```
$ ssh -i /home/vagrant/.ssh/openshift_key
52b823b34382ec52670003f6@blog-osbook.rhcloud.com ls
```

The -i option is used to tell the SSH client to pick a different SSH key.

## See also

▸  The *Working with the SSH key passphrases* recipe

# Working with the SSH key passphrases

In the *Uploading SSH keys using the web console* recipe, you learned how to create a new SSH key pair and upload it to an OpenShift account. The SSH key pair was created with an empty passphrase. The passphrase is a password to protect the private key. The empty passphrase avoids reentering a passphrase every time you use the key, but it might cause some security concerns. This recipe will walk you through the process of securing your SSH keys while avoiding having to re-enter the passphrase every time you use the key.

## Getting ready

To step through this recipe, you will need the OpenSSH SSH connectivity tools installed on your machine.

To make sure that the OpenSSH client tool is installed, run the following command:

```
$ ssh -V

OpenSSH_6.2p2, OpenSSL 1.0.1e-fips 11 Feb 2013
```

The output of the preceding command will depend on the operating system and OpenSSH version installed on your machine. If you get `ssh: command not found`, then the OpenSSH tools are not installed on your machine.

This recipe will use the WordPress application created in the *Uploading SSH keys using the web console* recipe.

## How to do it...

Perform the following steps to use SSH key passphrases:

1.  Passphrases can be added during key creation time or to an existing key without regenerating a new key pair. As you have already created the key pair in the *Uploading SSH keys using the web console* recipe, we will reuse this key pair. You will use `ssh-keygen` to add a key pair to the existing key:

    ```
    $ ssh-keygen -p
    Enter file in which the key is (/home/vagrant/.ssh/id_rsa):
    Key has comment '/home/vagrant/.ssh/id_rsa'
    Enter new passphrase (empty for no passphrase): <Enter passphrase>
    Enter same passphrase again: <Enter passphrase again>
    Your identification has been saved with the new passphrase.
    ```

2.  Now, if you try to SSH into the application gear, you will be asked to enter the passphrase.

3.  Next, run the `ssh-agent` command. The `ssh-agent` command, which is a part of the OpenSSH toolbelt, is another tool that stores your passphrase securely so that you do not have to re-enter the passphrase. You can run the `ssh-agent` command by typing the following:

    ```
    $ ssh-agent $SHELL
    ```

4.  To add the passphrase, run the `ssh-add` utility:

    ```
    $ ssh-add
    Enter passphrase for /home/vagrant/.ssh/id_rsa: <Enter passphrase>
    Identity added: /home/vagrant/.ssh/id_rsa
    (/home/vagrant/.ssh/id_rsa)
    ```

5. Connect to the application gear to see the SSH agent in action. You will notice that you are not asked to enter the passphrase:

```
$ ssh 52b823b34382ec52670003f6@blog-osbook.rhcloud.com ls
app-deployments
app-root
git
mysql
php
phpmyadmin
```

6. Exit the shell to end the `ssh-agent` session. If you try to connect with the application gear now, you will be asked to enter the passphrase:

```
$ ssh 52b823b34382ec52670003f6@blog-osbook.rhcloud.com ls
Enter passphrase for key '/home/vagrant/.ssh/id_rsa':
```

## How it works...

The `ssh-agent` utility stores the SSH keys in memory. It caches the private keys and responds to the authentication queries from SSH clients. The `ssh-add` utility is used to add and remove keys from `ssh-agent`. In step 1, you added the passphrase to your existing key. By default, it will use the default key, `id_rsa`, in the `.ssh` folder, but you can provide another SSH key file using the `-i` option. Now, SSH into the application gear and you will be asked to enter the passphrase:

```
$ ssh 52b823b34382ec52670003f6@blog-osbook.rhcloud.com ls
Enter passphrase for key '/home/vagrant/.ssh/id_rsa':
```

Step 2 starts the agent by forking the existing shell. It sets some environment variables required by the SSH agent. Next, in step 3, you add the SSH key into the agent. It asks for the passphrase to decrypt the private key. After decryption, it adds the private key to the agent's cache.

Finally, in step 4, you connect to the application gear using the `ssh` client. This time you will not be asked to enter the passphrase as the agent already cached the private key.

You can terminate the agent or log out from the shell to end the session.

## See also

▶ The *Uploading SSH keys using the web console* recipe

# Cloning the application to the local machine

Every OpenShift application has a private Git repository that houses the application source code. OpenShift uses Git not only as a version control system but also to build and deploy the application using Git's action hooks. In this recipe, you will learn how to get the source code of the OpenShift application on your local machine.

## Getting ready

You will need Git installed on the operating system before stepping through this recipe. For Debian-based Linux distributions, you can install Git with `apt-get install git` as the root. If you are on Fedora or any other Red Hat-based system, you can install Git with `yum install git-core` as the root. Mac and Windows users can download the Git package from the official download site at `http://git-scm.com/downloads`.

This recipe will use the WordPress application created in the *Creating a WordPress application using the web console* recipe.

## How to do it...

Perform the following steps to clone the repository:

1. Go to the **Applications** tab in the web console at `https://openshift.redhat.com/app/console/applications` and click on the application to view its details, as shown in the following screenshot:

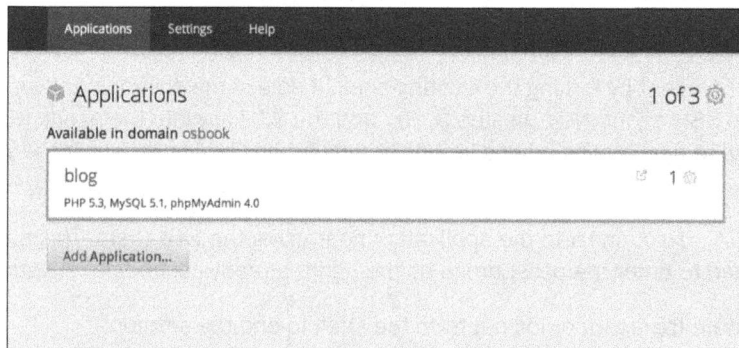

2. Copy the Git repository URL mentioned on the application detail web page, as shown in the following screenshot:

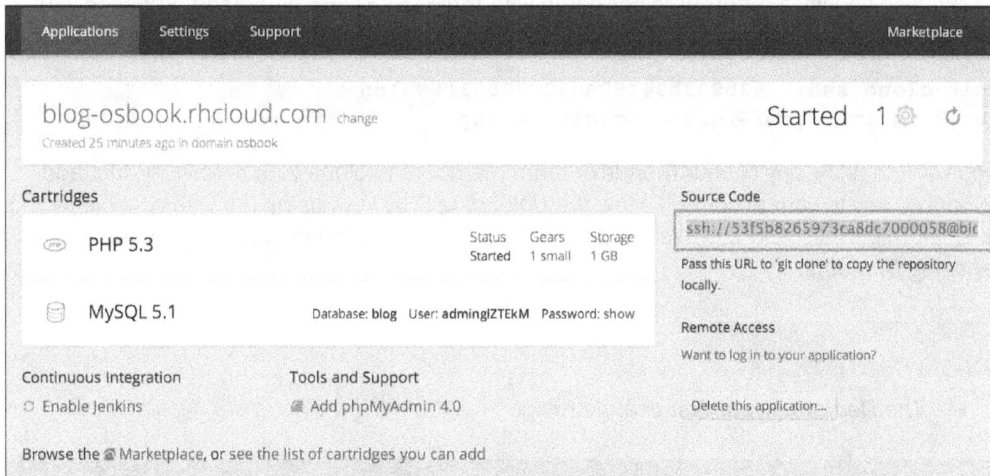

3. Open a command-line terminal, go to a convenient location on your machine, and execute the `git clone` command. Replace the repository URL with your application Git URL:

```
$ git clone ssh://52b823b34382ec52670003f6@blog-
osbook.rhcloud.com/~/git/blog.git/
```

## How it works...

The first and second steps helped us to locate the application Git repository URL. As discussed in the preceding section, OpenShift uses Git as revision control and a source code management system. Every application has a private Git repository. A Git repository contains all the information needed to retain and manage the revisions and history of a project. OpenShift uses the SSH transport protocol to work with Git repositories. To create a secure communication channel between the local machine and application gear, Git uses the SSH key setup discussed in the *Uploading SSH keys using the web console* recipe. Nobody will be able to clone your application repository unless you add their public SSH key to your account.

In step 3, you cloned the application Git repository using the `clone` command. The `git clone` command created a new Git repository based on the original application repository URL. The difference between Git and other version control systems is that Git clones the full copy of the repository, in addition to the working copy, of all the files in the repository. The `clone` command will create a new directory on your local filesystem with the same name as the application.

## There's more...

You can also specify a different folder name with the `git clone` command. Suppose you want to clone the application in the `myapp` folder. To do this, execute the following command:

```
$ git clone ssh://52b823b34382ec52670003f6@blog-
osbook.rhcloud.com/~/git/blog.git/ myapp
```

If you want to allow any of your friends or team members to clone your repository, just add their public key to your account. Follow the *Uploading SSH keys using the web console* recipe to upload the public SSH key. We will discuss team collaboration in detail in *Chapter 2, Managing Domains*.

## See also

▶ The *Deploying your first change* recipe

# Deploying your first change

In the *Cloning the application to the local machine* recipe, you learned how to clone an OpenShift application Git repository using the `git clone` command. The next logical step after cloning the repository is to make a change, commit it, and finally deploy it. In this recipe, you will learn how to deploy the source code changes to OpenShift applications.

## Getting ready

To step through this recipe, you will need Git installed on your local machine.

## How to do it...

Perform the following steps to deploy your first change:

1. Go to the OpenShift web console and navigate to the PHP 5.4 application creation page at `https://openshift.redhat.com/app/console/application_ type/cart!php-5.4`.
2. Enter the name of the application. I have used `myapp` as the application name.
3. Click on the **Create Application** button to create a new application.
4. Clone the application's Git repository on your local machine by following the steps mentioned in the *Cloning the application to the local machine* recipe.

5. Open the `index.php` file inside the application source code root directory. Go to the following line of code in `index.php`:

   `<h1>Welcome to your PHP application on OpenShift</h1>`

   Replace the preceding line of code with this:

   `<h1>Updated the application</h1>`

6. Commit the change to the local repository using Git:

   ```
   $ git commit -am 'modified index.php'
   ```

7. Push the changes to the remote repository hosted on the OpenShift application gear using the following Git command:

   ```
   $ git push origin master
   ```

8. After `git push` successfully completes, open the `http://myapp-{domain-name}.rhcloud.com/` application in your favorite browser. You will see your first change.

## How it works...

The OpenShift deployment process is based around Git. From step 1 to step 4, you created a PHP 5.4 application using the web console and cloned the application on your local machine. In step 5, you made a simple change to the `index.php` file. This change has not yet been committed to the local repository. Git, being a distributed version control system, has a concept of local and remote repositories. You can continue working (making changes and committing them) on your local machine as long as you want, and when you are ready, you can push the changes to the remote Git repository.

In step 6, you committed the change to your local Git repository using the `git commit` command. You used the `-a` and `-m` options. The `-a` option tells the `git` command to automatically stage the modified and deleted files, but new files are not touched. To commit a new file, you have to first stage the file using the `git add` command and then commit it:

```
$ git add test.html
$ git commit -m 'new html file'
```

Step 7 pushes the local commits to a remote repository. When you clone a repository, the cloned repository maintains a link back to its parent repository via a remote called `origin`. A remote is a handle or reference to another Git repository. The remote information is stored in a configuration file called `config` under the `.git` folder. You can open the `.git/config` file and view the `origin` remote information as follows:

```
[remote 'origin']
  url = ssh://52bbf209e0b8cd707000018a@myapp-osbook.rhcloud.com/~/git/
blog.git/
  fetch = +refs/heads/*:refs/remotes/origin/*
```

As shown in the preceding code, a remote consists of two different parts. The `url` part is the name of the remote repository in the form of a URL. The `fetch` part specifies how a reference should be mapped from the namespace of one repository into that of another.

The output of the `git push` command is as follows:

```
$ git push origin master
Counting objects: 7, done.
Compressing objects: 100% (4/4), done.
Writing objects: 100% (4/4), 404 bytes | 0 bytes/s, done.
Total 4 (delta 3), reused 0 (delta 0)
remote: Stopping PHP cartridge
remote: Waiting for stop to finish
remote: Stopping MySQL cartridge
remote: Stopping PHPMyAdmin cartridge
remote: Waiting for stop to finish
remote: Building git ref 'master', commit 3933f99
remote: Building PHP cartridge
remote: Preparing build for deployment
remote: Deployment id is b78e5efd
remote: Activating deployment
remote: Starting MySQL cartridge
remote: Starting PHPMyAdmin cartridge
remote: Database already configured.
remote: Starting PHP cartridge
remote: Result: success
remote: Activation status: success
remote: Deployment completed with status: success
To ssh://52bbf209e0b8cd707000018a@blog-
osbook.rhcloud.com/~/git/blog.git/
   e83c2a7..3933f99  master -> master
```

This is how the process works:

1. Git takes the `master` branch changes, compresses them, and transfers all the missing objects from your local repository to the remote repository named `origin`.

2. Next, a pre-receive action hook is invoked on the application gear. Git hooks are custom scripts, which Git will run at specific events like `push`. You can write scripts in bash, Perl, Python, Ruby, or whatever you have. The pre-receive hook receives a list of all (new or old) the refs that are to be updated. The pre-receive action hook in the application gear Git repository stops the PHP and other cartridges, checks the deployment integrity, and configures the deployment metadata.

3. Lastly, the postreceive action hook is invoked on the application gear. It receives a list of all the updated refs. The postreceive action hook in the application gear Git repository archives the application repository, builds the application, starts the PHP and other cartridges, and then finally deploys the application.

## There's more...

Instead of using the `git push origin master` command, you can also use `git push`. The `origin` part is the default remote and `master` is the default branch, so they are not required.

## See also

▸ The *Cloning the application to the local machine* recipe

# Checking the application's gear quota and limits

In this recipe, you will learn how to check the application resource limits.

## Getting ready

To step through this recipe, you will need the OpenSSH SSH connectivity tools installed on your machine. This recipe will use the WordPress application created in the *Creating a WordPress application using the web console* recipe.

## How to do it...

To check the resources consumed by your application, run the following command. Here, you replace the SSH URL with your application SSH URL. To find the SSH URL of your application, refer to the *Uploading SSH keys using the web console* recipe.

```
$ ssh 52bbf209e0b8cd707000018a@blog-osbook.rhcloud.com quota -s
```

## How it works...

The OpenShift applications run inside gears that have limited resources. Every gear, depending on its size, has a definite amount of resources. The `quota -s` command can be used to check the resources consumed by the application and the limits imposed on the gear.

The output of the `quota  -s` command is shown as follows:

```
Disk quotas for user 52bbf209e0b8cd707000018a (uid 2187):
     Filesystem  blocks    quota    limit    grace    files    quota
limit    grace
/dev/mapper/EBSStore01-user_home01
                    124M       0    1024M             2898         0
80000
```

The first column is the name of the filesystem that has quota enabled for it. The second column shows how many blocks the user is currently using. The fourth column tells us the storage limit. Gears in free tier have access to 1 GB of disk storage. The sixth column tells us the number of files created by the application. The eighth column shows the maximum number of files a user can create. Gears can create a maximum of 80,000 files. The gears also have limited RAM memory. Small gears have 512 MB of RAM, medium gears have 1 GB of RAM, and large gears have 2 GB of RAM. The medium and large gears are only available in the Bronze and Silver commercial plans.

## There's more...

You can also view how much disk space your gear is using by running the ***du*** command:

```
$ ssh 52bbf209e0b8cd707000018a@blog-osbook.rhcloud.com 'du -sh *'


17M     app-deployments
```

# Installing the OpenShift rhc command-line client

The `rhc` client is the most powerful and feature-rich command-line client utility, which users can use to work with OpenShift. It is built using Ruby programming language and packaged as a Ruby gem. The `rhc` source code is available on GitHub at `https://github.com/openshift/rhc`.

## Getting ready

To install `rhc`, you will need to have Ruby 1.8.7 or above installed on your machine. You can check whether Ruby is installed on your machine by running the following command:

```
$ ruby --version
ruby 2.0.0p247 (2013-06-27 revision 41674) [x86_64-linux]
```

The output of the preceding command will depend on the operating system and Ruby version installed on your machine. If you receive `ruby: command not found`, then Ruby is not installed on your machine. Install Ruby on your operating system. You can download the package for your operating system from the official website at `https://www.ruby-lang.org/en/downloads/`.

## How to do it...

Open a new command-line terminal and run the following command:

```
$ gem install rhc
```

This command will install the `rhc` gem required to work with OpenShift.

## How it works...

OpenShift packages the `rhc` command-line utility as a gem. A gem is a reusable piece of code or a command-line utility to help automate tasks. `RubyGems` is a package manager for the Ruby programming language that provides a standard format for distributing Ruby programs and libraries. This software allows a developer to download, install, and use software packages on their machine. The `gem` command allows you to work with `RubyGems`.

When you run the `gem install` command, the `gem` command-line tool fetches the package and its dependencies from the central repository and installs them. The central gem repository is available at `http://rubygems.org`.

After the command successfully finishes, you can check the version of `rhc` using the following command:

```
$ rhc --version
rhc 1.27.4
```

## There's more...

The `gem install` command also generates the documentation for the installed packages. You can use the Ruby `ri` command-line tool to view the documentation offline. For example, if you want to list all the classes for which `ri` can show documentation, then run the following command:

```
$ ri --list
```

This command will list all the classes and their methods for which you can view the documentation. To view the documentation of the `CLI` class method of the `RHC` class, execute the following command:

```
$ ri RHC::CLI
```

The output will be the documentation for the `CLI` method, as follows:

```
= RHC::CLI
(from gem rhc-1.27.4)
-------------------------------------------------------------------------
-----
Run and execute a command line session with the RHC tools.


You can invoke the CLI with:

  bundle exec ruby -e 'require 'rhc/cli'; RHC::CLI.start(ARGV);' --
<arguments>
```

You can disable the documentation generation by using the following command:

```
$ gem install rhc --no-document
```

## See also

> ▸ The *Setting up an OpenShift account using rhc* recipe
> ▸ The *Updating rhc* recipe

# Setting up an OpenShift account using rhc

In the *Installing the OpenShift rhc command-line client* recipe, you learned how to install the `rhc` command-line client. After installation, the first operation you have to perform is to set up the OpenShift account. In this recipe, you will learn how to set up your account using `rhc`.

## Getting ready

To complete this recipe, you will need to have `rhc` installed on your machine. Refer to the *Installing the OpenShift rhc command-line client* recipe for instructions.

## How to do it...

To set up an OpenShift account, open a command-line terminal and run the following command:

```
$ rhc setup
```

## How it works...

Before you can use the `rhc` client to work with OpenShift, you have to set up the account.

The `setup` command does the following:

1. It first asks you to provide your OpenShift credentials to authenticate with `openshift.redhat.com`.

2. After successful authentication, `rhc` asks whether it should create an authorization token. An authorization token allows you to access the OpenShift server without entering the password with every command. It stores the token in the `.openshift` folder under the user's `home` directory. By default, the token is valid for 30 days, which means that after this you have to authenticate it again.

3. Next, the `setup` command creates a file called `express.conf` in the `.openshift` folder under the user's `home` directory. The `express.conf` file stores the basic configuration required by `rhc` such as the OpenShift server location, your OpenShift username, and whether or not to create and use authorization tokens.

4. If no SSH key exists in the `.ssh` folder at `~/.ssh`, then the `rhc setup` command will generate a new key pair using the `ssh-keygen` utility.

5. After generating the new SSH key pair, `rhc` will upload the public SSH key to the OpenShift server. OpenShift copies the public key into an authorization file on the application gear called `authorized_keys` at `~/.ssh/authorized_keys`. In the *Uploading SSh keys using the web console* recipe, you uploaded the public SSH key using the web console. It will prompt you to provide the name of the key or use the default name generated by the `setup` command.

6. Next, `rhc` checks if Git has been installed. The `rhc setup` command will run a simple check against your local configuration and credentials to confirm that the configurations have been completed. It will also run a series of tests to check whether `ssh` has been configured properly and whether your system can communicate with OpenShift servers.

7. Finally, `rhc` asks the user to create a domain if one is not already created. In the *Creating OpenShift domains using the web console* recipe, you created the domain using the web console.

## There's more...

You can run the `rhc setup` command anytime while working with OpenShift. Every time you run the `rhc setup` command, it will use the configuration properties defined in the `express.conf` file. If you want to generate a new, clean configuration, you can use the `--clean` option. This will run the `setup` command again, ignoring any saved configuration options stored in `express.conf`:

```
$ rhc setup --clean
```

## See also

▸ The *Enabling the autocomplete feature in an rhc command-line client* recipe

▸ The *Viewing the account details using rhc* recipe

▸ The *Specifying a different OpenShift server hostname* recipe

# Enabling the autocomplete feature in an rhc command-line client

The `rhc` command-line utility supports autocompletion. This involves `rhc` predicting a command that the user wants to type in without them actually typing it completely. This is very helpful for new users who do not know all the commands supported by `rhc`. In this recipe, you will learn how to enable autocomplete for the `rhc` command-line client.

> The autocomplete feature does not work for Windows Terminal.

## Getting ready

To step through this recipe, you will need to have `rhc` installed on your machine. Refer to the *Installing the OpenShift rhc command-line client* recipe for instructions.

## How to do it...

To enable autocompletion, perform the following steps:

1. Run the `rhc setup` command again with the `autocomplete` option:

   ```
   $ rhc setup --autocomplete
   ```

2. The previous step will generate a file named `bash_autocomplete` in the `.openshift` folder at `~/.openshift`. To enable autocompletion, you have to add the `~/.openshift/bash_autocomplete` line to the `.bashrc` or `.bash_profile` file present in your user's home directory. The `.bashrhc` file on my Fedora box is as follows:

   ```
   # .bashrc
   . ~/.openshift/bash_autocomplete
   # Source global definitions
   if [ -f /etc/bashrc ]; then
   ```

```
. /etc/bashrc

fi

# User specific aliases and functions
```

3. Note that on Mac OS X, you have to add `~/.openshift/bash_autocomplete` to your `~/.bash_profile`. On Mac OS X, the new Terminal windows and tabs are always considered login shells, so this is a necessary step for OS X users.

4. Reload or restart the shell to allow these changes to take effect.

## How it works...

You should try to understand what you have done in the preceding section. In step 1, you ran the `setup` command with the `autocomplete` option. This generated a bash script called `bash_autocomplete` in the `.openshift` folder at `~/.openshift`. This bash script defines a custom completion function called `_rhc` for the `rhc` command-line client. Bash will execute this function when the `rhc` tab key is typed at the prompt and will display possible completions.

In step 2, you sourced the `bash_autocomplete` file by adding `~/.openshift/bash_autocomplete` to the `.bashrc` script. This will make sure that the autocompletion functionality is available for each shell.

Finally, in step 3, you restarted the shell to load the `_rhc` function. Now, if you type `rhc` and then press the *Tab* key, it will show you all the `rhc` commands:

```
$ rhc

account                  app-tidy                    deployment-list
member-list // removed all commands for brevity
```

## There's more...

Most of the `rhc` commands have options, which you can provide. To view all the options for a command, type in `--` and press *Tab*. For example, to view all the `rhc setup` command options, type in `rhc setup --` and press *Tab*:

```
$ rhc setup --

--autocomplete       --clean              --create-token       --no-create-
token   --server
```

## See also

▸ The *Setting up an OpenShift account using rhc* recipe

# Viewing the account details using rhc

In this recipe, you will learn how to view your account details using `rhc`.

## Getting ready

To complete this recipe, you will need to have `rhc` installed on your machine. Refer to the *Installing the OpenShift rhc command-line client* recipe for instructions.

## How to do it...

To view the account details, run the `rhc account` command as follows:

```
$ rhc account
```

This is all you need to do to view the account details.

## How it works...

The `rhc account` command shows details about the currently logged-in user. When you run the command, it makes a REST call to the OpenShift REST API using the authentication token generated during `rhc setup`. The REST API returns a JSON response, which `rhc` will render in a human-readable format:

```
$ rhc account
Login openshift.cookbook@gmail.com on openshift.redhat.com
-------------------------------------------------------------
  ID:                   52b8112ae0b8cdc308000018
  Plan:                 Free
  Gears Used:           0
  Gears Allowed:        3
  Domains Allowed:      1
  Allowed Gear Sizes:   small
  SSL Certificates:     no
```

The account details include whom you are logged in as, which OpenShift server you are connected to, your OpenShift user ID, the OpenShift plan you are using, the number of gears as well as the gear size used and allowed, the number of domains allowed, and whether you can use SSL certificates or not.

You can also view the account details in the web console by navigating to the account web page at `https://openshift.redhat.com/app/account`.

## There's more...

You can also view details of any of your other OpenShift accounts by passing the -1 or --rhlogin option. The -1 or --rhlogin option is a global option available with every command. When you use -1 or --rhlogin, you force the rhc client to use the user-specified login:

```
$ rhc account --rhlogin user@example.com
```

You can log out from your current session on the server by using the rhc account-logout command. This ends the user's current session and deletes the authorization token files in the .openshift folder at ~/.openshift:

```
$ rhc account-logout
```

You can also use rhc logout as a short alternative to rhc account-logout.

## See also

▸ The *Setting up an OpenShift account using rhc* recipe

# Specifying a different OpenShift server hostname

This recipe talks about how you can configure a different OpenShift server hostname. By default, when you set up your OpenShift account using the rhc setup command, rhc is configured to work with the public OpenShift PaaS hosted at openshift.redhat.com. However, it is possible to use a different OpenShift installation, which can be either an OpenShift Enterprise or an OpenShift Origin installation.

## Getting ready

To step through this recipe, you will need to have rhc installed on your machine. Refer to the *Installing the OpenShift rhc command-line client* recipe for instructions.

## How to do it...

Open a command-line terminal and run the following command to use a different OpenShift server hostname:

```
$ rhc setup --server <My OpenShift Installation Hostname>
```

Replace <My OpenShift Installation Hostname> with the OpenShift server hostname.

## How it works...

The `rhc setup` command takes an option, `--server`, which allows a user to specify the server hostname. When you run the `rhc setup` command with the new server location, the `setup` command will perform all the actions required to configure your OpenShift account to work with the new server. The `setup` command will overwrite the `express.conf` file in `~/.openshift` with the new server hostname. The `rhc` client will get configured to work with the new OpenShift server.

## There's more...

You can also configure the server by directly editing the `express.conf` file at `~/.openshift/express.conf`. The `libra_server` property is as follows:

```
# The OpenShift server to connect to
libra_server=openshift.redhat.com
```

Change the preceding code to a new server hostname:

```
# The OpenShift server to connect to
libra_server=<Your OpenShift Installation>
```

## See also

- ▶ The *Setting up an OpenShift account using rhc* recipe
- ▶ The *Viewing the account details using rhc* recipe

# Updating rhc

The OpenShift command-line tool, `rhc`, is the most powerful and popular way to work with OpenShift. In this recipe, you will learn how to update `rhc` to the latest version. OpenShift Online has a three-week release cycle, and most of the time, the `rhc` client tool is also updated to either support a new feature or fix a bug. So, it always helps if you use the latest version of `rhc`.

## Getting ready

To be ready for this recipe, you will need an already installed `rhc`. No other prerequisites are required.

## How to do it...

To update the `rhc` gem, run the `gem update` command:

```
$ gem update rhc
```

This is all you need to do to update the `rhc` command line to the latest version.

## How it works...

`rhc` is a Ruby gem and `RubyGems` is a package manager like many other package managers. It uses a central repository, which hosts installable packages. When you run the `gem update` command, this command-line tool fetches the latest packages from the central repository and installs them.

## There's more...

When you start working with `rhc`, you will soon have multiple versions of the `rhc` gem installed on your machine. You can uninstall all the previous versions using the `cleanup` command. This command will uninstall old versions of installed gems in the local repository:

```
$ gem cleanup rhc
```

## See also

▶ The *Installing the OpenShift rhc command-line client* recipe

# 2
# Managing Domains

This chapter presents a number of recipes that will show you how to get started with creating and managing domains. You will also learn how domains can help you work as a team and collaborate on a project. The specific recipes of this chapter are:

- ▶ Creating a domain using rhc
- ▶ Renaming a domain using rhc
- ▶ Viewing domain details using rhc
- ▶ Adding viewer members to a domain using rhc
- ▶ Adding an editor member to a domain using rhc
- ▶ Adding an admin member to a domain using rhc
- ▶ Viewing all the members in a domain using rhc
- ▶ Removing members from a domain using rhc
- ▶ Restricting gear sizes for a domain using rhc
- ▶ Leaving a domain using rhc
- ▶ Deleting a domain using rhc

# Introduction

A **domain** represents a unique name for each user within which each user application must exist. OpenShift users cannot create an application until they have a valid domain. The domain name becomes a part of the application URL. For example, if your domain name is `foo` and your application name is `bar`, the application URL will be `http://bar-foo.rhcloud.com`. Every OpenShift account must have at least one domain associated with it. The OpenShift Online free tier does not allow a user to create more than one domain, but you can create more than one domain in paid tiers. The domains make it possible for users to choose any valid name for their application. They allow two or more users to have the same name for their applications. For example, user A can have an application named `bar` in domain `foo`, and similarly, user B can also have an application named `bar` in domain `test`. Once a user has a valid domain, he/she can use any valid name for their application.

Team collaboration is one of the essential features of modern-day software development. Whether you are working on an open source project or an enterprise project, you need to collaborate and work with others. A group of people may work together to make a software project a success. A domain makes it possible to work as a team because you can add other users to your domain, giving them privileges to work with your application. This makes it very easy for different users to collaborate on a project and work together. You can add a user to your domain either as a viewer, editor, or an admin. Recipes 4 through 6 will cover these in detail.

A domain also helps us incorporate the concept of environments in our applications. You can have different domains for different environments. One can be used as a development environment, one as a quality assurance environment, and another for production. This allows you to give different people access to different domains. Your developers can have access to development and quality assurance domains but not to the production domain.

# Creating a domain using rhc

In the *Creating OpenShift domains using the web console* recipe of *Chapter 1, Getting Started with OpenShift*, you learned how to create a domain using the web console. In this recipe, you will learn how to create a domain using the rhc command line.

## Getting ready

To complete this recipe, you will need to have rhc installed on your machine. Please refer to the *Installing the OpenShift rhc command-line client* recipe in *Chapter 1, Getting Started with OpenShift,* for instructions. If you are using OpenShift's free plan, you have to first delete the domain you created in the *Creating OpenShift domains using the web console* recipe of *Chapter 1, Getting Started with OpenShift,* before continuing with this recipe. This is required because you cannot have more than one domain with OpenShift's free plan. To delete a domain, run the command shown as follows. This command is explained in the *Deleting a domain using rhc* recipe in this chapter:

```
$ rhc delete-domain <domain_name> --force
```

## How to do it...

To create a domain name, open a new command-line terminal and run the following command. Please provide a unique domain name.

```
$ rhc create-domain --namespace <unique_domain_ame>
```

> If you get the `You may not have more than 1 domain` error when you run this command, delete the existing domain associated with your account. In the free tier, you cannot create more than one domain.

## How it works...

You can use the `rhc domain-create` or `rhc create-domain` command to create a new domain name. The only required argument to create a domain is a unique alphanumeric name. Please note that a domain can contain, at most, 16 alphanumeric characters and cannot have spaces or symbols.

The output of the `rhc create-domain` command is shown as follows:

```
$ rhc create-domain --namespace osbook
Creating domain 'osbook' ... done
You may now create an application using the 'rhc create-app' command
```

You can avoid using the `--namespace` option by typing the following command. The `rhc` command-line client is intelligent and understands that you are only providing the mandatory argument:

```
$ rhc domain-create osbook
```

## There's more...

All OpenShift commands have help associated with them. To understand the usage of the `rhc create-domain` command and all the options available with it, you can use the `-h` or `--help` option. We will look at the other options in the later recipes.

```
$ rhc create-domain --help
Usage: rhc domain-create <namespace>
```

## See also

▸ The *Creating OpenShift domains using the web console recipe* in *Chapter 1, Getting Started with OpenShift*

▸ The *Renaming a domain using rhc* recipe

▸ The *Viewing domain details using rhc* recipe

▸ The *Deleting a domain using rhc* recipe

# Renaming a domain using rhc

Following the creation of a domain, you might need to rename it. Let's suppose you want to rename your existing name to reflect its environment. For instance, you may rename the `osbook` domain name to `devosbook` in order to indicate `devosbook` as your development environment.

## Getting ready

To complete this recipe, you will need to have rhc installed on your machine. Please refer to the *Installing the OpenShift rhc command-line client* recipe in *Chapter 1, Getting Started with OpenShift*, for instructions.

## How to do it...

To rename a domain, open a new command-line terminal and run the following command. You should provide a unique, new domain name:

```
$ rhc rename-domain <old_domain_name> <new_domain_name>
```

## How it works...

To rename a domain, you have to first make sure there are no applications associated with it. If there are any applications associated with a domain, you have to first delete them. To learn how to delete an application, refer to the *Deleting the application* recipe in *Chapter 3, Creating and Managing Applications*. The rename-domain command first deletes the old domain before creating a new one using the new domain name. To rename the osbook domain to devosbook, you need to run the following command:

```
$ rhc domain-rename osbook devosbook
Renaming domain 'osbook' to 'devosbook' ... done
```

## There's more...

You can also rename a domain using the web console. Visit your domain web page at `https://openshift.redhat.com/app/console/domain/{domain-name}` and click on **Change**, as shown in the following screenshot. Please replace {domain-name} with your OpenShift account domain name.

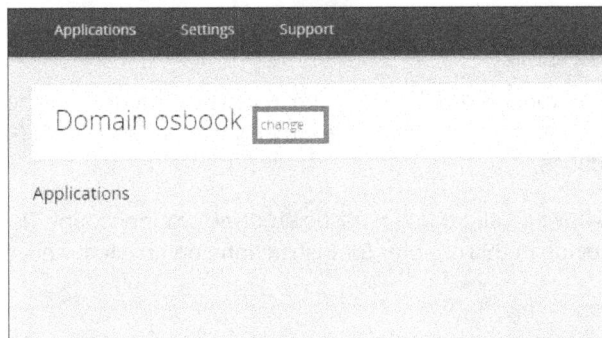

This will direct you to another web page where you can enter the new domain name, as seen in the following screenshot. Enter the new domain name and click on **Save**.

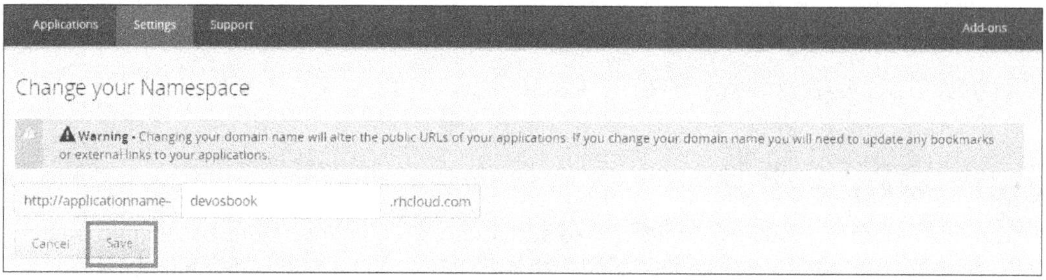

## See also

▸ The *Creating OpenShift domains using the web console* recipe in *Chapter 1, Getting Started with OpenShift*

▸ The *Renaming a domain using rhc* recipe

▸ The *Viewing domain details using rhc* recipe

▸ The *Deleting a domain using rhc* recipe

# Viewing domain details using rhc

In this recipe, you will learn how to view the details associated with a domain.

## Getting ready

To complete this recipe, you will need to have rhc installed on your machine. Please refer to the *Installing the OpenShift rhc command-line client* recipe in *Chapter 1, Getting Started with OpenShift*, for instructions.

Also, you will need to have a valid domain associated with your account. Refer to the *Creating a domain using rhc* recipe in this chapter for instructions on how to create a new domain.

## How to do it...

To view domain details, open a new command-line terminal and run the following command:

```
$ rhc show-domain --namespace <your domain name>
```

## How it works...

The `rhc show-domain` command returns the details of a domain and its applications. The output of the command is shown as follows. The details include the domain name, the owner's e-mail ID, other domain members, and the information of all the applications within it:

```
$ rhc show-domain --namespace devosbook
Domain devosbook (owned by openshift.cookbook@gmail.com)
--------------------------------------------------------

Created: 9:49 AM
Allowed Gear Sizes: small
Members: shekhar.redhat@gmail.com (edit)


blog @ http://blog-devosbook.rhcloud.com/ (uuid:
52d56620e0b8cd9911000166)
------------------------------------------------------------------------
--
Domain: devosbook
Created: 11:30 AM
Gears: 1 (defaults to small)
Git URL: ssh://52d56620e0b8cd9911000166@blog-devosbook.rhcloud.com/~/git/
blog.git/
Initial Git URL: git://github.com/openshift/wordpress-example.git
SSH: 52d56620e0b8cd9911000166@blog-devosbook.rhcloud.com
Deployment: auto (on git push)


php-5.3 (PHP 5.3)
-----------------
Gears: Located with mysql-5.1


mysql-5.1 (MySQL 5.1)
---------------------
Gears: Located with php-5.3
Connection URL: mysql://$OPENSHIFT_MYSQL_DB_HOST:$OPENSHIFT_MYSQL_DB_
PORT/
Database Name: blog
```

```
Password: teic7xz7JUFv

Username: adminiabcAWU
```

**You have 1 application in your domain.**

The `--namespace` option is optional. If you do not specify the `--namespace` option, OpenShift will first try to find the domain name from the Git repository configuration file in the current directory. It considers the directory from which you run the command as an OpenShift application Git repository. It uses the `git config --get rhc.domain-name` command to find the domain name. As we are not running the command inside an OpenShift application's Git repository, OpenShift will make a `GET` REST API request to fetch all the domains associated with the user. The user details and authorization token information will be retrieved from the `~/.openshift` folder. After finding all the domains associated with the user, a `GET` REST API call will be made to fetch details for each domain. Finally, the output will be shown to the user.

## There's more...

You can also view all the domains you have access to by running the `rhc list-domain` command:

```
$ rhc list-domain

Domain devosbook (owned by openshift.cookbook@gmail.com)

-------------------------------------------------------

Created: 9:49 AM

Allowed Gear Sizes: small

Members: shekhar.redhat@gmail.com (edit)


Domain ndtv123 (owned by shekhar.redhat@gmail.com)

--------------------------------------------------

Created: 12:08 PM

Allowed Gear Sizes: small

Members: openshift.cookbook@gmail.com (view)
```

As you can see, the `openshift.cookbook@gmail.com` user has access to two domains. The `openshift.cookbook@gmail.com` user owns the `devosbook` domain, but it is the only member of the `ndtv123` domain.

If a user only wants to view his/her domain, he/she can use the `--mine` argument, as shown in the following command-line output. To view all the options available for a command, you can pass the `--help` option:

```
$ rhc list-domain --mine
Domain devosbook (owned by openshift.cookbook@gmail.com)
--------------------------------------------------------

Created: 9:49 AM
Allowed Gear Sizes: small
Members: shekhar.redhat@gmail.com (edit)


You have access to 1 domain.
```

## See also

- The *Creating a domain using rhc* recipe
- The *Viewing domain details using rhc* recipe
- The *Deleting a domain using rhc* recipe

# Adding viewer members to a domain using rhc

Let's suppose you are a system administrator of your organization, where your job is to make sure all the production applications are running smoothly. Ideally, you would not want all the developers in your organization to have access to the production environment. Giving everyone access to the production environment is waiting for the inevitable to happen. What you should remember is that you can have different domains for different environments. The domain corresponding to the production deployment will be controlled by system administrators rather than developers. OpenShift allows you to give different access levels to a different group of people. You, along with other system administrators, can enjoy admin access to the production domain, whereas developers can only have viewer access, if required. Developers will be added to the production domain in the read-only mode. They can view the information about it and its applications, but they cannot make any changes. They also can't use Git to clone the source code or deploy changes. Viewers are also not allowed to SSH into the application gear.

## Getting ready

To complete this recipe, you will need to have rhc installed on your machine. Please refer to the *Installing the OpenShift rhc command-line client* recipe in *Chapter 1, Getting Started with OpenShift*, for instructions.

You will need two OpenShift accounts to work through this recipe. Please refer to the *Creating an OpenShift Online account* recipe in *Chapter 1, Getting Started with OpenShift*, for OpenShift account registration instructions.

## How to do it...

Let's suppose we have two OpenShift users, `openshift.cookbook@gmail.com` and `openshift.cookbook.test@gmail.com`. You may want to add `openshift.cookbook.test@gmail.com` as a viewer to the `prodosbook` domain of `openshift.cookbook@gmail.com`. The `prodosbook` domain corresponds to the production environment of your application. To do this, execute the following command:

```
$ rhc add-member openshift.cookbook.test@gmail.com --namespace prodosbook
--role view
```

## How it works...

The `add-member` command allows you to add members to your domain. A user can be added to one of the three roles: `view`, `edit`, or `admin`. In this recipe, we may want to add `openshift.cookbook.test@gmail.com` as a viewer, so we use the `--role` option to give the user the view role.

The syntax of the `rhc add-member` command is shown as follows:

```
$ rhc add-member <login> --namespace <namespace> --role <role>
```

The breakup of the command is as follows:

- ► `login`: This is the e-mail ID or short name of the OpenShift account you want to add as a member
- ► `namespace`: This is the domain name in which you want to add a member
- ► `role`: This refers to the access level you want to give to a member

You can view the added user by viewing the domain details:

```
$ rhc show-domain
```

```
Domain prodosbook (owned by openshift.cookbook@gmail.com)
------------------------------------------------------
Created: Jan 14 9:49 AM
Allowed Gear Sizes: small
Members: openshift.cookbook.test@gmail.com (view)
```

```
blog @ http://blog-prodosbook.rhcloud.com/ (uuid:
52d681815973ca43d600009a)
----------------------------------------------------------------------
// app details .. removed for brevity
You have 1 application in your domain.
```

If the openshift.cookbook.test@gmail.com user tries to clone the application to their local machine, they will receive the permission denied error shown as follows:

```
$ rhc git-clone blog -l openshift.cookbook.test@gmail.com
Cloning into 'blog'...
Permission denied (publickey,gssapi-keyex,gssapi-with-mic).
fatal: The remote end hung up unexpectedly
Unable to clone your repository. Called Git with: git clone
ssh://52d681815973ca43d600009a@blog-prodosbook.rhcloud.com/~/git/blog.
git/ "blog"
You can also use the OpenShift account user id instead of the OpenShift
login.
$ rhc add-member --ids 52d6784e5004462a80000235 --namespace prodosbook
--role view
To get the id for an OpenShift account, you can use the rhc account
command.
$ rhc account
Login openshift.cookbook.test@gmail.com on openshift.redhat.com
--------------------------------------------------------------
ID: 52d6784e5004462a80000235
```

Plan: Free

Gears Used: 0

Gears Allowed: 3

Domains Allowed: 1

Allowed Gear Sizes: small

SSL Certificates: no

You can also add multiple members to your domain in one go, as shown:

```
$ rhc add-member openshift.cookbook.test@gmail.com shekhar.redhat@gmail.
com --namespace prodosbook --role view
```

This also works for OpenShift account IDs as well by entering the following command:

```
$ rhc member-add --ids 52d6784e5004462a80000235 52d6784e5004462a80000236
--namespace prodosbook --role view
```

## There's more...

The OpenShift web console also allows users to add members. You can do this by going to `https://openshift.redhat.com/app/console/domain/{domain-name}` and replacing `{domain-name}` with your account domain name. Then, click on the **Add members...** web link:

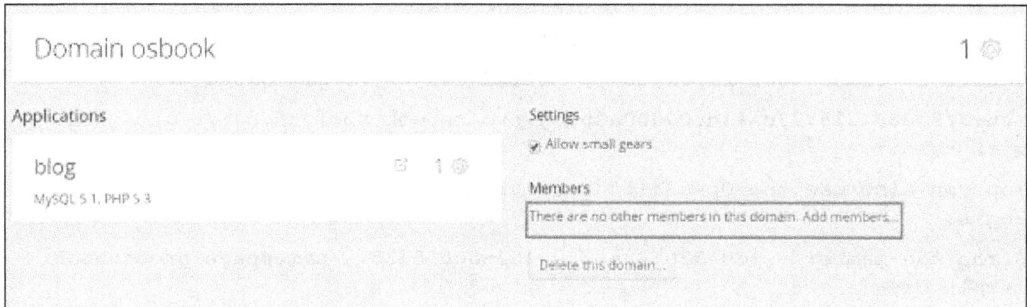

Enter the user login details and the role you want to give to the user before clicking on **Save**:

Settings
☑ Allow small gears

Members
👤 openshift.cookbook@gmail.c...   Owner

openshift.cookbook.test@gma   | Can view                ▼ | ✖

Add a user...

Cancel   Save

What can members do?
**View** – Read-only access to the domain and its applications.
**Edit** – Add, edit, control and delete applications in the domain, including SSH and Git access
**Administer** – Everything except change allowed gear sizes and the domain name.

## See also

 ▶   The *Adding an editor member to a domain using rhc* recipe
 ▶   The *Adding an admin member to a domain using rhc* recipe
 ▶   The *Viewing all the members in a domain using rhc* recipe

# Adding an editor member to a domain using rhc

Imagine that you are leading a software development team that uses OpenShift for development. During development, you would like all the developers in your team to be able to create, delete, push, or even SSH into application gear. However, you would not want users to rename or delete a domain, as this might impact other developers in your team or other teams. Another thing you would not like is to allow developers to change gear sizes. You can restrict development domains to only use small gears to save money. In this scenario, you will give developers an editor role that gives them the freedom to work with applications but not domains.

## Getting ready

To complete this recipe, you will need to have rhc installed on your machine. Please refer to the *Installing the OpenShift rhc command-line client* recipe in *Chapter 1, Getting Started with OpenShift*, for instructions.

You will need two OpenShift accounts to work through this recipe. Please refer to the *Creating an OpenShift online account* recipe in *Chapter 1, Getting Started with OpenShift*, for OpenShift account registration instructions.

## How to do it...

To add the `openshift.cookbook.test@gmail.com` user as an editor to the `devosbook` domain of `openshift.cookbook@gmail.com`, run the following command:

```
$ rhc add-member openshift.cookbook.test@gmail.com --namespace devosbook
--role edit
```

## How it works...

The edit role allows a user to perform the following actions on a domain:

- ▶ A user can create applications under the domain
- ▶ A user can delete applications under the domain
- ▶ A user can view logs of the application
- ▶ A user can perform other application-related actions such as start, stop, and restart
- ▶ A user can push the source code using Git
- ▶ A user can SSH into the application gear using SSH

When you run the `rhc add-member` command with the edit role, OpenShift will firstly add a new member to a domain with an edit role and then copy the user public SSH key to the OpenShift gear `~/.ssh/authorized_keys` file. This allows an editor to perform SSH-related operations such as code deployment using Git and SSH to the application gear.

To check whether the editor has been added successfully, you can view the domain details:

```
$ rhc show-domain
Domain devosbook (owned by openshift.cookbook@gmail.com)
-------------------------------------------------------
Created: Jan 14 9:49 AM
Allowed Gear Sizes: small
Members: openshift.cookbook.test@gmail.com (edit)
```

## There's more...

You can also use the web console to add the editor to your application. Just follow the steps mentioned in the *Adding viewer members to a domain using rhc* recipe in this chapter.

## See also

- ▶ The *Adding viewer members to a domain using rhc* recipe
- ▶ The *Adding an admin member to a domain using rhc* recipe
- ▶ The *Viewing all the members in a domain using rhc* recipe

# Adding an admin member to a domain using rhc

Consider a situation where a new system administrator joins your team. As the new system admin is also responsible for making sure your production apps are running smoothly, you would like to add the new system admin as an administrator. You can do this by giving the new user an admin role.

## Getting ready

To complete this recipe, you will need to have rhc installed on your machine. Please refer to the *Installing the OpenShift rhc command-line client* recipe in *Chapter 1, Getting Started with OpenShift*, for instructions.

You will need two OpenShift accounts to work through this recipe. Please refer to the *Creating an OpenShift Online account* recipe in *Chapter 1, Getting Started with OpenShift*, for OpenShift account registration instructions.

## How to do it...

To add the `openshift.cookbook.test@gmail.com` user as an administrator to `prodosbook` of the `openshift.cookbook@gmail.com` domain, run the following command:

```
$ rhc add-member openshift.cookbook.test@gmail.com --namespace osbook
--role admin
```

## How it works...

The admin role allows a user to perform the following actions on a domain:

  ▸ Everything an editor can do such as performing actions related to applications

  ▸ Perform operations on a domain such as adding members to a domain

When you run the `rhc add-member` command with an admin role, OpenShift will add a new member to a domain with an admin role and then copy the public SSH key to the OpenShift gear `~/.ssh/authorized_keys` file. This allows an editor to perform SSH-related operations.

To check whether the administrator has been added successfully, you can view the domain details by inserting the following command:

```
$ rhc domain-show


Domain prodosbook (owned by openshift.cookbook@gmail.com)
--------------------------------------------------------
Created: Jan 14 9:49 AM
Allowed Gear Sizes: small
Members: openshift.cookbook+test@gmail.com (admin)
```

## There's more...

You can also use the web console to add the editor to your application. Just follow the steps mentioned in the *Adding viewer members to a domain using rhc* recipe in this chapter.

## See also

  ▸ The *Adding viewer members to a domain using rhc* recipe

  ▸ The *Adding an admin member to a domain using rhc* recipe

  ▸ The *Viewing all the members in a domain using rhc* recipe

# Viewing all the members in a domain using rhc

There may be a situation when you want to view all the members in a domain. If so, you should follow this recipe.

## Getting ready

To complete this recipe, you will need to have rhc installed on your machine. Please refer to the *Installing the OpenShift rhc command-line client* recipe in *Chapter 1, Getting Started with OpenShift*, for instructions.

You will need two OpenShift accounts to work through this recipe. Please refer to the *Creating an OpenShift Online account* recipe in *Chapter 1, Getting Started with OpenShift*, for OpenShift account registration instructions.

## How to do it...

To view all the members added to the `osbook` domain, run the following command:

```
$ rhc list-member --namespace osbook
```

## How it works...

The result of the `rhc list-member` command is shown as follows:

```
Login Role

---------------------------------- -------------

openshift.cookbook@gmail.com admin (owner)

openshift.cookbook.test@gmail.com admin
```

The `rhc list-member` command makes a GET request to fetch all the information about the `osbook` domain. The rhc client then parses the **JSON** response and shows the relevant information to the user.

## There's more...

You can also use a shortcut command to fetch all the members in a domain:

```
$ rhc members --namespace osbook
```

## See also

- ▶  The *Adding viewer members to a domain using rhc* recipe
- ▶  The *Adding an admin member to a domain using rhc* recipe
- ▶  The *Viewing all the members in a domain using rhc* recipe

# Removing members from a domain using rhc

Let's suppose you are a system admin and suddenly your application starts behaving weird. You looked at the logs but you were not able to understand them. To fix this issue, you had to give a developer access to look at the logs. The developer was able to understand the problem, and now you want to remove the developer membership.

## Getting ready

To complete this recipe, you will need to have rhc installed on your machine. Please refer to the *Installing the OpenShift rhc command-line client* recipe in *Chapter 1, Getting Started with OpenShift*, for instructions.

You will need two OpenShift accounts to work through this recipe. Please refer to the *Creating an OpenShift Online account* recipe in *Chapter 1, Getting Started with OpenShift*, for OpenShift account registration instructions.

## How to do it...

To remove the `openshift.cookbook.test@gmail.com` user from the `osbook` domain of `openshift.cookbook@gmail.com`, run the following command:

```
$ rhc remove-member openshift.cookbook.test@gmail.com --namespace osbook
```

## How it works...

The `rhc member-remove` command does two things:

- It removes the `openshift.cookbook.test@gmail.com` public SSH key from the authorized keys registry so that `openshift.cookbook.test@gmail.com` can't perform SSH operations such as `git clone` and SSH into application gears.
- It removes the `openshift.cookbooktest@gmail.com` member from the `osbook` domain.

You can verify that `openshift.cookbook.test@gmail.com` is removed from the members' list by inserting the following command:

```
$ rhc members --namespace osbook
Login Role

---------------------------- -------------

openshift.cookbook@gmail.com admin (owner)
```

## There's more...

You can remove all the members from a domain by using the `--all` flag:

```
$ rhc remove-member --all --namespace osbook
```

## See also

- ▶ The *Adding viewer members to a domain using rhc* recipe
- ▶ The *Adding an admin member to a domain using rhc* recipe
- ▶ The *Viewing all the members in a domain using rhc* recipe

# Restricting gear sizes for a domain using rhc

As you start using different domains for different environments, you will feel the need to restrict gear sizes for different domains. In particular, you would like to use small gears for development and large gears for production. When you create an application, you can specify the gear size for that application. This does not help much as it applies only to that application. To avoid using large gears for development, you would want to restrict the development domain only to small gears.

## Getting ready

To complete this recipe, you will need to have rhc installed on your machine. Please refer to the *Installing the OpenShift rhc command-line client* recipe in *Chapter 1, Getting Started with OpenShift*, for instructions.

## How to do it...

To restrict the `devosbook` domain to only small gears, run the following command:

```
$ rhc configure-domain --allowed-gear-sizes small --namespace devosbook
```

## How it works...

By default, when you create a new domain, it gains access to all the gear sizes available for your account. When you sign up for a free account, you receive access to only small gears, meaning what you can do is limited. However, in the commercial version, you can get access to bigger gear sizes. The `rhc configure-domain` command allows you to restrict a domain to specific gear sizes.

The `rhc configure-domain` command requires you to specify a list of gear sizes you want to allow in a domain. The namespace is optional. If you do not specify a domain name, the domain associated with the user specified in `~/.openshift/express.conf` will be configured. You can also specify multiple gear sizes:

```
$ rhc configure-domain --allowed-gear-sizes small,medium --namespace
devosbook
```

## There's more...

You can also configure a domain to not allow any application creation by using the `--no-allowed-gear-sizes` option. You will use this option to disallow application creation for a domain or to block a domain name for later use. For example, I could create another domain, osbook2, for the second version of this book and configure it with the `--no-allowed-gear-sizes` option:

```
$ rhc configure-domain --no-allowed-gear-sizes --namespace osbook
```

## See also

- ▸ The *Adding viewer members to a domain using rhc* recipe
- ▸ The *Adding an admin member to a domain using rhc* recipe
- ▸ The *Viewing all the members in a domain using* rhc recipe

# Leaving a domain using rhc

You have now become a member of a domain that corresponds to the production environment. You have completed your work and now you want to leave the production domain.

## Getting ready

To complete this recipe, you will need to have rhc installed on your machine. Please refer to the *Installing the OpenShift rhc command-line client* recipe in *Chapter 1, Getting Started with OpenShift*, for instructions.

## How to do it...

To leave a domain, you should run the following command. All the users are allowed to leave the domain they are a member of:

```
$ rhc leave-domain --namespace prodosbook -l openshift.cookbook.test@
gmail.com
```

## How it works...

The `rhc leave-domain` command requires only one mandatory argument, which is `--namespace`, the namespace you want to leave. It then removes the user from the domain members. The rhc client makes a REST delete request to remove the member from the namespace.

## See also

- ▶ The *Adding viewer members to a domain using rhc* recipe
- ▶ The *Adding an admin member to a domain using rhc* recipe
- ▶ The *Viewing all the members in a domain using rhc* recipes

# Deleting a domain using rhc

You created a domain for testing and now you no longer require it. Naturally, you would like to delete the domain.

## Getting ready

To complete the steps in this recipe, you will need rhc to be installed on your machine.

## How to do it...

You should run the following command to delete a domain:

```
$ rhc delete-domain --namespace testosbook
```

> Once the domain is deleted, there is no way to undo it. So, please use this command with precaution.

## How it works...

The `rhc delete-domain` command will delete the domain by making a REST delete call to the OpenShift service. If your domain contains an application, you will not be able to delete the domain. Instead, you will get an error message:

```
$ rhc delete-domain --namespace testosbook

Deleting domain 'testosbook' ... Domain contains applications. Delete
applications first or set force to true.
```

Therefore, to delete a domain with an application, you have to pass a `-force` flag. This will delete the domain and all the applications associated with it.

## There's more...

The OpenShift web console also allows you to delete members from a domain. Go to `https://openshift.redhat.com/app/console/domain/{domain-name}` and replace `{domain-name}` with the domain name in which you want to delete a member. Click on the **Delete this domain...** button to delete it. This is shown in the following screenshot:

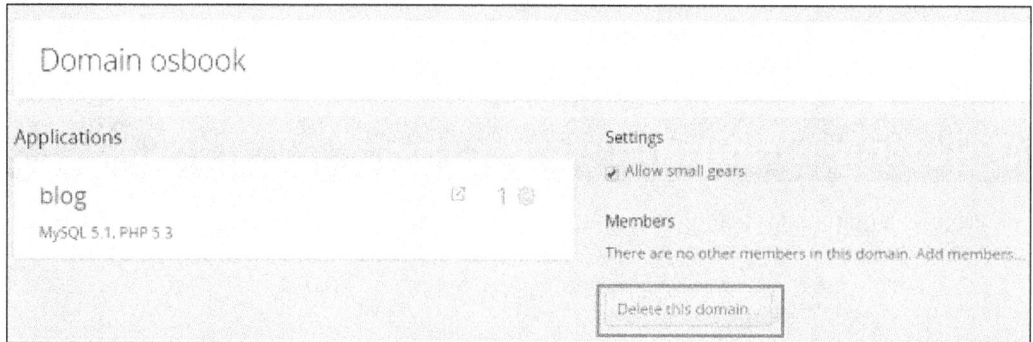

Domain osbook

Applications

blog

MySQL 5.1, PHP 5.3

Settings

☑ Allow small gears

Members

There are no other members in this domain. Add members.

Delete this domain...

## See also

▶ The *Renaming a domain using rhc* recipe

# 3
# Creating and Managing Applications

This chapter presents a number of recipes that show you how to get started with application development using the rhc command-line client. You will learn how to create your own OpenShift application using a single command, how to use application management operations such as start, stop, and delete, how to set up your own domain name for your application, and how to track and roll back deployments.

The specific recipes within this chapter are:

- ▸ Creating an OpenShift application using the rhc command-line client
- ▸ Specifying your own template Git repository URL
- ▸ Starting/stopping/restarting an application
- ▸ Adding and managing add-on cartridges
- ▸ Adding a cron cartridge to an application
- ▸ Using downloadable cartridges with OpenShift applications
- ▸ Viewing application details
- ▸ Cloning the application Git repository using rhc
- ▸ SSH into the application gear using rhc
- ▸ Running a command in the application's SSH session using rhc
- ▸ Setting application-specific environment variables
- ▸ Taking and restoring application backups
- ▸ Tracking and rolling back application deployments
- ▸ Configuring the default Git branch for deployment

- ▸ Doing manual deployments
- ▸ Configuring and doing binary deployments
- ▸ Using your own custom domain name
- ▸ Cleaning up the application
- ▸ Deleting the application

# Introduction

OpenShift (or any other **Platform as a Service** (**PaaS**)) is based on one core principle, in that it should simplify the application life cycle management, including application scaling to help developers build their business applications faster. They all help developers achieve higher productivity by provisioning, managing, and scaling the infrastructure as well as application stack for them. It enables software developers to take their ideas, write code on the local machine, and then deploy the application to the cloud in minutes. PaaS can take you a long way without requiring much work by providing a good foundation to your next big business idea. PaaS can also help enforce best practices, such as continuous integration, in your application from inception. In addition, PaaS can also help you get quick feedback from the customer, and you can iterate faster.

OpenShift provides application developers all the services and tools required to develop and deploy their applications. Apps running on OpenShift can leverage their managed stack, and they do not require system admins to manage the underlying platform in order to keep their apps secure and reliable. OpenShift provides commands that can help application developers take backups of their applications periodically. To understand how application developers can take backups, refer to the *Taking and restoring application backups* recipe.

The `rhc` command-line tool provides all the commands required to work with your application. To view all the application-related commands, open a command-line terminal and run the following command:

```
$ rhc app -h
Usage: rhc app <action>
Creates and controls an OpenShift application. To see the list of all
applications use the rhc domain show command. Note that

delete is not reversible and will stop your application and then remove
the application and repo from the remote server. No

local changes are made.
```

We will cover all these commands in this chapter, so stay tuned!

Every OpenShift application runs inside a gear, which is a container built using SELinux, Control Groups, and pam_namespace Linux technologies. Let's look at all these technologies one by one:

- **SELinux:SELinux** (**Security Enhanced Linux**) is a Linux kernel security module originally developed by the United States National Security Agency. OpenShift uses SELinux to achieve gear isolation and a hardened security layer around gears. This limits application gears from accessing parts of the system they should not access, such as the lower-level system and other application gears running on the same node. In a multitenant environment, such as OpenShift, this behavior is very important to ensure security and reliability when running multiple applications on the same infrastructure.

- **Control Groups**: OpenShift uses **Control Groups** (**cgroups**), a Linux kernel feature, to allocate resources such as CPU time, memory, bandwidth, or a combination of these resources among process groups. The amount of RAM and disk space a gear is allocated depends on the gear size. In the free tier, you only have access to small gears, which have 512 MB RAM and 1 GB of disk space. We will look at gear size in the *Creating an OpenShift application using the rhc command-line client* recipe.

- **pam_namespace**: pam_namespace is used to allow each user or session to maintain its own namespace for directory structures, keeping them from being able to view or impede upon each other's namespace. By using this, OpenShift is able to provide the `/tmp` directory to each gear.

A gear runs different software components (or cartridges) for your application. A cartridge is what makes a gear useful, that is, it provides the software components that an application might need. Every OpenShift application requires one web cartridge and can have zero or more add-on and downloadable cartridges. There are three types of cartridges:

- **Web cartridge**: These are used to serve web requests. You can't create an OpenShift application without a web cartridge. You have to specify the web cartridge at application creation time. They are available for Java, PHP, Python, Ruby, Node.js, and Perl, where you can list all the web cartridges by running the following command:

```
$ rhc cartridges|grep web

jbossas-7           JBoss Application Server 7              web
jbosseap-6 (*)      JBoss Enterprise Application Platform 6 web
jenkins-1           Jenkins Server                         web
nodejs-0.10         Node.js 0.10                           web
nodejs-0.6          Node.js 0.6                            web
perl-5.10           Perl 5.10                              web
php-5.3             PHP 5.3                                web
zend-5.6            PHP 5.3 with Zend Server 5.6           web
php-5.4             PHP 5.4                                web
```

| | | |
|---|---|---|
| zend-6.1 | PHP 5.4 with Zend Server 6.1 | web |
| python-2.6 | Python 2.6 | web |
| python-2.7 | Python 2.7 | web |
| python-3.3 | Python 3.3 | web |
| ruby-1.8 | Ruby 1.8 | web |
| ruby-1.9 | Ruby 1.9 | web |
| jbossews-1.0 | Tomcat 6 (JBoss EWS 1.0) | web |
| jbossews-2.0 | Tomcat 7 (JBoss EWS 2.0) | web |
| diy-0.1 | Do-It-Yourself 0.1 | web |

▶ **Add-on cartridge**: These are additional cartridges provided by OpenShift. You can add them depending on your requirement, that is, if you need a database in your application, you will need to add the MySQL, PostgreSQL, or MongoDB add-on cartridge. You can list all the add-on cartridges by running the following command:

```
$ rhc cartridges|grep addon
```

| | | |
|---|---|---|
| 10gen-mms-agent-0.1 | 10gen Mongo Monitoring Service Agent | addon |
| cron-1.4 | Cron 1.4 | addon |
| jenkins-client-1 | Jenkins Client | addon |
| mongodb-2.2 | MongoDB 2.2 | addon |
| mysql-5.1 | MySQL 5.1 | addon |
| mysql-5.5 | MySQL 5.5 | addon |
| metrics-0.1 | OpenShift Metrics 0.1 | addon |
| phpmyadmin-4 | phpMyAdmin 4.0 | addon |
| postgresql-8.4 | PostgreSQL 8.4 | addon |
| postgresql-9.2 | PostgreSQL 9.2 | addon |
| rockmongo-1.1 | RockMongo 1.1 | addon |
| switchyard-0 | SwitchYard 0.8.0 | addon |
| haproxy-1.4 | Web Load Balancer | addon |

▶ **Downloadable cartridge**: This enables developers to write their own cartridges. They can write their own cartridges and make them available via a public Git repository. These can then be installed using the rhc add-cartridge command. We will cover these in the *Using downloadable cartridges with OpenShift applications* recipe in this chapter.

Every OpenShift application has at least a private Git repository and web cartridge. It may have zero or more add-on cartridges, with the possibility of zero or more downloadable cartridges. An OpenShift application has built-in support for the Git version control system, automated dependency management, persistent data directory for file upload or storing other files, and deployment rollback.

An application can be a scalable or nonscalable application. A **scalable** application runs on multiple gears and scales horizontally depending on the number of concurrent users. We will look at scalable applications in *Chapter 11, Logging and Scaling Your OpenShift Applications*. In the current chapter, we will cover nonscalable applications. A **nonscalable application** runs inside a single gear, and all the cartridges are added to that gear. These are good for development purposes, but for production, high-traffic applications, you should consider scalable applications.

# Creating an OpenShift application using the rhc command-line client

In this recipe, you will learn how to create an OpenShift application using rhc. We will create a PHP 5.4 application just for demonstration. This chapter will be language-agnostic and will only cover concepts that apply to all the application types. Different programming languages supported by OpenShift will be covered later in the book.

## Getting ready

To step through this recipe, you will need the rhc command-line client installed on your machine. Please refer to the *Installing the OpenShift rhc command-line client* recipe in *Chapter 1, Getting Started with OpenShift*, for details. Also, you should set up your OpenShift account using rhc by following the *Setting up an OpenShift account using rhc* recipe in *Chapter 1, Getting Started with OpenShift*.

## How to do it...

To create a PHP 5.4 OpenShift application named `myapp`, open a new command-line terminal and run the following command:

```
$ rhc create-app --app myapp --type php-5.4
```

You can also avoid typing the `--app` and `--type` options where OpenShift will automatically figure them out, as follows:

```
$ rhc create-app myapp php-5.4
```

You can also write the command as follows:

```
$ rhc app-create myapp php-5.4
```

All the rhc commands can take either the `rhc <noun>-<verb>` or `rhc <verb>-<noun>` form.

## How it works...

Let's go through all the steps performed by the `rhc create-app` command:

1.  The `rhc create-app` command requires two mandatory options: `--app` and `--type`. You are not required to pass these options with the command, but you are required to provide their values as shown in the `rhc create-app myapp php-5.4` command. These two options specify the application name and the web cartridge the application will use. The OpenShift server checks whether the application name and web cartridge name are correct. A valid application name must contain only alphanumeric characters and can be, at the most, 32 characters in length. You can view all the available web cartridges using the following command:

    ```
    $ rhc cartridges|grep web
    ```

2.  After making sure the application name and web cartridge name are correct, it will check whether sufficient gears are available in your domain to create an application. In the free tier, you only have access to three gears, so if you try to create an application after you have consumed all three, you will receive an error response. For example, if you have already created three applications and you try to create the fourth application, you will get the error response, `user has already reached the gear limit of 3`.

3.  If you have sufficient resources to create an application, rhc will make a `HTTP POST` request to create an application. The rhc command-line client is a wrapper around the OpenShift REST API. The OpenShift server will receive the POST request and allocate a gear for your application. The amount of RAM and disk space a gear is allocated depends on the gear size. In the free tier, you only have access to small gears, which have 512 MB of RAM and 1 GB of disk space. If you are in the paid tier, you can specify bigger gear sizes with the `--gear` option. The valid values for `--gear` at the time of writing are small, medium, and large.

4.  Next, OpenShift will install the web cartridge required by your application. In the application created previously, it will install the PHP 5.4 language runtime and Apache web server to serve your web requests and perform the required configuration.

5.  The OpenShift server will also create a private Git repository for your application. The Git repository will have a template application depending on the web cartridge type. You can specify your own template application using `--from-code`. This is covered in the next recipe.

6.  Once the application is created with all the required cartridges, the OpenShift server will create a public URL for your application and register it with the DNS. The public URL is a combination of the application name and the domain name. For the application created previously, the URL will be `http://myapp-osbook.rhcloud.com`. Here, `myapp` is the application name, and `osbook` is the domain name. You can also use your own custom domain name with OpenShift applications. This is covered in the *Using your own custom domain name* recipe.

7. After the application DNS name is available, rhc will use the Git command-line to clone the application Git repository on your local machine.

8. Finally, you will be shown the details of your application. You can view the running application at `http://myapp-{domain-name}.rhcloud.com/`. Please replace `{domain-name}` with your account domain name. An example is shown as follows:

```
Your application 'myapp' is now available.

  URL:        http://myapp-osbook.rhcloud.com/

  SSH to:     52ef686d4382ec39f500001a@myapp-osbook.rhcloud.com

  Git remote: ssh://52ef686d4382ec39f500001a@myapp-osbook.rhcloud.
com/~/git/myapp.git/

  Cloned to:  /home/vagrant/dev/apps/myapp
```

Let's look at the `myapp` application directory on your local machine. After the application is created, a directory with a name that is identical to the application name is created on your local machine. It houses the source code of the template application created by OpenShift, as follows:

```
$ ls -a

.git   .openshift index.php
```

Let's look at each of these components one by one as follows:

1. The `.git` directory stores the Git repository of the `myapp` application. This directory contains the complete history of the repository. The `.git/config` file contains the configuration for the repository. The rhc command-line tool also adds the application-specific metadata to the `.git/config` file. The application-specific metadata is under the rhc section:

```
[rhc]

app-id = 52ef686d4382ec39f500001a

app-name = myapp

domain-name = osbook
```

2. The `.openshift` directory stores OpenShift-specific files. The `.openshift` directory has three subdirectories—`action_hooks`, `cron`, and `markers`:

   ❑ The `action_hooks` directory stores the executable scripts, which gives application developers an entry point into various applications and platform life cycle operations. An example of using an action hook would be to send an e-mail after the application is deployed.

   ❑ The `cron` directory stores the executable scripts, which can be scheduled to run periodically. We will cover this in detail in the *Adding a cron cartridge to an application* recipe later in this chapter.

❑ The `markers` directory allows a user to specify settings such as hot deployment, debugging, and the version of Java to be used. As these settings are specific to web cartridges, we will cover them in detail in web-cartridge-specific chapters.

3. The `index.php` file contains a simple PHP application that you see when you visit the application URL.

> At the time of writing this book, applications in the free tier will idle out after 24 hours of inactivity. Inactivity means no HTTP request has been made to your application URL from outside the gear. When idling, it takes a few seconds for the gear to wake up and start processing web requests.

## There's more

The `rhc` command-line tool will raise an exception if the application creation takes more than 120 seconds. To overcome errors related to timeout, you can specify the `--timeout` option as shown in the following code. The timeout value is in seconds:

```
$ rhc app-create myapp php-5.4 --timeout 300
```

You can also configure the timeout in the `~/.openshift/express.conf` file, as shown in the following code. This will apply to all the commands:

```
# The default timeout for network operations
timeout=300
```

## See also

► The *Creating a WordPress application using the web console* recipe in *Chapter 1, Getting Started with OpenShift*

► The *Specifying your own template Git repository URL* recipe

► The *Adding a cron cartridge to an application* recipe

► The *Viewing application details* recipe

► The *Using your own custom domain name* recipe

# Specifying your own template Git repository URL

In the *Creating an OpenShift application using the rhc command-line client* recipe, we created an application that used a template source code provided by OpenShift. Let's suppose you want OpenShift to use your Git repository to populate the initial contents of the application. This can be accomplished using the --from-code option at application creation time.

## Getting ready

To complete this recipe, you will need the rhc command-line client installed on your machine. Please refer to the *Installing the OpenShift rhc command-line client* recipe in *Chapter 1, Getting Started with OpenShift*, for details. You should also complete the setup on your OpenShift account using rhc by following the *Setting up an OpenShift account using rhc* recipe in *Chapter 1, Getting Started with OpenShift*.

## How to do it...

To create an application that uses initial content from your own Git repository, use the --from-code option:

```
$ rhc create-app javaapp jbosseap-6 --from-code https://github.com/
OpenShift-Cookbook/chapter3-recipe2.git
```

> The Git repository URL should be a public Git repository; otherwise, application creation will fail as OpenShift cannot access the repository.

## How it works...

When you create an OpenShift application using the --from-code option, the OpenShift server will first clone the Git repository provided with the --from-code option and then use that repository source code to populate the initial contents of the application. The Git repository URL should be a public Git repository; otherwise, OpenShift will not be able to clone the repository and will instead raise an exception. Following this, OpenShift will build the source code, create an artifact, and then deploy the artifact to the server. An artifact is a by-product produced during the development of software, for example, in the case of Java applications, it could be either a **Java Archive (JAR)**, **Web Archive (WAR)**, or **Enterprise Archive (EAR)** file.

In the previous command, we created a JBoss EAP application that used a public Git repository URL as its initial code. After the application is successfully created, you can view the application running at `http://javaapp-{domain-name}.rhcloud.com/`. The application is a simple demonstration of the article extraction library called Boilerpipe (which you can access at `https://code.google.com/p/boilerpipe/`). It takes a URL and gives you the title and relevant text from the URL.

## See also

 ▸  The *Creating a WordPress application using the web console* recipe in *Chapter 1, Getting Started with OpenShift*

 ▸  The *Creating an OpenShift application using the rhc command-line client* recipe

# Starting/stopping/restarting an application

The rhc command-line client provides commands to start, stop, and restart an application. In this recipe, you will learn how to perform these commands using rhc.

## Getting ready

To step through this recipe, you will need rhc installed on your machine. Also, we will make use of the OpenShift application created in the *Creating an OpenShift application using the rhc command-line client* recipe.

## How to do it...

To start an application, run the following command:

```
rhc start-app --app myapp
```

To stop an application, run the following command:

```
rhc stop-app --app myapp
```

To restart an application, run the following command:

```
rhc restart-app --app myapp
```

The `--app` option is not required if you are running the command from within the application Git repository. When you run the command within the repository, rhc will find the domain name and the application name from the `.git/config` Git repository configuration file. It uses the `git config --get rhc.domain-name` command to find the domain name and `git config -get rhc.app-name` to find the application name.

## How it works...

The rhc start/stop/restart app commands allow you to manage the application using rhc. The rhc client makes a POST HTTP request to stop the application, which stops the web and add-on cartridges. Every OpenShift gear has an executable called the gear available on it. When the server receives the POST request, it executes the gear stop command to stop the PHP 5.4 cartridge. After the application has successfully stopped, the curl request to the application URL will return a 503 error:

```
$ curl http://myapp-osbook.rhcloud.com
<!DOCTYPE HTML PUBLIC "-//IETF//DTD HTML 2.0//EN">
<html><head>
<title>503 Service Temporarily Unavailable</title>
</head><body>
<h1>Service Temporarily Unavailable</h1>
<p>The server is temporarily unable to service your
request due to maintenance downtime or capacity
problems. Please try again later.</p>
<hr>
<address>Apache/2.2.22 (Red Hat Enterprise Web Server) Server at myapp-osbook.rhcloud.com Port 80</address>
</body></html>
```

The rhc start-app command makes a POST HTTP request to start the application. The OpenShift server will receive the POST request and invoke the gear start command on the application gear. The gear start command will first start all the add-on cartridges before starting the web cartridge.

The rhc restart-app command first stops the application by invoking the gear stop command on the application gear, and then starts the application by calling the gear start command on the application gear.

## There's more...

The rhc stop-app command only stops the web and add-on cartridge processes, but if you want to kill all the processes running in your application gear, you should use the rhc force-stop-app command. This command will kill all the processes running inside the gear. This is very useful when people start running their own processes inside the application. In those cases, the rhc app-stop command will not help:

```
$ rhc force-stop-app --app myapp
```

## See also

> ▸ The *Creating an OpenShift application using the rhc command-line client* recipe
>
> ▸ The *Viewing application details* recipe

# Adding and managing add-on cartridges

In the *Creating an OpenShift application using the rhc command-line client* recipe, you learned how to create a new OpenShift application using a web cartridge. Apart from web cartridges, OpenShift also supports a number of add-on cartridges. These cartridges provide functionalities, such as databases, monitoring, cron jobs, database web clients, and others.

In this recipe, you will learn how to install the MySQL 5.5 cartridge to the PHP 5.4 application that you created in the *Creating an OpenShift application using the rhc command-line client* recipe.

## Getting ready

To complete this recipe, you will need rhc installed on your machine. Also, we will make use of the OpenShift application created in the *Creating an OpenShift application using the rhc command-line client* recipe.

## How to do it...

To add the MySQL 5.5 cartridge to our application, run the following command:

```
$ rhc cartridge-add --app myapp --cartridge mysql-5.5
```

If you want to start a cartridge, run the following command:

```
$ rhc cartridge-start --app myapp --cartridge mysql-5.5
```

To stop a cartridge, run the following command:

```
$ rhc cartridge-stop --app myapp --cartridge mysql-5.5
```

To restart a cartridge, run the following command:

```
$ rhc cartridge-restart --app myapp --cartridge mysql-5.5
```

You can also view a cartridge status using the following command:

```
$ rhc cartridge-status --app myapp --cartridge mysql-5.5
```

Finally, to remove a cartridge, run the following command:

```
$ rhc cartridge-remove --app myapp --cartridge mysql-5.5 --confirm
```

The `--confirm` option is used to confirm the cartridge removal. If you don't specify the `--confirm` option, OpenShift will ask you to confirm your action.

## How it works...

All the cartridge-specific commands are available under `rhc cartridge`. To view all the actions you can perform on a cartridge, run the following command:

```
$ rhc cartridge -h
List of Actions
   add          Add a cartridge to your application
   list         List available cartridges
   reload       Reload the cartridge's configuration
   remove       Remove a cartridge from your application
   restart      Restart a cartridge
   scale        Set the scale range for a cartridge
   show         Show useful information about a cartridge
   start        Start a cartridge
   status       Get current the status of a cartridge
   stop         Stop a cartridge
   storage      View/manipulate storage on a cartridge
```

The `rhc cartridge-add` command makes an HTTP POST request to add the MySQL 5.5 cartridge to the `myapp` application. The command-line tool runs within the context of the current directory of your command line and interacts with OpenShift REST API. This helps you to get away with specifying the application name using the `--app` option with every command. The server receives the POST request and installs the MySQL binary on the application gear. After successfully creating the application, you will receive the following result:

```
mysql-5.5 (MySQL 5.5)
---------------------
  Gears:          Located with php-5.4
  Connection URL: mysql://$OPENSHIFT_MYSQL_DB_HOST:$OPENSHIFT_MYSQL_DB_
PORT/
  Database Name:  myapp
  Password:       2L5FIzuyZrXa
  Username:       adminyEY1pty


Added mysql-5.5 to application myapp
MySQL 5.5 database added.  Please make note of these credentials:
```

```
      Root User:  adminyEY1pty
  Root Password:  2L5FIzuyZrXa
  Database Name:  myapp


Connection URL: mysql://$OPENSHIFT_MYSQL_DB_HOST:$OPENSHIFT_MYSQL_DB_
PORT/
```

You can manage your new MySQL database by also embedding phpmyadmin.
The phpmyadmin username and password will be the same as the MySQL
credentials above.

The rest of the commands are self-explanatory, so they require little discussion.

> Please be aware that the `rhc remove-cartridge` command is an irreversible action, and you *cannot* recover data after removing the cartridge.

## There's more...

You can also view the details of a cartridge using the `rhc cartridge` command:

```
$ rhc show-cartridge mysql --app myapp
Using mysql-5.5 (MySQL 5.5) for 'mysql'
mysql-5.5 (MySQL 5.5)
---------------------
  Gears:          Located with php-5.4
  Connection URL: mysql://$OPENSHIFT_MYSQL_DB_HOST:$OPENSHIFT_MYSQL_DB_
PORT/
  Database Name:  myapp
  Password:       2L5FIzuyZrXa
  Username:       adminyEY1pty
```

## See more

- The *Creating an OpenShift application using the rhc command-line client* recipe
- The *Viewing application details* recipe
- The *Adding a cron cartridge to an application* recipe

# Adding a cron cartridge to an application

In this recipe, you will learn how to add the cron add-on cartridge to your application. The cron cartridge will write the output of the `quota` command to a file every hour. The database and other cartridges will be covered later in this book.

## Getting ready

To prepare for this recipe, you will need rhc installed on your machine. Also, we will make use of the OpenShift application created in the *Creating an OpenShift application using the rhc command-line client* recipe.

## How to do it...

Perform the following steps to add a cron cartridge to your application:

1.  Open a new command-line terminal and run the following command:

    ```
    $ rhc add-cartridge --cartridge cron --app myapp
    ```

2.  Create a new file `quota.txt` in the application root directory and populate it with the following code. On a *nix machine, you can use the `cat` command, as shown in the following command line:

    ```
    $ echo "# Quote File" >> quota.txt
    ```

    On Windows machines, you can use filesystem explorer to create a new file. After creating the file, write # Quota File to it.

3.  After adding the cron cartridge, create a new file named `quota.sh` in the `.openshift/cron/hourly` folder, and add the following content to it:

    ```
    #!/bin/bash
    date >> $OPENSHIFT_REPO_DIR/quota.txt
    quota -s >> $OPENSHIFT_REPO_DIR/quota.txt
    echo "**************************************************
    ******************************" >> $OPENSHIFT_REPO_DIR/quota.txt
    ```

4.  Make the `quota.sh` script executable by running the following command. On *nix machines, you can run the following command:

    ```
    $ chmod +x .openshift/cron/hourly/quota.sh
    ```

    On Windows machines, you have to use the following command as the chmod command is not available on them:

    ```
    $ git update-index --add --chmod=+x .openshift/cron/hourly/quota.sh
    ```

5.  Add the `quota.sh` script to the Git repository, and then commit the changes to the local Git repository:

    ```
    $ git add .
    $ git commit -am "added hourly script to output quota limits"
    ```

6. Push the changes to OpenShift service:

   ```
   $ git push
   ```

7. After the changes are deployed, you will see the quota information at `http://myapp-{domain-name}.rhcloud.com/quota.txt`.

## How it works...

Every OpenShift application has a cron directory under the `.openshift` directory. This directory is used to define jobs that should run every minute, hourly, daily, weekly, or monthly. Cron jobs are not invoked until you add the cron cartridge to the application using the `rhc add-cartridge` command. They are useful to automatically perform tasks in the background at regular intervals. You can use them to take database backups, clean up log files, send e-mails, and much more.

In step 1, you added the cron cartridge to the `myapp` application. Next, in step 3, you defined a `quota.sh` bash script that should run every hour. The `quota.sh` script appends the date and quota information to the `quota.txt` file in the `php` directory under the OpenShift repository location. `$OPENSHIFT_REPO_DIR` is an environment variable that points to the location of the application source code directory. In step 4, you made the `quota.sh` script executable, without which the OpenShift service would not be able to execute the script. In the next three steps, you committed the change to the local Git repository and then pushed the changes to your application Git repository hosted on the OpenShift application gear. OpenShift will first stop the entire cartridge, build the application, deploy it to the Apache server, and then finally start all the cartridges. After the cron cartridge is started, it will write to the `quota.txt` file every hour. You can view the quota details by going to `http://myapp-{domain-name}.rhcloud.com/quota.txt`:

```
Tue Feb  4 02:57:14 EST 2014 Disk quotas for user
52f08f184382ecb8e9000239 (uid 2675):        Filesystem  blocks     quota
limit    grace    files    quota    limit    grace /dev/mapper/EBSStore01-
user_home01                     9760       0    1024M           359
0    80000    *******************************************************
*********************************** Tue Feb  4 03:57:14 EST 2014 Disk
quotas for user 52f08f184382ecb8e9000239 (uid 2675):        Filesystem
blocks    quota    limit    grace    files    quota    limit    grace /dev/
mapper/EBSStore01-user_home01                     9760       0    1024M
359      0    80000    *******************************************
**************************************************
```

> The default timeout for a cron job is 5 minutes, which means that your job should be complete within 5 minutes, or else it will be terminated.
>
> You can run longer jobs in the background using `nohup`:
>
> ```
> nohup /path-to/script > $OPENSHIFT_LOG_DIR/logfile 2>&1 &
> ```

## There's more...

OpenShift currently only supports scheduling jobs every minute, or at hourly, daily, weekly, or monthly intervals. To run a job at a specific time or specific intervals, such as running a daily job at 8:30 PM, create a job that runs every minute, and then add the following code. This job will execute itself only when the time is 8:30 PM:

```
#!/bin/bash
if [ `date +%H:%M` == "20:30" ]
then
    date >> $OPENSHIFT_REPO_DIR/quota_20h_30m.txt
quota -s >> $OPENSHIFT_REPO_DIR/quota_20h_30m.txt
echo "*****************************">> $OPENSHIFT_REPO_DIR/
quota_20h_30m.txt
fi
```

## See also

> ▸  The *Creating an OpenShift application using the rhc command-line client* recipe

# Using downloadable cartridges with OpenShift applications

In this recipe, you will learn how to use a third-party downloadable cartridge with OpenShift applications.

## Getting ready

To step through this recipe, you will need rhc installed on your machine. Also, we will make use of the OpenShift application created in the *Creating an OpenShift application using the rhc command-line client* recipe.

## How to do it...

To add the Monit downloadable cartridge, use the `rhc add-cartridge` command as shown in the following command. Please replace `email@address.com` with your valid email address:

```
$ rhc cartridge-add --app myapp https://raw.githubusercontent.com/
openshift-cartridges/openshift-origin-cartridge-monit/master/metadata/
manifest.yml --env MONIT_ALERT_EMAIL=email@address.com
```

The --env option is used to set the environment variable required by this cartridge. The cartridge required the MONIT_ALERT_EMAIL environment variable, which is used to configure e-mail that would be used to send alert notifications. Environment variables will be covered in detail in the *Setting application-specific environment variables* recipe.

## How it works...

To install a third-party downloadable cartridge to your application, you need to provide the rhc command-line client with the URL to its manifest file called manifest.yml. This file exists under the metadata directory in the cartridge source repository, and contains a URL pointing to the actual contents of the cartridge. The list of actively maintained third-party cartridges can be found at https://www.openshift.com/developers/download-cartridges. Another good way to find downloadable cartridges is to search GitHub (https://github.com/search?q=%22openshift+cartridge%22), as most cartridges are hosted on GitHub.

You can later remove the cartridge by running the rhc remove-cartridge command:

```
$ rhc remove-cartridge monit --confirm
```

## See also

- ▶ The *Creating an OpenShift application using the rhc command-line client* recipe
- ▶ The *Adding and managing add-on cartridges* recipe
- ▶ The *Adding a cron cartridge to an application* recipe

# Viewing application details

In this recipe, you will learn how to view all the details related to an application.

## Getting ready

To step through this recipe, you will need rhc installed on your machine. Also, we will make use of the OpenShift application created in the *Creating an OpenShift application using the rhc command-line client* recipe.

## How to do it...

The rhc show-app command can be used to view the information details about the application, as follows:

```
$ rhc show-app --app myapp
```

The `--app` option is not required if you are running the command within the application Git repository.

## How it works...

The `rhc show-app` command returns all the details about an application. The output of the command is shown as follows. The details include the application creation time, application name, public URL, Git repository URL, SSH URL, and details about all the cartridges:

```
rhc show-app --app myapp
myapp @ http://myapp-osbook.rhcloud.com/ (uuid: 52f08f184382ecb8e9000239)
--------------------------------------------------------------------
   Domain:     osbook
   Created:    1:56 AM
   Gears:      1 (defaults to small)
   Git URL:    ssh://52f08f184382ecb8e9000239@myapp-osbook.rhcloud.com/~/
git/myapp.git/
   SSH:        52f08f184382ecb8e9000239@myapp-osbook.rhcloud.com
   Deployment: auto (on git push)

   php-5.4 (PHP 5.4)
   -----------------
     Gears: Located with cron-1.4

   cron-1.4 (Cron 1.4)
   -------------------
     Gears: Located with php-5.4
```

You can also view the state of the application by passing in the `--state` option, as shown in the following command. The valid application states are `started`, `stopped`, and `building`:

```
$ rhc show-app --app myapp --state
Cartridge php-5.4, cron-1.4 is started
```

If you only want to view the SSH information and state of all the gears in the application, you can use the `--gears` option with the `rhc app-show` command:

```
$ rhc show-app--app --gears
ID                        State    Cartridges       Size  SSH URL
----------------------    -------  ---------------  ----  ----------------
------------------------------
52f08f184382ecb8e9000239 started php-5.4 cron-1.4 small
52f08f184382ecb8e9000239@myapp-osbook.rhcloud.com
```

The previous command is very useful when you are working with scalable applications, as it provides you with information about all the application gears with a single command.

## See more

  ▸  The *Creating an OpenShift application using the rhc command-line client* recipe
  ▸  The *Cloning the application Git repository using rhc* recipe

# Cloning the application Git repository using rhc

In the *Cloning the application to the local machine* recipe in *Chapter 1, Getting Started with OpenShift*, you learned how to clone the Git repository using the Git command-line tool. This recipe had a couple of steps—first, to copy the Git repository URL from the web console and second, to use the `git-clone` command to clone the Git repository. The rhc command-line tool can help you save some keystrokes. In this recipe, you will learn how to use rhc to clone the Git repository.

## Getting ready

To step through this recipe, you will need rhc installed on your machine. Also, we will use the OpenShift application created in The *Creating an OpenShift application using the rhc command-line client* recipe.

## How to do it...

To clone the `myapp` application on your local machine using rhc, run the following command:

```
rhc git-clone --app myapp
```

## How it works...

The `rhc git-clone` command first makes a HTTP GET request to fetch the details about the `myapp` application. The application details include the Git repository URL. The `rhc git-clone` command then uses the `git clone <GIT_REPOSITORY_URL>` command to clone the application.

> The `rhc git-clone` command requires Git to be installed on your machine to work.

## There's more...

You can also tell the `rhc git-clone` command to clone the repository to a specific directory using the `--repo` option. The following command will clone the repository inside the `tmp/myapp` folder:

```
$ rhc git-clone --app myapp --repo ../tmp/myapp
```

## See more

- The *Creating an OpenShift application using the rhc command-line client* recipe
- The *Cloning the application to the local machine* recipe in *Chapter 1, Getting Started with OpenShift*

# SSH into the application gear using rhc

In this recipe, you will learn how to use rhc to SSH into the application gear.

## Getting ready

In order to complete this recipe, you will need rhc installed on your machine. Also, you will need to make use of the OpenShift application created in The *Creating an OpenShift application using the rhc command-line client* recipe.

## How to do it...

To SSH into the application gear, open a new command-line terminal and run the following command:

```
$ rhc ssh --app myapp
```

The `--app` option is not required if you are running the command within the application Git repository.

## How it works...

Every OpenShift application gear acts and behaves like a virtual server that you can access using SSH. A gear is assigned a unique user ID and is associated with a SELinux context. When you run the `rhc ssh` command, a secure communication channel is opened between the node hosting the gear and the local machine where you are presented with a limited shell within the environment, as shown in the following command. I have removed part of the output for brevity:

```
Connecting to 52f08f184382ecb8e9000239@myapp-osbook.rhcloud.com ...


    Welcome to OpenShift shell
This shell will assist you in managing OpenShift applications.

    !!! IMPORTANT !!! IMPORTANT !!! IMPORTANT !!!
    Shell access is quite powerful and it is possible for you to
    accidentally damage your application.  Proceed with care!
    If worse comes to worst, destroy your application with "rhc app
delete"
    and recreate it
    !!! IMPORTANT !!! IMPORTANT !!! IMPORTANT !!!

    Type "help" for more info.
[myapp-osbook.rhcloud.com 52f08f184382ecb8e9000239]\>
```

If you run the `ls` command, you will only see all the directories available under your application user home directory:

```
[myapp-osbook.rhcloud.com 52f08f184382ecb8e9000239]\> ls
app-deployments  app-root  cron  git  php
```

## There's more...

By default, the SSH connection will timeout after 5 minutes of inactivity, and you will be logged out of the SSH session. You can turn off connection timeout by unsetting the TMOUT environment variable:

```
[myapp-osbook.rhcloud.com 52f08f184382ecb8e9000239]\> unset TMOUT
```

> If other people access your machine and you don't want them to access your OpenShift application by just typing the `rhc ssh` command, I would recommend you use the SSH key passphrase to restrict access. We discussed SSH key passphrases in the *Working with the SSH key passphrases* recipe in *Chapter 1, Getting Started with OpenShift.*

## See more

- ▸ The *Creating an OpenShift application using the rhc command-line client* recipe
- ▸ The *Uploading SSH keys using the web console* recipe in *Chapter 1, Getting Started with OpenShift*
- ▸ The *Working with the SSH key passphrases* recipe in *Chapter 1, Getting Started with OpenShift*

# Running a command in the application's SSH session using rhc

In this recipe, you will learn how to view the gear directory listing without performing SSH into the server using rhc.

## Getting ready

To step through this recipe, you will need rhc installed on your machine. Also, we will use the OpenShift application created in the *Creating an OpenShift application using the rhc command-line client* recipe.

## How to do it...

To run the `ls` command without performing SSH into the application server, you should run the following command:

```
$ rhc app-ssh --app myapp --command ls
```

The `rhc ssh` command is a short hand for `rhc app-ssh`. Both these commands allow you to SSH into an application gear.

## How it works...

The `rhc app-ssh` command internally uses the SSH command-line client to connect with the application gear. With the SSH command-line client, you can specify the command:

```
$ ssh username@server.com command
```

The rhc command-line client provides a `--command` option that allows you to specify a command you want to run on the server:

```
$ rhc app-ssh --app myapp --command ls
```

```
app-deployments
```

```
app-root
```

```
cron
```

```
git
```

```
php
```

## There's more...

If you want to run the command on all the gears in your application, you should use the `--gears` option with the `rhc app-ssh` command. This would be useful when working with scalable applications. Have a look at the following command:

```
$ rhc app-ssh --app myapp --gears --command ls
```

## See more

- ▶ The *Creating an OpenShift application using the rhc command-line client* recipe
- ▶ The *SSH into the application gear using rhc* recipe

# Setting application-specific environment variables

It is very common that people deploy their application in multiple environments, such as testing, staging, and production. Usually, the configuration differs between these environments to ensure that you are using the right service for the right environment. Consider an example where you want to send e-mails in your application. In the production environment, you would like to use the cloud e-mail service, such as Sendmail (accessible at `https://www.sendmail.com/`), but in the development environment, you would like to use an open source version of Sendmail. Environment variables provide a programming language and operating-system-agnostic solution to these kinds of problems.

Hard coding configuration values in the source code is never a good idea, as it leads to strong coupling between your code and the values, compromising the security of your app if your code falls into the wrong hands. The environment variables allow you to use the same application code in different environments leading to portable code.

OpenShift also exposes some environment variables you should use in your application, rather than hard coding their values. For example, if you want to write a file in your OpenShift application, you should use the OPENSHIFT_DATA_DIR environment variable to access the location of the persistent directory. Every OpenShift cartridge also exposes its own set of environment variables. For example, the PostgreSQL cartridge exposes environment variables for the username, password, host, port, and so on. You should not hard code the database configuration properties in your source code but take advantage of environment variables. You can view all the OpenShift and cartridge-specific environment variables by running the following command. The rhc ssh command is a shorthand for rhc app-ssh. Both these commands allow you to SSH into an application gear:

```
$ rhc ssh --command env
MANPATH=/opt/rh/php54/root/usr/share/man:
OPENSHIFT_PHP_IDENT=redhat:php:5.4:0.0.10
OPENSHIFT_GEAR_MEMORY_MB=512
SELINUX_ROLE_REQUESTED=
GEM_HOME=/var/lib/openshift/52f08f184382ecb8e9000239/.gem
OPENSHIFT_DEPLOYMENT_TYPE=git
SHELL=/usr/bin/oo-trap-user
TMPDIR=/tmp/
SSH_CLIENT=117.207.187.145 15958 22
OPENSHIFT_DEPLOYMENTS_DIR=/var/lib/openshift/52f08f184382ecb8e9000239/
app-deployments/
OPENSHIFT_TMP_DIR=/tmp/
SELINUX_USE_CURRENT_RANGE=
OPENSHIFT_REPO_DIR=/var/lib/openshift/52f08f184382ecb8e9000239/app-root/
runtime/repo/
OPENSHIFT_HOMEDIR=/var/lib/openshift/52f08f184382ecb8e9000239/
OPENSHIFT_GEAR_NAME=myapp
PHPRC=/var/lib/openshift/52f08f184382ecb8e9000239/php//configuration/etc/
php.ini
OPENSHIFT_PYPI_MIRROR_URL=http://mirror1.ops.rhcloud.com/mirror/python/
web/simple
OPENSHIFT_CRON_DIR=/var/lib/openshift/52f08f184382ecb8e9000239/cron/
```

```
OPENSHIFT_APP_SSH_PUBLIC_KEY=/var/lib/openshift/52f08f184382ecb
8e9000239/.openshift_ssh/id_rsa.pub

OPENSHIFT_CLOUD_DOMAIN=rhcloud.com

USER=52f08f184382ecb8e9000239

..// Removed for brevity
```

As you can see in the result of the previous command, the list also includes environment variables specific to the cron cartridge that we added in the previous recipe.

In this recipe, you will learn how you can create application-specific environment variables.

## Getting ready

To complete this recipe, you will need rhc installed on your machine. Also, you will need to use the OpenShift application created in the *Creating an OpenShift application using the rhc command-line client* recipe.

## How to do it...

Perform the following steps to set application-specific environment variables:

1. To create an application-specific environment variable, open a new command-line terminal and run the following command:

   ```
   rhc env-set --app myapp --env MY_APP_ENV="Hello OpenShift
   Environment Variables"
   ```

2. To test the environment variable, open the index.php file in the myapp folder, as follows:

   ```
   <hgroup>
   <h1>Welcome to your PHP application on OpenShift</h1>
   </hgroup>
   ```

   Then, make the following changes in the file:

   ```
   <hgroup>

   <h1>

   <?php

   echo($_ENV["MY_APP_ENV"]);

   ?>

   </h1>
   </hgroup>
   ```

3. Finally, commit the changes and push it into application gear:

```
git commit -am "added environment variable in index.php"
git push
```

4. After a successful push, go to `http://myapp-osbook.rhcloud.com/` to view the change.

## How it works...

The `rhc env-set` command allows a developer to set their application-specific environment variables. This is what happens when you run the `rhc env-set` command:

1. The `rhc` command-line client makes an HTTP POST request with the environment variable data in the body.

2. The OpenShift broker receives the request and performs some validation. If the validation check fails, the user would be presented with an error message.

3. After passing the validation checks, the broker will create tasks to update all the application gears with a new environment variable.

4. Once done, the user will be shown the success message:

```
Setting environment variable(s) ... done
```

> The environment variable will not be available until you restart the application. So, after setting the environment, restart the app using the `rhc app-restart` command.

Not only can you set one environment variable at a time, but you can also set multiple environment variables in one go:

```
rhc env-set -app myapp -env MY_APP_ENV1=test1 MY_APP_ENV2=test2
```

There is another alternative to setting up multiple environment variables that use a file to store environment variables and the passing of the file to the `rhc env-set` command. You should create a new file named `envs.txt` and enter one environment variable per line:

```
MY_APP_ENV1=test
MY_APP_ENV2=
```

Now, you can pass the `envs.txt` file to the `rhc env-set` command, as follows:

```
rhc env-set -app myapp envs.txt
```

If you want to view all the application-specific environment variables, run the following command:

```
rhc env-list -app myapp
```

## There's more...

To update the environment variable value, you should run the `rhc env-set` command with a new value, as follows:

```
rhc env-set --app myapp --env MY_APP_ENV="Hello World"
```

To remove an environment variable, run the following command:

```
$ rhc env-remove --env MY_APP_ENV –confirm
```

## See more

▸ The *Creating an OpenShift application using the rhc command-line client* recipe
▸ The *Viewing application details* recipe

# Taking and restoring application backups

In the real world, things can go wrong at any time, and you should always have a backup of your entire application that you can apply to restore the application to a happy state. An OpenShift application consists of a Git repository, one or more databases, environment variables, and a persistent data directory you should make a backup of. You can make database backups using command-line tools, such as `mysqldump`, `pg_dump`, and `mongoexport`, but those only make backups of the respective databases. We will cover database backups in later chapters. In this recipe, you will learn how to use rhc to make and restore backups.

## Getting ready

In order to prepare yourself for this recipe, you will need rhc installed on your machine. Also, you will need to make use of the application created in the *Creating an OpenShift application using the rhc command-line client* recipe.

## How to do it...

1. To make a backup of your application, open a command-line terminal and run the following command:

```
$ rhc snapshot-save --app myapp --filepath myapp-backup.tar.gz
```

2. Make a change to `index.php` under the `php` directory. Change the header to the following:

```
<h1>
    Welcome to your PHP application running on OpenShift
</h1>
```

3. Commit the change to the local repository and push the changes to the application's remote Git repository to deploy the changes, as follows:

```
$ git commit -am "updated header in index.php"
```

```
$ git push
```

4. Go to `http://myapp-{domain-name}.rhcloud.com/` to view your change.

5. To restore your application from the backup, run the following command:

```
$ rhc restore-snapshot --filepath myapp-backup.tar.gz
```

6. Now, after applying the backup, if you visit the application URL at `http://myapp-{domain-name}.rhcloud.com/`, you will notice that the change we made got reverted, as we applied the snapshot that was taken before making the change in step 2.

## How it works...

Let's now understand what you did in the steps mentioned in the previous section. In step 1, you ran the `rhc snapshot-save` command to make the application backup. The `rhc` tool first retrieves the application details by making an HTTP GET request to the OpenShift broker. The application details include the SSH URL of the application. After getting the SSH URL, the `rhc` command-line client executes a `ssh <application_ssh_url>'snapshot'>../backup/myapp-backup.tar.gz` command to back up the application. This uses the SSH command-line functionality of running a command on a remote server. The output of the snapshot command is written to the `myapp-backup.tar.gz` file on your local machine. This `rhc snapshot-save` command does not require the `--filepath` option and will, by default, create a TAR file with a name as that of the application and write it to the current directory. This command first stops the application before creating a backup of all the directories under your application gear home directory. This includes the application Git repository, data directory, all the cartridges and their data, and environment variables. You can list the content of the `tar.gz` file using the following command:

```
$ tar -ztf myapp-backup.tar.gz
```

Through step 2 to step 4 of the previous list of steps to be performed, you made a small change in `index.php`, pushed the change to your application gear, and then viewed the change by going to your application URL. This is done in order to test the restore functionality.

Step 5 restored the application backup you made in step 1 using the `rhc snapshot-restore` command. The rhc command-line client first makes the HTTP GET request to get the SSH URL of the application. After getting the SSH URL, the rhc command-line client executes the `cat '../backup/myapp-backup.tar.gz' | ssh <application_ssh_url>'restore INCLUDE_GIT'` command to restore the backup. The command pipes the standard output of the `cat` command to the standard input of the SSH command. The restore commands will stop the application before replacing all the directories in the application gear home directory with the one in the backup archive.

Finally, in step 6, you verified that the change you made in step 2 was reverted, because you applied a backup that didn't reflect the change made in step 2.

> The `rhc snapshot` commands stop the application and then run the `save` or `restore` commands.

## There's more...

The `rhc snapshot` commands can also take another option, which is `--ssh`. This can be used to specify a different SSH client and/or to pass SSH options. Suppose you want to print SSH debug information; you can use the SSH client `-v` option:

```
rhc snapshot-save --app myapp --filepath ../backup/myapp-backup.tar.gz
--ssh 'ssh -v'
```

This will print all the SSH debug information. For brevity, I am only showing part of the output:

```
Creating and sending tar.gz
debug1: client_input_channel_req: channel 0 rtype exit-status reply 0
debug1: client_input_channel_req: channel 0 rtype eow@openssh.com reply 0
debug1: channel 0: free: client-session, nchannels 1
debug1: fd 1 clearing O_NONBLOCK
Transferred: sent 2688, received 207872 bytes, in 19.0 seconds
Bytes per second: sent 141.2, received 10915.6
debug1: Exit status 0
RESULT:
Success
```

## See also

- The *Creating an OpenShift application using the rhc command-line client* recipe
- The *Tracking and rolling back application deployments* recipe

# Tracking and rolling back application deployments

When you deploy the source code using `git push`, OpenShift executes a new build, creates a deployment, deploys it to the respective server, and then starts your application container. By default, it will only track the last deployment of your application, which means you can't roll back to a previous deployment. In this recipe, you will learn how to configure your application to track multiple deployments and roll back to a particular deployment.

## Getting ready

To step through this recipe, you will need to have rhc installed on your machine.

## How to do it...

Perform the following steps to learn how to configure applications to track multiple deployments and roll back to a previous version:

1. Create a new PHP 5.4 application just like we created in the *Creating an OpenShift application using the rhc command-line client* recipe, as follows:

   ```
   $ rhc create-app--app myapp php-5.4
   ```

2. To enable an OpenShift application to track 10 deployments (for instance), you should run the following command:

   ```
   $ rhc configure-app --app myapp --keep-deployments 10
   ```

3. Make a change to `index.php` in the application directory:

   ```
   <h1>

       Configured the application to track 10 deployments

   </h1>
   ```

4. Commit the change and push the change to the application gear as follows:

   ```
   $ git commit -am "enabled deployment tracking"
   $ git push
   ```

5. View the change at `http://myapp-{domain-name}.rhcloud.com`.

6. List all the deployments tracked by the application by running the following command:

   ```
   $ rhc deployment-list --app myapp

   7:42 PM, deployment fbaa7582
   7:47 PM, deployment ac5d6f39
   ```

7. To roll back to the deployment with the ID `fbaa7582`, run the following command:

```
$ rhc deployment-activate --app myapp --id fbaa7582
```

8. You can verify that rollback has happened by again running the `rhc deployment-list` command:

```
$ rhc deployment-list --app myapp
7:42 PM, deployment fbaa7582
7:47 PM, deployment ac5d6f39 (rolled back)
7:50 PM, deployment fbaa7582 (rollback to 7:42 PM)
```

## How it works...

In step 1, you created a new PHP 5.4 application, and then in step 2, you configured the application to track 10 deployments using the `rhc app-configure` command. Then, from step 2 through to step 5, you made a simple change in `index.php` and deployed that change to the application gear. When you push the code to an application gear, a new deployment is created with the ID `ac5d6f39` and is stored in the `app-deployments` folder, under the application gear home directory. You can view the deployments stored under the `app-deployments` directory, as shown in the following command. Every deployment is stored inside a directory with its name as the current timestamp. The current active deployment is stored under the current directory:

```
$ rhc ssh --command "ls ~/app-deployments"
2014-02-09_09-11-31.636
2014-02-09_09-17-22.896
by-id
current
```

In step 6, you then listed all the deployments using the `rhc deployment-list` command. The `rhc deployment-list` command lists down all the deployments tracked. The first deployment with the ID `fbaa7582` is the initial deployment that happened when you created the application. The second deployment with the ID `ac5d6f39` is the deployment that happened after making a change in `index.php`.

Step 7 involved rolling back the code to deployment with the ID `fbaa7582` using the `rhc deployment-activate` command. Under the hoods, the `rhc deployment-activate` command runs the `ssh <application_ssh_url> 'gear activate --all fbaa7582'` command on the application gear to activate the deployment.

Finally, in step 8, you ran the `rhc deployment-list` command to view the information about the rollback that happened in step 7.

## There's more...

You can also enable deployment tracking during application creation, as follows:

```
$ rhc create-app myapp php-5.4 --keep-deployments 10
```

You can also view application configuration details using the `rhc show-app` command:

```
$ rhc show-app --app myapp --configuration
myapp @ http://myapp-osbook.rhcloud.com/ (uuid: 52f78c895973ca4cbc000113)
-------------------------------------------------------------------------
  Deployment:         auto (on git push)
  Keep Deployments:   10
  Deployment Type:    git
  Deployment Branch:  master
```

## See also

  ▸   The *Creating an OpenShift application using the rhc command-line client* recipe
  ▸   The *Taking and restoring application backups* recipe

# Configuring the default Git branch for deployment

Every OpenShift application has an associated remote Git repository. When you push the source code to an application gear using `git push`, you are pushing the source code to a Git remote named `origin` and branch named `master`. Every application is configured to autodeploy when code is pushed to the master branch on a remote origin. But it might so happen that you would like to use the master branch for development while using the production branch for deployment. In this recipe, you will learn how to configure an OpenShift application, where you will use a branch named `production` for deployment and a master for development.

## Getting ready

In order to complete this recipe, you will need rhc installed on your machine. Also, you will need to make use of the OpenShift application created in the *Creating an OpenShift application using the rhc command-line client* recipe.

## How to do it...

Perform the following steps to configure a different branch for deployment:

1. Open a command-line terminal and change the directory to the location where `myapp` application exists.

2. Create a new branch with the name `production` using the Git command-line client:

   ```
   $ git branch production
   ```

3. Configure the `myapp` OpenShift application to use the `production` branch for deployment:

   ```
   $ rhc configure-app --deployment-branch production
   ```

4. Open the `index.php` file in the application directory and change the header to the following:

   ```
   <h1>
   Configured the 'production' branch for auto-deployment
   </h1>
   ```

5. Commit the change to the local repository, and then push the changes to the master branch. As we have configured the application to deploy the production branch, only the code will be pushed, so autodeployment will not happen:

   ```
   $ git commit -am "updated index.php"
   ```

   ```
   $ git push
   ```

6. Next, check out the production branch, and merge the master branch changes:

   ```
   $ git checkout production
   ```

   ```
   $ git merge master
   ```

7. Now, push the changes to application gear, and the changes will get deployed:

   ```
   $ git push origin production
   ```

8. Now, if you go to `http://myapp-{domain-name}.rhcloud.com`, you will view the changes made in step 4.

## How it works...

OpenShift leverages the Git action hooks for application deployment. By default, deployment occurs every time you push the source code to the master branch. In step 1, you changed the directory to the `myapp` application location on your command-line tool. Step 2 helped you to create a new branch named `production` for future deployments. You can list all the branches in your Git repository using the `git branch` command:

```
$ git branch
* master
  production
```

In step 3, you configured the application to use the production branch for application deployment. You will get the following output upon successful completion of the command:

```
Configuring application 'myapp' ... done

myapp @ http://myapp-osbook.rhcloud.com/ (uuid: 52f78c895973ca4cbc000113)
- - - - - - - - - - - - - - - - - - - - - - - - - - - - - - - - - - - - - - - - - - - -
    Deployment:          auto (on git push)
    Keep Deployments:    10
    Deployment Type:     git
    Deployment Branch:   production


Your application 'myapp' is now configured as listed above.
```

The output shows that the deployment branch is changed to `production`.

In step 4, you made a change to `index.php` in which you committed and pushed the changes to the master branch in step 5. One thing you will notice is that the `git push` command only pushes the bits to the application gear, but it does not invoke the deployment. The application deployment does not happen, because in step 3, you configured the deployment of the application when to changes are pushed to the production branch. The output of the `git push` command is as follows:

```
Counting objects: 7, done.

Delta compression using up to 8 threads.

Compressing objects: 100% (4/4), done.

Writing objects: 100% (4/4), 427 bytes, done.

Total 4 (delta 2), reused 0 (delta 0)

To ssh://52f78c895973ca4cbc000113@myapp-osbook.rhcloud.com/~/git/myapp.git/
    8252402..9e4ac48  master -> master
```

In step 6, you checked out the production branch and merged the changes that you made in the master branch. You pushed the changes to the production branch in step 7, which will invoke the autodeployment, and the changes will be deployed to the application. The `git push origin production` command is shown as follows:

```
$ git push origin production
Total 0 (delta 0), reused 0 (delta 0)
remote: Stopping PHP 5.4 cartridge (Apache+mod_php)
remote: Waiting for stop to finish
remote: Building git ref 'production', commit 9e4ac48
remote: Checking deplist.txt for PEAR dependency..
remote: Preparing build for deployment
remote: Deployment id is 8c2a41a8
remote: Activating deployment
remote: Starting PHP 5.4 cartridge (Apache+mod_php)
remote: -----------------------
remote: Git Post-Receive Result: success
remote: Activation status: success
remote: Deployment completed with status: success
To ssh://52f78c895973ca4cbc000113@myapp-osbook.rhcloud.com/~/git/myapp.
git/
 * [new branch]      production -> production
```

Finally, you viewed that changes were actually deployed by visiting the application.

## There's more...

What if you want to turn off automatic deployment altogether, that is, if you do not want to deploy even on the production branch, this can be achieved using the `--no-auto-deploy` option:

```
$ rhc configure-app --app myapp --no-auto-deploy
```

This will turn off autodeployment, and only code will be pushed to the Git repository hosted on the application gear. If you want to deploy code, you have to do manual deployment, as explained in the *Doing manual deployments* recipe.

## See also

> ▸ The *Creating an OpenShift application using the rhc command-line client* recipe
>
> ▸ The *Tracking and rolling back application deployments* recipe
>
> ▸ The *Doing manual deployments* recipe

# Doing manual deployments

In the *Configuring the default Git branch for deployment* recipe, under the *There's more...* section, we looked at how to turn off autodeployment using the `--no-auto-deploy` option with the `rhc app-configure` command. What do you do if you want to deploy the application after switching off autodeployment? One solution would be to reconfigure the application to autodeploy by running the `rhc app-configure –auto-deploy` command. This solution is good if you want to perform autodeployment from now on, but if you want to manage deployment yourself, the `--auto-deploy` option is not a solution. In this recipe, you will learn how to manually deploy the application to OpenShift.

## Getting ready

To complete this recipe, you will need rhc installed on your machine. Also, you will need the application you created in the *Creating an OpenShift application using the rhc command-line client* recipe.

## How to do it...

Perform the following steps to perform manual deployments:

1. Open a command-line terminal and change the directory to the `myapp` application.

2. Disable autodeployment of the application using the `--no-auto-deploy` option with the rhc `configure-app` command:

   ```
   $ rhc configure-app --app myapp --no-auto-deploy
   ```

3. Make a change to the application's `index.php`:

   ```
   <h1>
   Application configured with no-auto-deploy
   </h1>
   ```

4. Commit the change, and push it to the application gear. As autodeployment is turned off, the code will not be deployed:

   ```
   $ git commit –am "updated index.php"
   ```
   ```
   $ git push
   ```

5. To manually deploy the change, use the `rhc deploy` command to deploy the master branch:

   ```
   $ rhc deploy --app --ref master
   ```

6. View the change by visiting `http://myapp-{domain-name}.rhcloud.com`.

## How it works...

In step 1, you changed the directory to the `myapp` application location. To disable autodeployment, you used the `rhc configure-app` command with the `--no-auto-deploy` option. You can view the application details by running the `rhc show-app` command with the `--configuration` option:

```
$ rhc show-app --configuration
myapp @ http://myapp-osbook.rhcloud.com/ (uuid: 52f78c895973ca4cbc000113)
------------------------------------------------------------------------

  Deployment:          manual (use 'rhc deploy')
  Keep Deployments:    10
  Deployment Type:     git
  Deployment Branch:   master
```

As you can see in the previous command, the deployment has been set to manual. In steps 3 and 4, you made a change in `index.php` and then committed and pushed the change to the application gear. The autodeployment will not kick in, as we disabled it in step 2. The output of the `git push` command is shown as follows:

```
$ git push
Counting objects: 7, done.
Delta compression using up to 8 threads.
Compressing objects: 100% (4/4), done.
Writing objects: 100% (4/4), 421 bytes, done.
Total 4 (delta 2), reused 0 (delta 0)
To ssh://52f78c895973ca4cbc000113@myapp-osbook.rhcloud.com/~/git/myapp.git/
   9e4ac48..75ea3dc  master -> master
```

In step 5, you manually deployed the change using the `rhc deploy` command. The `rhc deploy` command needs a reference that can be either a Git tag, Git commit ID, or Git branch name. This step made use of the master branch for deployment. The `rhc deploy` command under the hood executed the `gear deploy master` command on the application gear. The output of step 5 is shown as follows:

```
$ rhc deploy --ref master
Deployment of git ref 'master' in progress for application myapp ...
Stopping PHP 5.4 cartridge (Apache+mod_php)
Waiting for stop to finish
Building git ref 'master', commit 75ea3dc
Checking deplist.txt for PEAR dependency..
```

```
Preparing build for deployment
Deployment id is c36cde4a
Activating deployment
Starting PHP 5.4 cartridge (Apache+mod_php)
Success
```

As you can see in the previous command, first cartridges are stopped, and then the application is built using the latest commit ID of the Git master branch before finally deploying the changes.

Finally, you can view the deployed application and verify that changes are deployed.

## There's more...

Instead of using the branch name, you can also use the Git commit ID or Git tag with the `rhc deploy` command. You can see how to use a commit ID with the `rhc deploy` command:

```
$ rhc deploy --ref 9e4ac482d87fdbcf82546afb5a58910be0b9ef19
```

## See also

▶ The *Creating an OpenShift application using the rhc command-line client* recipe

▶ The *Viewing application details* recipe

# Configuring and doing binary deployments

So far, we have looked at how easy it is to perform Git-based deployments with OpenShift, where you perform a `git push` command, and OpenShift builds and deploys the application. This is ideal if you want to perform source-based deployments. It may be that you want OpenShift to also manage your source code using Git. But there are cases when developers do not want to push their source code to OpenShift servers. In those cases, you can use binary deployments to deploy your binary artifact. This is ideal when you want to deploy binary artifacts, such as a `.war` file, as Git is not an efficient means for storing binaries.

## Getting ready

To step through this recipe, you will need rhc installed on your machine.

## How to do it...

Perform the following steps to perform binary deployment:

1. Open a command-line terminal and change the directory to an appropriate location. Then, create a new JBoss EAP 6 application using rhc, as shown in the following command. Note that we are using the `--no-git` option, as we do not want to use Git:

   ```
   $ rhc create-app javaapp jbosseap --no-git
   ```

2. Configure the application to use binary deployment. Also, switch off autodeploy, and configure the application to store two deployments. This will help if we want to roll back to a previous version later. Have a look at the following command:

   ```
   $ rhc configure-app --app javaapp --no-auto-deploy --keep-
   deployments 2 --deployment-type binary
   ```

3. Create a directory structure, as shown in the following commands:

   ```
   $ mkdir javaapp-binary-deployment
   ```
   ```
   $ cd javaapp-binary-deployment/
   ```
   ```
   $ mkdir -p build-dependencies/.m2 repo/deployments dependencies/
   jbosseap/deployments
   ```

4. Download or copy the WAR file to the `repo/deployments` folder:

   ```
   $ cd repo/deployments
   ```
   ```
   $ wget https://github.com/OpenShift-Cookbook/chapter3-recipe15/
   raw/master/ROOT.war --no check-certificate
   ```

5. Package the folder structure to an archive. You can use the ZIP, TAR, tar.gz, or tar.bz formats:

   ```
   $ cd ../../
   ```
   ```
   $ tar -czvf ../javaapp-archive.tar.gz ./
   ```

6. Deploy the new binary artifact using the `rhc deploy` command:

   ```
   rhc deploy --app javaapp --ref ../javaapp-archive.tar.gz
   ```

## How it works...

In step 1, you created a JBoss EAP 6 application named `javaapp`. You also specified the `--no-git` option with the `rhc app-create` command, as we do not want to clone the Git repository to the local machine. Next, in step 2, you configured the application to use binary deployment. OpenShift supports two types of deployment—Git and binary. The Git deployment type is the default deployment type and is invoked via a `git push` command. When you use this, the gear will build a deployment artifact and then deploy the artifact to the server.

With the binary deployment type, you have to provide the deployment archive, as the OpenShift gear will not be responsible for building the deployment. The binary deployment requires an archive that follows a specified directory format. In step 3, you created a directory structure specific to the JBoss EAP 6 application type. Have a look at the following commands:

```
$ tree -a
.
├── build-dependencies
│   └── .m2
├── dependencies
│   └── jbosseap
│       └── deployments
└── repo
    └── deployments


7 directories, 0 files
```

As we are performing binary deployment, you just downloaded the WAR file to the `repo/deployments` folder. Next, in step 5, you created a `tar.gz` archive with the repository structure. Finally, in step 6, you deployed the binary artifact using the `rhc deploy` command. You can also use the HTTP URL instead of the local file path, as shown in the following code:

```
$ rhc deploy --app javaapp --ref https://github.com/OpenShift-Cookbook/
chapter3-recipe15/raw/master/javaapp-archive.tar.gz
```

## There's more...

You can save a deployment snapshot anytime using the `rhc snapshot-save` command:

```
$ rhc snapshot-save --app javaapp --deployment
```

This will save a `javaapp.tar.gz` archive on your local machine. Then, you can deploy this artifact at any point in time using the `rhc deploy` command.

## See also

- The *Creating an OpenShift application using the rhc command-line client* recipe
- The *Viewing application details* recipe

# Using your own custom domain name

By default, all the applications created by OpenShift are subdomains of `rhcloud.com`. In this recipe, you will learn how to use your own domain name with the `myapp` application you created in the *Creating an OpenShift application using the rhc command-line client* recipe.

## Getting ready

To complete this recipe, you will need rhc installed on your machine. Also, we will make use of the OpenShift application created in the *Creating an OpenShift application using the rhc command-line client* recipe.

## How to do it...

1. The first step is to buy a domain name from a domain registration provider. I will use GoDaddy, as I have few domains registered there, but you can just as easily choose a different domain provider. I have bought the `openshift-cookbook.in` domain name for this demonstration.

2. Open your domain registration provider's DNS manager console, and add a CNAME record. The CNAME record lets you point one domain name to another. You can create a new CNAME record that will point to `www.subdomain` to `myapp-osbook.rhcloud.com`, as shown in the following screenshot:

| **openshift-cookbook.in** (Last saved 2/9/2014 1:12:21 PM MST) | | | Cancel | **Save Zone File** |
| --- | --- | --- | --- | --- |
| email | email.secureserver.net | | 1 Hour | |
| fax | login.secureserver.net | | 1 Hour | |
| files | login.secureserver.net | | 1 Hour | |
| ftp | @ | | 1 Hour | |
| imap | imap.secureserver.net | | 1 Hour | |
| mail | pop.secureserver.net | | 1 Hour | |
| mobilemail | mobilemail-v01.prod.mesa1.secureserver.net | | 1 Hour | |
| pop | pop.secureserver.net | | 1 Hour | |
| smtp | smtp.secureserver.net | | 1 Hour | |
| www | myapp-osbook.rhcloud.com | | 1 Hour | Undo |
| Quick Add | | | | |

3. After creating the CNAME record, you have to map your OpenShift application with the custom name. This is done using the `rhc alias` command. To create an alias for `www.openshift-cookbook.in`, run the following command. Please use your own domain name with the `rhc alias` command. Have a look at the following command:

```
$ rhc alias-add --app myapp www.openshift-cookbook.in
```

## How it works...

In step 2, you created a new CNAME entry for the www subdomain. OpenShift allows you to do this by pointing the **Canonical Name** (**CNAME**) entry to your DNS provider's settings to provide an alias for your domain name. CNAME specifies that the domain name is an alias of another domain name. In the previous example, www.openshift-cookbook.com becomes an alias for http://myapp-osbook.rhcloud.com. In step 3, you ran the rhc alias command, which allows you to use your own domain names to run your apps. Technically, what OpenShift has done under the hood is to set up a Vhost in Apache to handle the URL.

Now, if you go to your custom domain name, such as http://www.openshift-cookbook. in, you will see your OpenShift application home page.

This configuration works fine if you use the www subdomain, but it will not work if we remove www from the openshift-cookbook.in URL. It is very common that developers would require both root and www URLs to work. To make it work, you have to use domain forwarding so that when a request comes to openshift-cookbook.in, it will be forwarded to www. openshift-cookbook.in. Open the DNS provider web console and go to the **Forward** tab. Forward the requests coming to openshift-cookbook.in to http://www.openshift-cookbook.in, as follows:

It will take 30 minutes or so to reflect the forwarding change. After changes are propagated, go to openshift-cookbook.in, and you will be redirected to http://www.openshift-cookbook.in.

## There's more...

You can also set an alias using the OpenShift web console. Please refer to the OpenShift blog at https://www.openshift.com/blogs/how-to-configure-custom-domain-names-and-ssl-in-the-openshift-web-console for more information.

## See also

▶ The *Creating an OpenShift application using the rhc command-line client* recipe
▶ The *Viewing application details* recipe

# Cleaning up the application

As you start using OpenShift for application development, the different components, such as Git and cartridge log directories, which constitute an application, will start consuming disk space. In the OpenShift Online free tier, applications are allocated only 1 GB of disk space so that it becomes critical to use the disk space effectively to avoid disk quota errors. In this recipe, you will learn how to clean up your application periodically to avoid disk quota errors.

## Getting ready

To step through this recipe, you will need rhc installed on your machine. Also, we will use the OpenShift application created in the *Creating an OpenShift application using the rhc command-line client* recipe.

## How to do it...

To clean up the application, open a command-line terminal and run the following command:

```
$ rhc tidy-app --app myapp
```

## How it works...

The rhc tidy-app command helps to manage the application disk space. Under the hood, it performs three operations:

1. To start off, the rhc tidy-app command stops the application.
2. Next, it clears out the application tmp directory. The location of the tmp directory can be found by fetching the OPENSHIFT_TMP_DIR environment variable.
3. Next, it clears the log directory for each cartridge.

4. Then, it clears up the application Git repository on the server. The Git repository cleanup is done using two Git commands—git prune and git gc --aggressive. The git prune command removes all the unreachable objects from the Git repository object database. The git gc --aggressive command deletes any loose objects and compresses objects to use the disk space more efficiently.

5. Finally, it starts the application. The application is started even if the rhc tidy command has any exceptions.

## There's more...

You can also create a daily or weekly cron job that would run git gc periodically on the application gear. To do that, add the cron cartridge to the application. Refer to the *Adding a cron cartridge to an application* recipe. After adding the cartridge, create a new shell script named gc_cleanup.sh under the .openshift/cron/daily directory, and add the following contents to it:

```
#!/bin/bash
cd ~/git/$OPENSHIFT_APP_NAME.git
git prune
git gc --aggressive
echo "Ran Git cleanup at $(date)">> $OPENSHIFT_REPO_DIR/php/git-gc.txt
```

Commit the files and push them to the application gear. The daily cron job will perform Git cleanup every day.

## See also

▸ The *Creating an OpenShift application using the rhc command-line client* recipe
▸ The *Viewing application details* recipe

# Deleting the application

In this recipe, you will learn how to delete an OpenShift application.

## Getting ready

To step through this recipe, you will need rhc installed on your machine. Also, you will use the application created in the *Creating an OpenShift application using the rhc command-line client* recipe.

## How to do it...

To delete an application, open a command-line terminal and run the following command:

```
$ rhc delete-app --app myapp --confirm
```

## How it works...

The rhc -delete command deletes the application and all its data on the OpenShift server. You cannot roll back this command, so use it with caution. Under the hood, the rhc -delete command makes an HTTP DELETE request to delete the application.

## See also

▸ The *Creating an OpenShift application using the rhc command-line client* recipe

▸ The *Viewing application details* recipe

# 4
# Using MySQL with OpenShift Applications

This chapter presents a number of recipes that show you how to get started with the OpenShift MySQL database cartridge. You will learn how to add and manage the MySQL cartridge, how to take MySQL database backups, and how to use Amazon RDS MySQL support with OpenShift applications. The specific recipes within this chapter are:

- ► Adding a MySQL cartridge to your application
- ► Adding a phpMyAdmin cartridge to your application
- ► Accessing a MySQL database from your local machine
- ► Connecting to a MySQL cartridge from your local machine using MySQL Workbench
- ► Updating the MySQL max connections setting
- ► Updating the MySQL configuration settings
- ► Performing scheduled MySQL database backups
- ► Using an Amazon RDS MySQL DB instance with OpenShift

# Introduction

Every typical web application needs some sort of persistent data storage on the backend. OpenShift supports a number of options to store your data, including several third-party providers that liberate you from having to deal with hardware provisioning and database management. At the time of writing this book, OpenShift officially supports the MySQL, PostgreSQL, and MongoDB data stores. Apart from these supported databases, there are third-party downloadable database cartridges available for data stores, such as Redis and MariaDB. Red Hat does not support downloadable cartridges, so you have to use them at your own risk. This chapter will cover the MySQL cartridge in detail. *Chapter 5, Using PostgreSQL with OpenShift Applications*, and *Chapter 6, Using MongoDB and Third-party Database Cartridges with OpenShift Applications*, will cover the PostgreSQL and MongoDB cartridges respectively.

This chapter will use the PHP 5.4 application we created in *Chapter 3, Creating and Managing Applications*. If you do not have any OpenShift application running, then you can create a new OpenShift application by running the following command:

```
$ rhc create-app myapp php-5.4
```

In the preceding command, we created a nonscalable application, as we have not used the -s option. If the application is nonscalable, then the database cartridges are installed on the same gear as the primary application gear. If you created a scalable application, then the database cartridge is installed on its own gear. This allows a database to use all the available RAM and disk space. We will cover scalable applications in *Chapter 11, Logging and Scaling Your OpenShift Applications*.

OpenShift also provides a persistent data directory to store your data. The persistent data directory is not scalable and, hence, should not be used with scalable applications. For scalable applications, you should use a third-party service such as Amazon S3.

OpenShift supports stock-standard, security-hardened distributions of MySQL, PostgreSQL, and MongoDB databases. If something goes wrong, the OpenShift operation team is available to fix operational issues. Also, as you are using standard versions of databases, you are not locked inside OpenShift and can easily port your data if required. In this chapter, we will cover how to take periodic backups of your database cartridges to make sure you always have your data in case something goes wrong.

You can also use third-party database services, such as Amazon RDS, if running your database in OpenShift is not possible, or you have already invested in third-party services. Another reason you might like to use a third-party database service is that the OpenShift database cartridges are not scalable. So, for applications where you need horizontally scalable, highly available databases, you can use any of the third-party database services covered in this chapter. This chapter will cover how to use Amazon RDS with OpenShift applications. *Chapter 5, Using PostgreSQL with OpenShift Applications*, and *Chapter 6, Using MongoDB and Third-party Database Cartridges with OpenShift Applications*, will cover third-party PostgreSQL and MongoDB cloud database services.

# Adding a MySQL cartridge to your application

At the time of this writing, OpenShift supports two versions of the MySQL database. You can view the supported MySQL versions by running the following command:

```
$ rhc cartridges|grep mysql
mysql-5.1              MySQL 5.1                              addon
mysql-5.5              MySQL 5.5                              addon
```

## Getting ready

To prepare for this recipe, you will need the `rhc` command-line client installed on your machine. Please refer to the *Installing the OpenShift rhc command-line client* recipe in *Chapter 1, Getting Started with OpenShift*, for more details. Also, we will use the application created in the *Creating an OpenShift application using the rhc command-line client* recipe in *Chapter 3, Creating and Managing Applications*.

## How to do it...

Follow these steps to add the MySQL database cartridge to your OpenShift application and manage it:

1.  To add the MySQL 5.5 cartridge to the `myapp` application, open a new command-line terminal, change the directory to the `myapp` directory location, and execute the following command:

    ```
    $ rhc add-cartridge -c mysql-5.5 --app myapp
    ```

2.  This will install a new instance of the MySQL database on your application gear. The `-c` option is used to specify the cartridge name, and the `--app` option is used to specify the application name. The `--app` option is not required if you are running the command from within the application directory. The `-c` option is required, but you can get away from writing `-c` as the `rhc` command-line client is intelligent enough to infer that `mysql-5.5` is the cartridge name. This can be seen in the following command:

    ```
    $ rhc cartridge-add mysql-5.5
    ```

3.  You can view the cartridge details using the `rhc show-cartridge` command as shown in the following command line:

    ```
    $ rhc show-cartridge mysql
    Using mysql-5.5 (MySQL 5.5) for 'mysql'
    mysql-5.5 (MySQL 5.5)
    ```

```
---------------------
    Gears:           Located with php-5.4
    Connection URL:
mysql://$OPENSHIFT_MYSQL_DB_HOST:$OPENSHIFT_MYSQL_DB_PORT/
    Database Name:   myapp
    Password:        1Qkran3E1a4K
    Username:        adminjL3VBAM
```

4. To stop the MySQL database cartridge, use the `stop` command as shown in this command:

   ```
   $ rhc stop-cartridge mysql
   ```

5. To restart the MySQL database cartridge, use the `restart` command as shown in the following command:

   ```
   $ rhc restart-cartridge mysql
   ```

6. Finally, if you want to remove the MySQL database from your application, you can use the `remove` command as shown in this command:

   ```
   $ rhc remove-cartridge mysql --confirm
   ```

## How it works...

When you run the `rhc cartridge-add` command, `rhc` will make an HTTP POST request to the OpenShift server. The OpenShift server will receive the request and instantiate a new instance of the MySQL server for your application. After provisioning the MySQL server, the `rhc` client will show the database details on the command-line terminal as follows:

```
Adding mysql-5.5 to application 'myapp' ... done


mysql-5.5 (MySQL 5.5)
---------------------
  Gears:           Located with php-5.4
  Connection URL:
mysql://$OPENSHIFT_MYSQL_DB_HOST:$OPENSHIFT_MYSQL_DB_PORT/
  Database Name:   myapp
  Password:        1Qkran3E1a4K
  Username:        adminjL3VBAM


MySQL 5.5 database added.  Please make note of these credentials:

      Root User: adminjL3VBAM
  Root Password: 1Qkran3E1a4K
```

```
Database Name: myapp
```

Connection URL:
```
mysql://$OPENSHIFT_MYSQL_DB_HOST:$OPENSHIFT_MYSQL_DB_PORT/
```

You can view the MySQL installation by performing SSH into your application gear:

```
$ rhc ssh --app myapp
```

Then run the `ls` command to view the gear directory structure:

```
[myapp-osbook.rhcloud.com 52fb71aa5973caf609000026]\> ls -p
app-deployments/  app-root/  git/  mysql/  php/
```

The `mysql` directory hosts your `mysql` installation. The MySQL database is not shared with any other OpenShift application or user. It is only for your application, and only your application can access it.

You can connect to the `mysql` directory with your MySQL database using the `mysql` command-line client as shown in the following command:

```
[myapp-osbook.rhcloud.com 52fb71aa5973caf609000026]\> mysql
Welcome to the MySQL monitor.  Commands end with ; or \g.
Your MySQL connection id is 3
Server version: 5.5.32 MySQL Community Server (GPL)


Type 'help;' or '\h' for help. Type '\c' to clear the current input
statement.


mysql>
```

Now, you can run SQL commands against your MySQL server. To view all the databases, run the following command:

```
mysql> SHOW DATABASES;
+--------------------+
| Database           |
+--------------------+
| information_schema |
| myapp              |
| mysql              |
| performance_schema |
+--------------------+
4 rows in set (0.00 sec)
```

The `myapp` database corresponds to your application database. You can use this database for your application or create a new database using the `CREATE DATABASE` command. To view the uptime of your MySQL database, try running the following command:

```
mysql> SHOW STATUS LIKE 'Uptime';
+----------------+-------+
| Variable_name  | Value |
+----------------+-------+
| Uptime         | 2573  |
+----------------+-------+
1 row in set (0.00 sec)
```

The output shows that the MySQL server is up from the last 2573 seconds.

You can view all the available MySQL command-line utilities on the gear by typing `mysql` and hitting *Tab* twice:

```
[myapp-osbook.rhcloud.com 52fb71aa5973caf609000026]\> mysql
mysql                       mysql_convert_table_format  mysql_fix_
privilege_tables  mysqlslap
mysqlaccess                 mysqld_multi                mysqlhotcopy
mysqltest
mysqladmin                  mysqld_safe                 mysqlimport
mysql_tzinfo_to_sql
mysqlbinlog                 mysqldump                   mysql_install_db
mysql_upgrade
mysqlbug                    mysqldumpslow               mysql_secure_
installation ` mysql_waitpid
mysqlcheck                  mysql_find_rows             mysql_
setpermission        mysql_zap
mysql_config                mysql_fix_extensions        mysqlshow
```

# There's more...

You can also add MySQL cartridges from the OpenShift web console. Go to `https://openshift.redhat.com/app/console/applications`, and click on the `myapp` application for details. On the `myapp` application details web page, you will see the option to add the MySQL database as shown in the following screenshot. Click on the **Add MySQL 5.5** link to add the MySQL 5.5 cartridge.

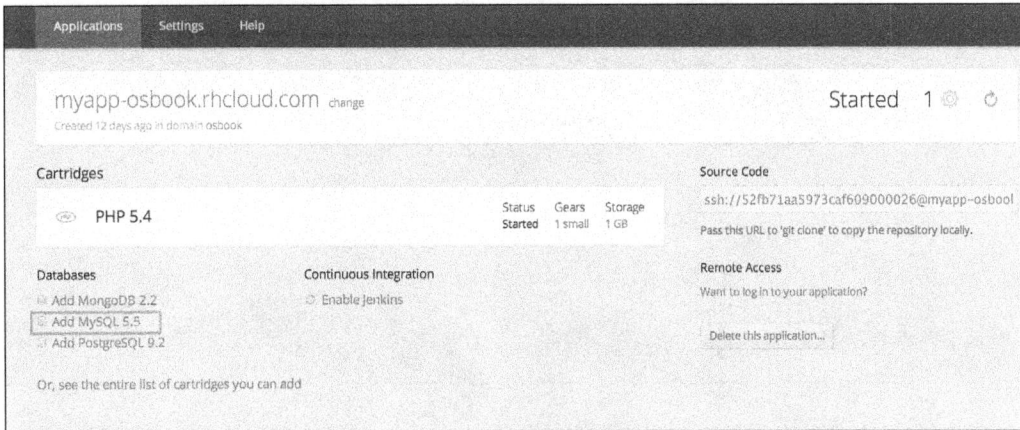

Next, click on the **Add Cartridge** button to add the MySQL 5.5 cartridge to your application as shown in the following screenshot:

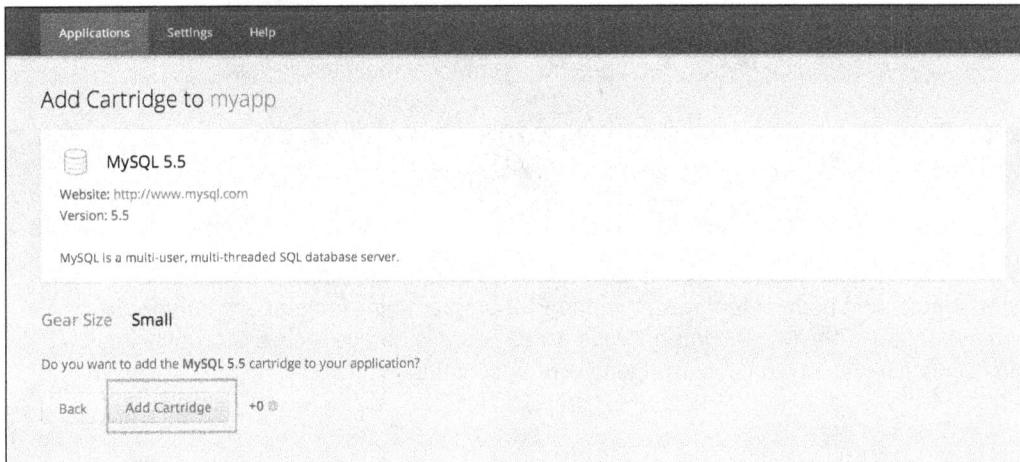

After installing the MySQL cartridge, you will be shown the MySQL database details as follows:

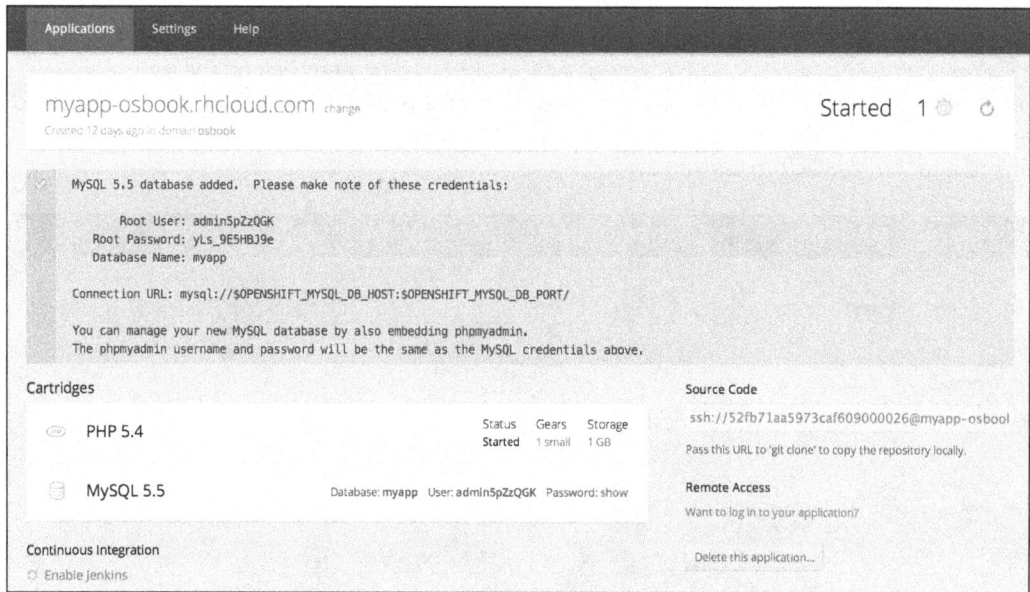

## See also

▸ The *Creating an OpenShift application using the rhc command-line client* recipe in *Chapter 3, Creating and Managing Applications*

▸ The *Adding a phpMyAdmin cartridge to your application* recipe

▸ The Accessing a MySQL database from your local machine recipe

# Adding a phpMyAdmin cartridge to your application

phpMyAdmin (which you can access at `http://www.phpmyadmin.net/`) is a free, open source, and popular tool written in the PHP programming language to handle the administration of the MySQL database via a web browser. In this recipe, you will learn how to install a phpMyAdmin cartridge to your application.

## Getting ready

To complete this recipe, you will need an application with a MySQL cartridge. Please refer to the *Adding a MySQL cartridge to your application* recipe in this chapter to learn how to add a MySQL cartridge.

## How to do it...

This recipe will walk you through all the steps required to add a phpMyAdmin cartridge to the OpenShift application:

1. To install the phpMyAdmin cartridge to the `myapp` application, open a new command-line terminal, change the directory to the `myapp` directory location, and execute the following command:

   **$ rhc add-cartridge phpmyadmin-4**

2. Note the username and password returned by the `rhc add-cartridge` command. You will need the credentials to log in to phpMyAdmin. The phpMyAdmin credentials are the same as your MySQL database credentials, and you can view them anytime by executing the `rhc show-app` command.

3. Log in to phpMyAdmin, accessible at `https://myapp-{domain-name}.rhcloud.com/phpmyadmin/`, using the credentials you got in step 1.

## How it works...

When you run the `rhc cartridge-add` command, the `rhc` client makes an HTTP POST request to the OpenShift server. The OpenShift server receives the request and installs the phpMyAdmin cartridge on the application gear. The phpMyAdmin cartridge works with all the supported application types (Java, Python, Node.js, Ruby, Perl, and PHP). You don't need to create PHP applications to use the phpMyAdmin cartridge. OpenShift will start an Apache process to run the phpMyAdmin application.

> You can only add a phpMyAdmin cartridge after you have added a MySQL cartridge to your application. If you try to add the phpMyAdmin cartridge before adding the MySQL cartridge, then you will get an error, `Cartridge 'phpmyadmin-4' cannot be added without mysql`. The dependency `mysql` can be satisfied with `mysql-5.5` or `mysql-5.1`.

## There's more...

You can also add the phpMyAdmin cartridge from the OpenShift web console. Go to `https://openshift.redhat.com/app/console/applications`, and add the phpMyAdmin cartridge.

## See also

- ► The *Adding a MySQL cartridge to your application* recipe
- ► The *Accessing a MySQL database from your local machine* recipe

# Accessing a MySQL database from your local machine

In the *Adding a MySQL cartridge to your application* recipe of this chapter, you learned how to access the MySQL database by performing an SSH into the application gear. In this recipe, you will learn how to connect with the MySQL database from your local machine.

## Getting ready

To complete this recipe, you will need an application with a MySQL cartridge. Please refer to the *Adding a MySQL cartridge to your application* recipe to learn how to install a MySQL cartridge. Also, you will need the `mysql` command-line client on your machine. You can download the MySQL community server (which includes the `mysql` command-line client) from the official website at `http://dev.mysql.com/downloads/mysql/`.

## How to do it...

Follow these steps to access the MySQL cartridge from your local machine:

1. Open a command-line terminal, and change the directory to the `myapp` application directory. Execute the following command to forward remote ports to the local machine:

   ```
   $ rhc port-forward --app myapp
   ```

2. The output of the preceding command will list down ports along with services that you could use to connect from your local machine. The output is as follows:

   ```
   Service Local               OpenShift

   ------- --------------- ---- --------------------

   httpd   127.0.0.1:8080  =>   127.12.123.129:8080
   mysql   127.0.0.1:3306  =>   127.12.123.130:3306
   Press CTRL-C to terminate port forwarding
   ```

3. Connect to the MySQL server from the local `mysql` command-line client as shown in the following command. You can get the username and password for the MySQL cartridge using the `rhc show-app` or `rhc cartridge-show mysql` command. The hostname and port are available in the output of the `rhc port-forward` command.

   ```
   $ mysql --user=<user> --password=<password> --host 127.0.0.1 --port 3306
   ```

4. Once connected to the MySQL server, you can run any valid SQL command as follows:

```
mysql> SHOW DATABASES;
+--------------------+
| Database           |
+--------------------+
| information_schema |
| myapp              |
| mysql              |
| performance_schema |
+--------------------+
4 rows in set (0.38 sec)
```

## How it works...

In step 1, you used the `rhc port-forward` command to forward all the remote ports to the local machine. The `rhc port-forward` command is a wrapper around the SSH port. Forwarding that makes a port on the remote machine available on your local machine. A port on the remote machine, which would otherwise be unavailable to you, can be used just as if it's on your local machine. The following command returns the list of ports that you can connect to from your local machine:

```
$ rhc port-forward --app myapp
Checking available ports ... done
Forwarding ports ...

To connect to a service running on OpenShift, use the Local address

Service Local              OpenShift
------- ---------------- ---- -------------------
httpd   127.0.0.1:8080   =>   127.9.255.129:8080
mysql   127.0.0.1:3306   =>   127.9.255.130:3306

Press CTRL-C to terminate port forwarding
```

As you can see from the preceding output, the MySQL process is available at port `3306` on the `127.0.0.1` host.

In step 2, you connected to the MySQL server from your local machine, passing in the username, password, host, and port of the database. After successful connection, you ran a SQL command in step 3.

To terminate port forwarding, just press *Ctrl + C* on the command-line terminal where the `rhc port-forward` command is running.

## See also

 ▶ The *Adding a MySQL cartridge to your application* recipe
 ▶ The *Connecting to a MySQL cartridge from your local machine using MySQL Workbench* recipe

# Connecting to a MySQL cartridge from your local machine using MySQL Workbench

In the *Accessing a MySQL database from your local machine* recipe, we showed you how to connect to the MySQL database from the `mysql` command line from your local machine using port forwarding. In this recipe, you will learn how to connect to the MySQL database from MySQL Workbench. MySQL Workbench is a visual database design tool that integrates SQL development, administration, database design, creation, and maintenance into a single integrated development environment for the MySQL database system.

## Getting ready

To complete this recipe, you will need an application with a MySQL cartridge. Please refer to the *Adding a MySQL cartridge to your application* recipe of this chapter to learn how to install the MySQL cartridge. Also, you will need MySQL Workbench on your local machine. You can download MySQL Workbench from the MySQL official website at `http://dev.mysql.com/downloads/tools/workbench/`.

## How to do it...

Follow these steps to connect to the MySQL cartridge from MySQL Workbench running on your local machine:

1. Open a command-line terminal, and change the directory to the `myapp` application directory. Execute the following command to forward the remote ports to the local machine:

   ```
   $ rhc port-forward --app myapp
   ```

2. Start the MySQL Workbench application, and you will see the following screenshot.

Click on the plus button to add a new MySQL connection.

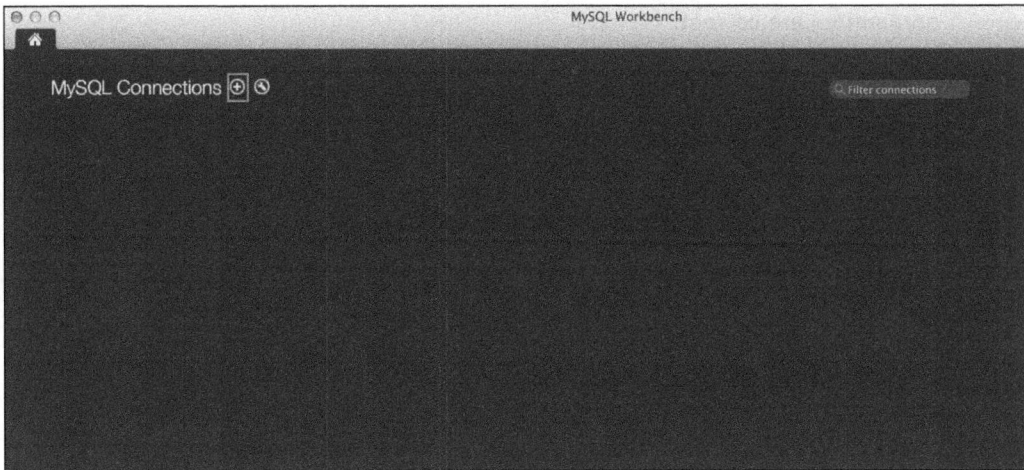

3. Set up a new connection by entering the MySQL database details. You can get the username and password for the MySQL cartridge using the `rhc show-app` or `rhc cartridge-show mysql` command. The hostname and port are available in the output of the `rhc port-forward` command. The following screenshot shows the **Setup New Connection** page:

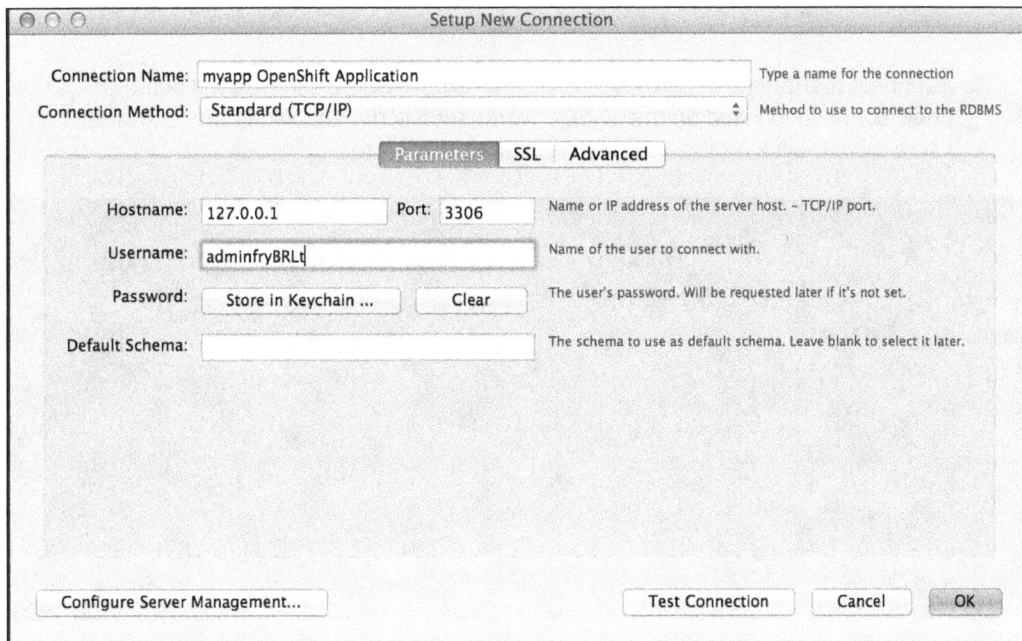

4. Next, test the connection by clicking on the **Test Connection** button. After successful connection, you will see the following dialog box with the message **Connection parameters are correct**:

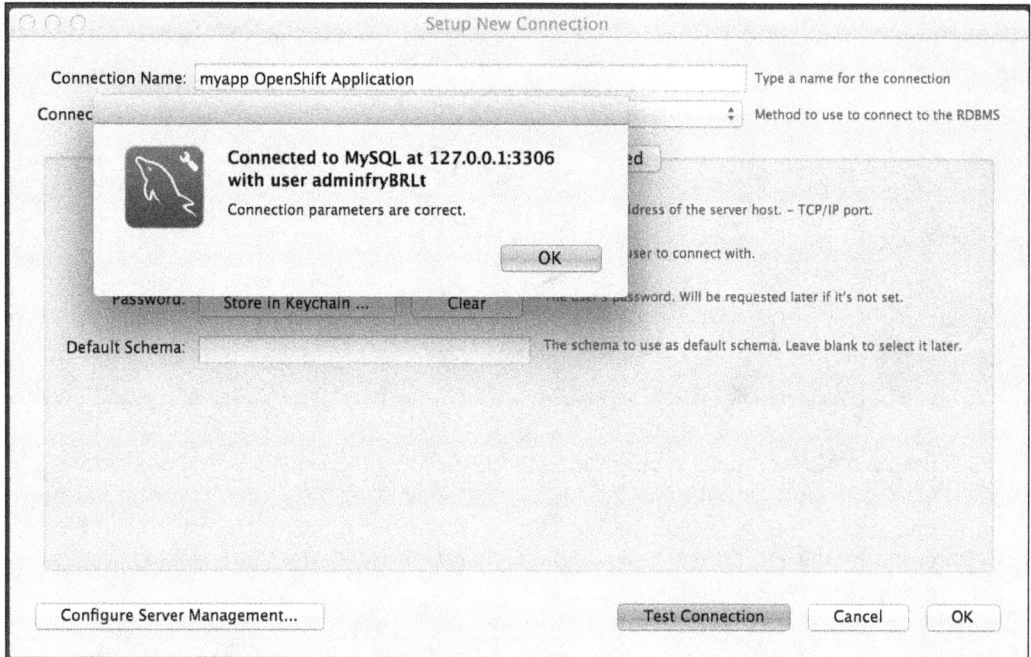

5. Connect to the MySQL cartridge by clicking on the **OK** button. You will see the new connection listed on the MySQL Workbench screen shown in the following screenshot. Click on the connection to open SQL Editor.

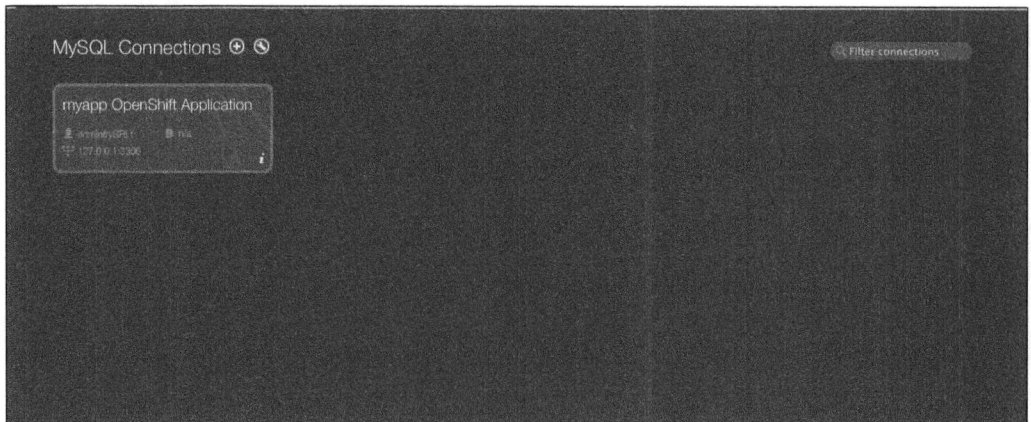

6. Now you can run any legitimate SQL query from within SQL Editor as shown in the following screenshot:

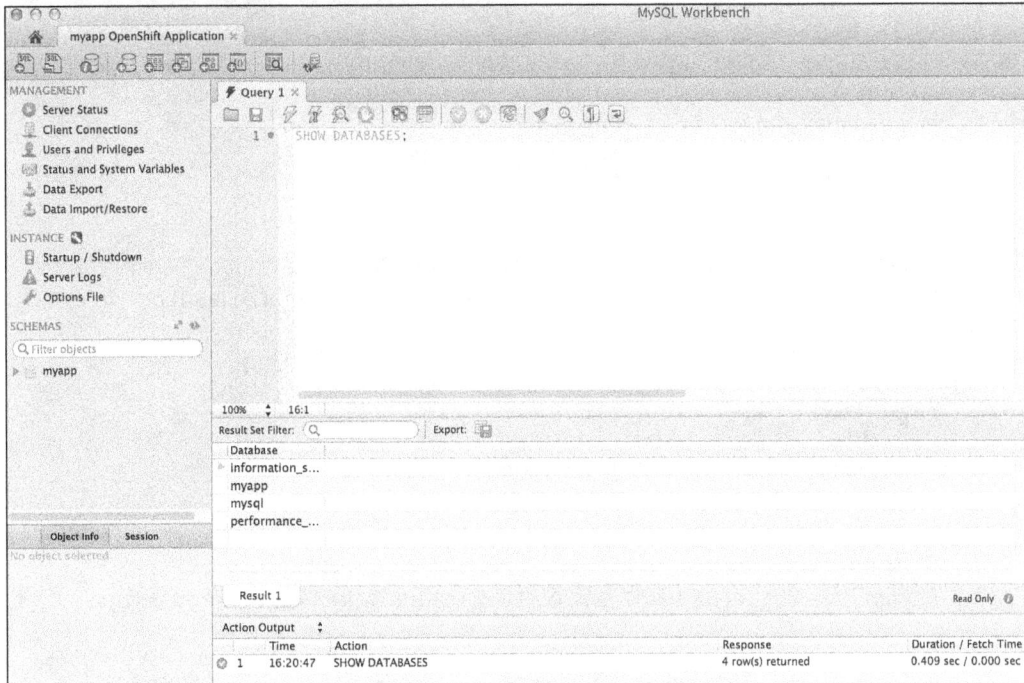

## How it works...

In step 1, you used the `rhc port-forward` command to forward all the remote ports to the local machine. This makes it possible to connect to the MySQL database running inside your application gear. From step 2 through to step 6, you created a new MySQL connection and connected with the MySQL cartridge from within MySQL Workbench. In Step 7, you executed a SQL query using SQL Editor to check whether that connection is getting data from the MySQL cartridge installed in your `myapp` application.

## See also

▶ The *Adding a MySQL cartridge to your application* recipe

▶ The *Accessing a MySQL database from your local machine* recipe

# Updating the MySQL max connections setting

The MySQL database will start giving too many connection errors when all the available connections are in use by other clients. In this recipe, you will learn how to update the MySQL cartridge max connections setting.

## Getting ready

To complete this recipe, you will need an application with a MySQL cartridge. Please refer to the *Adding a MySQL cartridge to your application* recipe of this chapter to learn how to install the MySQL cartridge.

## How to do it...

Follow these steps to update the MySQL max connection setting:

1.  To set the maximum connections to 200, open a command-line terminal, and run the following command:

    ```
    $ rhc env-set OPENSHIFT_MYSQL_MAX_CONNECTIONS=200 --app myapp
    ```

2.  After setting the environment variable, you have to restart the MySQL cartridge for changes to take effect using the following command:

    ```
    $ rhc cartridge-restart mysql --app myapp
    ```

## How it works...

The number of connections supported by the MySQL database is controlled by the max_connections system variable. The default value of max_connections is 151. You can see the current value by running the following SQL query against your MySQL database. To see max_connections for your OpenShift application, SSH into the application gear, and run the following command:

```
mysql> show variables like 'max_connections';
+-----------------+-------+
| Variable_name   | Value |
+-----------------+-------+
| max_connections | 151   |
+-----------------+-------+
```

One way to configure the `max_connections` system variable is to add `max_connections = 200` under the `[mysqld]` section in the `my.cnf` MySQL configuration file. This solution does not work with OpenShift as the `my.cnf` file is read-only. To allow users to change the `max_connections` value, OpenShift provides an environment variable called `OPENSHIFT_ MYSQL_MAX_CONNECTIONS` that can be used to set the `max_connections` system variable. In step 1, you set the `OPENSHIFT_MYSQL_MAX_CONNECTIONS` environment variable to `200`. The MySQL server will not read the new value unless you restart the database. So, in step 2, you restarted the database using the `rhc cartridge-restart` command. To verify whether the `max_connections` value is updated, you can run the following SQL command again:

```
mysql> show variables like 'max_connections';
+-------------------+-------+
| Variable_name     | Value |
+-------------------+-------+
| max_connections   | 200   |
+-------------------+-------+
```

This is the recommended way to update the MySQL `max_connections` system variable value. The only drawback with this approach is that you have to restart the MySQL database, which, depending on the circumstances, may not be the ideal way. Another way you could update the `max_connections` system variable is by issuing the following SQL command:

```
mysql> set global max_connections = 200;
```

This will take immediate effect and will not require a restart. However, this value will be lost once the MySQL database is restarted.

The best solution is to combine the two approaches. Run the `set global max_ connections = 200;` SQL command to make sure `max_connections` is instantly updated, and then create a new environment variable using the `rhc env-set` command. This means the next time your MySQL database is started, it will pick the value from the environment variable.

## See also

- The *Adding a MySQL cartridge to your application* recipe
- The *Updating the MySQL configuration settings* recipe

# Updating the MySQL configuration settings

The MySQL database stores its configuration settings in the `my.cnf` file. This file is located under the `conf` directory inside the MySQL cartridge installation. As mentioned in the previous recipe, OpenShift does not allow users to update the `my.cnf` configuration file. The solution is to use a set of environment variables to configure various settings of the MySQL database.

At the time of writing this book, you could configure the following MySQL settings through the environment variables:

| MySQL setting | OpenShift environment variable |
|---|---|
| lower_case_table_names | OPENSHIFT_MYSQL_LOWER_CASE_TABLE_NAMES |
| default-storage-engine | OPENSHIFT_MYSQL_DEFAULT_STORAGE_ENGINE |
| max_connections | OPENSHIFT_MYSQL_MAX_CONNECTIONS |
| ft_min_word_len | OPENSHIFT_MYSQL_FT_MIN_WORD_LEN |
| ft_max_word_len | OPENSHIFT_MYSQL_FT_MAX_WORD_LEN |
| innodb_use_native_aio | OPENSHIFT_MYSQL_AIO |
| default-time-zone | OPENSHIFT_MYSQL_TIMEZONE |
| table_open_cache | OPENSHIFT_MYSQL_TABLE_OPEN_CACHE |

## Getting ready

To complete this recipe, you will need an application with a MySQL cartridge. Please refer to the *Adding a MySQL cartridge to your application* recipe of this chapter to learn how to add a MySQL cartridge to your application.

## How to do it...

Follow these steps to update the MySQL `lower_case_table_names` configuration:

1. To set the `lower_case_table_names` setting, you should type the following command:

   ```
   $ rhc env-set OPENSHIFT_MYSQL_LOWER_CASE_TABLE_NAMES=1 --app myapp
   ```

2. After setting the environment variable, you have to restart the MySQL cartridge for changes to take effect using the following command:

   ```
   $ rhc cartridge-restart mysql --app myapp
   ```

## How it works...

The way it works is that OpenShift provides a set of environment variables that you can set to configure the MySQL configuration settings. After setting the environment variable, you have to restart the MySQL database so that it can use the new configuration value.

## See also

- ▸ The *Adding a MySQL cartridge to your application* recipe
- ▸ The *Updating the MySQL max connections setting* recipe

# Performing scheduled MySQL database backups

In this recipe, you will learn how to perform a scheduled backup of your MySQL database and upload it to Amazon S3.

## Getting ready

To complete this recipe, you will need an application with a MySQL cartridge. Please refer to the *Adding a MySQL cartridge to your application* recipe of this chapter to learn how to install the MySQL cartridge. Also, you need to have an Amazon AWS account. Visit `http://aws.amazon.com/`, and sign up for a new account if you don't have one already.

## How to do it...

Follow these steps to schedule a daily backup of your MySQL cartridge:

1. Go to `https://console.aws.amazon.com/s3/home`, and create a new bucket to store your database backups.

2. Add a `cron` cartridge to your application by running the following command:

   ```
   $ rhc add-cartridge cron --app myapp
   ```

3. SSH into the application gear, and download the `s3-bash` utility in `$OPENSHIFT_DATA_DIR`. Then, extract it to the `s3-bash` directory by running the following commands:

   ```
   $ rhc ssh --app myapp
   $ cd $OPENSHIFT_DATA_DIR
   $ wget http://s3-bash.googlecode.com/files/s3-bash.0.02.tar.gz
   $ mkdir s3-bash
   $ tar -xf s3-bash.0.02.tar.gz -C s3-bash
   ```

4. Create a new file called `AWSSecretAccessKeyIdFile` in the `$OPENSHIFT_DATA_DIR/s3-bash` directory, and store your Amazon access key secret to it. This is required by `s3-bash` to communicate with Amazon S3.

5. Create a script on your local machine at `.openshift/cron/minutely` named `database_backup.sh`, and add the following contents to it:

```
#!/bin/bash
if [ `date +%H:%M` == "23:50" ]
then
     FILE_NAME=$(date +"%Y%m%d%H%M")
     mysqldump --user $OPENSHIFT_MYSQL_DB_USERNAME -
p$OPENSHIFT_MYSQL_DB_PASSWORD --host
$OPENSHIFT_MYSQL_DB_HOST $BACKUP_DATABASE_NAME >
$OPENSHIFT_DATA_DIR/$FILE_NAME.sql
     echo "Took MySQL Dump" >>
$OPENSHIFT_CRON_DIR/log/backup.log
     $OPENSHIFT_DATA_DIR/s3-bash/s3-put -k
$AWS_ACCESS_KEY_ID -s $OPENSHIFT_DATA_DIR/s3-
bash/AWSSecretAccessKeyIdFile -T
$OPENSHIFT_DATA_DIR/$FILE_NAME.sql
/$AWS_S3_BUCKET/$FILE_NAME.sql
     echo "Uploaded dump to Amazon S3" >>
$OPENSHIFT_CRON_DIR/log/backup.log
     rm -f $OPENSHIFT_DATA_DIR/$FILE_NAME.sql
fi
```

6. The preceding script will run every day at `23:50` and run the `mysqldump` command to create the data dump file. The file is then transferred to Amazon S3 using the `s3-bash` API. Finally, after uploading the file, it deletes the SQL dump file from the application gear.

7. Create the following environment variables. Please refer to the Amazon EC2 documentation for detailed steps on how to create access keys and `S3 bucket`. You then run the following commands:

```
$ rhc env-set AWS_ACCESS_KEY_ID=< Your Amazon ACCESS_KEY_ID>
```

```
$ rhc env-set BACKUP_DATABASE_NAME=<Database you want to take
backup off>
```

```
$ rhc env-set AWS_S3_BUCKET=<Amazon S3 bucket name >
```

8. Following this, commit the code, and push it to the OpenShift application gear. The scheduled job will run every night at `23:50` (11:50 pm) to take database backup, and your backup will be uploaded to Amazon S3:

```
$ git commit -am "database backup script added"
```

```
$ git push
```

## How it works...

In step 1, you created a new Amazon S3 bucket to store your MySQL database backups. Amazon S3 is widely used to store static files and is an ideal choice for this job. Next, in step 2, you added the cron cartridge to your application. The cron cartridge will be used to perform daily backups at a particular time.

Amazon S3 exposes its REST service, which users can use to perform operations on S3 buckets. Amazon provides many programming languages wrapped around its REST API to make it easy for developers to integrate with their application. As we wanted to keep this recipe language agnostic, we used the Amazon s3-bash wrapper. Amazon does not officially support this wrapper but it works very well nonetheless. In step 3, you downloaded the s3-bash wrapper using the wget utility. The tar.gz file was stored in $OPENSHIFT_DATA_DIR. You then extracted the tar.gz file to the s3-bash directory.

In step 4, you created a file called AWSSecretAccessKeyIdFile to store the Amazon access key secret. The s3-bash wrapper uses this file for the AWS secret access key ID so that it does not appear in the list of running processes with ps.

In step 5, you created a bash script that will be executed every night at 11:50 pm. The script first takes the database backup using the mysqldump command and then uploads the file to Amazon S3. The filename is the current timestamp. Finally, after uploading the backup to S3, the script deletes the backup to save disk space. If your MySQL database is big, then you might want to compress the mysqldump output. You just have to update the mysqldump command in step 5 to the one shown in the following command:

```
mysqldump --user $OPENSHIFT_MYSQL_DB_USERNAME -
p$OPENSHIFT_MYSQL_DB_PASSWORD --host $OPENSHIFT_MYSQL_DB_HOST
$BACKUP_DATABASE_NAME | gzip -9 > $OPENSHIFT_DATA_DIR/$FILE_NAME.gz
```

In the preceding command, we have used gzip, a popular data compression program, to compress the mysqldump output.

In Step 6, you created three environment variables required by the backup script. Finally, you committed the changes in step 7 and pushed them to the OpenShift application gear.

## See also

▸   The *Adding a MySQL cartridge to your application* recipe

# Using an Amazon RDS MySQL DB instance with OpenShift

**Amazon Relational Database Service** (**Amazon RDS**) is a web service that makes it easy for you to set up, operate, and scale a relational database on top of Amazon EC2. It provides access to MySQL, Oracle, PostgreSQL, and Microsoft SQL Server database engines. In addition to the standard database features, RDS offers the following functionality:

- Automatic database patches
- Automated backup
- Point-in-time recovery
- Vertical scaling of a database instance via a single API call

In this recipe, you will learn how to use the Amazon RDS MySQL database service with your OpenShift applications.

## Getting ready

To complete this recipe, you will need an application with a MySQL cartridge. Please refer to the *Adding a MySQL cartridge to your application* recipe of this chapter to learn how to install the MySQL cartridge. Also, you need to have an Amazon AWS account. Visit `http://aws.amazon.com/`, and sign up for a new account if you don't have one already.

## How to do it...

Follow these steps to learn how to use the Amazon RDS MySQL database with your OpenShift applications:

1. Go to `https://console.aws.amazon.com/rds/home`, and then click on **Security Groups** as shown in the following screenshot:

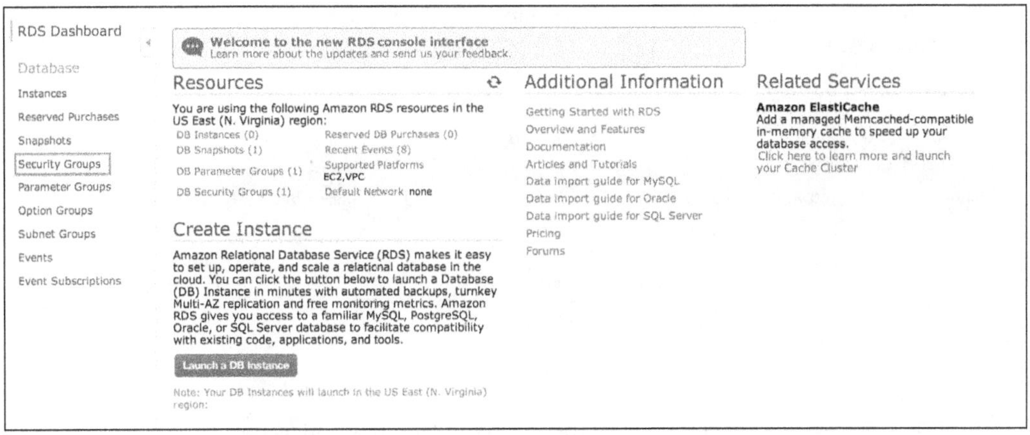

2. Click on the **Create DB Security Group** option to create a new security group, and then enter the details for your new security group (as shown in the following screenshot) before clicking on the **Add** button:

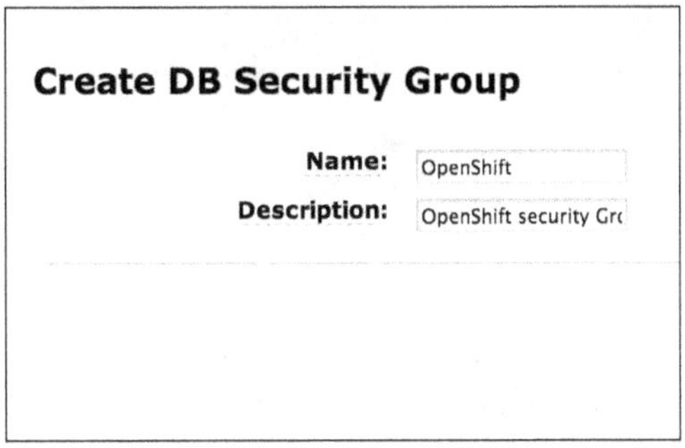

## Create DB Security Group

| | |
|---:|---|
| **Name:** | OpenShift |
| **Description:** | OpenShift security Gro |

3. The new security group will be visible in the security group list. Click on the details icon to view the security group details.

4. Next, configure the security group to permit ingress from all IPs. After entering the CIDR value 0.0.0.0/0, click on the **Add** button as shown in the following screenshot:

DB Security Groups > openshift

▼ Security Group Details

| Connection Type | Details | Status | Actions |
|---|---|---|---|
| CIDR/IP ⊕ | **CIDR:** 0.0.0.0/0<br>Our best estimate for the CIDR of your current machine is 117.200.63.15/32 . However, if your machine is behind a proxy/firewall, this estimate may be inaccurate and you may need to contact your network administrator. | | Add |

↻ Refresh Security Groups

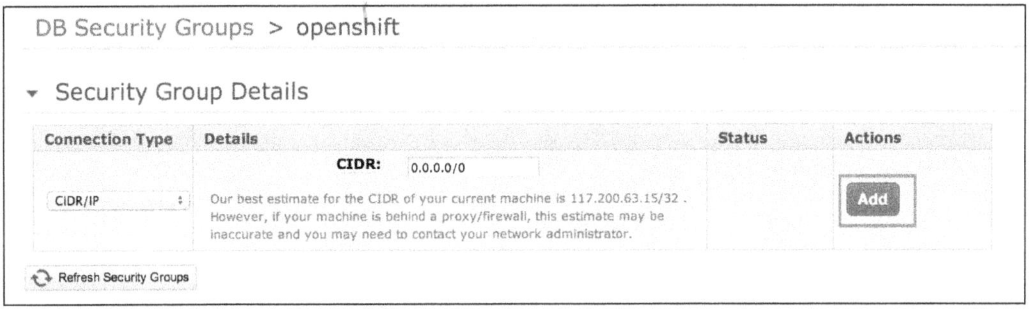

5.  After a few seconds, the new CIDR connection type will be visible under **Security Group Details**:

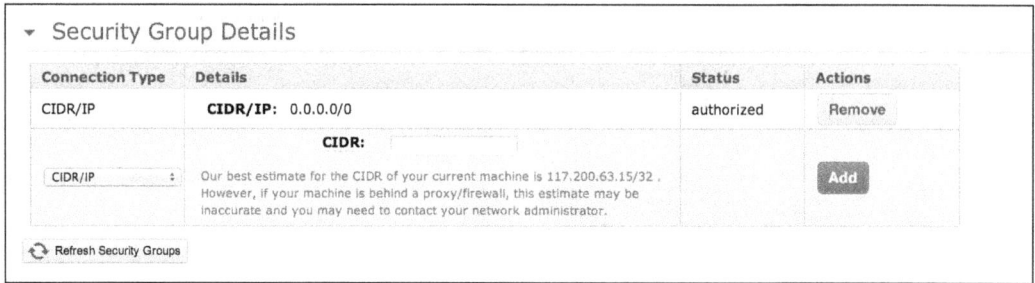

6.  Click on the **Instances** option in the left-hand side navigation bar, and then click on **Launch DB Instance**:

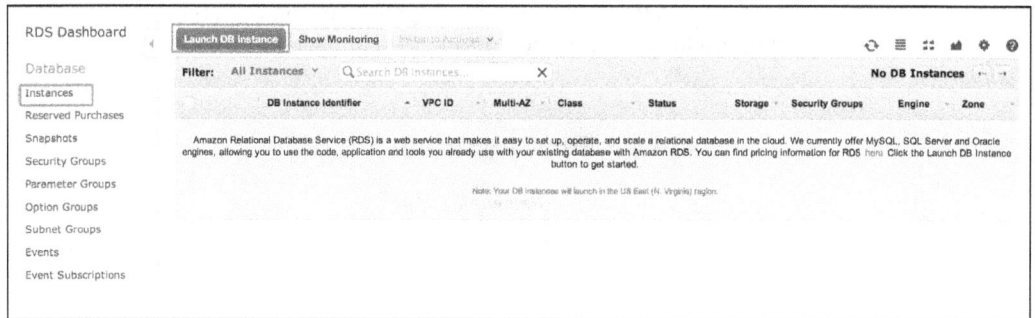

7.  Next, you have to choose the database engine that you want to work with. Select the **use MySQL database** option.

8.  Next, you have to choose whether you want to use this database for production or development purposes. We will choose **No**, but for production, it is recommended that you choose **Yes**.

9.  Then, enter the database details, which will include the MySQL version, database identifier, username, and password to connect to the MySQL database and many others as shown in the following screenshot:

| Step 1: | Engine Selection |
| Step 2: | Production? |
| **Step 3:** | **DB Instance Details** |
| Step 4: | Additional Config |
| Step 5: | Management Options |
| Step 6: | Review |

## DB Instance Details

To get started, choose a DB engine below and click Next Step

**DB Engine:** mysql

**License Model:** general-public-license

**DB Engine Version:** 5.5.33

**DB Instance Class:** db.t1.micro

**Multi-AZ Deployment:** No

**Auto Minor Version Upgrade:** ● Yes ○ No

Provide the details for your RDS Database Instance.

**Allocated Storage:*** 5 GB  (Minimum: 5 GB, Maximum: 3072 GB) Higher allocated storage may improve IOPS performance.

**Use Provisioned IOPS:** ☐

**DB Instance Identifier:*** mydb  (e.g. mydbinstance)

**Master Username:*** mydb1234  (e.g. awsuser)

**Master Password:*** ••••••••••••••••••  (e.g. mypassword)

Cancel    Previous    **Next Step**

10. On the **Additional Config** page, you have to provide the additional information that RDS needs to launch the MySQL database. You have to specify the database name, port, availability zone, DB security group, and so on. The DB security group is very important as we want to use the security group we created in step 3. Enter the details and click on **Next Step**. Have a look at the following screenshot:

| Step 1: | Engine Selection |
| Step 2: | Production? |
| Step 3: | DB Instance Details |
| **Step 4:** | **Additional Config** |
| Step 5: | Management Options |
| Step 6: | Review |

## Additional Config

Provide the optional additional configuration details below.

**Database Name:** mydb  (e.g. mydb)

Note: if no database name is specified then no initial MySQL database will be created on the DB Instance.

**Database Port:** 3306

**Choose a VPC:** Not in VPC  Only VPCs with a DB Subnet Group(s) are allowed

**Availability Zone:** us-east-1a

**Option Group:** default:mysql-5-5

If you have custom DB Parameter Groups or DB Security Groups you would like to associate with this DB Instance, select them below, otherwise proceed with default settings.

**Parameter Group:** default.mysql5.5

**DB Security Group(s):**
default
openshift

Cancel    Previous    **Next Step**

11. Next, on the **Management Options** page, you can specify the backup and maintenance options for your DB instance as shown in the following screenshot:

| Step 1: | Engine Selection |
| Step 2: | Production? |
| Step 3: | DB Instance Details |
| Step 4: | Additional Config |
| **Step 5:** | **Management Options** |
| Step 6: | Review |

## Management Options

**Enabled Automatic** ● Yes ○ No
**Backups:**

The number of days for which automated backups are retained.

Please note that automated backups are currently supported for InnoDB storage engine only. If you are using MyISAM, refer to detail here.

**Backup Retention Period:** [ 2 ⟳ ] days

The daily time range during which automated backups are created if automated backups are enabled

**Backup Window:** ○ Select Window ● No Preference

The weekly time range (in UTC) during which system maintenance can occur.

**Maintenance Window:** ○ Select Window ● No Preference

Cancel    Previous    **Next Step**

12. Finally, you can review the details of your DB instance on the **Review** page.

13. The creation and provisioning of the new MySQL DB instance will take a minute or so, and once done, it will be available under the list of DB instances, as you can see in the following screenshot:

| Launch DB Instance | Show Monitoring | | | | | | | | | |
|---|---|---|---|---|---|---|---|---|---|---|
| **Filter:** All Instances ▾ Q Search DB Instances... ✕ | | | | | | | Viewing 1 of 1 DB Instances ← → | | | |
| | DB Instance Identifier | VPC ID | Multi-AZ | Class | Status | Storage | Security Groups | Engine | Zone |
| ▸ Q mydb | | | No | db.t1.micro | available | 5 GB | openshift (active) | mysql | us-east-1a |

14. Before you can connect to the Amazon RDS MySQL DB instance, you should know the details of the newly created instance. The details of the MySQL DB instance can be found by clicking on the details icon in the DB instance list, as you can see in the following screenshot:

| **Filter:** All Instances ▾ Q Search DB instances... ✕ | | | | | | Viewing 1 of 1 DB Instances ← → | | | |
|---|---|---|---|---|---|---|---|---|---|
| | DB Instance Identifier | VPC ID | Multi-AZ | Class | Status | Storage | Security Groups | Engine | Zone |
| ▸ Q mydb | | | No | db.t1.micro | available | 5 GB | openshift (active) | mysql | us-east-1a |
| Go to Details Page | | | | | | | | | |

15. After clicking on the details page icon, you can view the MySQL hostname that you can connect to. The host information is next to **Endpoint**, and it will be a subdomain of `*.rds.amazonaws.com`, as shown in the following screenshot:

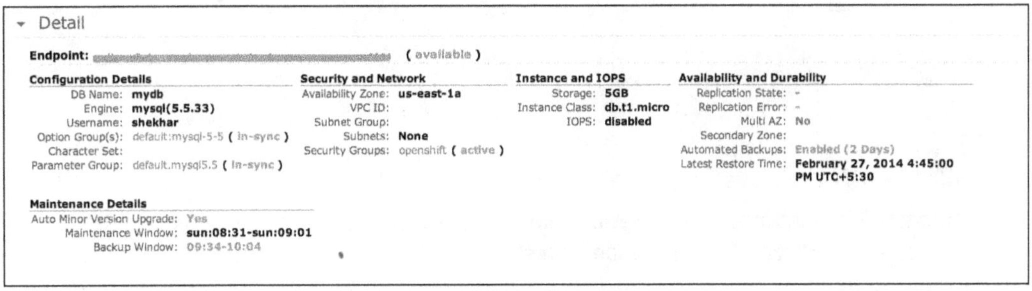

16. To connect to the MySQL DB instance, you will need to have the MySQL command-line client on the gear. Every OpenShift application gear already has the `mysql` command-line agent installed, so you don't have to do anything. Just SSH into the application gear using the `rhc ssh` command and then running the following command:

> The username and password corresponds to the one you created during step 10.

```
$ mysql --host <host_endpoint>.rds.amazonaws.com --port 3306 -
u <username> -p<password> <database_name>
```

17. Once connected, you can run any SQL command. To check the uptime of your MySQL database, you can run the following command:

```
Welcome to the MySQL monitor.  Commands end with ; or \g.

Your MySQL connection id is 12

Server version: 5.5.33-log Source distribution


Copyright (c) 2000, 2011, Oracle and/or its affiliates. All
rights reserved.


Type 'help;' or '\h' for help. Type '\c' to clear the current
input statement.


mysql> SHOW STATUS like 'Uptime';
+---------------+-------+
| Variable_name | Value |
```

```
+----------------+-------+
| Uptime         | 2227  |
+----------------+-------+
1 row in set (0.33 sec)

mysql>
```

## How it works...

Every Amazon RDS instance has a firewall that prevents any outside access to it. So, before you can create an Amazon RDS instance, you should create a new DB security group that gives access to an IP range. From step 1 through to step 6, you created a new security group that would allow all the IP addresses to connect to your Amazon MySQL DB instance. The 0.0.0.0/0 value allows all the IPs to access the database instance. This is important with environments such as OpenShift that do not provide static IPs.

Step 7 through to step 14 helped you create a new instance of Amazon RDS MySQL DB. You are required to provide details related to your DB instance, and Amazon RDS will provision a DB instance based on the details you entered. By step 14, you had a running MySQL DB instance that you could connect to from the outside world. You can connect to it from your local machine or the OpenShift application gear.

Step 15 and step 16 helped you to view the details of your MySQL DB instance. The most important detail is the hostname on which the MySQL DB instance is hosted. In step 17, you used the details to connect to the Amazon RDS MySQL DB instance using the mysql command-line client. In step 18, you ran a simple SQL query against your database to check its uptime.

## There's more...

You can make the MySQL database connection secure by configuring the RDS instance to only accept SSL-encrypted connections from authorized users. To configure SSL, execute the following SQL command. Please replace the username with your MySQL DB instance username:

```
mysql> GRANT USAGE ON *.* TO 'username'@'%' REQUIRE SSL;
```

Now, if you quit the connection and try to log in again using the mysql command mentioned in step 5, you will get an access denied error:

```
[myapp-osbook.rhcloud.com 530f227e50044604f9000060]\> mysql --host
<host_endpoint>.rds.amazonaws.com --port 3306 -u <username> -
p<password> <db_name>
ERROR 1045 (28000): Access denied for user 'username'@'ip-10-181-217-
44.ec2.internal' (using password: YES)
```

To connect to the MySQL DB instance, you have to first download the Amazon RDS CA certificate. Go to `$OPENSHIFT_DATA_DIR`, and run the following `wget` command:

```
[myapp-osbook.rhcloud.com]\> cd $OPENSHIFT_DATA_DIR

[myapp-osbook.rhcloud.com data]\> wget https://s3.amazonaws.com/rds-downloads/mysql-ssl-ca-cert.pem
```

Next, connect to RDS instance using mysql command-line as shown below. Please note the use of ssl_ca parameter to reference the public key.

```
  [myapp-osbook.rhcloud.com data]\> mysql --host <host_endpoint>.rds.amazonaws.com --port 3306 -u <username> -p<password> <db_name> --ssl_ca=mysql-ssl-ca-cert.pem

Welcome to the MySQL monitor.  Commands end with ; or \g.

Your MySQL connection id is 20

Server version: 5.5.33-log Source distribution

mysql>
```

## See also

- The *Adding a MySQL cartridge to your application* recipe

# 5
# Using PostgreSQL with OpenShift Applications

This chapter presents a number of recipes that show you how to get started with the OpenShift PostgreSQL database cartridge. You will learn how to add and manage the PostgreSQL cartridge, how to take backups of a PostgreSQL database, how to list and install PostgreSQL extensions, and how to use the EnterpriseDB PostgreSQL Cloud Database service with OpenShift applications. The specific recipes within this chapter are:

- ▶ Adding the PostgreSQL cartridge to your application
- ▶ Accessing the PostgreSQL cartridge from your local machine
- ▶ Connecting to the PostgreSQL cartridge using pgAdmin from your local machine
- ▶ Updating the PostgreSQL max_connections setting
- ▶ Using the .psqlrc configuration file to configure the OpenShift application psql shell
- ▶ Performing scheduled PostgreSQL database backups
- ▶ Using EnterpriseDB PostgreSQL Cloud Database with OpenShift
- ▶ Installing PostgreSQL extensions

## Introduction

PostgreSQL is a popular, open source relational database used by many web applications around the world. OpenShift supports a stock standard, security hardened version of PostgreSQL database. As you are using standard versions of databases, you are not locked inside OpenShift and can easily port your data if required.

This chapter will use the PHP 5.4 application we created in *Chapter 3, Creating and Managing Applications*. If you do not have any OpenShift application running, you can create a new OpenShift application by running the following command:

```
$ rhc create-app myapp php-5.4
```

You can also use third-party database services, such as EnterpriseDB Cloud Database, if running your database in OpenShift is not possible or you have already invested in third-party services. Another reason why you might like to use a third-party database service is that the OpenShift PostgreSQL cartridge is not scalable. So, for applications where you need horizontally scalable and highly available PostgreSQL service, you can use a third-party provider, such as EnterpriseDB, with your application.

# Adding the PostgreSQL cartridge to your application

At the time of writing this book, OpenShift supports two versions of the PostgreSQL database. You can view all the supported PostgreSQL versions by running the following command:

```
$ rhc cartridges|grep postgresql
postgresql-8.4        PostgreSQL 8.4                        addon
postgresql-9.2        PostgreSQL 9.2                        addon
```

In this recipe, you will learn how to add the PostgreSQL 9.2 cartridge to your OpenShift application.

## Getting ready

To complete this recipe, you will need the rhc command-line client installed on your machine. Please refer to the *Installing the OpenShift rhc command-line client* recipe in *Chapter 1, Getting Started with OpenShift*, for details. Also, we will use the application created in the *Creating an OpenShift application using the rhc command-line client* recipe in *Chapter 3, Creating and Managing Applications*.

## How to do it...

To install the PostgreSQL 9.2 cartridge to the myapp application, open a new command-line terminal, change the directory to the myapp directory location, and then execute the following command:

```
$ rhc add-cartridge --app myapp -c postgresql-9.2
```

This will install a new instance of PostgreSQL server on your application gear. The `-c` option is used to specify the cartridge name, and the `--app` option is used to specify the application name. The `--app` option is not required if you are running the command within the application directory. The `-c` option is required, but you can get away from writing `-c`, as the rhc command-line client is intelligent enough to infer that PostgreSQL 9.2 is the cartridge name. The command can be as simple as the following:

```
$ rhc cartridge-add postgresql-9
```

You can view the cartridge details using the `rhc show-cartridge` command as follows:

```
$ rhc cartridge-show postgresql
Using postgresql-9.2 (PostgreSQL 9.2) for 'postgresql'
postgresql-9.2 (PostgreSQL 9.2)
------------------------------
  Gears:           Located with php-5.4
  Connection URL: postgresql://$OPENSHIFT_POSTGRESQL_DB_HOST:$OPENSHIFT_
POSTGRESQL_DB_PORT
  Database Name:   myapp
  Password:        dPLehGi-UGQi
  Username:        admin8awrwrc
```

You can stop the PostgreSQL server using the `stop` command as follows:

```
$ rhc cartridge-stop postgresql
```

You can restart the PostgreSQL server using the `restart` command as follows:

```
$ rhc cartridge-restart postgresql
```

If you want to remove the PostgreSQL server from your application, you can use the `remove` command as follows:

```
$ rhc cartridge-remove postgresql --confirm
```

## How it works...

When you run the `rhc cartridge-add` command, rhc will make a HTTP POST request to the OpenShift server. The OpenShift server will receive the request and install a new instance of the PostgreSQL database on your application gear. After provisioning the PostgreSQL server, the rhc client will show the database details on the command-line terminal as follows:

```
Adding postgresql-9.2 to application 'myapp' ... done

postgresql-9.2 (PostgreSQL 9.2)
```

```
---------------------------------
   Gears:            Located with php-5.4
   Connection URL: postgresql://$OPENSHIFT_POSTGRESQL_DB_HOST:$OPENSHIFT_
POSTGRESQL_DB_PORT
   Database Name:  myapp
   Password:       dPLehGi-UGQi
   Username:       admin8awrwrc


PostgreSQL 9.2 database added.   Please make note of these credentials:

   Root User: admin8awrwrc
   Root Password: dPLehGi-UGQi
   Database Name: myapp
```

Connection URL: postgresql://$OPENSHIFT_POSTGRESQL_DB_HOST:$OPENSHIFT_
POSTGRESQL_DB_PORT

You can view the PostgreSQL installation by performing SSH into your application gear:

```
$ rhc ssh --app myapp
```

Then, run the `ls` command to view the gear directory structure, and you will see the `postgresql` directory:

```
[myapp-osbook.rhcloud.com 531069cd5973cad58c0000b6]\> ls -p

app-deployments/  app-root/  git/  php/  postgresql/
```

The `postgresql` directory is the location of your PostgreSQL installation, and it is not shared with any other OpenShift application or user. It is only for your application, and only your application can access it.

You can also connect with your PostgreSQL server using the `psql` command-line client:

```
[myapp-osbook.rhcloud.com 531069cd5973cad58c0000b6]\> psql
psql (9.2.4)
Type "help" for help.


myapp=#
```

Now you can run SQL commands against your PostgreSQL server. To view all the databases, run the following command:

```
myapp=# \list
                               List of databases
    Name     |     Owner     | Encoding |   Collate    |    Ctype     |
Access privileges
-------------+---------------+----------+--------------+--------------+-------
-----------------
 myapp       | admin8awrwrc  | UTF8     | en_US.UTF-8  | en_US.UTF-8  |
 postgres    | postgres      | UTF8     | en_US.UTF-8  | en_US.UTF-8  |
 template0   | postgres      | UTF8     | en_US.UTF-8  | en_US.UTF-8  | =c/
postgres          +
             |               |          |              |              |
postgres=CTc/postgres
 template1   | postgres      | UTF8     | en_US.UTF-8  | en_US.UTF-8  | =c/
postgres          +
             |               |          |              |              |
postgres=CTc/postgres
(4 rows)


myapp=#
```

The `myapp` database corresponds to your application database. You can use this database for your application or create a new database using the `CREATE DATABASE` command. To view the uptime of your PostgreSQL server, run the following command:

```
myapp=# select date_trunc('minute',current_timestamp - pg_postmaster_
start_time()) as "postgresql_uptime";
 postgresql_uptime
-------------------
 00:12:00
(1 row)
```

The output shows that the PostgreSQL server has been up for the last 12 minutes.

You can view all the available PostgreSQL command-line utilities available on the gear by typing `pg_` and pressing *Tab*. The *Tab* key enables the command-line completion functionality that allows the command-line program to automatically fill the rest of command:

```
[myapp-osbook.rhcloud.com 531069cd5973cad58c0000b6]\> pg_
pg_archivecleanup  pg_controldata     pg_dumpall         pg_resetxlog
pg_test_fsync
pg_basebackup      pg_ctl             pg_filedump        pg_restore
pg_test_timing
pg_config          pg_dump            pg_receivexlog     pg_standby
```

## There's more...

You can also add the PostgreSQL database from the OpenShift web console. Go to `https://openshift.redhat.com/app/console/applications`, and click on the `myapp` application for details. On the `myapp` application details web page, you will see the option to add the PostgreSQL database, as shown in the following screenshot. Click on **Add PostgreSQL 9.2** to add the PostgreSQL 9.2 cartridge.

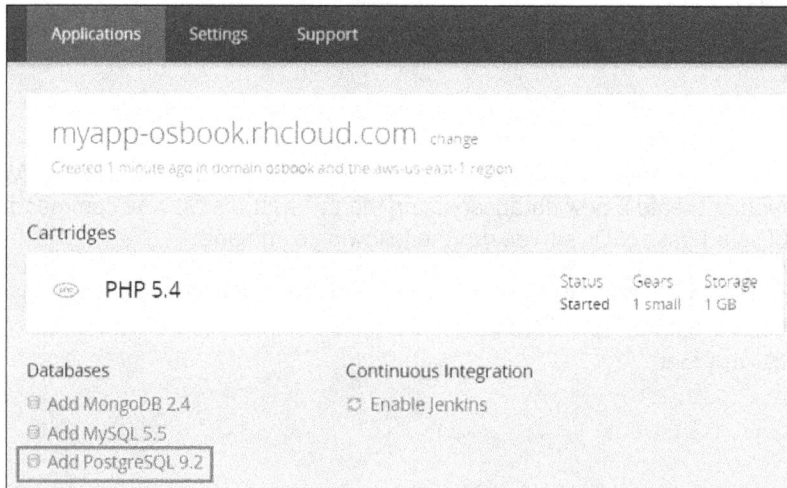

Next, you will be directed to the page to add the PostgreSQL cartridge. Click on **Add Cartridge** to add a PostgreSQL database to your application. Have a look at the following screenshot:

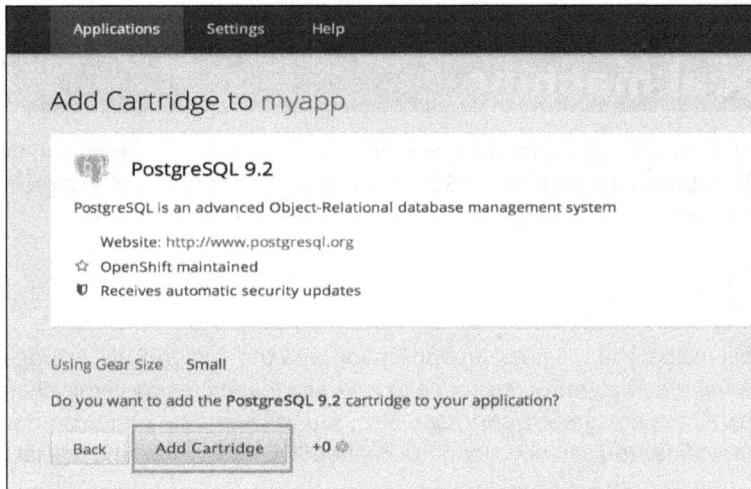

After installing the PostgreSQL cartridge, you will be shown the PostgreSQL database details as follows:

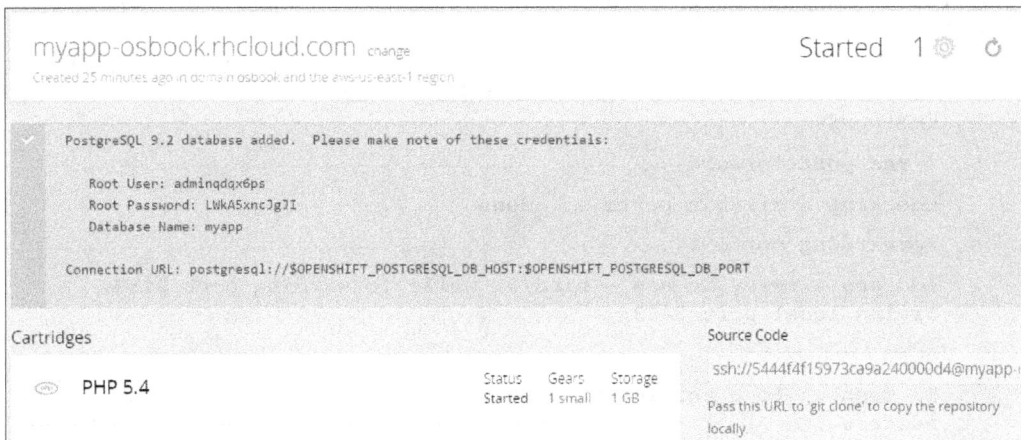

## See also

▶ The *Accessing the PostgreSQL cartridge from your local machine* recipe

# Accessing the PostgreSQL cartridge from your local machine

In the *Adding the PostgreSQL cartridge to your application* recipe, you learned how to access the PostgreSQL database by performing SSH into the application gear. In this recipe, you will learn how to connect with the PostgreSQL database from your local machine.

## Getting ready

To complete this recipe, you will need an application with the PostgreSQL cartridge. Please refer to the *Adding the PostgreSQL cartridge to your application* recipe in this chapter to learn how to install the PostgreSQL cartridge. Also, you will need the `psql` command-line client on your machine. You can download the PostgreSQL server from the official website, `http://www.postgresql.org/download/`.

## How to do it...

Perform the following steps to access the PostgreSQL cartridge from your local machine:

1.  Open a command-line terminal and change the directory to the `myapp` application directory. Execute the following command to forward remote ports to the local machine:

    ```
    $ rhc port-forward

    Checking available ports ... done

    Forwarding ports ...

    Address already in use - bind(2) while forwarding port 5432.
    Trying local port 5433


    To connect to a service running on OpenShift, use the Local
    address


    Service     Local                OpenShift
    ----------  --------------  ----  -----------------
    httpd       127.0.0.1:8080  =>    127.6.76.129:8080
    postgresql  127.0.0.1:5433  =>    127.6.76.130:5432
    ```

2.  Connect to the PostgreSQL server from the local machine using the `psql` command-line client as follows:

    ```
    $ psql --host <host> --port <port> --username <username> myapp
    ```

Please replace `<username>` with your PostgreSQL cartridge username and password. The host and port values can be found in the output of the `rhc port-forward` command. As you can see in step 1, PostgreSQL is available on the `127.0.0.1` host and port 5433. You can view the username and password by running the `rhc show-app` or `rhc cartridge-show postgresql` command.

3. Once connected, you can run any valid SQL command. The `\list` command shows the list of available databases:

```
adminvtxt5s8@127.0.0.1:5433 myapp#\list
                            List of databases
    Name     |    Owner     | Encoding |   Collate    |    Ctype     |
Access privileges
------------+--------------+----------+--------------+--------------
+-------
----------------
  myapp      | adminvtxt5s8 | UTF8     | en_US.UTF-8  | en_US.UTF-8  |
  postgres   | postgres     | UTF8     | en_US.UTF-8  | en_US.UTF-8  |
  template0  | postgres     | UTF8     | en_US.UTF-8  | en_US.UTF-8  |
=c/postgres          +
             |              |          |              |              |
postgres=CTc/postgres
  template1  | postgres     | UTF8     | en_US.UTF-8  | en_US.UTF-8  |
=c/postgres          +
             |              |          |              |              |
postgres=CTc/postgres
  (4 rows)
```

## How it works...

In step 1, you used the `rhc port-forward` command to forward all the remote ports to the local machine. The `rhc port-forward` command is a wrapper around the SSH port forwarding that makes a port on the remote machine available on your local machine. A port on the remote machine that would otherwise be unavailable to you can be used just as if it's on your local machine. The command returns the list of ports that you can connect from your local machine.

As you can see in step 1, the `postgresql` process is available at port 5433 on the `127.0.0.1` host.

In step 2, you connected to PostgreSQL from your local machine, passing in the username, password, host, and port of the database. After successful connection, you ran a SQL command in step 3.

To terminate port forwarding, just press *Ctrl + C* on the command-line terminal where the `rhc port-forward` command is running.

## See also

▸ The *Adding the PostgreSQL cartridge to your application* recipe
▸ The *Connecting to the PostgreSQL cartridge using pgAdmin from your local machine* recipe

# Connecting to the PostgreSQL cartridge using pgAdmin from your local machine

In the *Accessing the PostgreSQL cartridge from your local machine* recipe, you learned how to connect to the PostgreSQL cartridge from the `psql` command-line client from your local machine using port forwarding. In this recipe, you will learn how to connect to the PostgreSQL cartridge using pgAdmin from your local machine. pgAdmin is a comprehensive PostgreSQL database design and management system for Unix and Windows systems.

## Getting ready

To complete this recipe, you will need an application with the PostgreSQL cartridge. Please refer to the *Adding the PostgreSQL cartridge to your application* recipe in this chapter to learn how to add the PostgreSQL cartridge to your application. Also, you will need pgAdmin on your local machine. You can download pgAdmin from the official website, `http://www.pgadmin.org/download/`.

## How to do it...

Perform the following steps to connect the PostgreSQL cartridge using the pgAdmin client:

1. Open a command-line terminal, and change the directory to the `myapp` application directory. Execute the following command to forward remote ports to the local machine:

```
$ rhc port-forward --app myapp
```

2. Start the pgAdmin application, and click on the socket icon to create a new connection.

3. Set up a new connection by entering the PostgreSQL database details. You can get the username and password for the PostgreSQL cartridge using the `rhc show-app` or `rhc cartridge-show mysql` command. Have a look at the following screenshot:

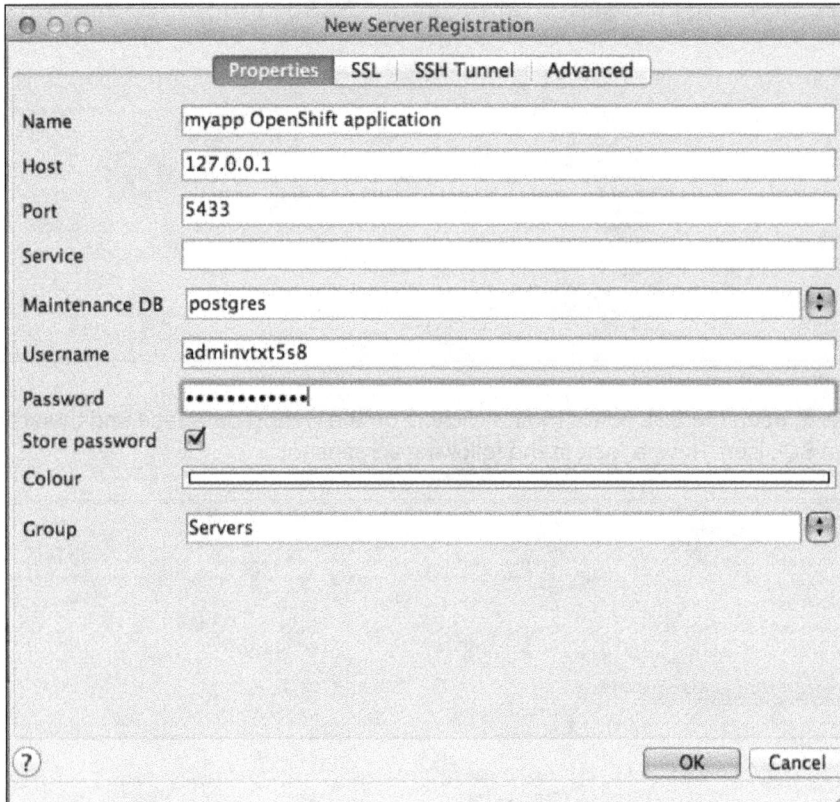

4. Connect to the PostgreSQL cartridge by clicking on the **OK** button.

5. You will see a connection listed in the left-hand side navigation pane, as shown in the following screenshot:

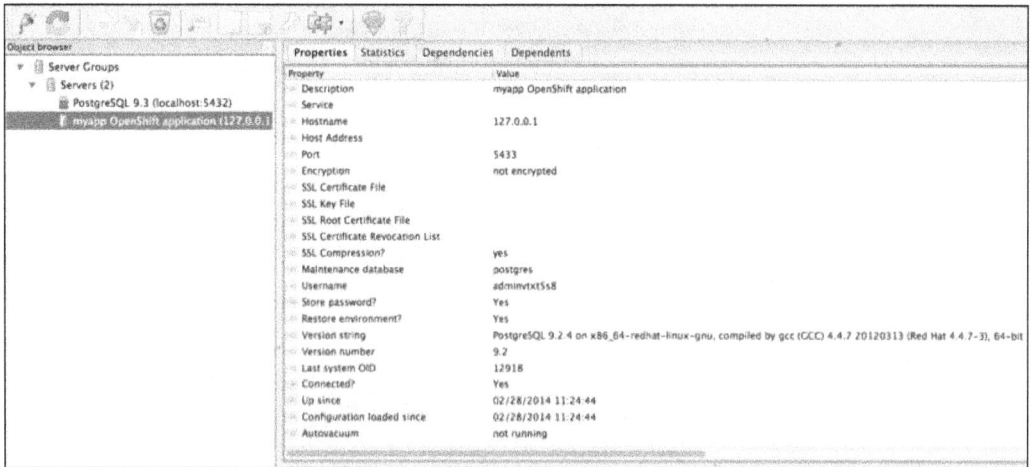

6. Next, open the SQL editor by first clicking on the `myapp` database and then clicking on SQL icon. Have a look at the following screenshot:

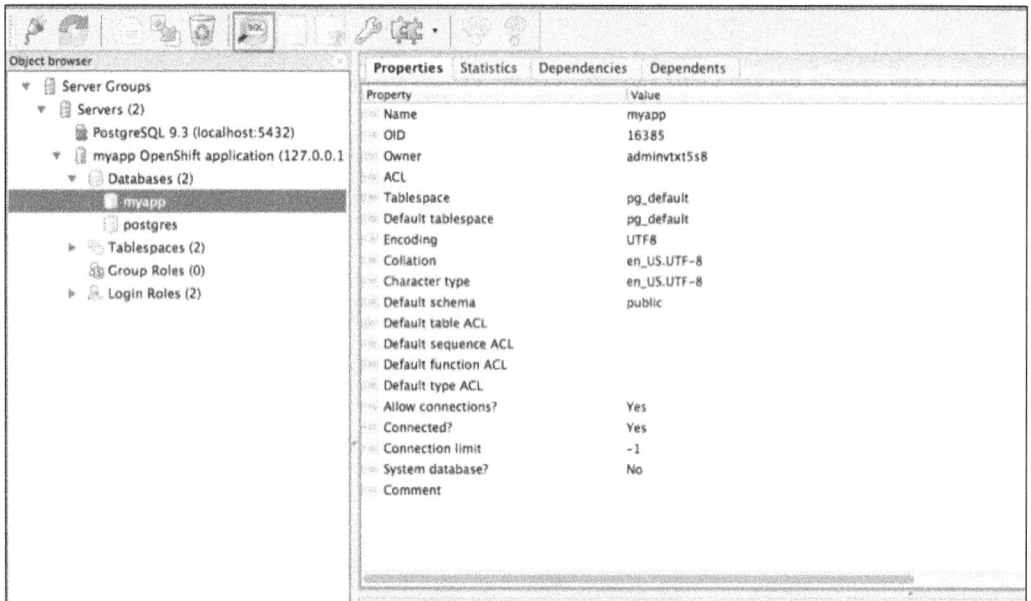

7.  Run the following SQL query inside the SQL editor to check the database uptime:

```
select date_trunc('minute',current_timestamp - pg_postmaster_
start_time()) as "postgresql_uptime";
```

## How it works...

In step 1, you used the `rhc port-forward` command to forward all the remote ports to the local machine. This makes it possible to connect to the PostgreSQL database running inside your application gear. Step 2 through step 6, you created a new PostgreSQL connection and connected with the PostgreSQL cartridge from within pgAdmin. In step 7, you executed a SQL query using the SQL editor to verify that the connection is getting data from the PostgreSQL cartridge installed in your `myapp` application.

## See also

▸ The *Adding the PostgreSQL cartridge to your application* recipe

▸ The *Accessing the PostgreSQL cartridge from your local machine* recipe

# Updating the PostgreSQL max_connections setting

The OpenShift PostgreSQL cartridge is configured to allow 100 client connections at the most. If the number of clients connected to the PostgreSQL server goes over this threshold, PostgreSQL will start giving the `FATAL too many connections` error. In this recipe, you will learn how to update the PostgreSQL cartridge `max_connections` setting.

The number of maximum connections is dictated by the `max_connections` setting in the `postgresql.conf` configuration file. OpenShift does not allow users to modify the `postgresql.conf` configuration file. The recommended way to change the `max_connections` setting is by setting an environment variable.

## Getting ready

To complete this recipe, you will need an application with the PostgreSQL cartridge. Please refer to the *Adding the PostgreSQL cartridge to your application* recipe in this chapter to learn how to install PostgreSQL cartridge.

## How to do it...

Perform the following steps to update the PostgreSQL `max_connections` setting:

1. To set the maximum connections to `200`, open a command-line terminal and run the following command:

```
$ rhc env-set OPENSHIFT_POSTGRESQL_MAX_CONNECTIONS=200 --app myapp
```

2. After setting the environment variable, you have to restart the PostgreSQL cartridge for changes to take effect as follows:

```
$ rhc cartridge-restart postgresql --app myapp
```

## How it works...

PostgreSQL database maintains its configuration in a file called `postgresql.conf` inside the `conf` directory of your installation. The `max_connections` configuration setting controls the maximum number of client connections allowed by the PostgreSQL server. You can view the `max_connection` setting by running a query against your PostgreSQL database. To see `max_connections` for your OpenShift PostgreSQL cartridge, SSH into the application gear, and run the following command:

```
myapp=# show max_connections;
 max_connections
-----------------
 100
(1 row)
```

OpenShift does not allow users to modify the `postgresql.conf` file for security reasons. To allow users to modify the `max_connections` setting, OpenShift provides an environment variable called `OPENSHIFT_POSTGRESQL_MAX_CONNECTIONS`, which can be used to set the `max_connections` system variable. In step 1, you set the `OPENSHIFT_POSTGRESQL_MAX_CONNECTIONS` environment variable to `200`. The PostgreSQL server will not read the new value unless you restart the database. So, in step 2, you restarted the database using the `rhc cartridge-restart` command. To verify that `max_connections` value is updated, you can run the SQL command again as follows:

```
myapp=# show max_connections;
 max_connections
-----------------
 200
(1 row)
```

## There's more...

The OPENSHIFT_POSTGRESQL_MAX_CONNECTIONS variable is not the only configuration property supported by the PostgreSQL cartridge. You can set the following properties using environment variables. To learn about these settings, please refer to the following documentation: https://wiki.postgresql.org/wiki/Tuning_Your_PostgreSQL_Server.

| Property | Environment variable |
|----------|---------------------|
| shared_buffers | OPENSHIFT_POSTGRESQL_SHARED_BUFFERS |
| datestyle | OPENSHIFT_POSTGRESQL_DATESTYLE |
| ssl | OPENSHIFT_POSTGRESQL_SSL_ENABLED |
| lc_messages | OPENSHIFT_POSTGRESQL_LOCALE |
| lc_monetary | OPENSHIFT_POSTGRESQL_LOCALE |
| lc_numeric | OPENSHIFT_POSTGRESQL_LOCALE |
| lc_time | OPENSHIFT_POSTGRESQL_LOCALE |

## See also

▸ The *Using the .psqlrc configuration file to configure the OpenShift application psql shell* recipe

▸ The *Accessing the PostgreSQL cartridge from your local machine* recipe

# Using the .psqlrc configuration file to configure the OpenShift application psql shell

PostgreSQL provides a startup file called .psqrc, which determines the behavior of the psql interactive command-line client. Just like bashrc, the psql client utility attempts to read and execute commands from the system-wide psqlrc file and the user's ~/.psqlrc file before starting up. In this recipe, you will learn how you can use your own .psqlrc configuration file to configure your OpenShift application psql shell.

## Getting ready

To complete this recipe, you will need an application with the PostgreSQL cartridge. Please refer to the *Adding the PostgreSQL cartridge to your application* recipe in this chapter to learn how to install the PostgreSQL cartridge.

## How to do it...

Perform the following steps to configure the psql shell:

1.  Change the directory to `myapp`, and then SSH into the application gear:

    ```
    $ rhc ssh --app myapp
    ```

2.  Create a new file in $OPENSHIFT_DATA_DIR named .psqlrc:

    ```
    [myapp-osbook.rhcloud.com 531069cd5973cad58c0000b6]\> touch
    $OPENSHIFT_DATA_DIR/.psqlrc
    ```

3.  Now let's configure the psql shell to store the history of commands you have entered so that you can run them again. This is achieved by setting the HISTFILE location as shown in the following command. The :DBNAME variable allows psql to store a different history for each database. We will also enable psql to print the time taken to execute each command. This is done using the \timing option. To customize the psql shell, add the following content to the .psqrc file:

    ```
    \set HISTFILE ~/app-root/data/.psql_history- :DBNAME
    \timing on
    ```

4.  Log out of the SSH session and create a new environment variable named PSQLRC to point to the new .psqlrc file location:

    ```
    $ rhc env-set PSQLRC<OPENSHIFT_DATA_DIR>data/.psqlrc
    ```

    Please replace OPENSHIFT_DATA_DIR with your OPENSHIFT_DATA_DIR location. You can get the location by running the following command:

    ```
    $ rhc ssh --app myapp --command 'cd $OPENSHIFT_DATA_DIR && pwd'
    ```

5.  SSH into the application gear again using the `rhc ssh` command, and then run the psql command. Run a query, and you will get the timing as well:

    ```
    adminvtxt5s8:myapp#SELECT pid, usename from pg_stat_activity;
       pid    |     usename
    --------+--------------
     354468 | adminvtxt5s8
    (1 row)


    Time: 85.372 ms
    ```

## How it works...

When psql is launched, it looks for a file called `psqlrc` and runs any command in the file to initialize the environment. On a *nix-based system, this file is called `.psqlrc` and is usually located under the user's home directory. From step 1 through step 3, you created a new file, `.psqlrc`, under `$OPENSHIFT_DATA_DIR`. We added a couple of configurations to the `.psqlrc` file. The first configuration makes sure that the SQL command history is stored in a file called `.psql_history` under `$OPENSHIFT_DATA_DIR`. The second configuration instructs psql to output the query execution time for each query.

In step 4, you created a new environment variable named `PSQLRC` that points to the `.psqlrc` location. Finally, in step 5, you logged in to the psql client and ran a query. After query execution, the psql client also showed the time taken to execute the query. As shown in the preceding command-line output, this query took approximately 86 ms.

## See also

▶ The *Adding the PostgreSQL cartridge to your application* recipe

▶ The *Accessing the PostgreSQL cartridge from your local machine* recipe

# Performing scheduled PostgreSQL database backups

In this recipe, you will learn how to perform a scheduled backup of your PostgreSQL database and upload it to Amazon S3.

## Getting ready

To complete this recipe, you will need an application with the PostgreSQL cartridge. Please refer to the *Adding the PostgreSQL cartridge to your application* recipe in this chapter to learn how to add the PostgreSQL cartridge. Also, you need to have the Amazon AWS account. Go to `http://aws.amazon.com/`, and sign up for a new account if you don't already have one.

## How to do it...

The following are the steps to perform daily scheduled backup of your PostgreSQL database:

1. Go to `https://console.aws.amazon.com/s3/home`, and create a new bucket to store your database backups.

2. Add the cron cartridge to your application by running the following command:

   ```
   $ rhc add-cartridge cron --app myapp
   ```

3. SSH into the application gear, and download the s3-bash utility in $OPENSHIFT_DATA_DIR. Extract it to the s3-bash directory. Have a look at the following commands:

```
$ rhc ssh --app myapp
$ cd $OPENSHIFT_DATA_DIR
$ wget http://s3-bash.googlecode.com/files/s3-bash.0.02.tar.gz
$ mkdir s3-bash
$ tar -xf s3-bash.0.02.tar.gz -C s3-bash
```

4. Create a new file named AWSSecretAccessKeyIdFile in the $OPENSHIFT_DATA_DIR/s3-bash directory, and store your Amazon secret access key to it. This is required by s3-bash to communicate with Amazon S3.

5. Create a script named database_backup.sh on your local machine in .openshift/cron/minutely, and add the following content to it:

```
#!/bin/bash
if [ `date +%H:%M` == "23:50" ]
then
    FILE_NAME=$(date +"%Y%m%d%H%M")
    pg_dump --username=$OPENSHIFT_POSTGRESQL_DB_USERNAME --no-
password --host=$OPENSHIFT_POSTGRESQL_DB_HOST $BACKUP_DATABASE_
NAME > $OPENSHIFT_DATA_DIR/$FILE_NAME.sql
    echo "Took PostgreSQL Dump" >> $OPENSHIFT_CRON_DIR/log/backup.
log
    $OPENSHIFT_DATA_DIR/s3-bash/s3-put -k $AWS_ACCESS_KEY_ID
-s $OPENSHIFT_DATA_DIR/s3-bash/AWSSecretAccessKeyIdFile -T
$OPENSHIFT_DATA_DIR/$FILE_NAME.sql /$AWS_S3_BUCKET/$FILE_NAME.sql
    echo "Uploaded dump to Amazon S3" >> $OPENSHIFT_CRON_DIR/log/
backup.log
    rm -f $OPENSHIFT_DATA_DIR/$FILE_NAME.sql
fi
```

The previous script will run every day at 23:50 and run the pg_dump command to create the data dump file. The file is then transferred to Amazon S3 using the s3-bash API. Finally, after uploading the file, it deletes the SQL dump file from the application gear.

6. Now, we have to set the environment variables so that our script can talk with Amazon S3 as shown in the following commands. If you are not sure how to access your security credentials, please refer to the documentation at http://docs.aws.amazon.com/general/latest/gr/getting-aws-sec-creds.html. Have a look at the following commands:

```
$ rhc env-set AWS_ACCESS_KEY_ID=< Your Amazon ACCESS_KEY_ID>
$ rhc env-set BACKUP_DATABASE_NAME=<Database you want to take
backup off>
$ rhc env-set AWS_S3_BUCKET=<Amazon S3 bucket name >
```

7. Commit the code, and push the code to the OpenShift gear. Every night at 23:50, a database backup would be done, and your backup would be uploaded to Amazon S3:

```
$ git commit -am "database backup script added"
$ git push
```

## How it works...

In the previous steps, you enabled daily backups of your PostgreSQL database cartridge. The recipe used the cron cartridge to upload database dumps to Amazon S3.

In step 1, you created a new Amazon S3 bucket to store your PostgreSQL database backups. Amazon S3 is widely used to store static files and is an ideal choice for this job. Next, you added the cron cartridge to the application. The cron cartridge will be used to perform daily backups at a particular time.

Amazon S3 exposes its REST service that users can use to perform operations on S3 buckets. Amazon provides wrappers of many programming languages around its REST API to make it easy for developers to integrate with their application. As we wanted to keep this recipe language-agnostic, we used the Amazon S3 bash wrapper. Amazon does not officially support this wrapper, but it works very well. In step 3, you downloaded s3-bash using wget. The tar.gz file was stored in $OPENSHIFT_DATA_DIR. You then extracted tar.gz to the s3-bash directory.

Next, in step 4, you created a file named AWSSecretAccessKeyIdFile to store the Amazon access key secret. The s3-bash wrapper uses a file for the AWS Secret Access Key ID so that it does not appear in the list of running processes with ps.

In step 5, you created a bash script that will be executed every night at 23:50. The script first takes the database backup using the pg_dump command and then uploads the file to Amazon S3. The filename is the current timestamp. Finally, after uploading the backup to S3, the script deletes the backup to save disk space.

In step 6, you created three environment variables required by the backup script. Finally, you committed the changes in step 7 and pushed them to the OpenShift application gear.

## See also

▶ The *Adding the PostgreSQL cartridge to your application* recipe

# Using EnterpriseDB PostgreSQL Cloud Database with OpenShift

In this recipe, you will learn how to use EnterpriseDB PostgreSQL Cloud Database with your OpenShift applications. You can also use the Amazon RDS PostgreSQL DB instance in the same way we used the Amazon RDS MySQL DB instance. EnterpriseDB Cloud Database allows you to set up a replicated, sharded, and highly available PostgreSQL cluster either on Amazon EC2 or the HP Cloud services. You can take periodic backups of your data and scale it horizontally without any administrative skills.

## Getting ready

To complete this recipe, you will need an OpenShift application. Refer to the *Creating an OpenShift application using the rhc command-line client* recipe in *Chapter 3*, *Creating and Managing Applications*, for more information.

## How to do it...

Perform the following steps to learn how to connect your OpenShift applications with the EnterpriseDB PostgreSQL database:

1. Go to `http://www.enterprisedb.com/cloud-database/amazon`, and click on **Get Started Now** in the free trial section.

2. Next, you will be directed to the signup page. Enter the valid details, and click on the submit button.

3. After successful signup, you will be redirected to the dashboard console as shown in the next screenshot. Here, you can launch a database cluster, see the resources you are consuming, or see the status update of the service. At the bottom of the dashboard, there are links to the tutorials and documentation about PostgreSQL CloudDB.

4. Now, we will create our first DB cluster on EnterpriseDB Cloud by clicking on **Launch DB Cluster**. This will open a pop up where you need to provide details of your cluster, as shown in the following screenshot. The details include the name of the cluster, PostgreSQL version, instance size of Amazon, number of nodes, and the master username and password.

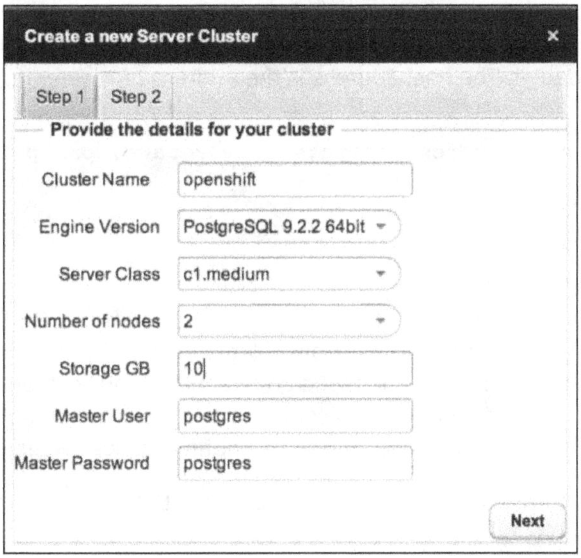

5. After entering cluster details, you can choose how many backups you want to keep and when you would like to take the backup. Use the default options.

6. Finally, click on the **Launch** button. This will initiate the process of creating a replicated DB cluster, as shown in the following screenshot. It will take a couple of minutes to launch the cluster, so please be patient. From the **Clusters** tab, you can get information about the database clusters you own. In the **Details** tab, you can see the address where master and replica are running.

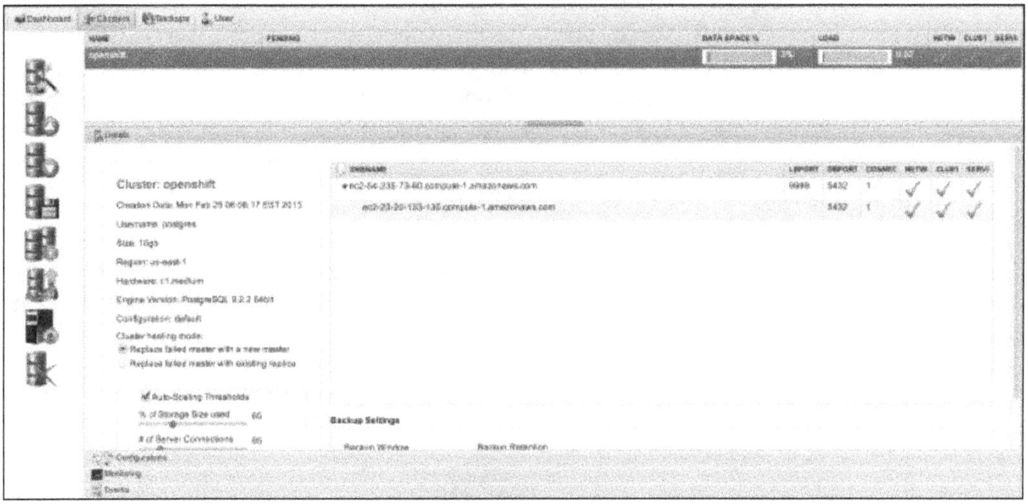

Creating a replicated DB cluster

7. To connect to the EnterpriseDB PostgreSQL Cloud DB, SSH into the application gear, and use the `psql` command to connect with Cloud DB. Every application gear has psql installed on it. The host address is the address of master that you can get from step 6.

```
$ psql -h host_address.compute-1.amazonaws.com -p 9999 -U postgres
-W postgres
```

## How it works...

Step 1 through step 6 helped you create a new instance of EnterpriseDB PostgreSQL Cloud DB instance. You are required to provide details related to your DB instance, and EnterpriseDB will provision a PostgreSQL DB instance based on the details you entered. By step 6, you had a running PostgreSQL DB instance that you could connect from the outside world. You can connect it from your local machine or from your OpenShift application gear.

In step 7, you used the database details to connect to the EnterpriseDB PostgreSQL instance using the psql command-line client.

## See also

▶ The *Adding the PostgreSQL cartridge to your application* recipe

# Installing PostgreSQL extensions

Extensions are add-ons that you can install in a PostgreSQL database to extend the functionality beyond the basic offering. You can find a list of PostgreSQL extensions available on the PostgreSQL Extension Network website, `http://www.pgxn.org/`. The OpenShift PostgreSQL cartridge comes in a bundle with a list of extensions. These extensions are not installed by default but are available to you if you need them. In this recipe, you will learn how to install an extension in your OpenShift PostgreSQL cartridge.

## Getting ready

To complete this recipe, you will need an application with the PostgreSQL cartridge. Please refer to the *Adding the PostgreSQL cartridge to your application* recipe in this chapter to learn how to add the PostgreSQL cartridge to your application.

## How to do it...

Perform the following steps to install an extension:

1. Open a new command-line terminal, and SSH into the application gear using the `rhc ssh` command. Once logged in, run the psql command-line utility to connect with the PostgreSQL cartridge.

2. From inside the psql shell, run the following command to view all the available extensions:

   ```
   # select * from pg_available_extensions;
   ```

3. Next, install the `fuzzystrmatch` extension by executing the following SQL command:

   ```
   # create extension fuzzystrmatch;
   ```

4. You can view all the installed extensions by running the `\dx` command:

   ```
   #\dx
                                    List of installed extensions
          Name       | Version |   Schema    |
   Description
   ----------------+---------+-------------+---------------------------
   ----------------------------
    fuzzystrmatch | 1.0     | public      | determine similarities and
   distance between strings
    plpgsql       | 1.0     | pg_catalog  | PL/pgSQL procedural
   language
   (2 rows)
   ```

5. You can remove the extension from your psql cartridge by running the following SQL command:

   ```
   # drop extension fuzzystrmatch;
   ```

## How it works...

Every OpenShift PostgreSQL cartridge has access to a list of extensions. These extensions are not installed by default, as not all the applications need these extensions. To view all the available extensions, you can use the `select * from pg_available_extensions` SQL command as shown in step 2. At the time of writing this book, the PostgreSQL cartridge is prepackaged with 51 extensions. These extensions can be installed by running the CREATE EXTENSION SQL command as shown in step 2. The CREATE EXTENSION command compiles and installs the extension. In step 3, you installed the `fuzzystrmatch` extension.

The `fuzzystrmatch` extension provides several functions to determine similarities and differences between strings. To view the details of the `fuzzystrmatch` extension, you can run the following command:

```
\dx+ fuzzystrmatch
                    Objects in extension "fuzzystrmatch"
                          Object Description
----------------------------------------------------------------------
---
 function difference(text,text)
 function dmetaphone_alt(text)
 function dmetaphone(text)
 function levenshtein_less_equal(text,text,integer)
 function levenshtein_less_equal(text,text,integer,integer,integer,integ
er)
 function levenshtein(text,text)
 function levenshtein(text,text,integer,integer,integer)
 function metaphone(text,integer)
 function soundex(text)
 function text_soundex(text)
(10 rows)
To find the levenshtein distance between Hello and Hallo, you can run
command shown below.
select levenshtein('Hello','Hallo');
 levenshtein
-------------
           1
(1 row)
```

You can drop an extension using the DROP EXTENSION command.

## See also

▶ The *Adding the PostgreSQL cartridge to your application* recipe

# 6
# Using MongoDB and Third-party Database Cartridges with OpenShift Applications

This chapter presents a number of recipes that show you how to get started with the OpenShift MongoDB cartridge. We will also look at how you can use downloadable cartridges for MariaDB and **Remote Dictionary Server** (**Redis**). The specific recipes within this chapter are:

- ▶ Adding a MongoDB cartridge to your application
- ▶ Adding a RockMongo cartridge to your application
- ▶ Accessing a MongoDB cartridge from your local machine
- ▶ Connecting to a MongoDB cartridge using Robomongo from your local machine
- ▶ Enabling the MongoDB cartridge REST interface
- ▶ Performing scheduled MongoDB database backups
- ▶ Using MongoLab MongoDB-as-a-Service with OpenShift
- ▶ Adding a MariaDB cartridge to your application
- ▶ Adding a Redis cartridge to your application

# Introduction

MongoDB is a popular and open source document-oriented NoSQL data store. It is designed for scalability and stores complex object graphs in a single document. It has support for dynamic queries, secondary indexes, fast atomic updates, aggregation, and inbuilt support for replication and sharding.

This chapter will use the PHP 5.4 application we created in *Chapter 3, Creating and Managing Applications*. If you do not have any OpenShift application running, then you can create a new OpenShift application by running the following command:

```
$ rhc create-app myapp php-5.4
```

# Adding a MongoDB cartridge to your application

In this recipe, you will learn how to add a MongoDB cartridge to your OpenShift application. MongoDB is a document-oriented, horizontally scalable, and NoSQL data store.

## Getting ready

To step through this recipe, you will need the `rhc` command-line client installed on your machine. Refer to the *Installing the OpenShift rhc command-line client* recipe in *Chapter 1, Getting Started with OpenShift* for details. Also, we will use the application created in the *Creating an OpenShift application using the rhc command-line client* recipe in *Chapter 3, Creating and Managing Applications*.

## How to do it...

To install the MongoDB cartridge to the `myapp` application, use the following steps:

1.  Open a new command-line terminal, then change the directory to the `myapp` directory location and execute the following command:

    ```
    $ rhc cartridge-add c mongodb-2.4 --app myapp
    ```

    This will install a new instance of MongoDB on your application gear. The `-c` option is used to specify the cartridge name and the `--app` option is used to specify the application name.

2.  You can view the cartridge details using the `rhc show-cartridge` command:

    ```
    $ rhc show-cartridge mongodb --app myapp
    Using mongodb-2.4 (MongoDB 2.4) for 'mongodb'
    ```

```
mongodb-2.4 (MongoDB 2.4)

-------------------------

  Gears:              Located with php-5.4

  Connection URL:
mongodb://$OPENSHIFT_MONGODB_DB_HOST:$OPENSHIFT_MONGODB_DB_POR
T/

  Database Name:    myapp

  Password:         DSdIxMVY8kd4

  Username:         admin
```

3.  You can also stop the MongoDB server using the `stop` command:

    `$ rhc stop-cartridge mongodb`

    You can restart the MongoDB server using the `restart` command:

    `$ rhc cartridge-restart mongodb`

4.  If you want to remove the MongoDB server from your application, you can use the `remove` command:

    `$ rhc cartridge-remove mongodb --confirm`

## How it works...

When you run the `rhc add-cartridge` command, `rhc` will make an HTTP POST request to the OpenShift server. The OpenShift server will receive the request and instantiate a new instance of the MongoDB database for your application. After provisioning the MongoDB database, the `rhc` client will show the database details on the command-line terminal.

You can view the MongoDB installation by performing an SSH into your application gear:

`$ rhc ssh --app myapp`

Then, run the `ls` command to view the gear directory structure and you will see the `mongodb` directory:

`[myapp-osbook.rhcloud.com 52fb71aa5973caf609000026]\> ls -p`

`app-deployments/  app-root/  git/  mongodb/  php/`

The `mongodb` directory is your `mongodb` installation, and it is not shared with any other OpenShift application or user. It is only for your application, and only your application can access it.

You can also connect with your MongoDB database by using the `mongo` command-line client, as shown in the following command. The *Accessing a MongoDB cartridge from your local machine* recipe will cover how to connect with MongoDB from your local machine:

```
[myapp-osbook.rhcloud.com 52fb71aa5973caf609000026]\> mongo
MongoDB shell version: 2.4.6
connecting to: 127.2.34.2:27017/admin
Welcome to the MongoDB shell.
For interactive help, type "help".
For more comprehensive documentation, see
   http://docs.mongodb.org/
Questions? Try the support group
   http://groups.google.com/group/mongodb-user
>
```

Now, you can run commands against your MongoDB database. To view all the databases, run the following command:

```
> show databases;
admin   0.03125GB
local   0.03125GB
myapp   0.03125GB
```

The `myapp` database corresponds to your application database.

You can view all the MongoDB command-line utilities available on the gear by typing in `mongo` and hitting *Tab* twice:

```
[myapp-osbook.rhcloud.com 52fb71aa5973caf609000026]\> mongo

mongo           mongod          mongoexport     mongoimport     mongoperf
mongos          mongostat

mongo_console   mongodump       mongofiles      mongooplog
mongorestore    mongosniff      mongotop
```

## There's more...

You can also add a MongoDB database from the OpenShift web console. Go to `https://openshift.redhat.com/app/console/applications`, and click on the **myapp** application for details. On the `myapp` application's details web page, you will see an option to add a MongoDB database. Click on the **Add MongoDB 2.4** option to add a MongoDB 2.4 cartridge.

▸ The *Adding a RockMongo cartridge to your application* recipe

# Adding a RockMongo cartridge to your application

RockMongo (`http://rockmongo.com/`) is a free, open source, and popular tool written in the PHP programming language to handle the administration of the MongoDB database via a web browser. As a web application, RockMongo makes it easy to administer the MongoDB server without any installation on your local machine. In this recipe, you will learn how to install a RockMongo cartridge on your application.

## Getting ready

To complete this recipe, you will need an application with a MongoDB cartridge. Refer to the *Adding a MongoDB cartridge to your application* recipe to learn how to install a MongoDB cartridge.

## How to do it...

The steps needed to add the RockMongo cartridge are as follows:

1. To install the RockMongo cartridge on the `myapp` application, open a new command-line terminal, then change the directory to the `myapp` directory location and execute the following command:

   ```
   $ rhc add-cartridge rockmongo --app myapp
   ```

2. Note the username and password returned by the `rhc cartridge-add` command. You will need these to log in to RockMongo. The RockMongo credentials are the same as your MongoDB database credentials, and you can view them anytime by executing the `rhc show-app` or `rhc cartridge-show mongodb-2.4` command.

3. Log in to RockMongo (`https://myapp-{domain-name}.rhcloud.com/rockmongo/`) using the credentials from step 1.

## How it works...

When you run the `rhc add-cartridge` command, the `rhc` client makes an HTTP POST request to the OpenShift server. The OpenShift server receives the request and installs the RockMongo cartridge on the application gear. The RockMongo cartridge works with all the supported application types (Java, Python, Node.js, Ruby, Perl, and PHP). You don't need to create PHP applications in order to use the RockMongo cartridge. OpenShift will start an Apache process to run the RockMongo application.

> You can only add the RockMongo cartridge after you have added a MongoDB cartridge to your application. If you try to add RockMongo before adding a MongoDB cartridge, then you will receive the `Cartridge 'rockmongo-1.1' can not be added without mongodb` error.

## There's more...

You can also add a RockMongo cartridge from the OpenShift web console. Go to `https://openshift.redhat.com/app/console/applications` and click on the `myapp` application. To install a RockMongo cartridge, click on the **Add RockMongo 1.1** web link.

## See also

▶ The *Accessing a MongoDB cartridge from your local machine* recipe

▶ The *Connecting to a MongoDB cartridge using Robomongo from your local machine* recipe

# Accessing a MongoDB cartridge from your local machine

In the *Adding a MongoDB cartridge to your application* recipe, you learned how to access a MongoDB database by performing an SSH into the application gear. In this recipe, you will learn how to connect with the MongoDB database from your local machine.

## Getting ready

To complete this recipe, you will need an application with a MongoDB cartridge. Refer to the *Adding a MongoDB cartridge to your application* recipe in this chapter to learn how to add a MongoDB cartridge. Also, you will need the `mongo` command-line client on your machine. You can download the MongoDB database from the official website at `http://www.mongodb.org/downloads/`.

## How to do it...

Perform the following steps to connect to a MongoDB cartridge from your local machine:

1. Open a command-line terminal and change the directory to the `myapp` application directory. Execute the following command to forward remote ports to the local machine:

```
$ rhc port-forward --app myapp
Checking available ports ... done
Forwarding ports ...
Address already in use - bind(2) while forwarding port 8080.
Trying local port 8081

To connect to a service running on OpenShift, use the Local
address

Service Local                OpenShift
------- ---------------- ---- ----------------
httpd   127.0.0.1:8080   =>   127.2.34.1:8080
httpd   127.0.0.1:8081   =>   127.2.34.3:8080
mongodb 127.0.0.1:27017  =>   127.2.34.2:27017

Press CTRL-C to terminate port forwarding
```

2. Open another command-line terminal and connect to the MongoDB database from the `mongo` command-line client from your local machine using the following command:

```
$ mongo --username <username> --password <password>
<host>:<port>/admin
```

3. Replace `<username>` and `<password>` with your MongoDB cartridge username and password. The host and port values can be found in the output of the `rhc port-forward` command. As you can see in step 1, the `MongoDB` database is available on the `127.0.0.1` host and `27017` port number. You can view the username and password by running the `rhc show-app` or `rhc cartridge-show mongodb-2.4` command.

4. Once connected to the MongoDB database, you can run any legitimate command, as follows:

```
> show databases
admin  0.03125GB
local  0.03125GB
myap   (empty)
myapp  0.03125GB
test   0.03125GB
```

## How it works...

In step 1, you used the `rhc port-forward` command to forward all the remote ports to the local machine. The `rhc port-forward` command is a wrapper around the SSH port forwarding that makes a port on the remote machine available on your local machine. A port on the remote machine, which would otherwise be unavailable to you, can be used as if it's on your local machine. The command returns the list of ports that you can connect from your local machine, as shown in step 1.

As you can see in the output, the `mongod` process is available on the `27017` port and `127.0.0.1` host.

In step 2, you connected to the MongoDB database from your local machine, passing in the username, password, host, and port of the database. After a successful connection, you ran a command in step 3.

To terminate port forwarding, just press *Ctrl + C* on the command-line terminal where the `rhc port-forward` command is running.

## See also

- ▶ The *Connecting to a MongoDB cartridge using Robomongo from your local machine* recipe
- ▶ The *Adding a MongoDB cartridge to your application* recipe

# Connecting to a MongoDB cartridge using Robomongo from your local machine

In the *Accessing a MongoDB cartridge from your local machine* recipe, you learned how to connect to a MongoDB cartridge using the `mongo` command-line client from your local machine. In this recipe, you will learn how to connect to a MongoDB cartridge using RoboMongo from your local machine. RoboMongo (`http://robomongo.org/`) is an open source, cross-platform MongoDB GUI management tool. We used RoboMongo because it is available across all the operating systems, and you can type in all the commands you type in the mongo shell in RoboMongo. It feels natural to developers who are used to the mongo shell.

## Getting ready

To complete this recipe, you will need an application with a MongoDB cartridge. Refer to the *Adding a MongoDB cartridge to your application* recipe in this chapter to learn how to add a MongoDB cartridge. Also, you will need the RoboMongo tool installed on your local machine. You can download the RoboMongo tool from its website at `http://robomongo.org/`.

## How to do it...

Perform the following steps to connect to RoboMongo with your MongoDB cartridge:

1. Open a command-line terminal and change the directory to the `myapp` application directory. Execute the following command to forward remote ports to the local machine:

   ```
   $ rhc port-forward --app myapp
   ```

2. Start the RoboMongo application, and you will see the following screenshot. Click on the connect icon in the top-left corner:

3. After clicking on the connect icon, you will see a new window with options to create a new connection. Click on the **Create** link to create a new connection:

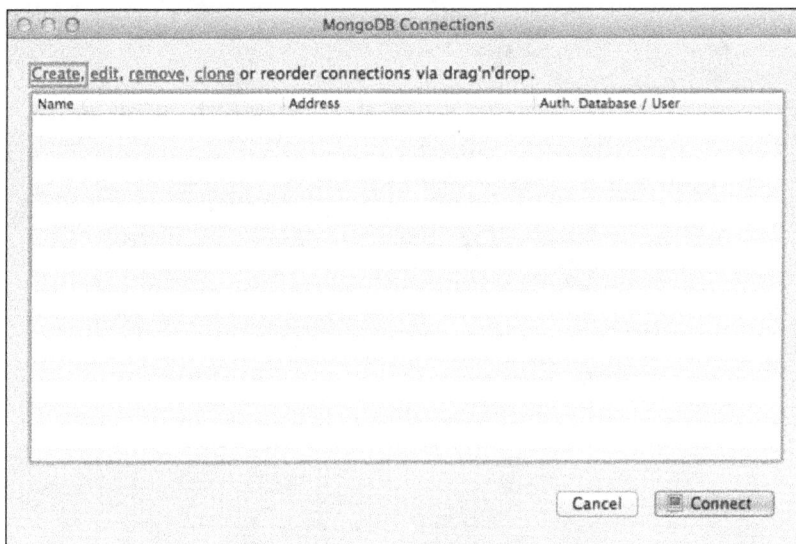

4.  Set up a new connection by entering the MongoDB database details. The host and port can be found in the output of the `rhc port-forward` command in step 1, as shown in the following screenshot:

5.  Click on the **Authentication** tab to enter the username and password required to connect with the MongoDB cartridge. You can view the MongoDB cartridge details using the `rhc show-app` or `rhc cartridge-show mongodb-2.4` command. The following screenshot shows the **Authentication** tab details:

6. Click on the **Save** button and you will see the new connection listed in the **MongoDB Connections** window:

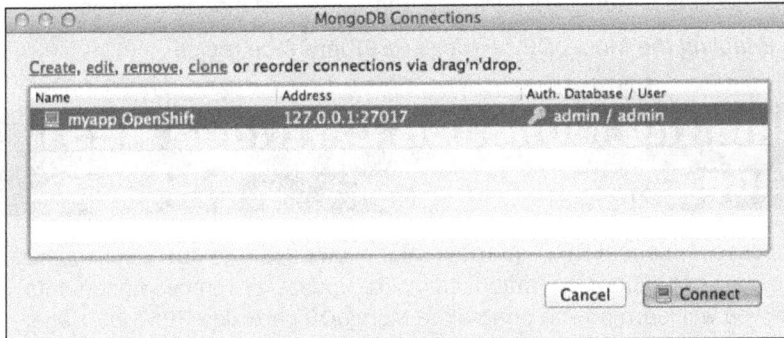

7. Click on the **Connect** button and you will be connected to the MongoDB cartridge.

8. Once connected to your MongoDB cartridge, you can click on any database and view all its collections. When you double-click on a collection, you can see the first 50 documents inside it. The following screenshot shows the documents inside the `msgs` collection:

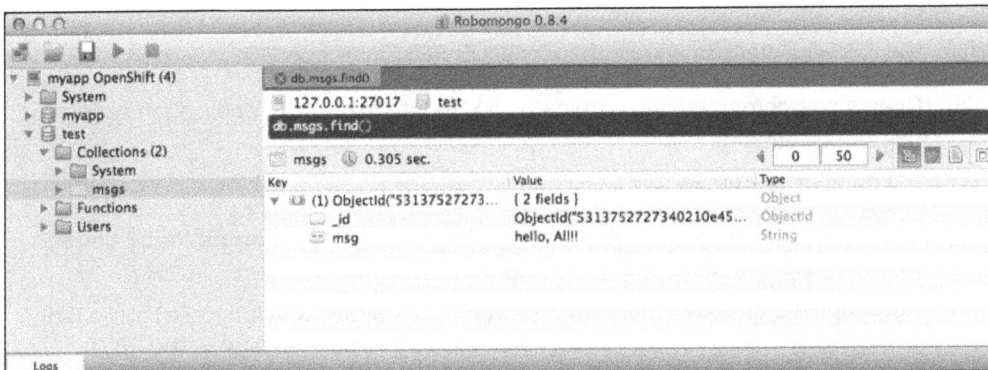

## How it works...

In step 1, you used the `rhc port-forward` command to forward all the remote ports to the local machine. This will make it possible to connect to the MongoDB database running inside your application gear. In steps 2 through 7, you created a new MongoDB connection and connected with the MongoDB cartridge from within RoboMongo. In step 8, you navigated to the **msgs** collection in the **test** database.

## See also

- ▶ The *Accessing a MongoDB cartridge from your local machine* recipe
- ▶ The *Enabling the MongoDB cartridge REST interface* recipe

# Enabling the MongoDB cartridge REST interface

MongoDB exposes a minimal REST interface that allows users to query collections. The interface does not expose operations to insert, update, or remove documents. In this recipe, you will learn how to enable the MongoDB cartridge REST interface.

## Getting ready

To complete this recipe, you will need an application with a MongoDB cartridge. Refer to the *Adding a MongoDB cartridge to your application* recipe in this chapter to learn how to add one.

## How to do it...

Perform the following steps to enable the MongoDB REST interface:

1. Open a new command-line terminal and SSH into the `myapp` application gear using the `ssh` command:

   ```
   $ rhc ssh --app myapp
   ```

2. Once inside the application gear, change the directory to `mongodb/conf` and edit the `mongodb.conf` file using Vim.

3. Now, we need to update the `nohttpinterface` property value to `false` so that MongoDB enables the HTTP frontend on the `28017` port. To enable the REST interface, you have to add a new property, `rest`, and set its value equal to `true`, as shown in the following code:

   ```
   nohttpinterface = false
   rest = true
   ```

4. Exit the SSH session and restart the MongoDB cartridge to allow the changes to take effect:

   ```
   $ rhc cartridge-restart –app mongodb-2.4
   ```

5. Execute the `rhc port-forward` command on your local machine to enable port forwarding. This will list all the applications that you can connect to from your local machine. The REST interface will be exposed at the `28017` port:

```
$ rhc port-forward

Checking available ports ... done

Forwarding ports ...

Address already in use - bind(2) while forwarding port 8080.
Trying local port 8081


To connect to a service running on OpenShift, use the Local
address


Service Local               OpenShift
------- ---------------- ---- ----------------

httpd   127.0.0.1:8080   =>  127.2.34.1:8080

httpd   127.0.0.1:8081   =>  127.2.34.3:8080

mongod  127.0.0.1:28017  =>  127.2.34.2:28017

mongodb 127.0.0.1:27017  =>  127.2.34.2:27017


Press CTRL-C to terminate port forwarding
```

6. Open `http://127.0.0.1:28017/` in a web browser. You have to authenticate using the MongoDB cartridge credentials. It uses the HTTP basic authentication.

7. Then, to view all the documents in the `msgs` collection in the `test` document, you can go to `http://127.0.0.1:28017/test/msgs/`. This will list a JSON document that contains all the messages in the `msgs` collection.

## How it works...

By default, MongoDB disables the REST interface. To enable the REST interface, you have to update the `mongodb.conf` MongoDB configuration file. In step 3, you updated the `mongodb.conf` file to enable the REST API. Then, you restarted the MongoDB cartridge in step 4 to reload the configuration. To connect with the REST interface from your local machine, you enabled port forwarding in step 5. The `rhc port-forward` command lists all the remote services that you can connect to from your local machine. The MongoDB REST interface is available on the `28017` port. In step 7, you viewed the details of the `msgs` collection in the `test` database by opening `http://127.0.0.1:28017/test/msgs/` in the browser.

## See also

 ▶  The *Using MongoLab MongoDB-as-a-Service with OpenShift* recipe
 ▶  The *Performing scheduled MongoDB database backups* recipe

# Performing scheduled MongoDB database backups

In this recipe, you will learn how to perform a scheduled backup of your MongoDB database and upload the backup to Amazon S3.

## Getting ready

To complete this recipe, you will need an application with a MongoDB cartridge. Refer to the *Adding a MongoDB cartridge to your application* recipe in this chapter to learn how to install one. Also, you need to have an Amazon AWS account. Go to `http://aws.amazon.com/` and sign up for a new account if you don't have one already.

## How to do it...

Perform the following steps to enable a daily scheduled backup of the MongoDB cartridge:

1. Go to `https://console.aws.amazon.com/s3/home` and create a new bucket to store your database backups.

2. Add the `cron` cartridge to your application by running the following command:

   ```
   $ rhc cartridge-add cron --app myapp
   ```

3. SSH into the application gear and download the `s3-bash` utility in `$OPENSHIFT_DATA_DIR`. Extract it to the `s3-bash` directory using the following commands:

   ```
   $ rhc ssh --app myapp
   $ cd $OPENSHIFT_DATA_DIR
   $ wget http://s3-bash.googlecode.com/files/s3-bash.0.02.tar.gz
   $ mkdir s3-bash
   $ tar -xf s3-bash.0.02.tar.gz -C s3-bash
   ```

4. Create a new file, `AWSSecretAccessKeyIdFile`, in the `$OPENSHIFT_DATA_DIR/s3-bash` directory and store your Amazon secret access key to it. This is required by `s3-bash` to communicate with Amazon S3.

5. Create a script on your local machine in `.openshift/cron/minutely/` `database_backup.sh` and add the following content to it:

```bash
#!/bin/bash
function load_env {
    [ -z "$1" ] && return 1
    [ -f "$1" ] || return 0

    local key=$(basename $1)
    export $key="$(< $1)"
}

for f in ~/.env/mongodb/*
do
  load_env $f
done

set -x
if [ 'date +%H:%M' == "23:50" ]
then
  FILE_NAME=$(date +"%Y%m%d%H%M")
  mongodump --host $OPENSHIFT_MONGODB_DB_HOST --port
$OPENSHIFT_MONGODB_DB_PORT --username
$OPENSHIFT_MONGODB_DB_USERNAME --password
$OPENSHIFT_MONGODB_DB_PASSWORD --db $OPENSHIFT_APP_NAME --
out $OPENSHIFT_DATA_DIR/$FILE_NAME
  cd $OPENSHIFT_DATA_DIR
  zip -r $FILE_NAME.zip $FILE_NAME
  echo "Took MongoDB Dump" >>
$OPENSHIFT_CRON_DIR/log/backup.log
  $OPENSHIFT_DATA_DIR/s3-bash/s3-put -k $AWS_ACCESS_KEY_ID
-s $OPENSHIFT_DATA_DIR/s3-bash/AWSSecretAccessKeyIdFile -T
$OPENSHIFT_DATA_DIR/$FILE_NAME.zip
/$AWS_S3_BUCKET/$FILE_NAME.zip
  echo "Uploaded dump to Amazon S3" >>
$OPENSHIFT_CRON_DIR/log/backup.log
  rm -f $OPENSHIFT_DATA_DIR/$FILE_NAME.zip
  rm -rf $OPENSHIFT_DATA_DIR/$FILE_NAME
fi
```

6. The preceding script will run every day at 23:50 (11:50 p.m.) and also run the `mongodump` command to create the database backup file. The file is then transferred to Amazon S3 using the `s3-bash` API. Finally, after uploading the file, it deletes the database dump file from the application gear.

7. Now, we have to set the environment variables so that our script can talk with Amazon S3. If you are not sure how to access your security credentials, then refer to the documentation at `http://docs.aws.amazon.com/general/latest/gr/getting-aws-sec-creds.html`. We run the following commands:

```
$ rhc env-set AWS_ACCESS_KEY_ID=< Your Amazon ACCESS_KEY_ID>

$ rhc env-set AWS_S3_BUCKET=<Amazon S3 bucket name >
```

8. Commit the code and push it to the OpenShift gear. Every night, at 23:50 (11:50 p.m.), database backup will be done and your backup will be uploaded to Amazon S3.

## How it works...

In step 1, you created a new Amazon S3 bucket to store your MongoDB database backups. Amazon S3 is widely used to store static files and is an ideal choice for this job. Next, you added the `cron` cartridge to the application. The `cron` cartridge will be used to perform daily backups at a particular time.

Amazon S3 exposes its REST service that users can use to perform operations on S3 buckets. Amazon provides many programming languages wrapped around their REST API to make it easy for developers to integrate with their application. As we wanted to keep this recipe's language agnostic, we used the Amazon S3 bash wrapper. Amazon does not officially support this wrapper, but it works very well. In step 3, you downloaded the `s3-bash` utility using `wget`. The `tar.gz` file was stored in `$OPENSHIFT_DATA_DIR`. You then extracted the `tar.gz` file to the `s3-bash` directory.

Next, in step 4, you created a file called `AWSSecretAccessKeyIdFile` to store the Amazon access key secret. The `s3-bash` wrapper uses a file for the AWS secret access key ID so that it does not appear in the list of running processes with `ps`.

In step 5, you created a bash script that will be executed every night at 23:50 (11:50 p.m.). The script first takes the database backup using the `mongodump` command and then uploads the file to Amazon S3. The filename is the current timestamp. Finally, after uploading the backup to S3, the script deletes the backup to save disk space.

Step 6 creates two environment variables required by the backup script. Finally, in step 7, you push the code to the application gear.

## See also

▶ The *Using MongoLab MongoDB-as-a-Service with OpenShift* recipe

# Using MongoLab MongoDB-as-a-Service with OpenShift

The MongoLab (`https://mongolab.com`) MongoDB-as-a-Service makes it easy for you to set up, operate, and scale a MongoDB database on top of various cloud providers. In addition to the standard MongoDB features, MongoLab also offers the following functionality:

▶ Running MongoDB on all the major cloud providers, such as Amazon, Google, Rackspace, and so on

▶ Highly available MongoDB

▶ Automated backups

▶ Monitoring support

In this recipe, you will learn how to use the MongoLab MongoDB-as-a-Service with your OpenShift applications.

## Getting ready

To complete this recipe, you will need an OpenShift application. Also, you need to have a MongoLab account. Go to `https://mongolab.com/` and sign up for a new account if you don't have one already.

## How to do it...

Perform the following steps to connect with the MongoLab MongoDB server from the OpenShift application:

1. After you have created a MongoLab account, you will be shown a screen to create your first database. Click on the **Create new** button:

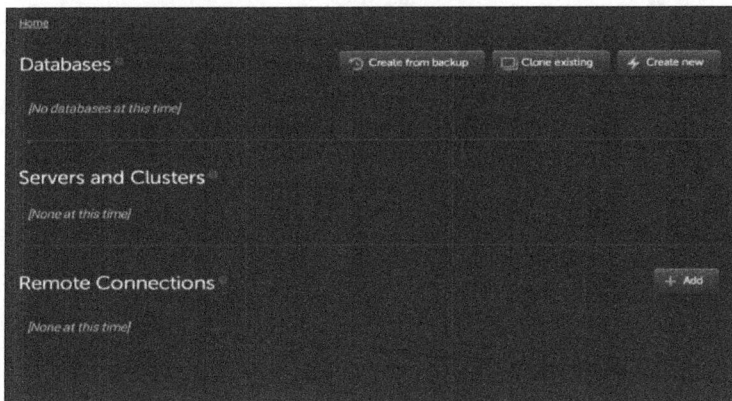

2. Enter the details of your MongoDB instance. In the following screenshot, the database name is `myapp` and Amazon EC2 is the cloud-hosting provider. We choose the US East coast data center, as this is where the OpenShift Online application instances are located. This helps to minimize the latency between the OpenShift application and the database instance:

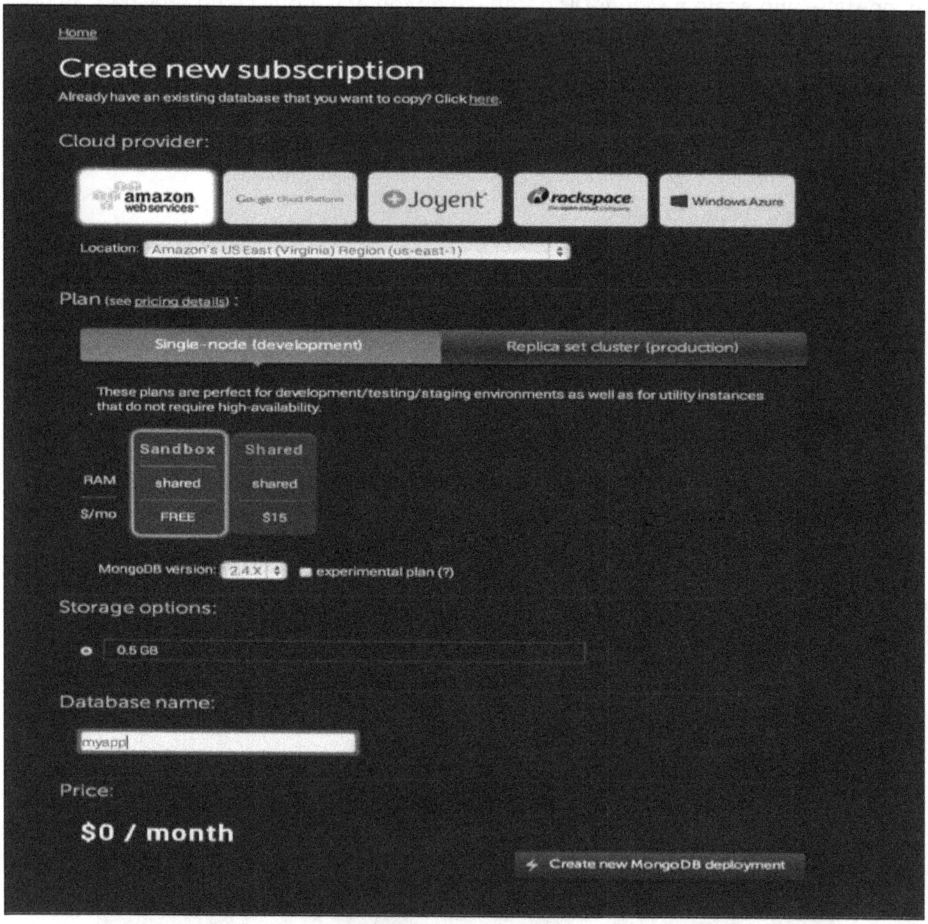

3. After the database is successfully provisioned, you will see it listed, as shown in the following screenshot:

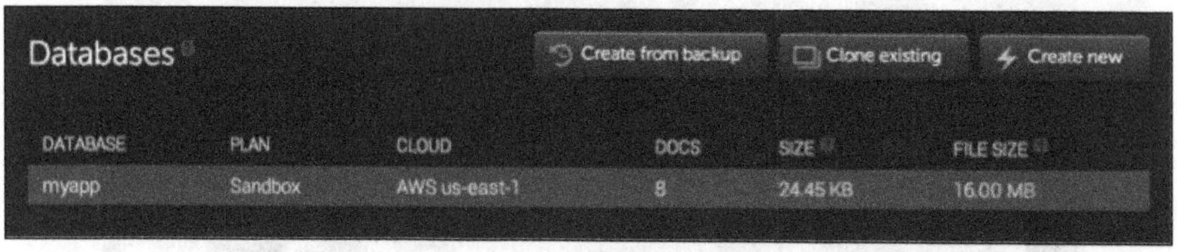

4. Click on the **myapp** database and you will be shown details of the database:

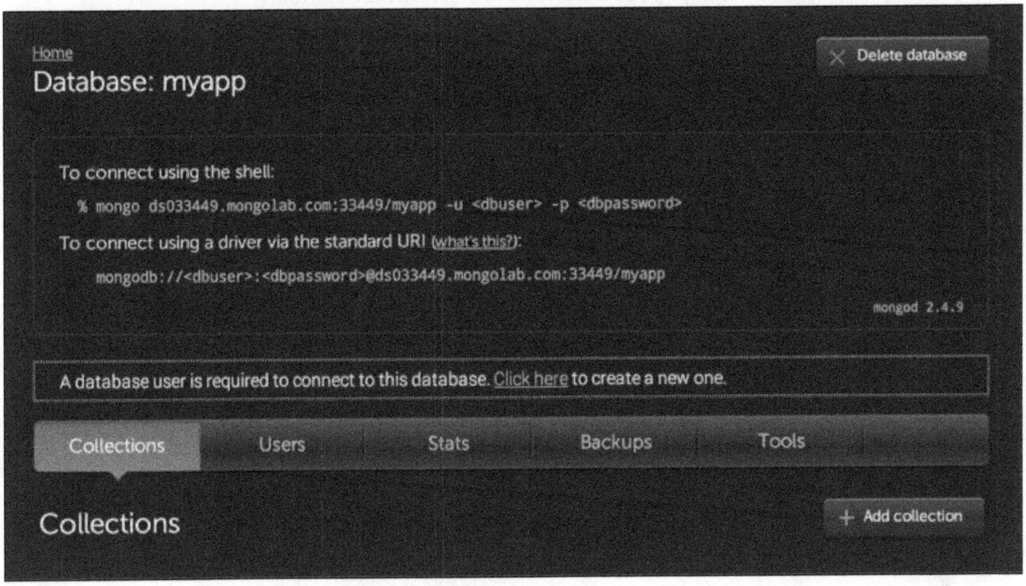

5. Before you can connect with the database, you need to create a database user. Click on the **Click here** link to create a new database user, as shown in the following screenshot:

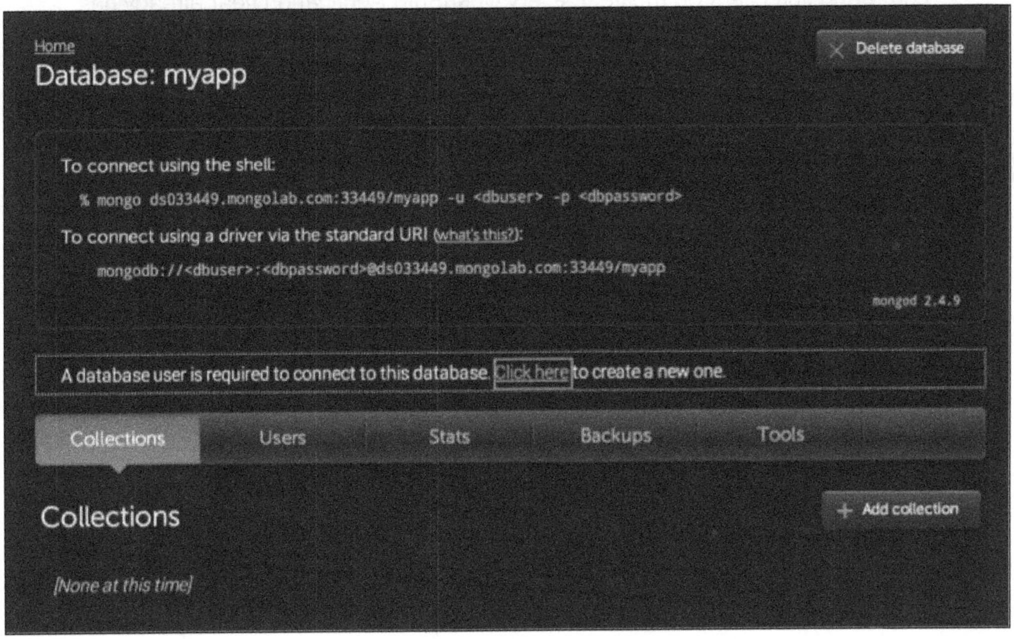

6. This will open a pop up, as shown in the following screenshot, where you have to enter the username and password for the new database user:

7. After creation, the database user will be shown on the database details page under the **Users** tab.

8. To connect to the MongoLab MongoDB instance, you will need to have the `mongo` command-line client on the gear. Every OpenShift application gear already has the `mongo` command-line client installed, so you don't have to do anything. Just SSH into the application gear using the `rhc ssh` command and then enter the following command. The username and password corresponds to the one you created during step 6. The host, port, and database name correspond to the information found in step 4:

```
$ mongo --host <host> --port <port> --username <username> --password <password> <database_name>
```

9. Once connected to the MongoLab MongoDB instance, you can run any valid MongoDB command, as follows:

```
> show collections
system.indexes
system.users
> db.msgs.insert({msg:"hello"})
>
> db.msgs.findOne()
{ "_id" : ObjectId("5315aa28317c39c58ecd4f04"), "msg" : "hello" }
```

## How it works...

Step 1 through 4 helped you create a new instance of the MongoLab MongoDB database instance. You are required to provide details related to your database instance, and MongoLab will provision a MongoDB database instance based on the details you entered. From step 5 through step 7, you created a new database user that will allow you to connect to the MongoDB database instance from the outside world.

In step 8, you used the database details to connect to the MongoDB instance from the OpenShift application gear using the `mongo` command-line client. Finally, you ran a few Mongo commands on the connected MongoLab MongoDB database instance. To learn how to connect to MongoLab with your PHP code, you can refer to the OpenShift official blog at `https://www.openshift.com/blogs/getting-started-with-mongodb-mongolab-php-and-openshift`.

## See also

▸ The *Adding a MongoDB cartridge to your application* recipe

# Adding a MariaDB cartridge to your application

In this recipe, you will learn how to add the MariaDB downloadable cartridge to your OpenShift application. MariaDB (`https://mariadb.org/`) is a community fork of the MySQL database. It is intended to be a drop-in replacement for the MySQL database.

## Getting ready

To step through this recipe, you will need the `rhc` command-line client installed on your machine. Refer to the *Installing the OpenShift rhc command-line client* recipe in *Chapter 1, Getting Started with OpenShift* for details. Also, we will use the application created in the *Creating an OpenShift application using the rhc command-line client* recipe in *Chapter 3, Creating and Managing Applications*.

## How to do it...

To install the MariaDB 5.5 downloadable cartridge on the `myapp` application, open a new command-line terminal, then change the directory to the `myapp` directory location and execute the following command:

```
$ rhc cartridge-add https://raw.github.com/openshift-
cartridges/mariadb-cartridge/master/metadata/manifest.yml --app myapp
```

The preceding command will install a new instance of the MariaDB server on your application gear.

You can view the cartridge details using the `rhc cartridge-show` command:

```
$ rhc cartridge-show mariadb
developercorey-mariadb-5.5 (MariaDB 5.5)
------------------------------------------
  From:              https://raw.github.com/openshift-
cartridges/mariadb-cartridge/master/metadata/manifest.yml
  Gears:             Located with php-5.4, cron-1.4
  Connection URL:
mysql://$OPENSHIFT_MARIADB_DB_HOST:$OPENSHIFT_MARIADB_DB_PORT/
  Database Name:     myapp
  Password:          wPG6vvBy6_L9
  Username:          admin7H6WdQN
```

You can also stop the MariaDB server using the `stop` command:

```
$ rhc cartridge-stop mariadb
```

You can restart the MariaDB server using the `restart` command:

```
$ rhc cartridge-restart mariadb
```

If you want to remove the MariaDB server from your application, you can use the `remove` command:

```
$ rhc cartridge-remove mariadb --confirm
```

## How it works...

When you run the `rhc cartridge-add` command, `rhc` will make an HTTP POST request to the OpenShift server. The OpenShift server will receive the request and instantiate a new instance of the MariaDB server for your application using the manifest file. After provisioning the MariaDB server, the `rhc` client will show the database details on the command-line terminal.

You can view the MariaDB installation by performing an SSH into your application gear:

```
$ rhc ssh --app myapp
```

Then, run the `ls` command to view the gear directory structure and you will see the `mariadb` directory:

```
[myapp-osbook.rhcloud.com 52fb71aa5973caf609000026]\> ls -p
app-deployments/  app-root/  cron/  git/  mariadb/  php/
```

The `mariadb` directory is your `mariadb` installation, and it is not shared with any other OpenShift application or user. It is only for your application, and only your application can access it.

You can also connect with your MariaDB server using the `mysql` command-line client. We used the `mysql` client because it is already installed and compatible with MariaDB.

Now, you can run SQL commands against your MariaDB server. To view all the databases, run the following command:

```
mysql> SHOW DATABASES;
+--------------------+
| Database           |
+--------------------+
| information_schema |
| myapp              |
| mysql              |
+--------------------+
3 rows in set (0.00 sec)
```

The `myapp` database corresponds to your application database.

## See also

> ▸ The *Adding a MongoDB cartridge to your application* recipe

# Adding a Redis cartridge to your application

In this recipe, you will learn how to add the Redis downloadable cartridge to your OpenShift application. Redis is an open source, advanced, NoSQL key value data store, written in the ANSI C programming language. It is an in-memory data store but also writes to the disk for durability.

## Getting ready

To step through this recipe, you will need the `rhc` command-line client installed on your machine. Refer to the *Installing the OpenShift rhc command-line client* recipe in *Chapter 1, Getting Started with OpenShift* for details. Also, we will use the application created in the *Creating an OpenShift application using the rhc command-line client* recipe in *Chapter 3, Creating and Managing Applications*.

## How to do it...

To install the Redis downloadable cartridge to the `myapp` application, open a new command-line terminal, then change the directory to the `myapp` directory location, and execute the following command:

```
$ rhc cartridge-add http://cartreflect-
claytondev.rhcloud.com/reflect?github=smarterclayton/openshift-redis-
cart --app myapp
```

This will install a new instance of the Redis server on your application gear.

You can view the cartridge details using the `rhc cartridge-show` command.

You can also stop the Redis server using the `stop` command:

```
$ rhc cartridge-stop redis
```

You can restart the Redis server using the `restart` command:

```
$ rhc cartridge-restart redis
```

If you want to remove the Redis server from your application, you can use the `remove` command:

```
$ rhc cartridge-remove redis --confirm
```

## How it works...

When you run the `rhc cartridge-add` command, `rhc` will make an HTTP POST request to the OpenShift server. The OpenShift server will receive the request and instantiate a new instance of the Redis server for your application using the manifest file. After provisioning the Redis server, the `rhc` client will show the database details on the command-line terminal, as follows:

```
Adding http://cartreflect-
claytondev.rhcloud.com/reflect?githubgithub=smarterclayton/openshift-
redis-cart to application 'myapp' ... done


smarterclayton-redis-2.6 (Redis)
----------------------------------

  From:  http://cartreflect-
claytondev.rhcloud.com/reflect?github=smarterclayton/openshift-redis-
cart
  Gears: Located with php-5.4
```

Redis is now configured with a default password
ZTNiMGM0NDI5OGZjMWMxND1hZmJmNGM4OTk2ZmI5

You can configure various Redis scaling and persistence modes by setting

environment variables - consult the cartridge README for more info.

You can view the Redis installation by performing an SSH into your application gear:

```
$ rhc ssh --app myapp
```

Then, run the `ls` command to view the gear directory structure, and you will see the redis directory:

```
[myapp-osbook.rhcloud.com 52fb71aa5973caf609000026]\> ls -p
app-deployments/  app-root/  git/  php/  redis/
```

The redis directory is your redis installation, and it is not shared with any other OpenShift application or user. It is only for your application, and only your application can access it.

You can also connect with your Redis server using the redis-cli command-line client:

```
[myapp-osbook.rhcloud.com 53121c645973ca7acf000018]\> redis-cli
$REDIS_CLI
redis 127.2.34.2:16379>
```

Now, you can run commands against your Redis server. To view the details about your Redis installation, you can run the INFO command:

```
redis 127.2.34.2:16379> INFO
# Server
redis_version:2.6.13
redis_git_sha1:00000000
redis_git_dirty:0
redis_mode:standalone
os:Linux 2.6.32-431.5.1.el6oso.bz844450.x86_64 x86_64
arch_bits:64
multiplexing_api:epoll
tcp_port:16379
uptime_in_seconds:874
uptime_in_days:0
hz:10
lru_clock:957695
// removed for brevity
```

## There's more...

To learn how to use Redis with a Java application, you can read my blog at `https://www.openshift.com/blogs/build-cloud-enabled-java-redis-applications-with-spring-on-openshift.`

## See also

  ▸   The *Adding a MariaDB cartridge to your application* recipe

# 7
# OpenShift for Java Developers

This chapter presents a number of recipes that show you how to get started with Java web application development on OpenShift. You will learn how to create and deploy **Java Enterprise Edition** (**Java EE**) applications on OpenShift using the JBoss EAP 6 and JBoss AS 7 application server cartridges. This chapter will also cover how to develop and host your Spring Framework applications on the Tomcat server. The specific recipes within this chapter are as follows:

- ▶ Creating and deploying Java EE 6 applications using the JBoss EAP and PostgreSQL 9.2 cartridges
- ▶ Configuring application security by defining the database login module in standalone.xml
- ▶ Installing modules with JBoss cartridges
- ▶ Managing JBoss cartridges using the management web interface and CLI
- ▶ Creating and deploying Spring applications using the Tomcat 7 cartridge
- ▶ Taking thread dumps of Java cartridges
- ▶ Choosing between Java 6 and Java 7
- ▶ Enabling hot deployment for Java applications
- ▶ Skipping the Maven build
- ▶ Forcing a clean Maven build
- ▶ Overriding the default Maven build command
- ▶ Installing the JAR file not present in the Maven central repository
- ▶ Developing OpenShift Java applications using Eclipse
- ▶ Using Eclipse System Explorer to SSH into the application gear
- ▶ Debugging Java applications in the Cloud

# Introduction

This chapter will explore how Java developers can get started with OpenShift to develop Java EE or Spring applications. Java is often thought of as the de facto open source, enterprise programming language. OpenShift supports the JBoss application server, which is a certified platform for Java EE 6 development. As an OpenShift Online user, you have access to both the community version of JBoss and commercial JBoss EAP 6 for free. The *Creating and deploying Java EE 6 applications using the JBoss EAP and PostgreSQL 9.2 cartridges* recipe will cover how to develop and deploy Java EE 6 applications on OpenShift. There is also a community-supported cartridge for WildFly, a certified Java EE 7 application server that you can use to deploy Java EE 7 applications. This chapter will not cover the WildFly cartridge.

A popular alternative to Java EE development is Spring Framework. Spring developers normally use Apache Tomcat to host their applications. OpenShift supports two versions of Tomcat: Apache Tomcat 6 and Apache Tomcat 7. The *Creating and deploying Spring applications using the Tomcat 7 cartridge* recipe will cover how to develop a Spring application and deploy it on OpenShift. Also, it is possible to run Apache Tomcat 8 (currently in beta) on OpenShift. You can read my blog to learn how to deploy Apache Tomcat 8 on OpenShift at `https://www.openshift.com/blogs/how-to-run-apache-tomcat-8-on-openshift`.

OpenShift uses Apache Maven to manage dependencies and build your OpenShift apps. All OpenShift Java applications are Maven-based applications. This chapter assumes that you are familiar with Apache Maven. In the event that you are not comfortable with Maven, then please refer to the documentation at `http://maven.apache.org/guides/getting-started/index.html`. This chapter will cover various aspects of using Apache Maven with OpenShift, such as how to use your own JARs (not hosted on the Maven central repository) with OpenShift, and so on. OpenShift also allows you to use other build tools, such as Apache Ant and Gradle. Please refer to my blogs on Apache Ant (`https://www.openshift.com/blogs/running-ant-builds-on-openshift`) and Gradle (`https://www.openshift.com/blogs/run-gradle-builds-on-openshift`) to learn how to use them with OpenShift applications.

Almost all Java developers use an IDE to build their applications. OpenShift has first-class support for the Eclipse IDE. The *Developing OpenShift Java applications using Eclipse* recipe will walk you through a step-by-step process of creating and managing an application from within Eclipse. You can even SSH into the application gear from within Eclipse. This will be covered in the *Using Eclipse System Explorer to SSH into the application gear* recipe.

If you want to run the examples on your local machine, then please install Java 7, Apache Maven, and Eclipse. The instructions to install Java for your operating system can be found at `http://www.java.com/en/download/help/download_options.xml`. Next, instructions to install Apache Maven can be found here: `http://maven.apache.org/download.cgi#Installation`. Finally, you can install Eclipse on your machine by following the instructions mentioned here: `http://wiki.eclipse.org/Eclipse/Installation`.

This chapter is based on the assumption that you know the basics of OpenShift application development and database cartridges. In the event that you are not comfortable with the basics, I will recommend that you first read *Chapter 3, Creating and Managing Applications* to *Chapter 6, Using MongoDB and Third-party Database Cartridges with OpenShift Applications* before continuing with this chapter.

In this chapter, we will develop a simple job portal application that will allow users to post job openings for a company. Users can create a company and then post jobs for that company. All the source code is on the *OpenShift-Cookbook* repository of the GitHub organization at `https://github.com/OpenShift-Cookbook`.

# Creating and deploying Java EE 6 applications using the JBoss EAP and PostgreSQL 9.2 cartridges

Gone are the days when Java EE or J2EE (as it was called in the olden days) was considered evil. Java EE now provides a very productive environment to build web applications. Java EE has embraced convention over configuration and annotations, which means that you are no longer required to maintain XML to configure each and every component. In this recipe, you will learn how to build a Java EE 6 application and deploy it on OpenShift. This recipe assumes that you have basic knowledge of Java and Java EE 6. If you are not comfortable with Java EE 6, please read the official tutorial at `http://docs.oracle.com/javaee/6/tutorial/doc/`.

In this recipe, you will build a simple job portal that will allow users to post job openings and view a list of all the persisted jobs in the system. These two functionalities will be exposed using two REST endpoints.

The source code for the application created in this recipe is on GitHub at `https://github.com/OpenShift-Cookbook/chapter7-jobstore-javaee6-simple`. The example application that you will build in this recipe is a simple version of the `jobstore` application with only a single domain class and without any application interface. You can get the complete `jobstore` application source code on GitHub as well at `https://github.com/OpenShift-Cookbook/chapter7-jobstore-javaee6`.

## Getting ready

To complete this recipe, you will need the `rhc` command-line client installed on your machine. Please refer to the *Installing the OpenShift rhc command-line client* recipe in *Chapter 1, Getting Started with OpenShift*, for details. Also, you will need an IDE to work with the application code. The recommended IDE to work with OpenShift is Eclipse Luna, but you can also work with other IDEs, such as IntelliJ Idea and NetBeans. Download and install the Eclipse IDE for Java EE developers from the official website at `https://www.eclipse.org/downloads/`.

## How to do it...

Perform the following steps to create the `jobstore` application:

1. Open a new command-line terminal, and go to a convenient location. Create a new JBoss EAP application by executing the following command:

   ```
   $ rhc create-app jobstore jbosseap-6
   ```

2. The preceding command will create a Maven project and clone it to your local machine.

3. Change the directory to `jobstore`, and execute the following command to add the PostgreSQL 9.2 cartridge to the application:

   ```
   $ rhc cartridge-add postgresql-9.2
   ```

4. Open Eclipse and navigate to the project workspace. Then, import the application created in step 1 as a Maven project. To import an existing Maven project, navigate to **File | Import | Maven | Existing Maven Projects**. Then, navigate to the location of your OpenShift Maven application created in step 1.

5. Next, update `pom.xml` to use Java 7. The Maven project created by OpenShift is configured to use JDK 6. Replace the properties with the one shown in the following code:

   ```
   <maven.compiler.source>1.7</maven.compiler.source>
   <maven.compiler.target>1.7</maven.compiler.target>
   ```

6. Update the Maven project to allow the changes to take effect. You can update the Maven project by right-clicking on the project and navigating to **Maven | Update Project**.

7. Now, let us write the domain classes for our application. Java EE uses JPA to define the data model and manage entities. The application has one domain class: `Job`. Create a new package called `org.osbook.jobstore.domain`, and then create a new Java class called `Job` inside it. Have a look at the following code:

   ```java
   @Entity
   public class Job {

   @Id
   @GeneratedValue(strategy = GenerationType.AUTO)
   private Long id;

   @NotNull
   private String title;

   @NotNull
   @Size(max = 4000)
   private String description;
   ```

```
@Column(updatable = false)
@Temporal(TemporalType.DATE)
@NotNull
private Date postedAt = new Date();

@NotNull
private String company;

//setters and getters removed for brevity


}
```

8. Create a `META-INF` folder at `src/main/resources`, and then create a `persistence.xml` file with the following code:

```xml
<?xml version="1.0" encoding="UTF-8"?>
<persistence xmlns:xsi="http://www.w3.org/2001/XMLSchema-
instance"

xsi:schemaLocation="http://java.sun.com/xml/ns/persistence
http://java.sun.com/xml/ns/persistence/persistence_2_0.xsd"
version="2.0"
xmlns="http://java.sun.com/xml/ns/persistence">

<persistence-unit name="jobstore" transaction-type="JTA">

<provider>org.hibernate.ejb.HibernatePersistence</provider>
<jta-data-
source>java:jboss/datasources/PostgreSQLDS</jta-data-
source>

<exclude-unlisted-classes>false</exclude-unlisted-
classes>

<properties>
<property name="hibernate.show_sql" value="true" />
<property name="hibernate.hbm2ddl.auto"
value="update" />
</properties>
</persistence-unit>

</persistence>
```

9. Now, we will create the `JobService` class that will use the JPA `EntityManager` API to work with the database. Create a new package called `org.osbook.jobstore.services`, and create a new Java class as shown in the following code. It defines the `save` and `findAll` operations on the `Job` entity.

```
@Stateless
public class JobService {

@PersistenceContext(unitName = "jobstore")
private EntityManager entityManager;

public Job save(Job job) {
entityManager.persist(job);
return job;
}

public List<Job> findAll() {
return entityManager
.createQuery("SELECT j from
org.osbook.jobstore.domain.Job j order by j.postedAt desc",
Job.class)
.getResultList();
}
}
```

10. Next, enable **Contexts and Dependency Injection (CDI)** in the `jobstore` application by creating a file with the name `beans.xml` in the `src/main/webapp/WEB-INF` directory as follows:

```
<?xml version="1.0"?>
<beans xmlns="http://java.sun.com/xml/ns/javaee"

  xmlns:xsi="http://www.w3.org/2001/XMLSchema-instance"
xsi:schemaLocation="http://java.sun.com/xml/ns/javaee
http://jboss.org/schema/cdi/beans_1_0.xsd"/>
```

11. The `jobstore` application will expose the REST JSON web service. Before you can write the JAX-RS resources, you have to configure JAX-RS in your application. Create a new package called `org.osbook.jobstore.rest` and a new class called `RestConfig`, as shown in the following code:

```
@ApplicationPath("/api/v1")
public class RestConfig extends Application {
}
```

12. Create a JAX-RS resource to expose the `create` and `findAll` operations of `JobService` as REST endpoints as follows:

```
@Path("/jobs")
public class JobResource {

@Inject
private JobService jobService;

@POST
@Consumes(MediaType.APPLICATION_JSON)
public Response createNewJob(@Valid Job job) {
job = jobService.save(job);
return Response.status(Status.CREATED).build();
}

@GET
@Produces(MediaType.APPLICATION_JSON)
public List<Job> showAll() {
return jobService.findAll();
}
}
```

13. Commit the code, and push it to the OpenShift application as shown in the following commands:

```
$ git add .
$ git commit -am "jobstore application created"
$ git push
```

14. After the build finishes successfully, the application will be accessible at `http://jobstore-{domain-name}.rhcloud.com`. Please replace `domain-name` with your own domain name.

15. To test the REST endpoints, you can use `curl`. `curl` is a command-line tool for transferring data across various protocols. We will use it to test our REST endpoints. To create a new job, you will run the following `curl` command:

```
$ curl -i -X POST -H "Content-Type: application/json" -H
"Accept: application/json" -d '{"title":"OpenShift
Evangelist","description":"OpenShift
Evangelist","company":"Red Hat"}'http://jobstore-{domain-
name}.rhcloud.com/api/v1/jobs
```

16. To view all the jobs, you can run the following `curl` command:

```
$ curl http://jobstore-{domain-name}.rhcloud.com/api/v1/jobs
```

## How it works...

In the preceding steps, we created a Java EE application and deployed it on OpenShift. In step 1, you used the `rhc create-app` command to create a JBoss EAP web cartridge application. The `rhc` command-line tool makes a request to the OpenShift broker and asks it to create a new application using the JBoss EAP cartridge. The anatomy of application creation was explained in the *Creating an OpenShift application using the rhc command-line client* recipe in *Chapter 3, Creating and Managing Applications*. Every OpenShift web cartridge specifies a template application that will be used as the default source code of the application. For Java web cartridges (JBoss EAP, JBoss AS7, Tomcat 6, and Tomcat 7), the template is a Maven-based application. After the application is created, it is cloned to the local machine using Git. The directory structure of the application is shown in the following command:

```
$ ls -a
.git .openshift README.md pom.xml deployments src
```

As you can see in the preceding command, apart from the `.git` and `.openshift` directories, this looks like a standard Maven project. OpenShift uses Maven to manage application dependencies and build your Java applications.

Let us take a look at what's inside the `jobstore` directory to better understand the layout of the application:

- ▶ **The src directory**: This directory contains the source code for the template application generated by OpenShift. You need to add your application source code here. The `src` folder helps in achieving source code deployment when following the standard Maven directory conventions.

- ▶ **The pom.xml file**: The Java applications created by OpenShift are Maven-based projects. So, a `pom.xml` file is required when you do source code deployment on OpenShift. This `pom.xml` file has a profile called `openshift`, which will be executed when you push code to OpenShift as shown in the following code. This profile will create a `ROOT` WAR file based upon your application source code.

```
<profiles>
<profile>
<id>openshift</id>
<build>
<finalName>jobstore</finalName>
<plugins>
<plugin>
<artifactId>maven-war-plugin</artifactId>
<version>2.1.1</version>
<configuration>
<outputDirectory>deployments</outputDirectory>
<warName>ROOT</warName>
```

```
</configuration>
</plugin>
</plugins>
</build>
</profile>
</profiles>
```

- ▶ **The deployments directory**: You should use this directory if you want to do binary deployments on OpenShift, that is, you want to deploy a WAR or EAR file directly instead of pushing the source code.

- ▶ **The .git directory**: This is a local Git repository. This directory contains the complete history of the repository. The `config` file in `.git/` contains the configuration for the repository. It defines a Git remote origin that points to the OpenShift application gear SSH URL. This makes sure that when you do `git push`, the source code is pushed to the remote Git repository hosted on your application gear. You can view the details of the origin Git remote by executing the following command:

```
$ git remote show origin
```

- ▶ **The .openshift directory**: This is an OpenShift-specific directory, which can be used for the following purposes:

    - ❑ The files under the `action_hooks` subdirectory allow you to hook onto the application lifecycle.

    - ❑ The files under the `config` subdirectory allow you to make changes to the JBoss EAP configuration. The directory contains the `standalone.xml` JBoss EAP-specific configuration file.

    - ❑ The files under the `cron` subdirectory are used when you add the cron cartridge to your application. This allows you to run scripts or jobs on a periodic basis.

    - ❑ The files under the `markers` subdirectory allow you to specify whether you want to use Java 6 or Java 7 or you want to do hot deploy or debug the application running in the Cloud, and so on.

In step 2, you added the PostgreSQL 9.2 cartridge to the application using the `rhc cartridge-add` command. We will use the PostgreSQL database to store the `jobstore` application data. Then, in step 3, you imported the project in the Eclipse IDE as a Maven project. Eclipse Kepler has inbuilt support for Maven applications, which makes it easier to work with Maven-based applications.

From step 3 through step 5, you updated the project to use JDK 1.7 for the Maven compiler plugin. All the OpenShift Java applications use OpenJDK 7, so it makes sense to update the application to also use JDK 1.7 for compilation.

In step 6, you created the `job` domain class and annotated it with JPA annotations. The `@Entity` annotation marks the class as a JPA entity. An entity represents a table in the relational database, and each entity instance corresponds to a row in the table. Entity class fields represent the persistent state of the entity. You can learn more about JPA by reading the official documentation at `http://docs.oracle.com/javaee/6/tutorial/doc/bnbpz.html`.

The `@NotNull` and `@Size` annotation marks are Bean Validation annotations. Bean Validation is a new validation model available as a part of the Java EE 6 platform. The `@NotNull` annotation adds a constraint that the value of the field must not be null. If the value is null, an exception will be raised. The `@Size` annotation adds a constraint that the value must match the specified minimum and maximum boundaries. You can learn more about Bean Validation by reading the official documentation at `http://docs.oracle.com/javaee/6/tutorial/doc/gircz.html`.

In JPA, entities are managed within a persistence context. Within the persistence context, the entity manager manages the entities. The configuration of the entity manager is defined in a standard configuration XML file called `persitence.xml`. In step 7, you created the `persistence.xml` file. The most important configuration option is the `jta-datasource-source` configuration tag. It points to `java:jboss/datasources/PostgreSQLDS`. When a user creates a JBoss EAP 6 application, then OpenShift defines a PostgreSQL datasource in the `standalone.xml` file. The `standalone.xml` file is a JBoss configuration file, which includes the technologies required by the Java EE 6 full profile specification plus Java Connector 1.6 architecture, Java XML API for RESTful web services, and OSGi. Developers can override the configuration by making changes to the `standalone.xml` file in the `.openshift/config` location of your application directory. So, if you open the `standalone.xml` file in `.openshift/config/` in your favorite editor, you will find the following PostgreSQL datasource configuration:

```
<datasource jndi-name="java:jboss/datasources/PostgreSQLDS"
enabled="${postgresql.enabled}" use-java-context="true" pool-
name="PostgreSQLDS"
use-ccm="true">
<connection-
url>jdbc:postgresql://${env.OPENSHIFT_POSTGRESQL_DB_HOST}:${env.OP
ENSHIFT_POSTGRESQL_DB_PORT}/${env.OPENSHIFT_APP_NAME}
</connection-url>
<driver>postgresql</driver>
<security>
<user-name>${env.OPENSHIFT_POSTGRESQL_DB_USERNAME}</user-name>
<password>${env.OPENSHIFT_POSTGRESQL_DB_PASSWORD}</password>
</security>
<validation>
<check-valid-connection-sql>SELECT 1</check-valid-connection-
sql>
```

```
<background-validation>true</background-validation>
<background-validation-millis>60000</background-validation-
millis>
<!--<validate-on-match>true</validate-on-match> -->
</validation>
<pool>
<flush-strategy>IdleConnections</flush-strategy>
<allow-multiple-users />
</pool>
</datasource>
```

In step 8, you created stateless **Enterprise JavaBeans (EJBs)** for our application service layer. The service classes work with the `EntityManager` API to perform operations on the `Job` entity.

In step 9, you configured CDI by creating the `beans.xml` file in the `src/main/webapp/WEB-INF` directory. We are using CDI in our application so that we can use dependency injection instead of manually creating the objects ourselves. The CDI container will manage the bean life cycle, and the developer just has to write the business logic. To let the JBoss application server know that we are using CDI, we need to create a file called `beans.xml` in our `WEB-INF` directory. The file can be completely blank, but its presence tells the container that the CDI framework needs to be loaded.

In step 10 and step 11, you configured JAX-RS and defined the REST resources for the `Job` entity. You activated JAX-RS by creating a class that extends `javax.ws.rs.ApplicationPath`. You need to specify the base URL under which your web service will be available. This is done by annotating the `RestConfig` class with the `ApplicationPath` annotation. You used `/api/v1` as the application path.

In step 12, you added and committed the changes to the local repository and then pushed the changes to the application gear. After the bits are pushed, OpenShift will stop all the cartridges and then invoke the `mvn -e clean package -Popenshift -DskipTests` command to build the project. Maven will build a `ROOT.war` file, which will be copied to the JBoss EAP `deployments` folder. After the build successfully finishes, all the cartridges are started. Then the new updated `ROOT.war` file will be deployed. You can view the running application at `http://jobstore-{domain-name}.rhcloud.com`. Please replace `{domain-name}` with your account domain name.

Finally, you tested the REST endpoints using `curl` in step 14.

## There's more...

You can perform all the aforementioned steps with just a single command as follows:

```
$ rhc create-app jobstore jbosseap postgresql-9.2 --from-code
https://github.com/OpenShift-Cookbook/chapter7-jobstore-javaee6-
simple.git --timeout 180
```

## See also

▸ The *Configuring application security by defining the database login module in standalone.xml* recipe

▸ The *Managing JBoss cartridges using the management web interface and CLI* recipe

# Configuring application security by defining the database login module in standalone.xml

In the *Creating and deploying Java EE 6 applications using the JBoss EAP and PostgreSQL 9.2 cartridges* recipe, you learned how to develop a Java EE 6 application on OpenShift. The application allows you to create company entities and then assign jobs to them. The problem with the application is that it is not secured. The Java EE specification defines a simple, role-based security model for EJBs and web components. JBoss security is an extension to the application server and is included by default with your OpenShift JBoss applications. You can view the extension in the JBoss `standalone.xml` configuration file. The `standalone.xml` file exists in the `.openshift/config` location. The following code shows the extension:

```
<extension module="org.jboss.as.security" />
```

OpenShift allows developers to update the `standalone.xml` configuration file to meet their application needs. You make a change to the `standalone.xml` configuration file, commit the change to the local Git repository, then push the changes to the OpenShift application gear. Then, after the successful build, OpenShift will replace the existing `standalone.xml` file with your updated configuration file and then finally start the server. But please make sure that your changes are valid; otherwise, the application will fail to start.

In this recipe, you will learn how to define the database login module in `standalone.xml` to authenticate users before they can perform any operation with the application.

The source code for the application created in this recipe is on GitHub at `https://github.com/OpenShift-Cookbook/chapter7-jobstore-security`.

## Getting ready

This recipe builds on the application created in the *Creating and deploying Java EE 6 applications using the JBoss EAP and PostgreSQL 9.2 cartridges* recipe. So, please refer to that recipe before continuing with this recipe.

## How to do it...

Perform the following steps to add security to your web application:

1. Create the OpenShift application created in the *Creating and deploying Java EE 6 applications using the JBoss EAP and PostgreSQL 9.2 cartridges* recipe using the following command:

   ```
   $ rhc create-app jobstore jbosseap postgresql-9.2 --from-code
   https://github.com/OpenShift-Cookbook/chapter7-jobstore-
   javaee6-simple.git --timeout 180
   ```

2. After the application creation, SSH into the application gear, and connect with the PostgreSQL database using the `psql` client. Then, create the following tables and insert the test data:

   ```
   $ rhc ssh
   ```

   ```
   $ psql
   ```

   ```
   jobstore=# CREATE TABLE USERS(email VARCHAR(64) PRIMARY KEY,
   password VARCHAR(64));
   ```

   ```
   jobstore=# CREATE TABLE USER_ROLES(email VARCHAR(64), role
   VARCHAR(32));
   ```

   ```
   jobstore=# INSERT into USERS values('admin@jobstore.com',
   'ISMvKXpXpadDiUoOSoAfww==');
   ```

   ```
   jobstore=# INSERT into USER_ROLES values('admin@jobstore.com',
   'admin');
   ```

3. Exit from the SSH shell, and open the `standalone.xml` file in the `.openshift/config` directory. Update the security domain with the following code:

   ```xml
   <security-domain name="other" cache-type="default">
   <authentication>
   <login-module code="Remoting" flag="optional">
   <module-option name="password-stacking"
   value="useFirstPass" />
   </login-module>
   <login-module code="Database" flag="required">
   <module-option name="dsJndiName"
   value="java:jboss/datasources/PostgreSQLDS" />
   <module-option name="principalsQuery"
   value="select password from USERS where email=?" />
   <module-option name="rolesQuery"
   value="select role, 'Roles' from USER_ROLES where
   email=?" />
   <module-option name="hashAlgorithm" value="MD5" />
   <module-option name="hashEncoding" value="base64" />
   ```

```
</login-module>
</authentication>
</security-domain>
```

4. Create the web deployment descriptor (that is, `web.xml`) in the `src/main/webapp/`
   `WEB-INF` folder. Add the following content to it:

```xml
<?xml version="1.0" encoding="UTF-8"?>
<web-app version="3.0"
xmlns="http://java.sun.com/xml/ns/javaee"
xmlns:xsi="http://www.w3.org/2001/XMLSchema-instance"
xsi:schemaLocation="http://java.sun.com/xml/ns/javaee
http://java.sun.com/xml/ns/javaee/web-app_3_0.xsd">

<security-constraint>
<web-resource-collection>
<web-resource-name>WebAuth</web-resource-name>
<description>application security constraints
</description>
<url-pattern>/*</url-pattern>
<http-method>GET</http-method>
<http-method>POST</http-method>
</web-resource-collection>
<auth-constraint>
<role-name>admin</role-name>
</auth-constraint>
</security-constraint>
<login-config>
<auth-method>FORM</auth-method>
<realm-name>jdbcRealm</realm-name>
<form-login-config>
<form-login-page>/login.html</form-login-
page>
<form-error-page>/error.html</form-error-
page>
</form-login-config>
</login-config>
<security-role>
<role-name>admin</role-name>
</security-role>

</web-app>
```

5. Create the `login.html` file in the `src/main/webapp` directory. The `login.html` page will be used for user authentication. The following code shows the contents of this file:

```
<!DOCTYPE html>
<html>
<head>
<meta charset="UTF-8">
<title>Login</title>
<link href="//cdnjs.cloudflare.com/ajax/libs/twitter-
bootstrap/3.1.1/css/bootstrap.css" rel="stylesheet">
</head>
<body>
<div class="container">
<form class="form-signin" role="form" method="post"
action="j_security_check">
<h2 class="form-signin-heading">Please sign in</h2>
<input type="text" id="j_username"
name="j_username" class="form-control" placeholder="Email
address" required autofocus>
<input type="password" id="j_password"
name="j_password" class="form-control"
placeholder="Password" required>
<button class="btn btn-lg btn-primary btn-block"
type="submit">Sign in</button>
</form>
</div>
</body>
</html>
```

6. Create an `error.html` file in the `src/main/webapp` directory. The `error.html` page will be shown after unsuccessful authentication. The following code shows the contents of this file:

```
<!DOCTYPE html>
<html>
<head>
<meta charset="US-ASCII">
<title>Error page</title>
</head>
<body>
<h2>Incorrect username/password</h2>
</body>
</html>
```

7. Commit the changes, and push them to the OpenShift application gear:

```
$ git add .
$ git commit -am "enabled security"
$ git push
```

8. Go to the application page at `http://jobstore-{domain-name}.rhcloud.com`, and you will be asked to log in before you can view the application. Use `admin@jobstore.com/admin` as the username-password combination to log in to the application.

## How it works...

Let's now understand what you did in the preceding steps. In step 1, you recreated the `jobstore` application we developed in the *Creating and deploying Java EE 6 applications using the JBoss EAP and PostgreSQL 9.2 cartridges* recipe. Next, in step 2, you performed an SSH into the application gear and created the `USERS` and `USER_ROLES` tables. These tables will be used by the JBoss database login module to authenticate users. As our application does not have the user registration functionality, we created a default user for the application. Storing the password as a clear text string is a bad practice, so we have stored the MD5 hash of the password. The MD5 hash of the `admin` password is `ISMvKXpXpadDiUoOSoAfww==`. If you want to generate the hashed password in your application, I have included a simple Java class, which uses `org.jboss.crypto.CryptoUtil` to generate the MD5 hash of any string. The `CryptoUtil` class is part of the picketbox library. The following code depicts this:

```
import org.jboss.crypto.CryptoUtil;

public class PasswordHash {

public static String getPasswordHash(String password) {
return CryptoUtil.createPasswordHash("MD5",
CryptoUtil.BASE64_ENCODING,
null, null, password);
}

public static void main(String[] args) throws Exception {
System.out.println(getPasswordHash("admin"));
}
}
```

In step 3, you logged out of the SSH session and updated the `standalone.xml` JBoss configuration file with the database login module configuration. There are several login module implementations available out of the box. This book will only talk about the database login module, as discussing all the modules is outside the scope of this book. You can read about all the login modules at `https://docs.jboss.org/author/display/AS7/Secur ity+subsystem+configuration`. The database login module checks the user credentials against a relational database. To configure the database login module, you have to specify a few configuration options. The `dsJndiName` option is used to specify the application datasource. As we are using a configured PostgreSQL datasource for our application, you specified the same `dsJndiName` option value. Next, you have to specify the SQL queries to fetch the user and its roles. Then, you have specified that the password will be hashed against an MD5 hash algorithm by specifying the `hashAlgorithm` configuration.

In step 4, you applied the database login module to the `jobstore` application by defining the security constraints in `web.xml`. This configuration will add a security constraint on all the web resources of the application that will restrict access to authenticated users with role admin. You have also configured your application to use FORM-based authentication. This will make sure that when unauthenticated users visit the website, they will be redirected to the `login.html` page created in step 5. If the user enters a wrong e-mail/password combination, then they will be redirected to the `error.html` page created in step 6.

Finally, in step 7, you committed the changes to the local Git repository and pushed the changes to the application gear. OpenShift will make sure that the JBoss EAP application server uses the updated `standalone.xml` configuration file. Now, the user will be asked to authenticate before they can work with the application.

## See also

- The *Creating and deploying Java EE 6 applications using the JBoss EAP and PostgreSQL 9.2 cartridges* recipe
- The *Installing modules with JBoss cartridges* recipe
- The *Managing JBoss cartridges using the management web interface and CLI* recipe

# Installing modules with JBoss cartridges

From version 7 of the JBoss application server, class loading is based on the JBoss Modules project. In this recipe, you will learn how to install the `Twitter4J` library as a module on the JBoss EAP 6 cartridge. The `modules` directory under the JBoss server home houses all the modules installed on the application server.

The source code for the application created in this recipe is on GitHub at `https://github.com/OpenShift-Cookbook/chapter7-recipe4`.

## Getting ready

This recipe builds on the application created in the *Creating and deploying Java EE 6 applications using the JBoss EAP and PostgreSQL 9.2 cartridges* recipe. So, please refer to that recipe before continuing with this recipe.

## How to do it...

Perform the following steps to install the `Twitter4J` library as a module:

1. Create the OpenShift application created in the *Creating and deploying Java EE 6 applications using the JBoss EAP and PostgreSQL 9.2 cartridges* recipe using the following command:

   ```
   $ rhc app-create jobstore jbosseap postgresql-9.2 --from-code
   https://github.com/OpenShift-Cookbook/chapter5-jobstore-
   javaee6.git --timeout 180
   ```

2. To install a new module, you have to create the module path under the `.openshift/config/modules` directory as follows:

   ```
   $ mkdir -p .openshift/config/modules/org/twitter4j/main
   ```

3. Download the `twitter4j-core` library from `http://mvnrepository.com/artifact/org.twitter4j/twitter4j-core/3.0.5`, and place it under the `.openshift/config/modules/org/twitter4j/main` directory.

4. Now, in the `main` folder, add a file named `module.xml`. This file contains the actual module definition as follows:

   ```
   <module xmlns="urn:jboss:module:1.1" name="org.twitter4j">
   <resources>
   <resource-root path="twitter4j-core-3.0.5.jar" />
   </resources>
   <dependencies>
   <module name="javax.api"/>
   </dependencies>
   </module>
   ```

5. Now, to use this module in your application, you have to first add its dependency in your `pom.xml` file. Make sure that the scope is provided, as the server will already have this dependency since you are adding it as a module:

   ```
   <dependency>
   <groupId>org.twitter4j</groupId>
   <artifactId>twitter4j-core</artifactId>
   <version>3.0.5</version>
   <scope>provided</scope>
   </dependency>
   ```

6. Secondly, you have to update the Maven WAR plugin configuration by adding the `org.twitter4j` module dependency in the `META-INF/MANIFEST.MF` location:

```
<plugin>
<artifactId>maven-war-plugin</artifactId>
<version>2.4</version>
<configuration>
<archive>
<manifestEntries>
<Dependencies>org.twitter4j</Dependencies>
</manifestEntries>
</archive>
<outputDirectory>deployments</outputDirectory>
<warName>ROOT</warName>
<failOnMissingWebXml>false</failOnMissingWebXml>
</configuration>
</plugin>
```

7. Finally, commit the changes, and push them to the application gear. Now, after the server restarts, JBoss will have the `twitter4j` library as a module.

## How it works...

In the preceding steps, you learned how to install a third-party library as a module. The alternative to using a third-party library is to add a compile scope dependency in `pom.xml` and then use the `twitter4j` library in your application. The advantage of using a module is that you do not have to bundle the JAR file with your application archive. If you are deploying multiple applications on a single server instance, then the server will only need one copy of the JAR file.

After creating the application in step 1, you created a directory structure required to define a module inside the `.openshift/config` directory in step 2. This directory is added to the module path of the JBoss EAP server associated with your OpenShift application. It has the same structure as the standard JBoss EAP `modules` directory. Inside `org.twitter4j.main`, you placed the `twitter4j-core-3.0.5.jar` file in step 3. In step 4, you created a file called `module.xml` inside the `org.twitter4j.main` directory. The `module.xml` file is used to define a module and its dependencies. The module name `org.twitter4j` corresponds to the module attribute that you will define in your application manifest. Next, you need to state the path to the `twitter4j-core` library and finally, its dependencies.

Next, in step 5, you added a provided scope dependency to the `twitter4j-core` library. The provided scope indicated that you expect the application container to provide the dependency at runtime. Also, provided dependencies are not packaged with web applications. This makes sure that the application archives are smaller in size and the application deploys faster. Also, in step 5, you updated the Maven WAR plugin configuration to add a dependency on the `org.twitter4j` module to the application archive `META-INF/MANIFEST.MF` file.

In step 6, you committed the changes and pushed them to the application gear.

In this recipe, I have not covered how to use the `Twitter4J` library. If you want to see `Twitter4J` in action, I have created an application for you, which will tweet after posting a job. To use the application, you have to first create a Twitter application. Go to `https://dev.twitter.com`, and create a new Twitter application. Give the application the read-and-write level access. Once you are done, create a new OpenShift application by running the following command. Please replace the environment variable values with your Twitter application values. You can find these values under the Twitter application's **API Keys** section.

```
$ rhc create-app jobstore jbosseap postgresql-9.2 --env
TWITTER_CONSUMER_KEY=$TWITTER_CONSUMER_KEY
TWITTER_CONSUMER_SECRET=$TWITTER_CONSUMER_SECRET
TWITTER_ACCESS_TOKEN_KEY=$TWITTER_ACCESS_TOKEN_KEY
TWITTER_ACCESS_TOKEN_SECRET=$TWITTER_ACCESS_TOKEN_SECRET --from-code
https://github.com/OpenShift-Cookbook/chapter7-recipe4.git
```

After the application is successfully created, a tweet will be sent after every job posting.

## See also

▶ The *Creating and deploying Java EE 6 applications using the JBoss EAP and PostgreSQL 9.2 cartridges* recipe

▶ The *Managing JBoss cartridges using the management web interface and CLI* recipe

# Managing JBoss cartridges using the management web interface and CLI

JBoss provides three different ways to manage the server: a web interface, a command-line client, and the XML configuration files. In this recipe, you will learn how to deploy WAR files to your JBoss cartridge using the web management interface and JBoss CLI.

## Getting ready

To complete this recipe, you will need to have the JBoss application server binary on your local machine. This is required to connect with the JBoss cartridge using `jboss-cli`. Download the JBoss AS7 binary from the official website at `http://www.jboss.org/jbossas/downloads`. Extract the ZIP file, and you will find the `jboss-cli` script in the `bin` folder.

In this recipe, we will use the `jobstore` application that we created in the *Creating and deploying Java EE 6 applications using the JBoss EAP and PostgreSQL 9.2 cartridges* recipe.

## How to do it...

Perform the following steps:

1. Open a new command-line terminal, and navigate to the directory where the `jobstore` application is located. Run the `rhc port-forward` command to forward the remote ports on your local machine:

   **$ rhc port-forward --app myapp**

   **To connect to a service running on OpenShift, use the Local address**

   ```
   Service     Local                OpenShift
   ---------   --------------  ----  ------------------
   java        127.0.0.1:3528   =>   127.8.104.129:3528
   java        127.0.0.1:4447   =>   127.8.104.129:4447
   java        127.0.0.1:5445   =>   127.8.104.129:5445
   java        127.0.0.1:8080   =>   127.8.104.129:8080
   java        127.0.0.1:9990   =>   127.8.104.129:9990
   java        127.0.0.1:9999   =>   127.8.104.129:9999
   postgresql  127.0.0.1:5433   =>   127.8.104.130:5432
   ```

   **Press CTRL-C to terminate port forwarding**

2. Open the management interface at `http://127.0.0.1:9990` in your favorite web browser. This information is available in the output of the `rhc port-forward` command.

3. In this recipe, we will deploy the WAR file of the application we created in the *Creating and deploying Java EE 6 applications using the JBoss EAP and PostgreSQL 9.2 cartridges* recipe using the JBoss management interface. Download the WAR file from `https://github.com/OpenShift-Cookbook/chapter7-recipe5/raw/master/ROOT.war` to your local machine.

4. After downloading the WAR file, navigate to **Runtime | Manage Deployments**, and remove the existing `ROOT.war` file by clicking on the **Remove** button as shown in the following screenshot. It will ask you to confirm the removal, and you can click on the **OK** button. Have a look at the following screenshot:

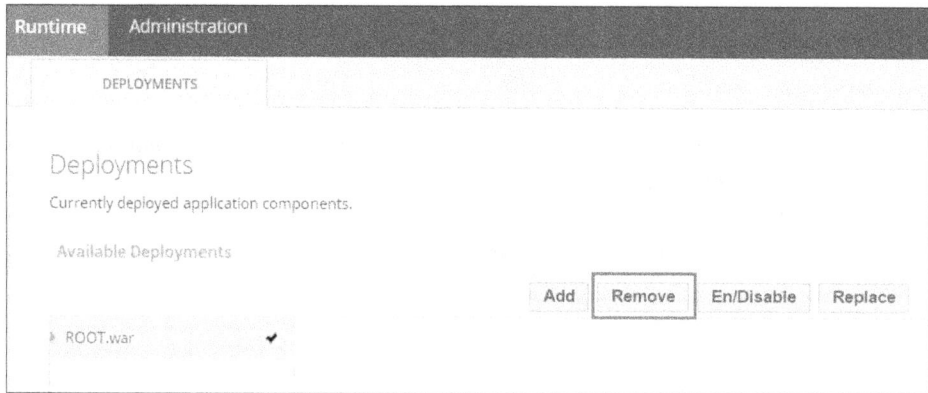

5. To deploy the WAR file, click on the **Add** button, and then upload the `ROOT.war` file from your local machine. After uploading the WAR file, you will be asked to verify the deployment name. Choose the default values, and click on the **Save** button as shown in the following screenshot:

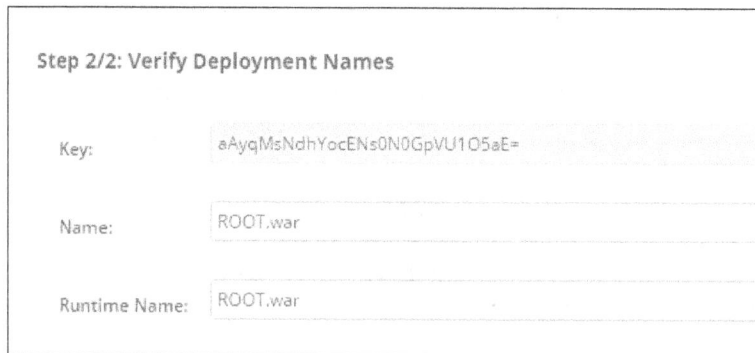

6. Uploading the WAR file does not initiate the deployment. You have to click on the **En/Disable** button to initiate the deployment. You will be asked to confirm your decision. Click on the **Confirm** button as shown in the following screenshot:

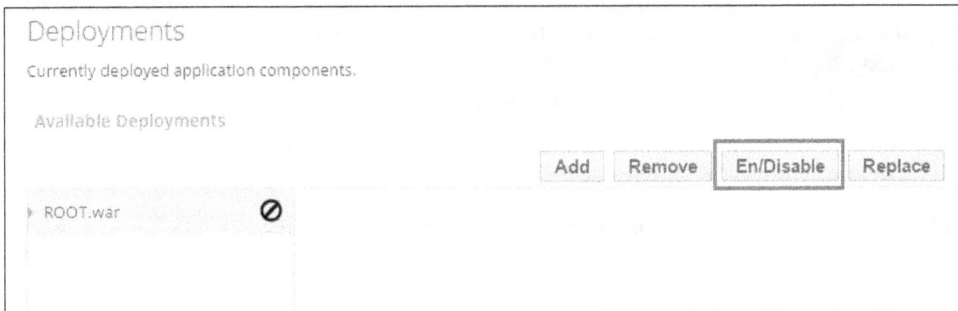

7. Now, if you go to `http://myapp-{domain-name}.rhcloud.com`, you will see your application deployed.

8. Another way to deploy an application is via the `jboss-cli` command-line interface. The `jboss-cli` script can be found in your local downloaded JBoss archive `bin` folder. Launch the `jboss-cli` client, and you will see the message shown in the following command:

```
$ ~/ jboss-eap-6.2/bin/jboss-cli.sh
```

```
You are disconnected at the moment. Type 'connect' to connect
to the server or 'help' for the list of supported commands.
```

```
[disconnected /]
```

9. To connect to the JBoss cartridge, type the `connect` command as follows:

```
[disconnected /] connect
[standalone@localhost:9999 /]
```

10. Now, you can check the deployed applications using the `deploy` command. Type `deploy`, and then press *Enter*:

```
[standalone@localhost:9999 /] deploy
```

```
ROOT.war
```

11. As you can see in the preceding command, `ROOT.war` is currently deployed. This WAR file was deployed using the web interface. To withdraw this WAR file, type the `undeploy` command:

```
[standalone@localhost:9999 /] undeploy ROOT.war
```

12. Now, if you go to `http://myapp-{domain-name}.rhcloud.com`, you will get a 404 error as the application is not deployed.

13. To deploy the application using `jboss-cli`, you can use the `deploy` command as shown in the following command line. Please make sure you have downloaded the application `ROOT.war` file as discussed in step 3. Have a look at the following command:

    ```
    [standalone@localhost:9999 /] deploy
    ~/chapter5/recipe8/jobstore/ROOT.war

    [standalone@localhost:9999 /]
    ```

14. Finally, you can see the application running at `http://myapp-{domain-name}.rhcloud.com`.

## How it works...

In the preceding steps, you learned how to manage your application deployment from the JBoss web management and command-line interface. In step 1, you ran the `rhc port-forward` command to enable SSH port forwarding. The `rhc port-forward` command forwarded all the remote ports running on the application gear to your local machine. In the output of the `rhc port-forward` command, you can see that the management interface is exposed on port `9090`.

From step 3 through step 5, you saw how to connect with the web interface from your local machine and undeploy the existing `ROOT.war` file. The web interface is a **Google Web Toolkit (GWT)** application accessible on port `9090`. Google Web Toolkit is an open source set of tools that allows Java developers to write complex JavaScript-based web applications in Java. OpenShift only exposes port `8080` to the outside world; all other ports are internal to the application gear and can only be connected via port forwarding. This is a secure setup as no one from the outside world will be able to connect with your application web management interface, because the `rhc port-forward` command will only work if their SSH keys are uploaded. The web console is divided into two main tabs: the **Profile** and the **Runtime** tab. The **Profile** tab gives access to all the subsystem configurations. You can edit the configuration without fiddling with XML. For example, you can go to `http://127.0.0.1:9990/console/App.html#datasources` to edit the `datasource` configuration. The **Runtime** tab can be used to manage application deployment, and you used it to undeploy the WAR file in step 5. You can learn more about the management interface from the documentation at `https://docs.jboss.org/author/display/AS7/Admin+Guide`.

In step 6, you uploaded the `ROOT.war` file to your JBoss cartridge. After upload, the deployment is listed in the **Deployments** table. The WAR file is not deployed by default; you have to click on the **En/Disable** button to enable the deployment of the application as you did in step 7.

Another way to deploy an application is using the `jboss-cli` command-line interface. In step 9, you launched the `jboss-cli` script. The `jboss-cli` console provides a built-in autocomplete feature using the *Tab* key. At any point in time, you can list all the available commands using the *Tab* key as shown in the following command. For brevity, only part of the output is shown:

```
[standalone@localhost:9999 /]
alias              connection-factory  help              ls
read-operation     version....
```

In step 9, you undeployed the existing `ROOT.war` file using the `undeploy` command. The `undeploy` command takes the application that is already deployed as an argument. Finally, in step 10, you deployed the `ROOT.war` file on your local machine to the JBoss cartridge running on OpenShift using the `deploy` command.

## See also

▶ The *Configuring application security by defining the database login module in standalone.xml* recipe

▶ The *Installing modules with JBoss cartridges* recipe

# Creating and deploying Spring applications using the Tomcat 7 cartridge

Spring Framework is a very popular alternative to Java EE web development. Java developers around the world use Spring Framework to build their enterprise applications. Spring Framework is often thought of as a lightweight alternative to Java EE, and Java developers normally use a lightweight web container, such as Apache Tomcat, for deployment. At the time of this writing, OpenShift supports two versions of Apache Tomcat: Apache Tomcat 6 and Apache Tomcat 7. They are shown using the following command:

```
$ rhc cartridges|grep Tomcat
jbossews-1.0          Tomcat 6 (JBoss EWS 1.0)              web
jbossews-2.0          Tomcat 7 (JBoss EWS 2.0)              web
```

In this recipe, you will learn how to develop a simple Spring Framework application from scratch using OpenShift's Tomcat 7 cartridge. The application exposes a REST endpoint. When a user makes an HTTP request to `/api/v1/ping`, then the applicaton will return a JSON response with the message `It works`.

The source code for the application created in this recipe is on GitHub at `https://github.com/OpenShift-Cookbook/chapter7-jobstore-spring`.

## Getting ready

To complete this recipe, you will need the `rhc` command-line client installed on your machine. Please refer to the *Installing the OpenShift rhc command-line client* recipe in *Chapter 1, Getting Started with OpenShift*, for details.

## How to do it...

Perform the following steps to create an application using Spring Framework:

1. Open a new command-line terminal, and go to a convenient location. Create a new Tomcat 7 and MySQL 5.5 application by executing the following commands:

   ```
   $ rhc create-appmyapp tomcat-7
   ```

   The preceding command will create a Maven-based project and clone it to your local machine.

2. Open Eclipse and navigate to the project workspace. Then, import the application created in step 1 as a Maven application. To import an existing Maven project, navigate to **File | Import | Maven | Existing Maven Projects**. Then browse to the location of your OpenShift Maven application created in step 1.

3. Next, update `pom.xml` to use Java 7. The Maven project created by OpenShift is configured to use JDK 6. Replace the properties with the one shown in the following code:

   ```
   <maven.compiler.source>1.7</maven.compiler.source>
   <maven.compiler.target>1.7</maven.compiler.target>
   ```

4. Update the Maven project to allow the changes to take effect. You can update the Maven project by right-clicking on the project and navigating to **Maven | Update Project**.

5. Add Spring Maven dependencies to your `pom.xml` file. These are the minimum dependencies that you need to write a REST JSON web service using Spring Framework. The code is as follows:

   ```
   <dependency>
   <groupId>org.springframework</groupId>
   <artifactId>spring-webmvc</artifactId>
   <version>4.0.3.RELEASE</version>
   </dependency>
   <dependency>
   <groupId>javax.servlet</groupId>
   <artifactId>javax.servlet-api</artifactId>
   <version>3.1.0</version>
   ```

```
<scope>provided</scope>
</dependency>
<dependency>
<groupId>com.fasterxml.jackson.core</groupId>
<artifactId>jackson-databind</artifactId>
<version>2.3.1</version>
</dependency>
```

6. Create a new package called `org.myapp.config`, and create a new class named `WebMvcConfig`:

```
@EnableWebMvc
@ComponentScan(basePackageClasses = PingResource.class)
@Configuration
public class WebMvcConfig extends WebMvcConfigurerAdapter {

    @Bean
    public MappingJackson2JsonView jsonView() {
        MappingJackson2JsonView jsonView = new
MappingJackson2JsonView();
        jsonView.setPrefixJson(true);
        return jsonView;
    }

}
```

7. Create another configuration class in the `org.myapp.config` package. This `@Configuration` class will be used for defining application beans, such as `datasource`, and so on. This will be covered later in this recipe. The code is as follows:

```
import org.springframework.context.annotation.Configuration;

@Configuration
public class ApplicationConfig {
}
```

8. From Servlet 3.0 onwards, the `web.xml` deployment descriptor is optional. Prior to Servlet 3.0, we configured the Spring MVC dispatcher servlet in `web.xml`, but now we can programmatically configure it using `WebApplicationInitializer`. Create a new class called `JobStoreWebApplicationInitializer` in the `org.myapp.config` package as follows:

```
public class JobStoreWebApplicationInitializer implements
WebApplicationInitializer {
    @Override
    public void onStartup(ServletContext servletContext)
throws ServletException {
```

```
        AnnotationConfigWebApplicationContext
webApplicationContext = new
AnnotationConfigWebApplicationContext();
        webApplicationContext.register(ApplicationConfig.class,
WebMvcConfig.class);

        Dynamic dynamc =
servletContext.addServlet("dispatcherServlet", new
DispatcherServlet(webApplicationContext));
        dynamc.addMapping("/api/v1/*");
        dynamc.setLoadOnStartup(1);
    }


}
```

9. Now, we will create a simple REST resource called `PingResource`. `PingResource` will be invoked when a request is made to `/api/v1/ping` and will respond with a JSON message. Create a new class called `PingResource` in the `org.myapp.rest` package. Have a look at the following code:

```
@Controller
@RequestMapping("/ping")
public class PingResource {


@RequestMapping(method=RequestMethod.GET,produces=MediaType
.APPLICATION_JSON_VALUE)
public @ResponseBody PingResponse ping(){
return new PingResponse("It works!!");
}
}
```

10. Also, create another class called `PingResponse` as shown in the following code:

```
public class PingResponse {

private String message;

public PingResponse(String message) {
this.message = message;
}

public String getMessage() {
return message;
}
}
```

11. Commit the changes and push them to the OpenShift application gear as follows:

```
$ git add .
$ git commit -am "Spring 4 application"
$ git push
```

12. You can test the `PingResource` using a command-line tool, such as `curl`, or by opening the `http://myapp-{domain-name}.rhcloud.com/api/v1/ping` location in your favorite browser. You should see the following JSON message:

```
$ curl http://myapp-osbook.rhcloud.com/api/v1/ping

{"message":"It works!!"}
```

## How it works...

In the preceding steps, we created a Spring application and deployed it to OpenShift. In step 1, you used the `rhc create-app` command to create Apache Tomcat 7 MySQL 5.5. Every OpenShift web cartridge specifies a template application that will be used as the default source code of the application. For Java-based web cartridges, such as JBoss EAP, JBoss AS7, Tomcat 6, and Tomcat 7, the template is a Maven-based application. After the application is created, the template application is cloned to the local machine using Git. The directory structure of the application is shown in the following command:

```
$ ls -a
.git .openshift README.md pom.xml webapps src
```

As you can see in the preceding command-line output, apart from the `.git` and `.openshift` directories, this looks like a standard Maven project. OpenShift uses Maven for managing application dependencies and building your Java applications.

The directory structure was explained in the *Creating and deploying Java EE 6 applications using the JBoss EAP and PostgreSQL 9.2 cartridges* recipe. Please refer to the recipe to get an understanding of the directory structure.

From step 3 through step 5, you made a few changes in `pom.xml`. You updated the project to use JDK 1.7 for the Maven compiler plugin. All the OpenShift Java applications use OpenJDK 7, so it makes sense to update the application to also use JDK 1.7 for compilation. Another change you made to `pom.xml` is that you updated the Maven WAR plugin configuration not to fail the build if `web.xml` is not found. Next, you added the Spring Web MVC dependencies to `pom.xml`. The Servlet 3.1.0 is provided, as this should exist in Apache Tomcat 7. The `jackson-databind` dependency is added to convert Java objects to JSON.

From step 6 through step 8, you configured the Spring Web MVC framework programmatically. Normally, we configure the Spring Web MVC dispatcher servlet in web.xml, but now, we can programmatically configure it using WebApplicationInitializer. From Spring 3.1, Spring provides an implementation of the ServletContainerInitializer interface called SpringServletContainerInitializer. The SpringServletContainerInitializer class delegates to an implementation of org. springframework.web.WebApplicationInitializer that you provide. There is just one method that you need to implement: WebApplicationInitializer#onStartup(Ser vletContext). You are handed the ServletContext parameter that you need to initialize.

From step 9 through step 11, you created a simple REST JSON resource called PingResource using Spring MVC. PingResource is available at the/api/v1/ping URL as defined using the @RequestMapping annotation.

## There's more...

You can perform all the preceding steps with just the following single command:

```
$ rhc create-app jobstore tomcat-7 mysql-5.5 --from-code
https://github.com/OpenShift-Cookbook/chapter7-spring-recipe.git --
timeout 180
```

## See also

▸   The *Taking thread dumps of Java cartridges* recipe

# Taking thread dumps of Java cartridges

In this recipe, you will learn how to take thread dumps of your Java cartridge applications. A thread dump lists all the Java threads that are currently active in a **Java Virtual Machine** (**JVM**). It can help you understand the state of every thread in the JVM at a particular point in time. It gives you a snapshot of exactly what's executing at a moment in time. Thread dumps are very useful to debug a deadlock condition or to understand resource usage.

> This command will work with all the four supported Java cartridges (Apache Tomcat 6, Apache Tomcat 7, JBoss AS7, and JBoss EAP).

## Getting ready

This recipe will request for a thread dump of the application created in the *Creating and deploying Java EE 6 applications using the JBoss EAP and PostgreSQL 9.2 cartridges* recipe. So, please refer to the aforementioned recipe before continuing with this recipe.

## How to do it...

Perform the following steps to take a thread dump of your Java application:

1. Open a new command-line terminal, and navigate to the directory where the `jobstore` application is located.

2. To take a thread dump of the `jobstore` application, run the following command:

   ```
   $ rhc threaddump --app jobstore
   ```

## How it works...

When you run the `rhc threaddump` command, the JBoss EAP cartridge initiates a thread dump. It first gets the process ID of the JBoss application server and then runs the `kill -3 <process id>` command. The `kill -3` command sends the HUP or BREAK signal to the Java process. The thread dump log will be placed in the `jbosseap.log` file in $OPENSHIFT_LOG_DIR/, which you can download on your local machine for analysis. You can also view the logfile using the `rhc tail` command, as mentioned in the following command output:

```
$ rhc tail -f app-root/logs/jbosseap.log -o '-n 250'
```

To download the thread dump file on your local machine, you can use the `rhc scp` command. The `rhc scp` command can be used to transfer files to and from your applications using SCP (http://en.wikipedia.org/wiki/Secure_copy). Run the following command to download the `jbosseap.log` file:

```
$ rhc scp jobstore download ./ app-root/logs/jbosseap.log
```

Now, you can use tools, such as samurai (http://yusuke.homeip.net/samurai/en/index.html), to analyze the thread dump on your local machine.

## There's more...

You can also take a thread dump of the Java application using the `jps` and `jstack` JVM tools. To do that, perform the following steps:

1. Open a command-line terminal and then SSH into the `jobstore` application gear as follows:

   ```
   $ rhc ssh --app jobstore
   ```

2. Once inside the application gear, run the `jps` utility to list all the available Java processes as follows:

   ```
   $ jps -l
   ```

3. The `jps` utility ships with JDK and lists all the Java process IDs.

4. The output of the `jps -1` command is as follows:

   ```
   59850 sun.tools.jps.Jps

   157027
   /var/lib/openshift/541ecec35004466ec000007f/jbosseap/jboss-
   modules.jar
   ```

5. Now, to take a thread dump of the Java process with ID `157027`, run the following command:

   ```
   $ jstack 157027 >> /tmp/threaddump.log
   ```

6. The `jstack` utility is also part of JDK and is used to take a thread dump of a Java process.

## See also

▶ The *Choosing between Java 6 and Java 7* recipe

▶ The *Enabling hot deployment for Java applications* recipe

▶ The *Creating and deploying Java EE 6 applications using the JBoss EAP and PostgreSQL 9.2 cartridges* recipe

# Choosing between Java 6 and Java 7

OpenShift supports both Java 6 and Java 7 to run your applications. By default, all the Java applications use OpenJDK 7, but you can configure your application to use OpenJDK 6 as well. To get the exact version of your Java installation, you can SSH into the application gear and run the `java -version` command or run the following command:

```
$ rhc ssh --app jobstore --command "java -version"
```

In this recipe, you will learn how you can choose among different supported versions of Java.

> This recipe will work with all the four supported Java cartridges (Apache Tomcat 6, Apache Tomcat 7, JBoss AS7, and JBoss EAP).

## How to do it...

Perform the following steps to switch to OpenJDK 6:

1. Create a new JBoss AS 7 application by running the following command. If you already have a Java application deployed on OpenShift, then you can use that as well.

   ```
   $ rhc create-app myapp jbossas-7
   ```

2. Once the application is created, you can check the default Java version by running the `java -version` command on the application gear as shown in the following command:

```
$ rhc ssh --command "java -version"
java version "1.7.0_51"
OpenJDK Runtime Environment (rhel-2.4.4.1.el6_5-i386 u51-b02)
OpenJDK Server VM (build 24.45-b08, mixed mode)
```

3. To configure your application to use Java 6, delete a marker file called `java7` in the `.openshift/markers` directory as follows:

```
$ rm -f .openshift/markers/java7
```

4. Commit the changes and push them to your application gear as follows:

```
$ git commit -am "switched to Java 6"
$ git push
```

5. After a successful build, run the `java -version` command again to verify that you are now using Java 6 as follows:

```
$ rhc ssh --command "java -version"
java version "1.6.0_30"
OpenJDK Runtime Environment (IcedTea6 1.13.1) (rhel-3.1.13.1.el6_5-i386)
OpenJDK Server VM (build 23.25-b01, mixed mode)
```

## How it works...

OpenShift uses the marker files to configure various aspects of the application, such as the Java version, hot deployment, debugging, and so on. The presence of a marker file in the `.openshift/markers` location tells OpenShift that you want to enable the feature. For example, every OpenShift application has a `java7` marker file in the `.openshift/markers` directory that informs OpenShift that it should use Java 7 for application deployment. When you perform code deployment using `git push`, OpenShift will set the JAVA_HOME environment variable depending on the Java version you want to use in your application.

To use Java 6, you just deleted the `java7` marker file. This informs OpenShift that it should fall back to Java 6. From now on, your application will use Java 6.

## See also

▶ The *Taking thread dumps of Java cartridges* recipe
▶ The *Enabling hot deployment for Java applications* recipe

# Enabling hot deployment for Java applications

Every time you make a change and push it to the OpenShift application gear, OpenShift stops your gear (that is, all the cartridges), copies the source code from your application Git repo to `app-root/runtime/repo`, performs a build, prepares the artifact, and finally starts your gear (that is, all the cartridges). This process takes time and does not suit rapid development. To enable rapid development and faster deployment, OpenShift supports hot deployment. Hot deployment means that you can deploy your changes without the need to restart all the application cartridges.

> This recipe will work with all the four supported Java cartridges (Apache Tomcat 6, Apache Tomcat 7, JBoss AS7, and JBoss EAP).

## How to do it...

Perform the following steps to enable hot deployment:

1. Open a new command-line terminal, and navigate to the directory where you want to create the application. To create a new JBoss EAP application, execute the following command. If you already have an OpenShift Java application, then you can work with that as well. Have a look at the following command:

   ```
   $ rhc create-app myapp jbosseap
   ```

2. To enable hot deployment, create a new file with the name `hot_deploy` inside the `.openshift/markers` directory. On *nix machines, you can create a new file using the `touch` command as shown in the following command. On Windows machines, you can use file explorer to create a new file. Have a look at the following code:

   ```
   $ touch .openshift/markers/hot_deploy
   ```

3. Add the new file to the Git repository index, commit it to the local repository, and then push the changes to the application's remote Git repository:

   ```
   $ git add .openshift/markers/hot_deploy
   $ git commit -am "enabled hot deployment"
   $ git push
   ```

4. In the `git push` logs, you will see a message that cartridges are not stopped because hot deployment is enabled as follows:

   ```
   remote: Not stopping cartridge jbosseap because hot deploy is enabled
   ```

## How it works...

The presence of the `hot_deploy` marker file informs OpenShift that you want to do hot deployment. Before stopping and starting the application cartridges, OpenShift checks for the existence of the `hot_deploy` marker file. For JBoss cartridges, hot deployment is achieved by using the JBoss deployment scanner. The scanner polls the `deployments` directory every 5 seconds to check for the existence of the WAR file. If the WAR file exists, it will undeploy the existing WAR file and deploy the new WAR file. You can configure the deployment scanner's `scan-interval` option in `.openshift/config/standalone.xml`:

```
<subsystem xmlns="urn:jboss:domain:deployment-scanner:1.1">
<deployment-scanner path="deployments" relative-
to="jboss.server.base.dir"
scan-interval="5000" deployment-timeout="300" />
</subsystem>
```

When your application is using hot deploy, then your application will have downtime starting when the JBoss deployment scanner recognizes the new WAR file, undeploys the old one, and deploys the new WAR file. Your application will be back online once the new file is deployed.

Hot deployment is ideal for development, and I recommend you should always use it during development.

> If you set new environment variables with hot deployment enabled, then you have to restart the application to allow the server to pick the new environment variables.

## See also

- ▸ The *Taking thread dumps of Java cartridges* recipe
- ▸ The *Choosing between Java 6 and Java 7* recipe

# Skipping the Maven build

Every OpenShift Java application is a Maven-based application. Whenever you run a `git push` command, a Maven build is performed, and the resulting archive (WAR or EAR) is deployed. There are scenarios where you don't want to do a Maven build with every push to the gear. These scenarios can be WAR deployment or executing only action hooks. In this recipe, you will learn how to skip the Maven build step during deployment.

[ This recipe will work with all the four supported Java cartridges (Apache Tomcat 6, Apache Tomcat 7, JBoss AS7, and JBoss EAP). ]

## Getting ready

To complete this recipe, you will need the `jobstore` application created in the *Creating and deploying Java EE 6 applications using the JBoss EAP and PostgreSQL 9.2 cartridges* recipe. Please refer to this recipe if you don't have a running OpenShift application.

## How to do it...

Perform the following steps to skip the Maven build:

1. Open a new command-line terminal, and navigate to the directory where the `jobstore` application is located. If you don't have a Java OpenShift application, then you can recreate a new application by following the steps mentioned in the *Creating and deploying Java EE 6 applications using the JBoss EAP and PostgreSQL 9.2 cartridges* recipe.

2. To skip a Maven build during deployment, create a marker file called `skip_maven_build` in the `.openshift/markers` directory. On *nix systems, you can use the `touch` command as shown in the following command. On Windows machines, you can use file explorer. Have a look at the following code:

   ```
   $ touch .openshift/markers/skip_maven_build
   ```

3. Add the new file to the Git repository index, commit it to the local repository, and then push the changes to the application's remote Git repository as follows:

   ```
   $ git add .openshift/markers/skip_maven_build
   $ git commit -am "skipmaven build"
   $ git push
   ```

## How it works...

The presence of the `skip_maven_build` marker informs OpenShift that it should not build the application. In the `git push` command output, you will see that the Maven build is skipped because of the presence of the `skip_maven_build` marker file:

```
remote: skip_maven_build marker found; build will be skipped
```

## There's more...

Another way to skip the Maven build is to delete the pom.xml file. If there is no pom.xml file, then OpenShift does not try to build the application.

## See also

▸ The *Forcing a clean Maven build* recipe

▸ The *Installing the JAR file not present in the Maven central repository* recipe

▸ The *Overriding the default Maven build command* recipe

# Forcing a clean Maven build

The first time you push your changes to the application gear, Maven will download all the dependencies and will store those dependencies in the .m2 directory under your application gear home directory. After the first push, OpenShift will reuse all the dependencies in the .m2 repository and will only download new dependencies. This saves build time and make application deployment faster. But, there are a few situations when you want to do a clean build. One situation can be when you want to download all the latest Maven dependencies. In this recipe, you will learn how you can inform OpenShift to perform a clean build.

> This recipe will work with all the four supported Java cartridges (Apache Tomcat 6, Apache Tomcat 7, JBoss AS7, and JBoss EAP).

## Getting ready

To complete this recipe, you will need the jobstore application created in the *Creating and deploying Java EE 6 applications using the JBoss EAP and PostgreSQL 9.2 cartridges* recipe. Please refer to this recipe if you don't have a running OpenShift application.

## How to do it...

Perform the following steps to force a clean Maven build of your Java application:

1. Open a new command-line terminal, and navigate to the directory where the jobstore application is located. If you don't have a Java OpenShift application, then you can recreate a new application by following the steps mentioned in the *Creating and deploying Java EE 6 applications using the JBoss EAP and PostgreSQL 9.2 cartridges* recipe.

2. To force a clean Maven build during deployment, create a marker file called force_clean_build inside the application's .openshift/markers directory. On *nix systems, you can use the touch command as shown in the following command. On Windows machines, you can use file explorer. Have a look at the following screenshot:

```
$ touch .openshift/markers/force_clean_build
```

3. Add the new file to the Git repository index, commit it to the local repository, and then push the changes to the application's remote Git repository as follows:

```
$ git add .openshift/markers/force_clean_build
$ git commit -am "force_clean_buildmarker added"
$ git push
```

## How it works...

The presence of the force_clean_build marker file informs OpenShift that you want to do a clean build. When you run a git push command, OpenShift will first delete the .m2 directory and then start the build process by invoking the mvn clean package -Popenshift -DskipTests command. Maven will now download all the dependencies again. You will see the following log message in the git push command output. Have a look at the following command:

```
remote: Force clean build enabled - cleaning dependencies
```

## See also

▸ The *Forcing a clean Maven build* recipe
▸ The *Installing the JAR file not present in the Maven central repository* recipe
▸ The *Overriding the default Maven build command* recipe

# Overriding the default Maven build command

OpenShift, by default, will execute the mvn -e clean package -Popenshift -DskipTests command to build the project. If you don't want to use the OpenShift Maven profile or want to run tests, then you have to tell OpenShift to run a different command. In this recipe, you will learn how you can tell OpenShift to use a different command.

## Getting ready

To complete this recipe, you will need the jobstore application created in the *Creating and deploying Java EE 6 applications using the JBoss EAP and PostgreSQL 9.2 cartridges* recipe. Please refer to this recipe if you don't have a running OpenShift application.

## How to do it...

Perform the following steps to override the default Maven build command:

1. Open a new command-line terminal, and navigate to the directory where the `jobstore` application is located.

2. To configure OpenShift to use a different build command, create a new environment variable with the name `MAVEN_ARGS`. The value of the `MAVEN_ARGS` environment variable is the Maven build phases you want to run, as shown in the following command:

```
$ rhc env-set MAVEN_ARGS="clean install"
```

## How it works...

Before running the build, OpenShift first checks whether the environment variable called `MAVEN_ARGS` is set. It uses the phases and goals defined in this environment variable to create a Maven command that will be used to build the project. If `MAVEN_ARGS` is not set, then it will set the default value, that is, `clean package -Popenshift -DskipTests`, else it will use the value of the `MAVEN_ARGS` environment variable.

Now, when you run the `git push` command, you will see an entry in the `git push` logs, as shown in the following command output:

```
remote: Found pom.xml... attempting to build with 'mvn -e clean
install'
```

## See also

▸ The *Forcing a clean Maven build* recipe

▸ The *Installing the JAR file not present in the Maven central repository* recipe

▸ The *Skipping the Maven build* recipe

# Installing the JAR file not present in the Maven central repository

OpenShift will download all the dependencies from the Maven central repositories specified in your `pom.xml` file. There are times when your application depends on the libraries that do not exist in any public Maven repository. In this recipe, you will learn how you can use the OpenShift action hooks to install a local JAR.

## Getting ready

To complete this recipe, you will need the `jobstore` application created in the *Creating and deploying Java EE 6 applications using the JBoss EAP and PostgreSQL 9.2 cartridges* recipe. Please refer to this recipe if you don't have a running OpenShift application.

## How to do it...

Perform the following steps to install the JAR file not present in the configured Maven repositories:

1. Open a new command-line terminal, and navigate to the directory where the `jobstore` application is located.

2. Create a `lib` directory in the root of your application directory, and add your local JAR file here. To demonstrate this recipe, I have created a simple library that you can download from `https://github.com/OpenShift-Cookbook/chapter7-recipe14/raw/master/lib/simplelogger-0.0.1.jar`.

3. Create a `pre_build` action hook inside the `.openshift/action_hooks` directory, and add the following content to it:

   ```
   #!/bin/bash
   ```

   The following command will install the JAR file to the local Maven repository located on the application gear:

   ```
   mvn install:install-file -
   Dfile=$OPENSHIFT_REPO_DIR/lib/simplelogger-0.0.1.jar -
   DgroupId=org.osbook -DartifactId=simplelogger -Dversion=0.0.1
   -Dpackaging=jar
   ```

4. Make sure the `pre_build` action hook is executable. You can make the `pre_build` action hook script executable by running the following command:

   ```
   $ chmod +x .openshift/action_hooks/pre_build
   ```

5. Add the dependency to the application's `pom.xml` file so that your application can use the library in the application source code as follows:

   ```
   <dependency>
   <groupId>org.osbook</groupId>
   <artifactId>simplelogger</artifactId>
   <version>0.0.1</version>
   </dependency>
   ```

## How it works...

In step 2, you created a `lib` directory inside the application source code root. You downloaded the `simplelogging` library and placed it in the `lib` directory. Next, in step 2, you created a `pre_build` action hook that installs the `simplelogging-0.0.1.jar` file into the application gear's `.m2` repository. The `pre_build` script is executed before the build step. This means your library will be available during the build.

> On Windows, the execute permissions on the action hooks will be lost during `git push`. You can fix the problem by running the following command:
>
> `git update-index --chmod=+x .openshift/action_hooks/*`

Finally, you added the library as a dependency in your application's `pom.xml` file so that you can use the library in your application.

## See also

- ▶ The *Forcing a clean Maven build* recipe
- ▶ The *Overriding the default Maven build command* recipe
- ▶ The *Skipping the Maven build* recipe

# Developing OpenShift Java applications using Eclipse

You can build, deploy, and manage your OpenShift Java applications right from within the Eclipse IDE using the JBoss Tools OpenShift plugin. This recipe will guide you through installation, setup, application creation, and managing your application from within Eclipse. In this recipe, you will develop a Java EE 6 PostgreSQL 9.2 application and deploy it on the JBoss EAP 6 application server running on OpenShift all from within Eclipse.

## Getting ready

Download the latest Eclipse package for your operating system from the official Eclipse website at `http://www.eclipse.org/downloads/`. At the time of this writing, the latest Eclipse package is Kepler.

It is very easy to install Eclipse; just extract the downloaded package, and we are done. On Linux and Mac, open a new command-line terminal, and type the following command:

```
$ tar -xzvf eclipse-jee-kepler-R-*.tar.gz
```

On Windows, you can extract the ZIP file using WinZip or 7-zip (`http://www.7-zip.org/download.html`) or any other software.

After we have extracted the Eclipse file, there will be a folder named `*eclipse*` in the directory where we extracted Eclipse. We can optionally create a shortcut to the executable file.

> It is recommended that you use the latest version of Eclipse, that is, Kepler, to work with OpenShift. Earlier versions are not supported and might not even work.

## How to do it...

Perform the following steps to create OpenShift applications using OpenShift Eclipse tooling:

1. After downloading and extracting the Eclipse Kepler IDE for Java EE, open Eclipse, and navigate to the project workspace. Navigate to **Help | Eclipse Marketplace**.

2. In the search box, type `jboss tools`, and then click on the **Go** button. After clicking on the **Go** button, we will see **JBoss Tools (Kepler)** as the first result. Now click on the **Install** button. Have a look at the following screenshot:

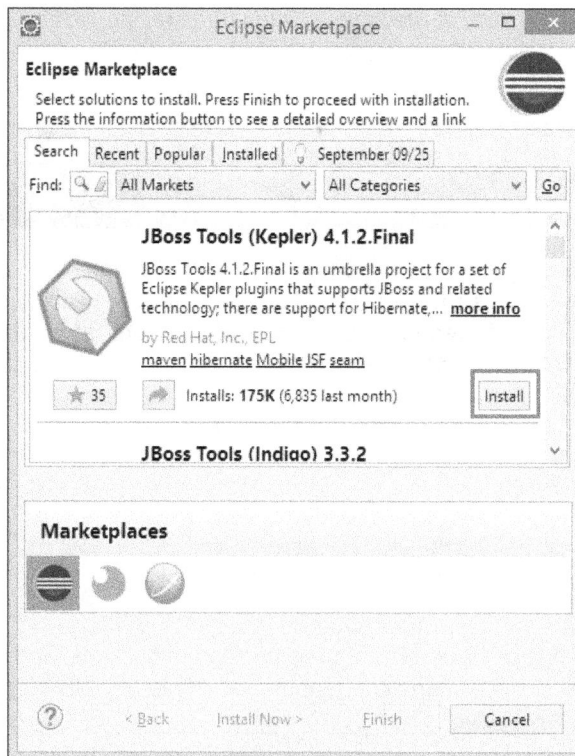

3. After clicking on the **Install** button, you will get a list of plugins that you can install. As the purpose of this recipe is to demonstrate the OpenShift Eclipse support, we will only select **JBoss OpenShift Tools** from the list. After selecting **JBoss OpenShift Tools**, click on the **Confirm** button. Have a look at the following screenshot:

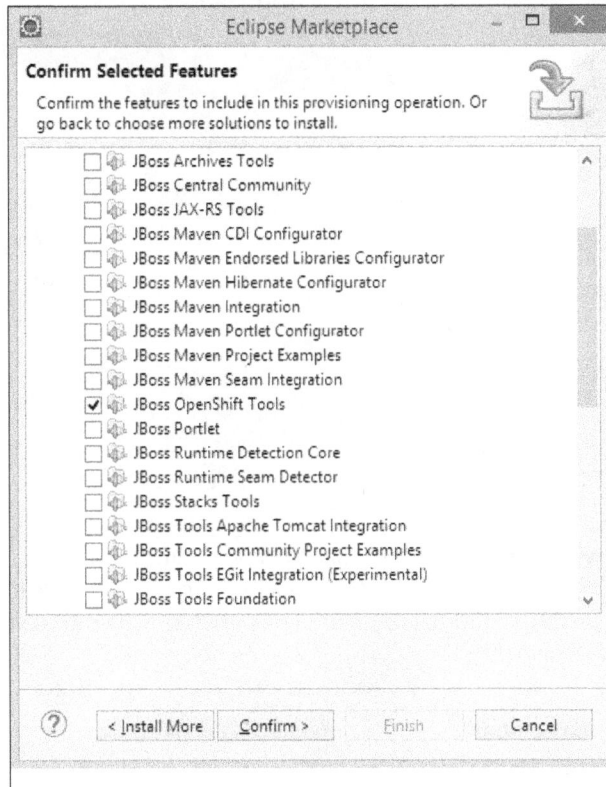

4. Accept the license by clicking on the **I accept the terms of the license agreement** radio button, and then click on the **Finish** button.

5. As the JBoss Tools OpenShift plugin is unsigned, you will get a security message. Click on the **OK** button, and restart Eclipse to apply the changes.

6.  Now that you've installed the OpenShift Eclipse plugin, you have everything required to start building the application. Create a new OpenShift application by navigating to **File | New | Other | OpenShift Application**:

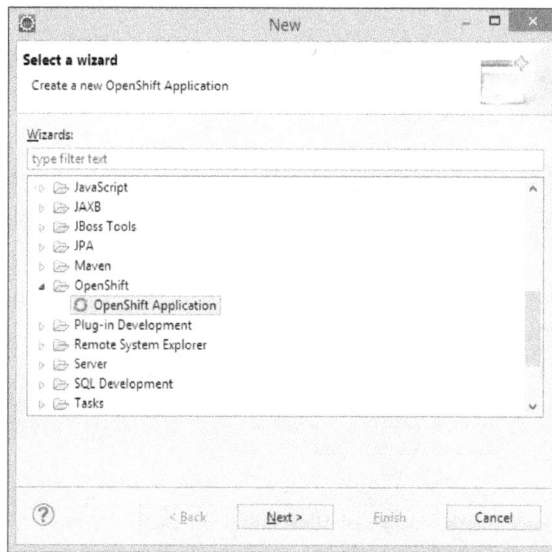

7.  Click on the **Next** button, and you will be asked to provide your OpenShift account credentials. If you do not have an OpenShift account, you can click on the sign up **here** link on the wizard to create a new OpenShift account. Have a look at the following screenshot:

8. Enter your OpenShift account details. Also, check the **Save password** checkbox so that we do not have to enter the password with every command. Click on the **Next** button. Have a look at the following screenshot:

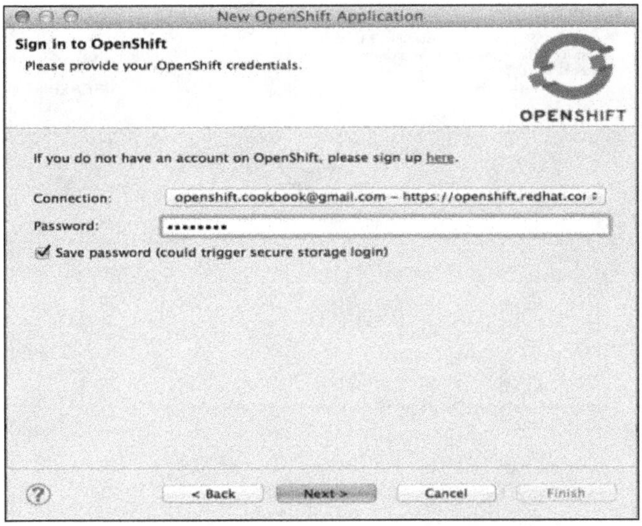

9. After clicking on the **Next** button, you will be asked to enter additional information for password recovery. I choose **No**, but you can choose **Yes** as well.

10. Next, you will be asked to create a new OpenShift domain if you don't have a domain associated with your account already. The domain name is the unique namespace, and all the user applications will exist under this namespace. This is shown in the following screenshot:

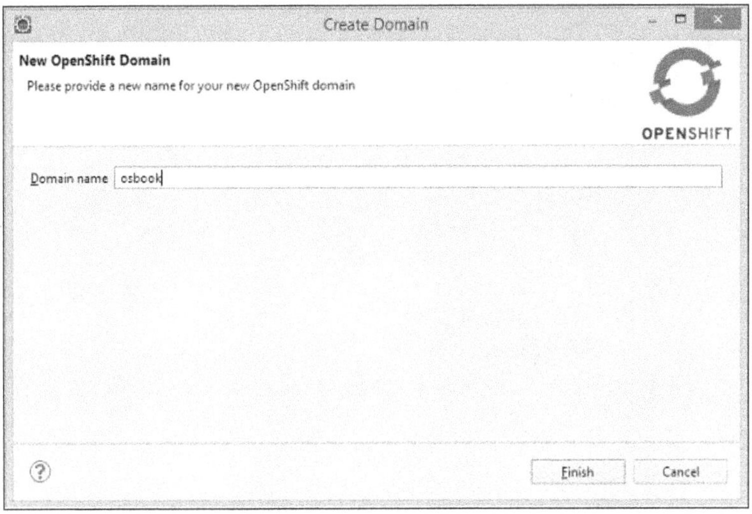

11. Next, you will be asked to upload your public SSH keys to OpenShift, as shown in the following screenshot:

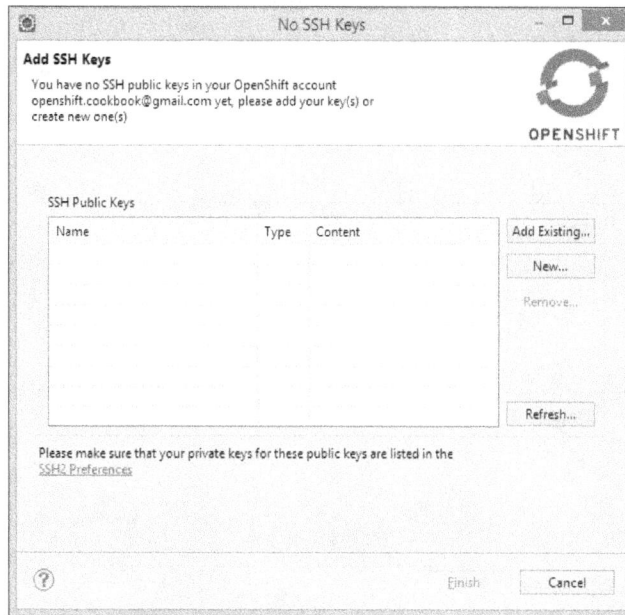

12. You can either upload your existing SSH keys or create a new SSH key by clicking on the **New** button. Let's create a new key by clicking on the **New** button. We need to provide a name for the key and a name for the private and public key filenames. I have used my name as the key name and filename. Have a look at the following screenshot:

13. Now, you will be directed to the application creation wizard where you have to enter the application details. The details include the name of the application, the type of the application, the gear profile (whether you want a small, medium, or large instance; in a free tier, you have access only to small instances), whether you want a scalable application or a nonscalable application, and whether you want to embed any or multiple cartridges, such as MySQL, PostgreSQL, MongoDB, and others. For our application, we will select the JBoss EAP and PostgreSQL cartridges. We will name the application `jobstore` as shown in the following screenshot:

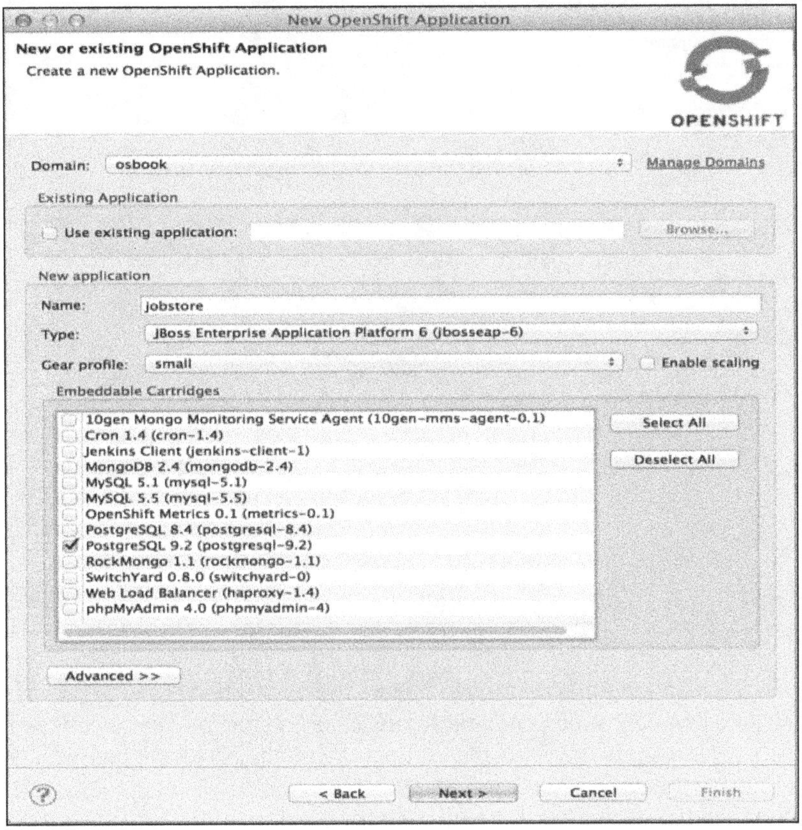

14. Next, you have to set up a `jobstore` application and configure the server adapter settings. Choose the default and click on **Next**.

15. The next screen will ask us to specify the location where we want to clone the Git repository and the name of the Git remote. Have a look at the following screenshot:

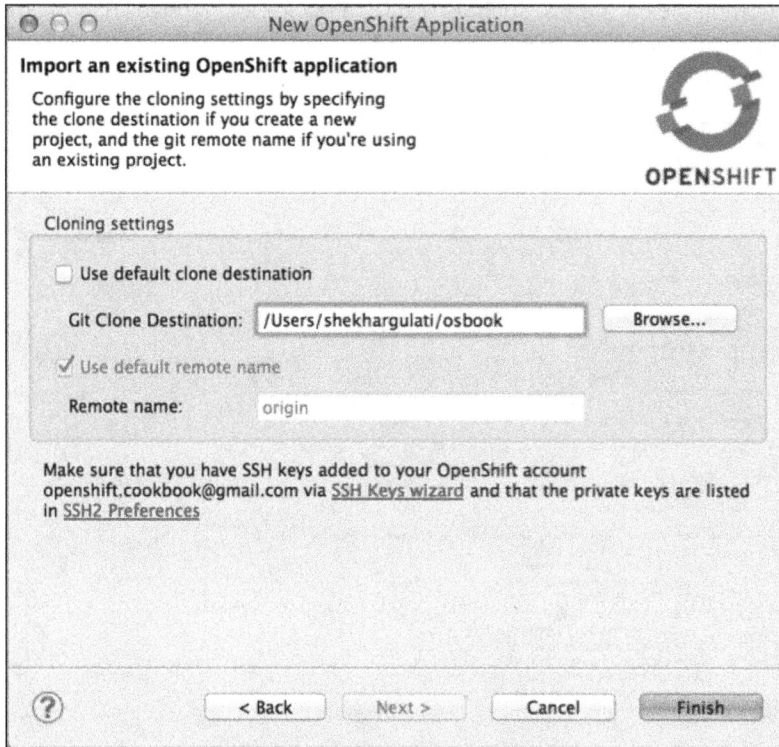

16. Finally, click on the **Finish** button to initiate the application creation process. This will create an application container for us, called a gear, and set up all the required SELinux policies and cgroup configuration. OpenShift will install the PostgreSQL cartridge on the application gear, and the JBoss Tools OpenShift plugin will show an information box with the PostgreSQL details.

17. Finally, the project is imported as a Maven project in the Eclipse workspace. After importing the application to Eclipse, you will be asked whether you want to publish the uncommitted changes. You might start wondering why it is asking you to publish changes. The reason is that when a project is imported into Eclipse, JBoss Tools creates a new file called `.jsdtscope` under the `.settings` directory. As the file is not ignored, the OpenShift Eclipse plugin asks you for a deployment. You can easily ignore the file by navigating to the **Git Staging** view. To open the **Git Staging** view, navigate to **Window|Show View|Other|Git|Git Staging**. Have a look at the following screenshot:

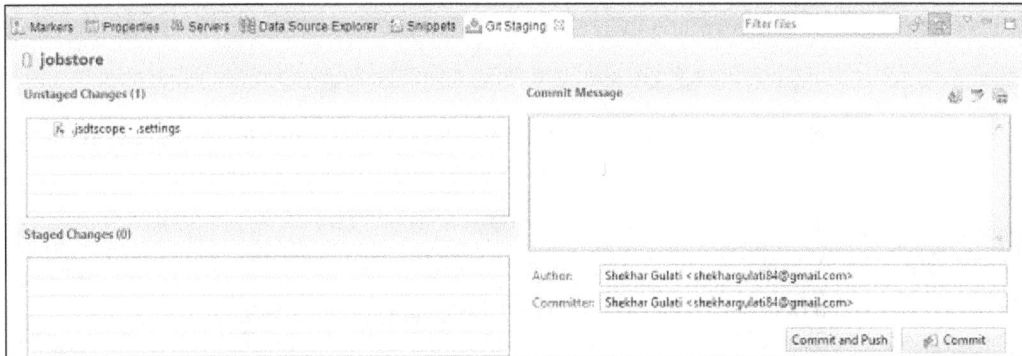

18. Right-click on the `.jsdtscope` file under the **Git Staging** view, and then choose **Ignore**. Have a look at the following screenshot:

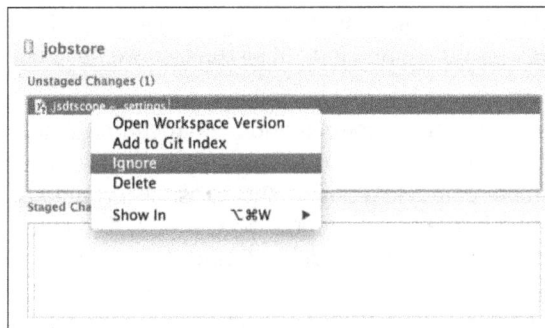

19. Next, open the **OpenShift Explorer** view. Navigate to **Window|Show View|Other|JBoss Tools|OpenShift Explorer**. This will open up a new view as shown in the following screenshot:

20. Now, right-click on the application, and then click on the **Show in Web Browser** option. This will open up the template application in the default browser.

## How it works...

The preceding steps help you to create OpenShift Java applications using Eclipse. In this recipe, I used the JBoss EAP cartridge, but you can do the same for the Tomcat or JBoss AS7 cartridge. The preceding steps are self-explanatory and do not require any explanation. Now, I will explain to you how your development workflow should work. The recommended way to work with OpenShift Eclipse tooling is split into two steps, which are as follows:

1. Write code for functionality, and then commit the code to a Git local repository using the **Git Staging** view. The **Git Staging** view gives a graphical view to the changes, and you can easily compare and look at all the files we have changed.

2. In the **Git Staging** view, you have two options. You can either commit the changes to the local repository or do a commit and push together. When you perform `git commit` and `push` together, the code is pushed to a Git remote called `origin`. The `origin` remote points to a private Git repository created by OpenShift. When the code is pushed to the remote repository, OpenShift will kick off the build. The problem with the **Git Staging** view **Commit and Push** button is that you will not be able to monitor the application build logs. To view the application build logs, you should use the server view publication mechanism. We will use the server configured for the `jobstore` OpenShift application. To publish the changes, right-click on the server, and click on **Publish**. This internally does a `git push`. The advantage of this approach is that it will open up a new console view, where we can monitor the application build progress.

Let's make a small change to the application to better understand the development workflow discussed in the previous section. Open the `index.html` file, and consider the following code:

```
<h1>
    Welcome to OpenShift, JBossEAP6.0 Cartridge
</h1>
```

And change it to:

```
<h1>
Welcome to JobStore application
</h1>
```

Go to the **Git Staging** view, and you will see the change shown in the following screenshot:

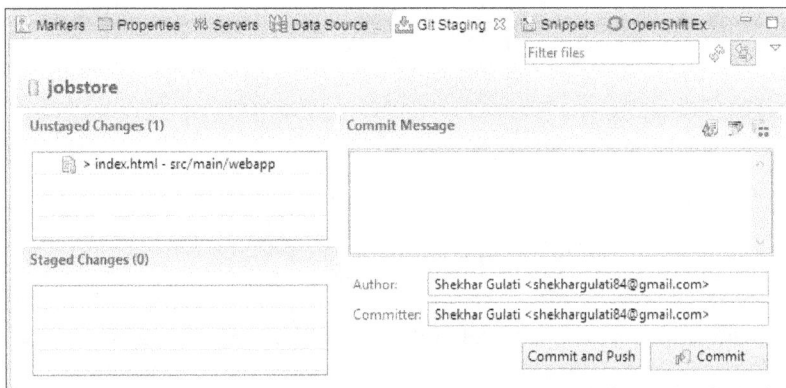

Next, drag the change to **Staged Changes**, and write a commit message. Have a look at the following screenshot:

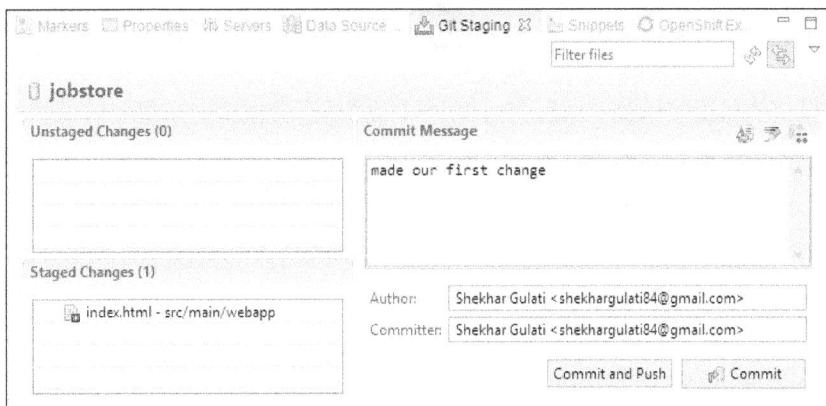

Commit the change by clicking on the **Commit** button. As I mentioned before, do not use **Commit and Push**, as that will trigger application deployment and will not show the build log. The build log is very useful when the build fails.

Go to the **Servers** view, and you will see a server configured for the `jobstore` application.

Right-click on the application server, and then click on **Publish**. Have a look at the following screenshot:

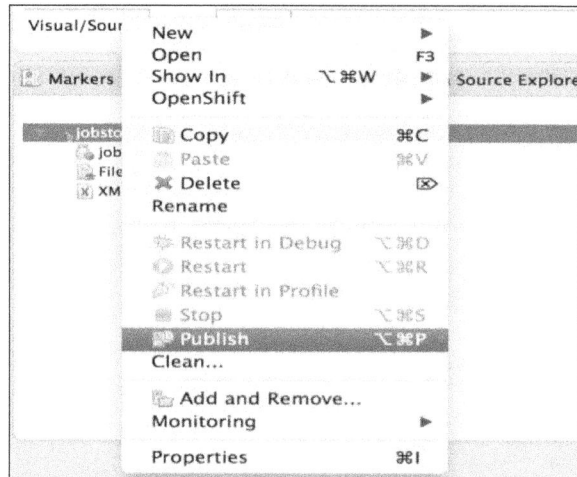

You will get a dialog where you have to confirm whether you want to publish the changes or not. Click on **Yes**, and it will open a new **Console** view where we can track the build progress. Have a look at the following screenshot:

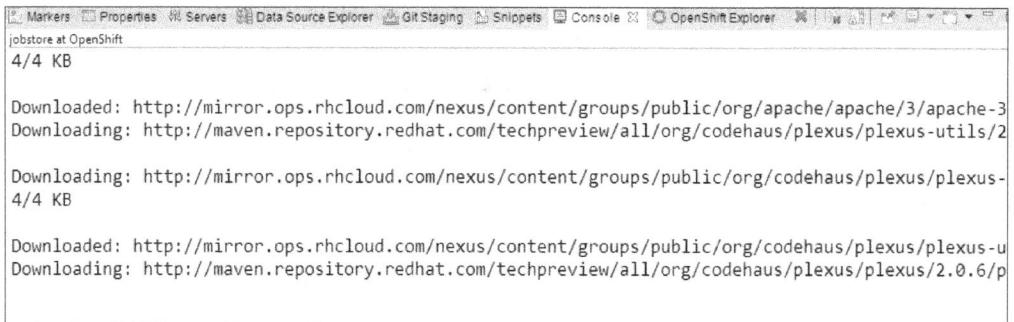

To view the logfiles of the JBoss EAP application server, go to the **OpenShift Explorer** view, and right-click on the application. Click on **Tail files...**. Have a look at the following screenshot:

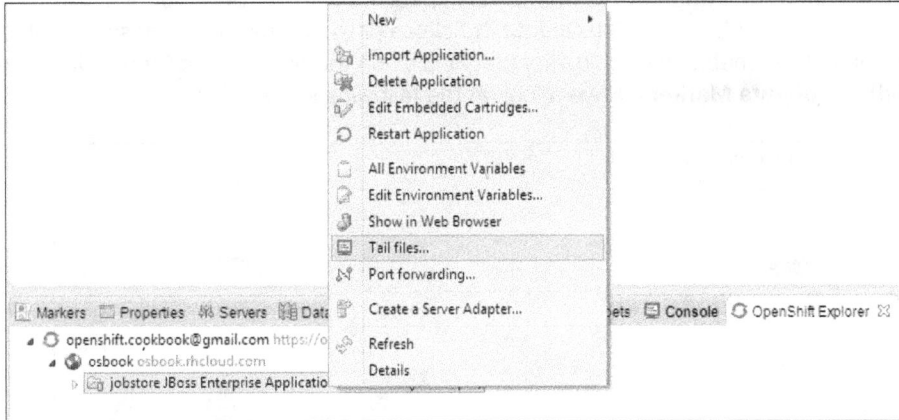

Next, you will configure to tail only the JBoss EAP `server.log` file. By default, it will tail all the logfiles, which includes the database logfiles as well, as shown in the following screenshot:

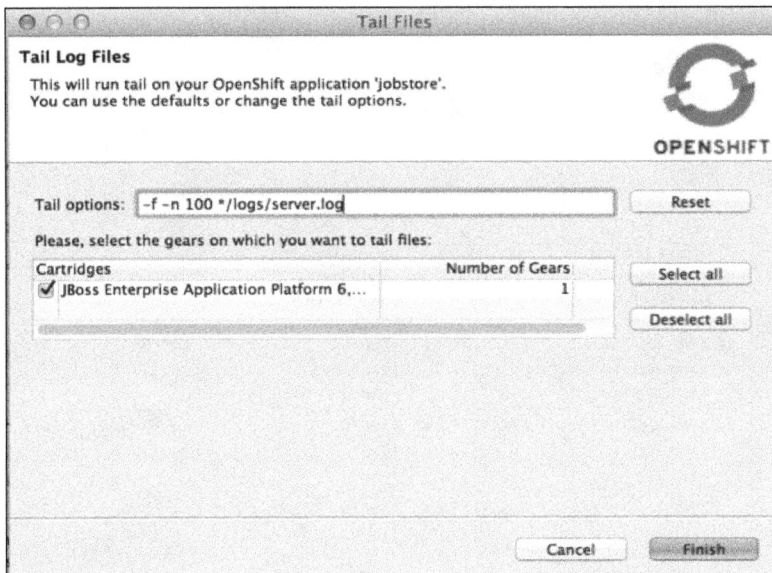

It will open up another console view where it will tail only the JBoss EAP `server.log` file.

Finally, we can view the change in the browser by right-clicking on the **jobstore** server, and then navigating to **Show In | Web Browser**. This will open up the default web browser, where we can view the change that we made in `index.html`.

You can do a lot more with the OpenShift Eclipse plugin. For faster development, you should enable hot deployment. The OpenShift Eclipse plugin makes it very easy to enable hot deployment. To enable hot deployment, right-click on the project, and then navigate to **OpenShift | Configure Markers**. Have a look at the following screenshot:

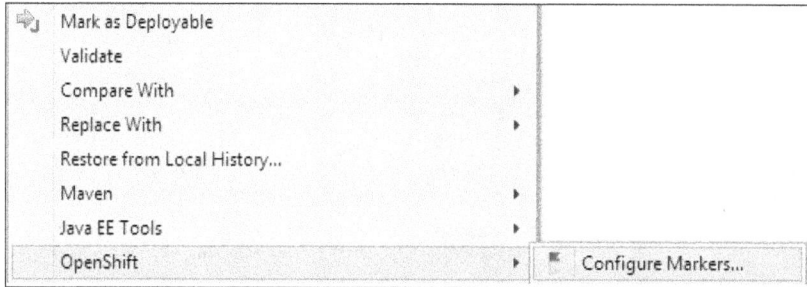

Then, you will see a view where you can configure which OpenShift markers you want to enable for the application. Select the **Hot Deploy** marker. Have a look at the following screenshot:

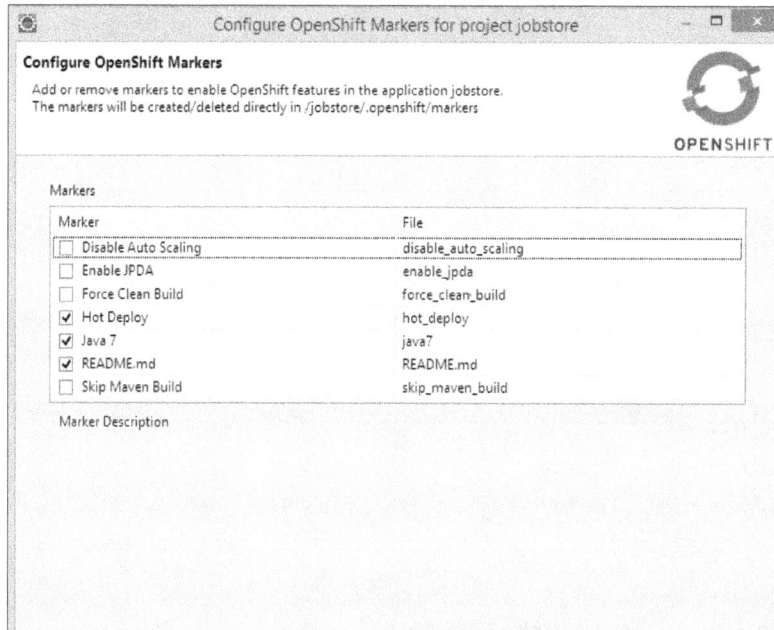

This will create a new empty file called `hot_deploy` in the `.openshift/markers` directory. You can commit the changes by going to the **Git Staging** view. Go to the **Servers** view, and publish this change. The build log will show that the cartridges are not stopped as hot deploy is enabled. Have a look at the following build log:

```
Not stopping cartridge jbosseap because hot deploy is enabled
Not stopping cartridge postgresql because hot deploy is enabled
```

## See also

▶ The *Using Eclipse System Explorer to SSH into the application gear* recipe

▶ The *Debugging Java applications in the Cloud* recipe

# Using Eclipse System Explorer to SSH into the application gear

In this recipe, you will learn how you can SSH into the application gear from within Eclipse.

## Getting ready

This recipe requires you to have Eclipse with the JBoss Tools OpenShift plugin installed. Please refer to the *Developing OpenShift Java applications using Eclipse* recipe for more information.

## How to do it...

Perform the following steps to learn how to SSH into the application gear from within Eclipse:

1. Create a new application using the OpenShift Eclipse plugin. Refer to the *Developing OpenShift Java applications using Eclipse* recipe for instructions.

2. Navigate to **Window | Open Perspective | Other | Remote System Explorer** to open the **Remote System Explorer** perspective. Have a look at the following screenshot:

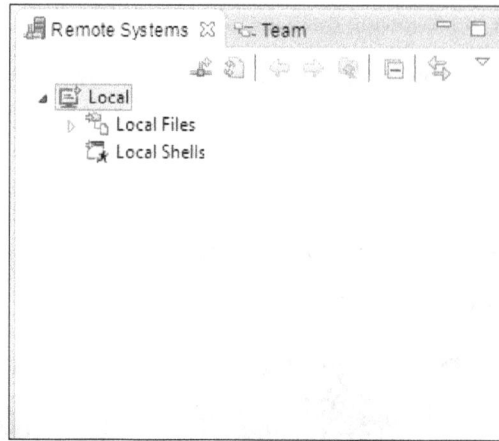

3. Go to **OpenShift Explorer** and copy the SSH connection details as shown in the following screenshot:

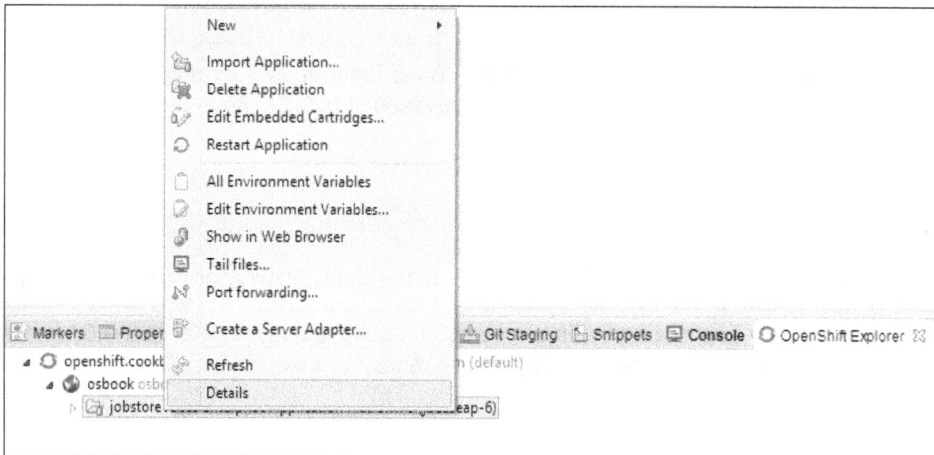

4. Copy the SSH details as shown in the following screenshot:

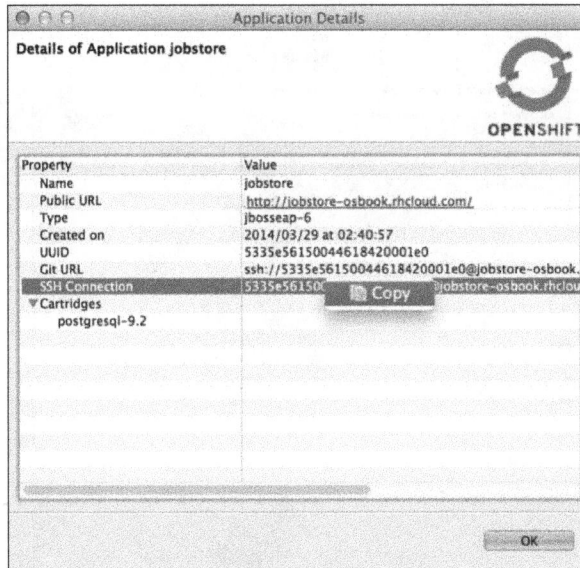

5. Go back to the **Remote System Explorer** perspective, and define a new connection to the remote system as shown in the following screenshot:

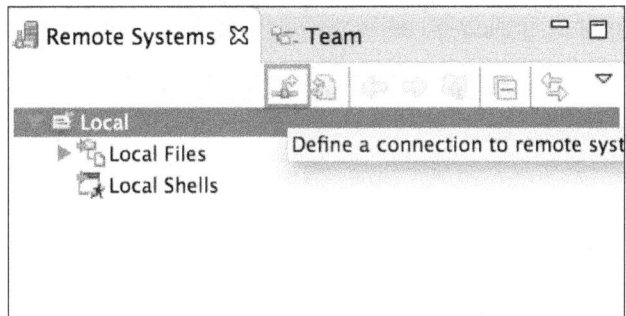

6. Next, it will ask you to select the remote system type. Select the **SSH Only** option as shown in the following screenshot:

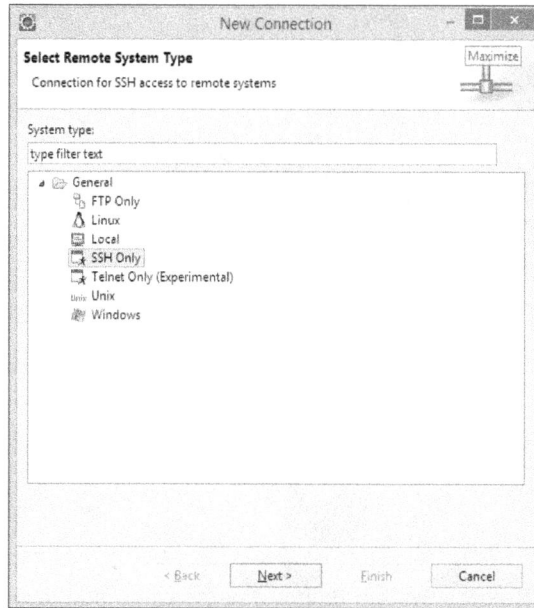

7. Next, you will be asked to enter the details of the new connection. Enter the hostname of your application as shown in the following screenshot:

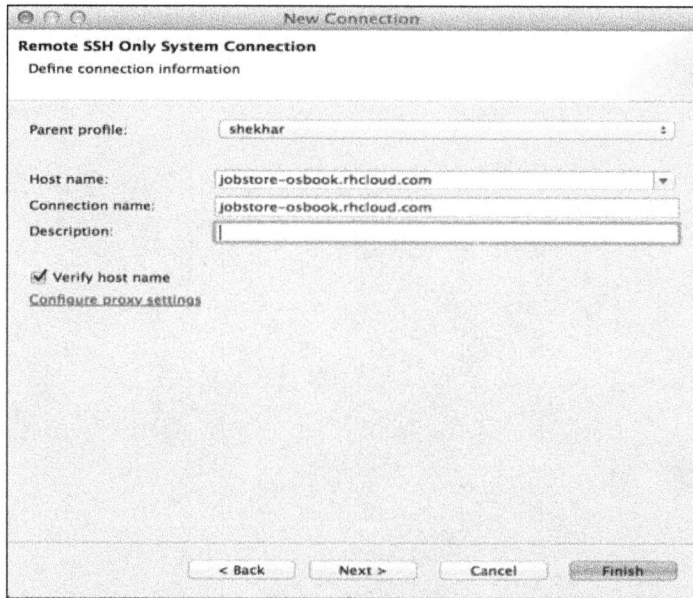

8. Click on the **Finish** button to create a new connection. The connection will be listed in the left-hand side bar.

9. To open an SSH terminal, navigate to **Ssh Terminals | Launch Terminal** as follows:

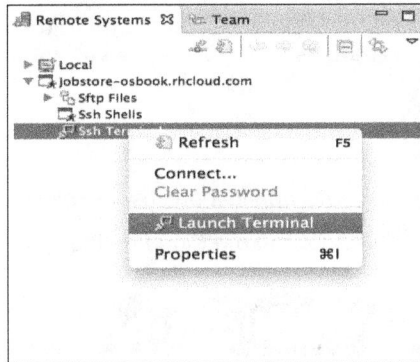

10. Next, you will be asked to enter the user ID with which you want to connect. The user ID is the UUID part of the SSH connection URL. Click on **OK**. Have a look at the following screenshot:

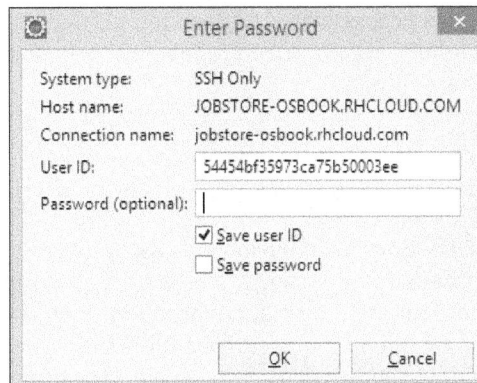

11. Launch the terminal again, and you will see an SSH terminal as shown in the following screenshot:

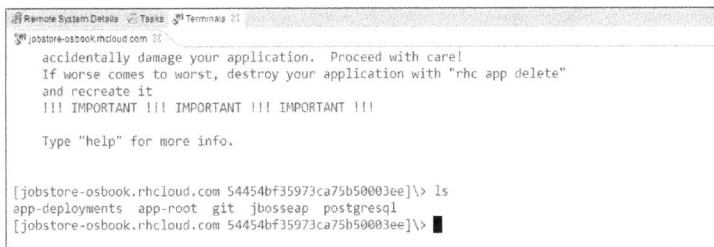

## How it works...

In the preceding steps, you used Eclipse Remote System Explorer to SSH into the OpenShift application gear. Remote System Explorer comes bundled with Eclipse Kepler for Java EE. Remote System Explorer allows you to connect and work with a variety of remote systems. To learn more about Remote System Explorer, you can refer to the documentation at `http://help.eclipse.org/kepler/index.jsp?nav=%2F56`.

## See also

▶ The *Developing OpenShift Java applications using Eclipse* recipe

▶ The *Debugging Java applications in the Cloud* recipe

# Debugging Java applications in the Cloud

In this recipe, you will learn how to debug Java applications running on OpenShift.

## Getting ready

This recipe requires you to have Eclipse with the JBoss Tools OpenShift plugin installed. Please refer to the *Developing OpenShift Java applications using Eclipse* recipe for more information.

## How to do it...

Perform the following steps to learn how to debug your Java applications:

1. In the *Developing OpenShift Java applications using Eclipse* recipe, you learned how to create a Java application using the Eclipse plugin. The application that we developed used the OpenShift template application as its starting point. As you might know, in the `rhc` command line, you can use the `--from-code` option to specify your own template application. Let's create a new Java application using Eclipse that uses the application we created in the *Creating and deploying Java EE 6 applications using the JBoss EAP and PostgreSQL 9.2 cartridges* recipe using Eclipse. Create a new OpenShift application by navigating to **File | New | Other | OpenShift Application**. After validating your account, you will get a screen where you need to enter the application details. Please select the **JBoss EAP** and **PostgreSQL 9.2** cartridges. To specify the Git repository, click on the **Advanced** button, and then uncheck the **Use default source code** checkbox.

In the input box, specify the URL of the Git repository as shown in the following screenshot:

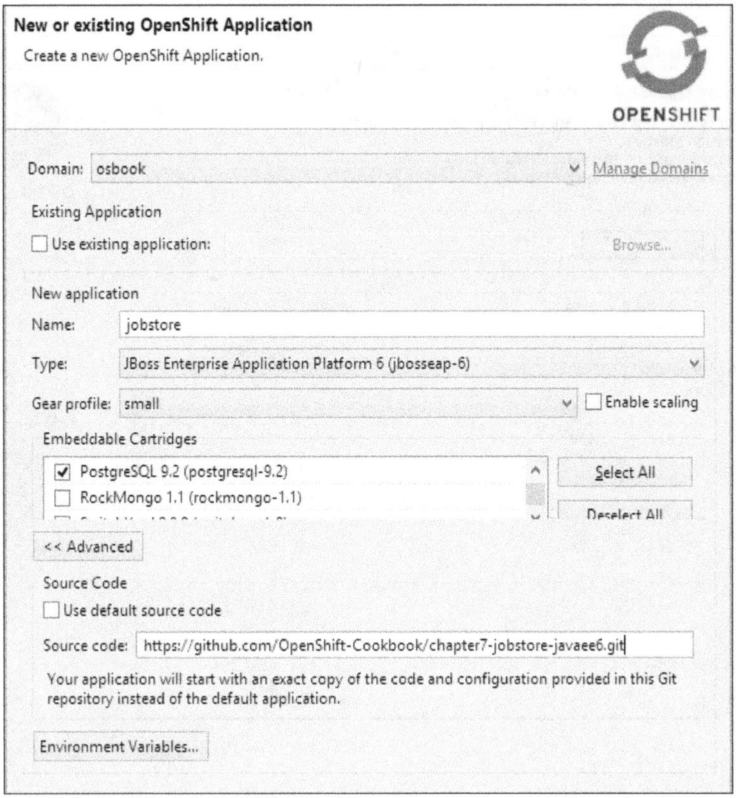

2. Next, you have to set up a `jobstore` application and configure the server adapter settings. Choose the default and click on **Next**.

3. The next screen will ask us to specify the location where you want to clone the Git repository and the name of the Git remote. Specify a writable directory, and click on **Finish**.

4. Now, a new application instance will be created using the selected cartridges and Git repository. Finally, the project will be imported into Eclipse as a Maven project.

5. To enable debugging, you have to create a new marker file called `enable_jpda` inside the `.openshift/markers` directory. The Eclipse plugin can help us create the file. Right-click on the project, and navigate to **OpenShift | Configure Markers...**.

6. This will open a dialog where you can select the marker files. Select the **Enable JPDA** marker as shown in the following screenshot. This will create a new file called `enable_jpda` inside the `.openshift/markers` directory.

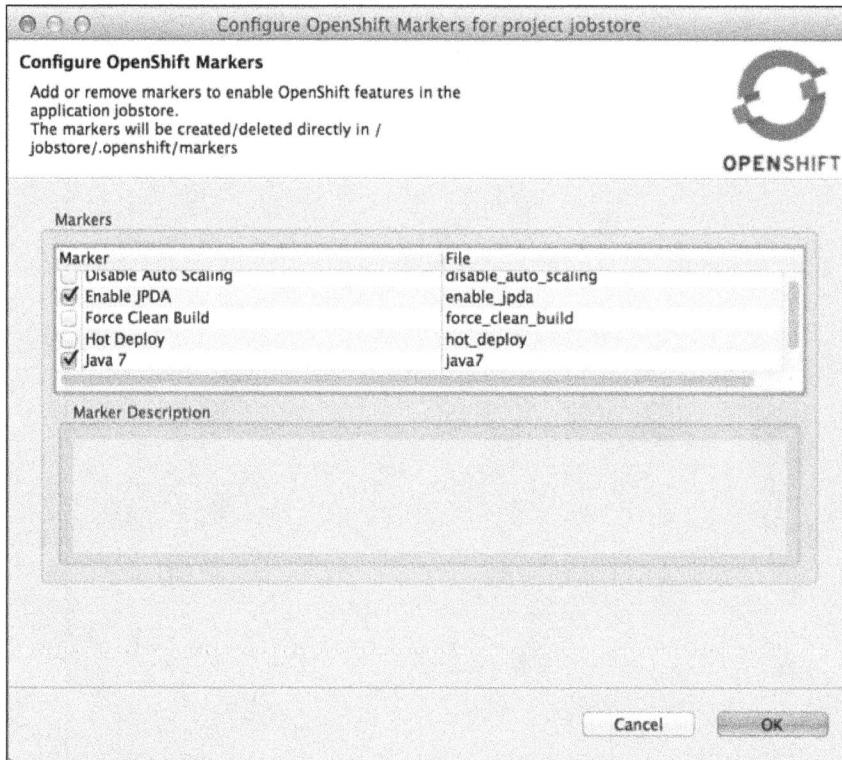

7. Go to the **Git Staging** view, and commit the change. Have a look at the following screenshot:

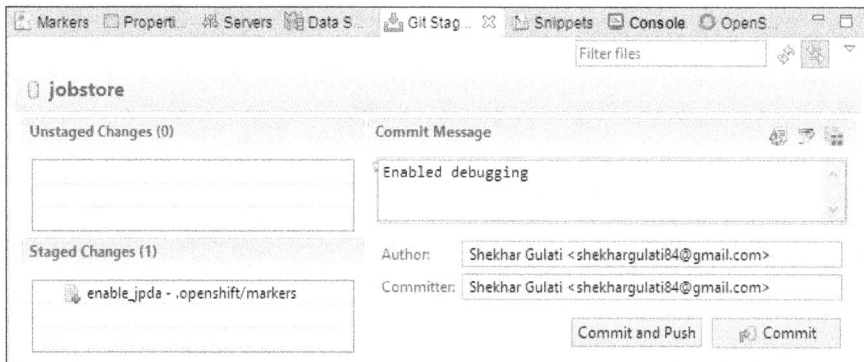

8.  After committing the change, go to the **Servers** view, and publish your changes. This will start the server with JPDA enabled.

9.  Now, enable port forwarding so that you can connect with the JPDA port. Go to the **OpenShift Explorer** view, and right-click on the project to enable port forwarding. Have a look at the following screenshot:

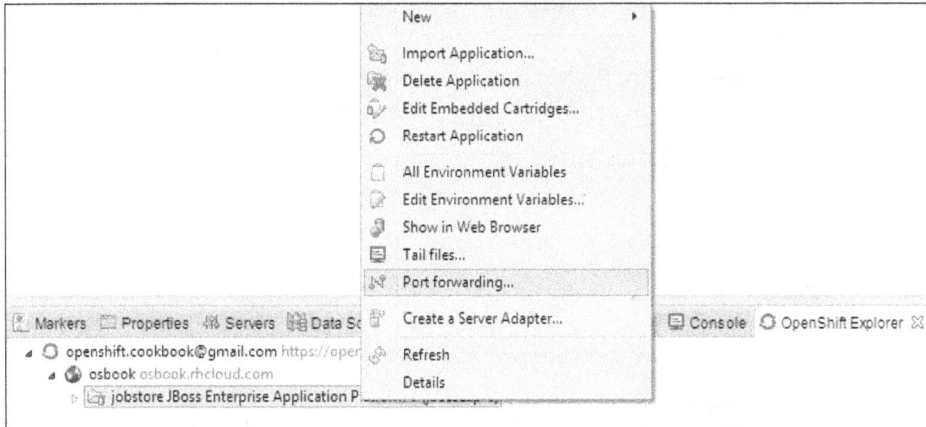

10. This will open a dialog where you can configure port forwarding. Click on the **Start All** button to enable port forwarding. The port `8787` is used to debug. This is shown in the following screenshot:

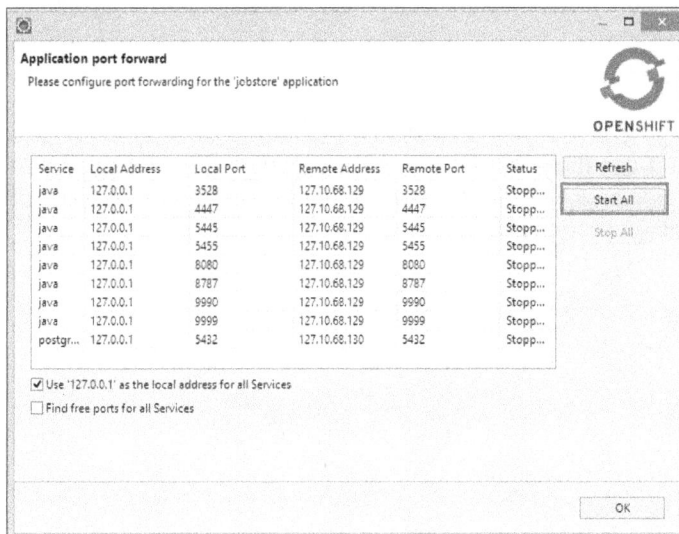

11. Now, we will add the breakpoint to the `CompanyResource` class at line number 32. After setting the debug point, create a new debug configuration by right-clicking on the debug point, navigating to **Debug Configurations|Remote Java Application|New** and giving it a name, and enter the port as `8787` as shown in the following screenshot:

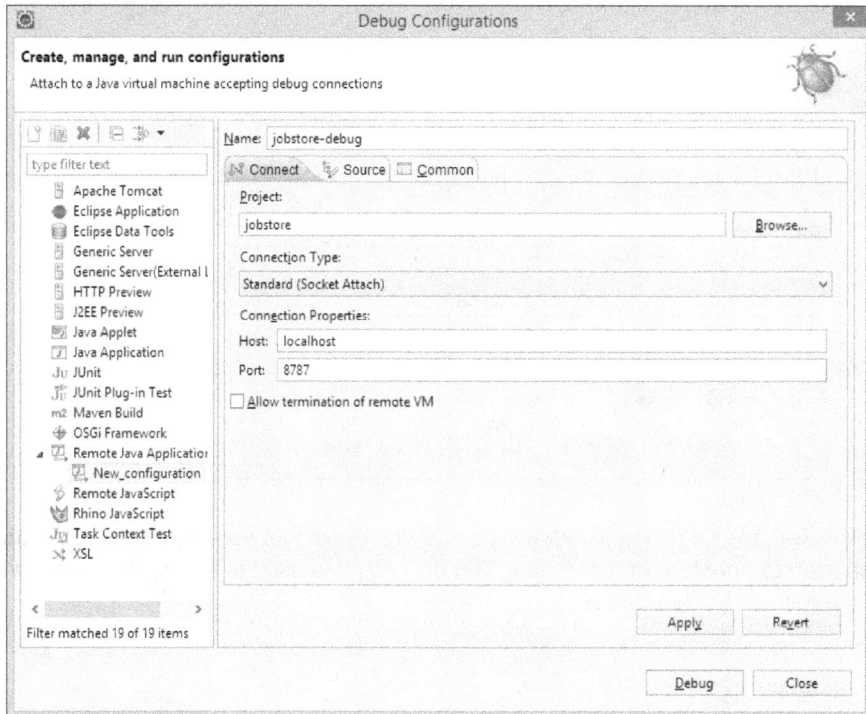

12. After entering all the details, click on the **Debug** button. Open the debug perspective, and you will see the remote debugger in action. Please note that it will take some time to enable remote debugging, so please be patient. This is shown in the following screenshot:

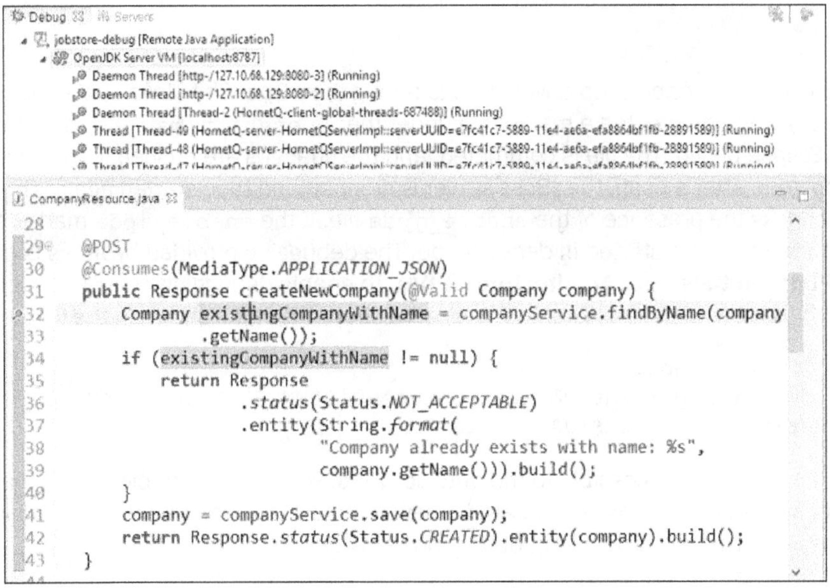

13. Now, go to `http://jobstore-{domain-name}.rhcloud.com/#companies/new` and create a new company. This will invoke the breakpoint as shown in the following screenshot:

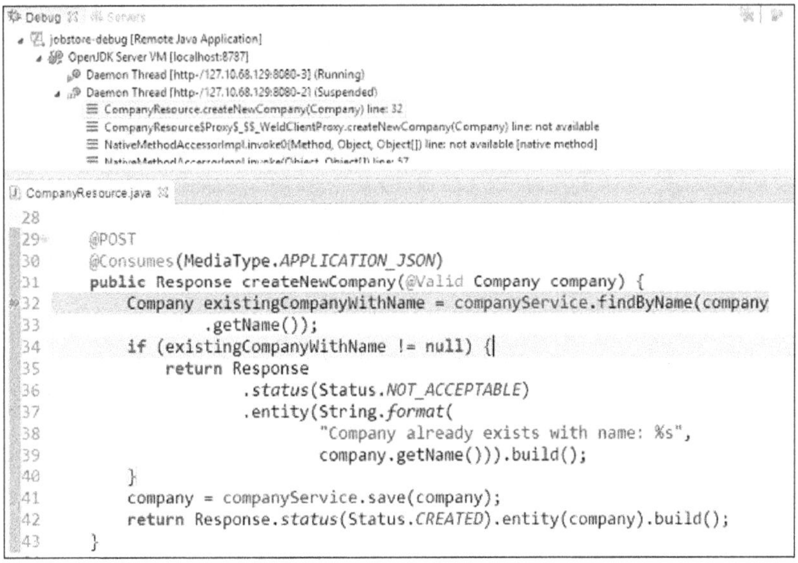

## How it works...

The preceding steps enable Java developers to debug their OpenShift Java applications. To enable debugging, you created a marker file under the `.openshift/markers` directory using the Eclipse plugin. The file is committed, and the changes are pushed to the OpenShift application gear. After a push, the JBoss server is stopped and then started again. The JBoss cartridge checks the presence of the `enable_jpda` file. If the `enable_jpda` marker file exists, then the server is started in debug mode. The debugging provided by JBoss is based on the **Java Platform Debugger Architecture** (**JPDA**). To enable debugging, the JBoss server is started with the `JAVA_OPTS` environment variable set to the value shown in the following code:

```
JAVA_OPTS="-Xdebug -
Xrunjdwp:transport=dt_socket,address=${OPENSHIFT_JBOSSEAP_IP}:8787
,server=y,suspend=n ${JAVA_OPTS}"
```

As the port `8787` is not accessible to the outside world, you have to enable port forwarding. After enabling port forwarding, you created a new remote Java application that will connect to the JBoss EAP cartridge running in debug mode.

## See also

- ▶ The *Developing OpenShift Java applications using Eclipse* recipe
- ▶ The *Using Eclipse System Explorer to SSH into the application gear* recipe

# 8

# OpenShift for Python Developers

This chapter presents a number of recipes that will help you to get started with Python web application development on OpenShift. This chapter contains the following recipes:

- ▸ Creating your first Python application
- ▸ Managing Python application dependencies
- ▸ Creating and deploying Flask web applications using Python and PostgreSQL cartridges
- ▸ Enabling hot deployment for Python applications
- ▸ Forcing a clean Python virtual environment
- ▸ Accessing an application's Python virtual environment
- ▸ Using Gevent with Python applications
- ▸ Installing a custom Python package
- ▸ Using the .htaccess file to configure Apache

## Introduction

Python is a general-purpose, high-level, easy-to-use, popular programming language. It is an interpreted language that emphasizes source code readability using strict indentation to determine code blocks. Python is very commonly used as a scripting language, but it is also very popular in the web application development and scientific computing world. There are various powerful web application frameworks, such as Django, Flask, Bottle, and Tornado, available to help developers build awesome web applications using the Python programming language.

OpenShift provides Python web developers with a hosting platform to deploy their web applications. At the time of writing this book, it supports three versions of Python—2.6, 2.7, and 3.3. You can view all the available Python versions by running the following command:

```
$ rhc cartridges |grep python
python-2.6          Python 2.6                              web
python-2.7          Python 2.7                              web
python-3.3          Python 3.3                              web
```

The *Creating your first Python application* recipe will help you take your first steps toward developing Python applications on OpenShift. OpenShift supports Apache with the `mode_wsgi` HTTP server module (`https://code.google.com/p/modwsgi/`) to run your Python web applications. Python applications can choose any of the supported versions and run within a virtualenv tool. A virtualenv tool is an isolated and private copy of your Python installation, which will be only used for that project without affecting the system's global Python installation. The *Accessing an application's Python virtual environment* recipe will show you how to access the virtual environment by connecting to the application gear using SSH.

We will also cover various ways in which you can manage application dependencies in Python applications. You can use `requirements.txt` or `setup.py` or both to manage application dependencies. This will be covered in the *Managing Python application dependencies* recipe.

The example application in this chapter will be developed using the Flask web framework and PostgreSQL database. I choose Flask because of its popularity and ease of use. You can use any other web framework, such as Bottle, web2py, and Django. The *Creating and deploying Flask web applications using Python and PostgreSQL cartridges* recipe will cover step-by-step how to write Flask web applications on OpenShift. All the source code is available on the OpenShift-Cookbook GitHub organization (`https://github.com/OpenShift-Cookbook`).

It is also feasible to use a standalone WSGI server, such as Gevent or Gunicorn, with OpenShift Python applications. The *Using Gevent with Python applications* recipe will cover this in detail.

If you want to run the examples on your local machine, please install Python, pip, and virtualenv. pip is a command-line tool to install and manage Python packages. The instructions to install Python for your operating system can be found at `http://docs.python-guide.org/en/latest/index.html`. Instructions to install pip can be found at `http://pip.readthedocs.org/en/latest/installing.html`. Finally, you can install virtualenv on your machine by following the instructions mentioned at `http://docs.python-guide.org/en/latest/dev/virtualenvs/`.

This chapter assumes that you are comfortable with the Python web development basics, OpenShift application basics, and how to work with OpenShift database cartridges. In case you are not comfortable with these topics, I recommend that you first read *Chapter 3, Creating and Managing Applications*, through *Chapter 6, Using MongoDB and Third-party Database Cartridges with OpenShift Applications*, before continuing with this chapter.

# Creating your first Python application

In this recipe, you will learn how to create an OpenShift Python application using the rhc command-line tool. We will create a Python 3.3 application and then understand the template application created by OpenShift.

## Getting ready

To walk through this recipe, you will need the rhc command-line client installed on your machine. Please refer to the *Installing the OpenShift rhc command-line client* recipe in *Chapter 1, Getting Started with OpenShift*, for details.

## How to do it...

Perform the following steps to create your first Python application:

1. Open a new command-line terminal, and change the directory to a convenient location where you want to create the application.

2. To create a new Python 3.3 application, run the following command:

   ```
   $ rhc create-app myapp python-3.3
   ```

3. You can replace Python 3.3 with Python 2.6 or Python 2.7 to create applications that use the respective Python versions.

4. Open your favorite web browser, and go to `http://myapp-{domain-name}.rhcloud.com` to view the application. Please replace `{domain-name}` with your OpenShift account domain name. You will see the OpenShift template application in your browser as follows:

Welcome to your Python application on OpenShift

**Deploying code changes**

OpenShift uses the Git version control system for your source code, and grants you access to it via the Secure Shell (SSH) protocol. In order to upload and download code to your application you need to give us your public SSH key. You can upload it within the web console or install the RHC command line tool and run `rhc setup` to generate and upload your key automatically.

**Working in your local Git repository**

If you created your application from the command line and uploaded your SSH key, rhc will automatically download a copy of that source code repository (Git calls this 'cloning') to your local system.

If you created the application from the web console, you'll need to manually clone the repository to your local system. Copy the application's source code Git URL and then run:

```
$ git clone <git_url> <directory_to_create>

# Within your project directory
# Commit your changes and push to OpenShift

$ git commit -a -m 'Some commit message'
$ git push
```

- Learn more about deploying and building your application
- See the README file in your local application Git repository for more information on the options for deploying applications.

**Managing your application**

**Web Console**

You can use the OpenShift web console to enable additional capabilities via cartridges, add collaborator access authorizations, designate custom domain aliases, and manage domain memberships.

**Command Line Tools**

Installing the OpenShift RHC client tools allows you complete control of your cloud environment. Read more on how to manage your application from the command line in our User Guide.

**Development Resources**

- Developer Center
- User Guide
- OpenShift Support
- Stack Overflow questions for OpenShift
- IRC channel at #openshift on freenode.net
- Git documentation

## How it works...

When you run the `rhc create-app` command, OpenShift broker will receive the request and will initiate the application creation process. The application creation process was explained in detail in the *Creating an OpenShift application using the rhc command-line client* recipe in *Chapter 3*, *Creating and Managing Applications*. To run your Python applications, OpenShift needs to know the Python version you want to use. In step 2, you specified that OpenShift should create a Python 3.3 application with `myapp` as the application name. OpenShift will use these details along with a few defaults to create the `myapp` application. The defaults include a small gear size, non-scalable application, and the use of the current directory to clone the Git repository. To run Python-3.3-based web applications, OpenShift will install Python 3.3 language runtime and configure the Apache server with the `mod_wsgi` module. The `mod_wsgi` module provides an implementation of the **Web Server Gateway Interface** (**WSGI**) specification, allowing the Apache web server to host Python web applications that support the Python WSGI interface. The WSGI specification describes a simple interface between web servers and web applications or frameworks for the Python programming language. Most of the popular web frameworks (http://wsgi.readthedocs.org/en/latest/frameworks.html) in the Python community support the WSGI interface. This makes it very easy for developers to run their choice of framework on OpenShift, as it provides the Apache `mod_wsgi` deployment environment.

> You can also run Python web applications on alternative Python web servers, such as Gevent. This will be covered in the *Using Gevent with Python applications* recipe.

Apart from installing Python and configuring Apache with `mod_wsgi`, every OpenShift application uses virtualenv and pip to manage application dependencies. A virtualenv tool is an isolated and private copy of your Python installation, which will be only used for that project without affecting the system's global Python installation. You can install packages in a virtualenv tool using pip, and virtualenv will ensure the application has access only to the package that it needs. Another advantage of virtual environments is that they don't require administrative rights.

Now, let's look at the template application created by OpenShift as follows:

```
$ cd myapp && ls -ap
$ .git/.openshift/ requirements.txt   wsgi.py  setup.py
```

The template application has three files—`requirements.txt`, `wsgi.py,` and `setup.py`—apart from the `.openshift` and `.git` directories. We have already talked about `.openshift` and `.git` in the *Creating an OpenShift application using the rhc command-line client* recipe in *Chapter 3, Creating and Managing Applications*, so I will not cover them here. Let's talk about the three application files one by one:

- `requirements.txt`: The `requirements.txt` file is used to specify libraries that your application depends on. The pip package manager will install all the application dependencies mentioned in `requirements.txt`. This is a regular text file with one dependency per line. The format is `[package name]==[package version]`. The sample `requirements.txt` file is shown as follows:

  ```
  Flask==0.10.1
  Jinja2==2.7.2
  MarkupSafe==0.21
  Werkzeug==0.9.4
  itsdangerous==0.24
  ```

- `setup.py`: The `setup.py` file allows developers to more easily build and distribute python packages that will be imported as dependencies by other projects. It allows you to specify project-specific metadata, such as name and description, as well as specify dependencies. The sample `setup.py` file is shown as follows:

  ```
  from setuptools import setup
  setup(name='MyAwesomeApp',
          version='1.0',
          description='My Awesome OpenShift Application',
          author='Shekhar Gulati',
          author_email='shekhargulati84@gmail.com',
          url='http://www.python.org/sigs/distutils-sig/',
          install_requires=['Flask>=0.7.2', 'MarkupSafe'],
          )
  ```

- `wsgi.py`: The `wsgi.py` file is a WSGI-compatible application created by OpenShift. This file is mandatory if you want to use the Apache `mod_wsgi` server to host your Python web application. This file contains the code `mod_wsgi` module, which will execute on startup to get the application object. The application object is a callable that takes two parameters—`environ` and `start_response`. The `environ` parameter is a dictionary containing environment variables, and `start_response` is a callable that takes two required parameters: `status` and `response_headers`.

You can check the exact version of Python running inside the application gear by running the following command:

```
$ rhc ssh --command 'python -V'
Python 3.3.2
```

## There's more...

By default, a Python application expects `wsgi.py` to be available at the application's root directory. If you want to change the directory layout and use a different location for `wsgi.py`, you can set the `OPENSHIFT_PYTHON_WSGI_APPLICATION` environment variable to specify a different location, as shown in the following command. You can view the list of available environment variables for a Python application at `https://access.redhat.com/ documentation/en-US/OpenShift_Online/2.0/html/User_Guide/ Python_Environment_Variables.html`.

```
$ rhc env-set OPENSHIFT_PYTHON_WSGI_APPLICATION=wsgi/wsgi.py
```

## See also

- ▸ The *Managing Python application dependencies* recipe
- ▸ The *Enabling hot deployment for Python applications* recipe
- ▸ The *Creating and deploying Flask web applications using Python and PostgreSQL cartridges* recipe

# Managing Python application dependencies

OpenShift gives the Python developer two options to specify their application dependencies. You can specify application dependencies either in the `install_requires` element in `setup.py`, in `requirements.txt`, or both. When dependencies are specified in both the `setup.py` and `requirements.txt` files, OpenShift will install all the libraries mentioned in both the files. The `setup.py` file is required when you want to distribute your library as a package that others can use. All the packages listed on PyPi need to have the `setup.py` script in their root directory. As you do not want to distribute your web applications as a package, there is no need to use the `setup.py` file. I recommend that you use `requirements.txt` for your OpenShift applications. The reason why `setup.py` exists is that OpenShift initially only supported `setup.py` and later added support for the `requirements.txt` file. So to make sure that the existing application continues to work on OpenShift, we need to support both the options. In this recipe, you will learn how to use `requirements.txt` to specify application dependencies. The source code of the application created in this recipe is available on GitHub (`https://github.com/ OpenShift-Cookbook/chapter8-recipe2`).

## Getting ready

This recipe is based on the assumption that you have read the *Creating your first Python application* recipe. To walk through this recipe, you will need the rhc command-line client installed on your machine. Please refer to the *Installing the OpenShift rhc command-line client* recipe in *Chapter 1, Getting Started with OpenShift*, for details. This recipe will require you to have virtualenv installed on your machine. You can install virtualenv on your machine by following the instructions mentioned at `http://docs.python-guide.org/en/latest/dev/virtualenvs/`.

## How to do it...

Perform the following steps to build a `Hello World` Flask web application that will demonstrate how you can work with application dependencies:

1. Open a new command-line terminal, and run the following command to create a new Python application:

   ```
   $ rhc create-app myapp python-3.3
   ```

   If you want to create Python 2.6 or Python 2.7 applications, use `python-2.6` or `python-2.7` as the web cartridge name instead of `python-3.3`.

2. Change the directory to `myapp`, and delete the `setup.py` file as follows:

   ```
   $ cd myapp
   $ rm -f setup.py
   ```

3. Create a new virtual environment by running the following command:

   ```
   $ virtualenv venv --python=python3.3
   ```

4. Before you can work with the virtual environment, you have to activate it. To activate the virtual environment, run the following command:

   ```
   $ . venv/bin/activate
   ```

5. Once you have activated virtualenv, you can begin installing modules without affecting the system's default Python interpreter. Install the Flask module by running the following command:

   ```
   $ pip install flask
   ```

6. Create a new Python file named `hello.py` in the `myapp` directory, and populate it with the following code:

```
from flask import Flask
app = Flask(__name__)

@app.route('/')
def index():
  return 'Hello World!'

if __name__ == '__main__':
  app.run()
```

7. To run this application on your local machine, run the following command:

**$ python hello.py**

8. Next, open your favorite web browser, and go to `http://127.0.0.1:5000`. You will see **Hello World!** displayed in the browser.

9. To deploy this application on OpenShift, we have to declare all the dependencies in `requirements.txt`. The following command will write all of your application dependencies in `requirements.txt`:

**$ pip freeze > requirements.txt**

10. The preceding command will populate `requirements.txt` with all the application dependencies. This includes transitive dependencies as well. The `requirements.txt` file will look as shown in the following code:

**Flask==0.10.1**

**Jinja2==2.7.2**

**MarkupSafe==0.23**

**Werkzeug==0.9.4**

**distribute==0.7.3**

**itsdangerous==0.24**

> Please make sure that the distribute version is 0.7.3, as earlier versions do not work with Python 3.3. Earlier versions of the distribute are not compatible with Python 3.3, so you might face trouble if you use them.

11. Also, we have to update the `wsgi.py` file to load the Flask application instead of the default one created by OpenShift. Delete all the content in the `wsgi.py` file, and replace it with the one shown in the following code:

```
#!/usr/bin/env python
from hello import app as application
```

12. Create a new file named `.gitignore` in the `myapp` directory, and add the `venv` directory to be ignored. We do not want to push the virtual environment to OpenShift; OpenShift will create the virtual environment based on the dependencies mentioned in the `requirements.txt` file. The `.gitignore` file is created as follows:

```
$ cat .gitignore
venv/
```

13. Now commit the code to the local repository, and then push changes to application gear. OpenShift will install all the packages specified in the `requirements.txt` file and make them available to the application via the virtual environment as follows:

```
$ git add .
$ git commit -am "Hello World Flask application"
$ git push
```

14. Now, you can see the application running at `http://myapp-{domain-name}.rhcloud.com`. Please replace `{domain-name}` with your application domain name. You will see **Hello World** in your browser.

## How it works...

In the previous steps, you created a simple Flask framework web application that uses `requirements.txt` to specify application dependencies. Flask is a micro web framework for the Python programming language. It is an easy-to-learn framework with extensive documentation, which can be found at `http://flask.pocoo.org/docs`.

In step 1, you created a Python 3.3 application with the name `myapp`. Read the *Creating your first Python application* recipe to understand the Python application created by OpenShift. As you will use `requirement.txt` to specify application dependencies, you deleted the `setup.py` file in step 2. If you wish, you can keep the `setup.py` file and specify your application metadata in it. The application metadata includes the name, description, version, and so on, of the application. I recommend that you specify application dependencies in only one file to avoid dependency hell (`http://en.wikipedia.org/wiki/Dependency_hell`).

Step 3 created a new virtual environment using the Python 3.3 interpreter. To use a virtual environment, you have to first activate it using the command shown in step 4. The virtual environment is the ideal way to work with Python applications, as it avoids polluting the system global Python installation.

You installed the Flask web framework using pip in step 5, as we are going to develop a web application that uses this framework. The Flask framework will be installed in the virtual environment and will become available to your application.

In step 6, you created a new Python file named `hello.py` and added the source code for the `Hello World` application. The code shown in step 6 does the following:

- In line 1, you imported the `Flask` class from the `flask` module.

- In line 2, you created an instance of the `Flask` class. This instance will be that of the WSGI application.

- Then, you defined a route for the root (`/`) URL. The route tells the Flask framework that it should invoke the `index()` function when a request is made to the root URL. The `index()` function will simply render **Hello World!** in the browser.

- Finally, if the name of the application module is equal to `'__main__'`, the development server will be launched. The `__name__ == '__main__'` expression is used to ensure the development server is started only when the script is executed directly using the `python hello.py` command.

Step 7 started the development web server by executing the `hello.py` script. This will start the development server and launch the Flask application.

In step 8, you used the `pip freeze` command to add all the dependencies to the `requirements.txt` file. OpenShift will download all the dependencies mentioned in this file and populate the application virtual environment with them. OpenShift uses Apache mod_wsgi to run your Python applications. The entry point of mod_wsgi is the `wsgi.py` file. This file should contain the code that will provide the application object on startup. In step 9, you replaced the content of the `wsgi.py` file so that it uses the Flask application object instead of the application object created by the template.

Finally, you committed the code to the local Git repository and pushed the code to the OpenShift application gear. OpenShift will first stop the Apache server, download all the dependencies mentioned in the `requirements.txt` file inside a virtual environment, and then finally start the Apache server. The part of the `git push` output is shown as follows:

```
$ git push
Counting objects: 9, done.
Writing objects: 100% (6/6), 695 bytes, done.
Total 6 (delta 0), reused 0 (delta 0)
remote: Stopping Python 3.3 cartridge
remote: Building git ref 'master', commit 128311d
remote: Activating virtenv
remote: Checking for pip dependency listed in requirements.txt file..
```

```
remote: Downloading/unpacking Flask==0.10.1 (from -r /var/lib/openshift/5
36f59b3e0b8cd628600138b/app-root/runtime/repo/requirements.txt (line 1))

remote: Downloading/unpacking Jinja2==2.7.2 (from -r /var/lib/openshift/5
36f59b3e0b8cd628600138b/app-root/runtime/repo/requirements.txt (line 2))

...

remote: Successfully installed Flask Jinja2 MarkupSafe Werkzeug
itsdangerous setuptools distribute

remote: Cleaning up...

remote: Starting Python 3.3 cartridge (Apache+mod_wsgi)

remote: Application directory "/" selected as DocumentRoot

remote: Application "wsgi.py" selected as default WSGI entry point

remote: Deployment completed with status: success
```

## There's more...

If you want to use `setup.py` instead of `requirements.txt`, you can delete `requirement.txt` or keep it empty and specify all the requirements under the `install_requires` element, as shown in the following code. The full source code of the application is available on GitHub at `https://github.com/OpenShift-Cookbook/chapter8-recipe2-setup.py`.

```
from setuptools import setup

setup(name='MyApp',
      version='1.0',
      description='My OpenShift App',
      author='Shekhar Gulati',
      author_email='shekhargulati84@gmail.com',
      url='http://www.python.org/sigs/distutils-sig/',
      install_requires=['Flask>=0.10.1'],
      )
```

## See also

► The *Creating your first Python application* recipe

► The *Enabling hot deployment for Python applications* recipe

► The *Creating and deploying Flask web applications using Python and PostgreSQL cartridges* recipe

# Creating and deploying Flask web applications using Python and PostgreSQL cartridges

In this recipe, you will develop a simple job portal application using the Python Flask web framework (http://flask.pocoo.org/) and the PostgreSQL database. I have chosen Flask because it is a very easy-to-use and popular web framework. You can run any web framework, such as Django, Bottle, Zope, and Tornado, on OpenShift. The example application will allow users to post job openings and view a list of all the persisted jobs in the system. These two functionalities will be exposed using the two REST endpoints. The source code for this recipe is available on GitHub at https://github.com/OpenShift-Cookbook/chapter8-jobstore-simple.

## Getting ready

This recipe is based on the assumption that you have read previous recipes in this chapter. To walk through this recipe, you will need the rhc command-line client installed on your machine. Please refer to the *Installing the OpenShift rhc command-line client* recipe in *Chapter 1, Getting Started with OpenShift*, for details. Also, if you want to run the application on your local machine, you will need to have Python, pip, and virtualenv installed on your machine. Please refer to the introduction section for links to installation instructions for respective software.

## How to do it...

To create the application, perform the following steps:

1. Open a new command-line terminal, and navigate to a convenient location where you want to create the application. Create a new Python 2.7 and PostgreSQL 9.2 OpenShift application, and type the following command:

   ```
   $ rhc create-app jobstore python-2.7 postgresql-9.2
   ```

2. After the application is created, change the directory to `jobstore`, and delete the `setup.py` file:

   ```
   $ cd jobstore
   $ rm -f setup.py
   ```

3. Also, create a `.gitignore` file, and add the following to it:

   ```
   venv/
   *.pyc
   ```

4. Create a new virtual environment for the `jobstore` application. Run the following command to create the virtual environment, and then activate it:

```
$ virtualenv venv --python=python2.7
$ . venv/bin/activate
```

5. Now that the virtual environment is activated, you can install the application dependencies. This application uses the Flask web framework. To install the dependencies in the virtual environment, run the following command:

```
$ pip install flask
```

6. Create a new file named `jobstore.py`, which will house the application source code. The following code is a simple Flask application that renders an `index.html` file when a request is made to the root URL:

```
from flask import Flask, render_template, jsonify, request,
Response

app = Flask(__name__)
app.config['PROPAGATE_EXCEPTIONS'] = True

@app.route('/')
def index():
    return render_template('index.html')

if __name__ == '__main__':
    app.run(debug=True)
```

7. In the previous code, the index route will render `index.html` when a request is made to the root URL. By default, Flask looks for templates in the `templates` directory inside the application folder. The `render_template()` function provided by the Flask framework integrates the Jinja 2 template engine with the application. To make sure this code works, create a new directory named `templates` in the application source code repository as follows:

```
$ mkdir templates
```

8. Now, create a new `index.html` file inside the `templates` directory, and add the following content to it:

```
<!DOCTYPE html>
<html lang="en">
<head>
<meta charset="UTF-8">
<title>JobStore</title>
<link href="//cdnjs.cloudflare.com/ajax/libs/twitter-
bootstrap/3.1.1/css/bootstrap.css" rel="stylesheet">
</head>
```

```
<body>
  <div class="container">
    <div class="row">
      <h2>JobStore application expose Two REST End Points</h2>
      <ul>
        <li>
          To create a Job, make a HTTP POST request to <code>/api/
v1/jobs</code>
        </li>
        <li>
          To view all Jobs, make a HTTP GET request to <code>/api/
v1/jobs</code>
        </li>
      </ul>
    </div>
  </div>

</body>
</html>
```

9. You can test the application when you start the Python server by running the following command:

```
$ python jobstore.py
```

10. To view the application, go to `http://127.0.0.1:5000/` in your favorite browser. You will see `index.html` rendered in your browser.

11. The main responsibility of this application is to store the job data in the database. Python has support functionalities for various database frameworks that makes it very easy to work with a variety of databases. Among them, SQLAlchemy is the most popular and powerful relational database framework that supports various RDBMS backends. To use SQLAlchemy with Flask applications, you have to first install the Flask SQLAlchemy extension. The Flask SQLAlchemy extension simplifies working with SQLAlchemy inside Flask applications. To install Flask SQLAlchemy, run the following `pip` command:

```
$ pip install flask-sqlalchemy
```

12. Now that you have installed the Flask SQLAlchemy extension, the next task is to write the configuration code so that the `jobstore` application can connect to the PostgreSQL database. Add the following content to `jobstore.py`. You can view the full source code on GitHub at `https://github.com/OpenShift-Cookbook/chapter8-jobstore-simple/blob/master/jobstore.py`.

```
from flask.ext.sqlalchemy import SQLAlchemy

app.config['SQLALCHEMY_DATABASE_URI'] = os.environ['OPENSHIFT_
POSTGRESQL_DB_URL']
```

```
app.config['SQLALCHEMY_COMMIT_ON_TEARDOWN'] = True

db = SQLAlchemy(app)
```

13. In the preceding code, you added two configuration options to the Flask application configuration object. `SQLALCHEMY_DATABASE_URI` points to the database connection URL. OpenShift exposes the PostgreSQL database connection URL using the `OPENSHIFT_POSTGRESQL_DB_URL` environment variable. The `SQLALCHEMY_COMMIT_ON_TEARDOWN` option enables automatic commits of database changes at the end of each request. Finally, you instantiated the `db` object from the `SQLAlchemy` class, passing it the application object. This `db` object provides access to all the database-related functionalities.

14. Next, you will write a model class to represent the `Job` table in the PostgreSQL database. The model represents a persistent entity stored in the database. The `db` instance that we got in step 7 provides a base class that a model can extend. Apart from this, the `db` object also provides helper functions to define the structure of a model class. The `Job` model is shown as follows:

```python
class Job(db.Model):
    __tablename__ = 'jobs'
    id = db.Column(db.Integer(), primary_key=True)
    title = db.Column(db.String(64), index=True, nullable=False)
    description = db.Column(db.Text())
    posted_at = db.Column(db.DateTime(), nullable=False,
default=datetime.utcnow)
    company = db.Column(db.String(100), nullable=False)

    def __repr__(self):
      return 'Job %s' % self.title

    def to_json(self):
      job_json = {
        'id' : self.id,
        'title': self.title,
        'description' : self.description,
        'posted_at' : self.posted_at,
        'company':self.company
      }
      return job_json


    @staticmethod
    def from_json(job_json):
      title = job_json.get('title')
      description = job_json.get('description')
```

```
        company = job_json.get('company')
        return Job(title=title, description=description,company=compa
ny)
```

The `__tablename__` variable is used to define the name of the table in the database. The `db.Column()` function is used to define the class variables that will be mapped to columns in the database table. You also defined a couple of helper functions that will help convert to and from JSON. These methods will be useful when we build the REST API.

15. Now you will write a couple of REST endpoints that will expose a couple of functionalities. The first endpoint will allow users to list all the jobs inside the database, and the second endpoint will allow users to create a new job. The REST endpoints are shown as follows:

```
@app.route('/api/v1/jobs')
def all_jobs():
  jobs = Job.query.all()
  return jsonify({'jobs':[job.to_json() for job in jobs]})


@app.route('/api/v1/jobs', methods=['POST'])
def post_job():
  job = Job.from_json(request.json)
  db.session.add(job)
  db.session.commit()
  return jsonify(job.to_json()) , 201
```

In the previous code, the `all_jobs()` function queries the database for all the Job rows. The result from the database is converted to JSON and returned to the user. The `jsonify()` function is provided by Flask and creates a response with the JSON representation and the `application/json` MIME type.

The `post_job()` function first converts the JSON request to the Job object and then writes it to the database. Finally, it returns the persisted job to the user.

16. As discussed in the *Managing Python application dependencies* recipe, you have to update the `wsgi.py` file to load the Flask application instead of the default created by OpenShift. Delete all the content in the `wsgi.py` file, and replace it with the one shown in the following code:

```
#!/usr/bin/python
import os
virtenv = os.environ['OPENSHIFT_PYTHON_DIR'] + '/virtenv/'
virtualenv = os.path.join(virtenv, 'bin/activate_this.py')
try:
    execfile(virtualenv, dict(__file__=virtualenv))
except IOError:
    pass
```

```
from jobstore import app as application
from jobstore import *
db.create_all()
```

17. The last thing to do before we can deploy the application is specify the dependencies in `requirements.txt`. Run the following command to populate the application `requirements.txt` file:

    ```
    $ pip freeze > requirements.txt
    ```

18. Now, commit the code and push the application changes to the application gear as follows:

    ```
    $ git add .
    ```

    ```
    $ git commit -am "jobstore application created"
    ```

    ```
    $ git push
    ```

19. The application will be up and running at `http://jobstore-{domain-name}.rhcloud.com`.

20. To test the REST endpoints, you could use cURL. To create a new `Job` instance, run the following cURL command:

    ```
    $ curl -i -X POST -H "Content-Type: application/json" -H "Accept:
    application/json" -d '{"title":"OpenShift Evangelist","descriptio
    n":"OpenShift Evangelist","company":"Red Hat"}' http://jobstore-
    {domain-name}.rhcloud.com/api/v1/jobs
    ```

21. To view all the jobs, you can run the following cURL command:

    ```
    $ curl http://jobstore-osbook.rhcloud.com/api/v1/jobs
    ```

## How it works...

In the previous steps, you created a Python web application and deployed it on OpenShift. From steps 1 through 4, you first created a new Python 2.7 OpenShift application, created a virtual environment for the project, and finally activated the virtual environment. The application uses the Python Flask framework, so you installed it using pip in step 5.

In steps 6 through 8, you created a Flask web application that renders the `index.html` file. The code shown in step 4 does the following:

▶ You imported all the required classes and functions.

▶ Then, you created an instance of the `Flask` class. The only required argument is the name of the main module or package of the application. The correct value is __name__ in most cases.

▶ Then, you defined a route for the root URL using the `app.route` decorator. A route allows you to bind HTTP requests to function calls based on the URL requested. The index function will render `index.html` in the browser.

▸ Finally, if the name of the application module is equal to '_ _main_ _', the development server is launched. The __name__ == '__main__' expression is used to ensure the development server is started only when the script is executed directly using the python jobstore.py command. You tested the application on your local machine in step 10.

In steps 11 through 14, you first installed the Flask SQLAlchemy extension and then did the following:

▸ First, you imported the SQLAlchemy class from the Flask-SQLAlchemy extension.

▸ Then, you configured the URL of the application database using SQLALCHEMY_DATABASE_URI in the Flask configuration object. You also used another useful option, SQLALCHEMY_COMMIT_ON_TEARDOWN, to configure the automatic commits of the database changes at the end of each request.

▸ Next, you created an instance of the SQLAlchemy class that provides access to all the SQLAlchemy APIs.

▸ Then, you defined the Job model class using the SQLAlchemy API. The company class extends the db.Model base class and uses the db.Column constructor to define the structure of the model class. The __tablename__ variable is used to define the name of the table in the database.

▸ Finally, you defined a couple of helper functions that will help convert to and from JSON. These methods will be useful when we build the REST API.

In step 15, you defined REST endpoints for the Job model class. The code listing shown in step 15 does the following:

▸ When a user makes a GET request to /api/v1/jobs, the all_jobs() function is invoked. The function finds all the jobs using the SQLAlchemy API, iterates over the result set, and then converts it into JSON.

▸ When a user makes a POST request to /api/v1/jobs, a new job is created. The JSON data is exposed as the request.json Python dictionary. Then, the request.json dictionary is converted into the Job object using the from_json method. The data is then persisted into the database using the db.session API.

In step 16, you replaced the content of the wsgi.py file so that it uses the Flask application object instead of the application object created by the template. Finally, you committed the code to your local Git repository and then pushed the changes to the OpenShift application gear. Once deployed, you can go to http://jobstore-{domain-name}.rhcloud.com and work with the application.

## There's more

You can do all the previously performed steps with just a single command. The Git repository mentioned in the command contains the source code for this recipe as follows:

```
$ rhc create-app jobstore python-2.7 postgresql-9.2 --from-code https://
github.com/OpenShift-Cookbook/chapter8-jobstore-simple.git
```

## See also

- ▶ The *Creating your first Python application* recipe
- ▶ The *Enabling hot deployment for Python applications* recipe

# Enabling hot deployment for Python applications

Every time you make a change to your application source code and push the changes to the OpenShift application gear Git repository, OpenShift first stops your gear (which stops all the cartridges installed on the gear), copies the source code from your application Git repository to `app-root/runtime/repo`, performs a build, prepares the artifact, and finally starts your gear (which starts all the cartridges). This process takes time and does not suit rapid development and deployment. To enable rapid development and faster deployments, OpenShift supports hot deployment. Hot deployment means that you can deploy your changes without the need to restart all the application cartridges.

In this recipe, you will learn how you can enable hot deployment for Python applications.

This recipe will work with all the three supported Python versions.

## How to do it...

Perform the following steps to enable hot deployment for your application:

1. Create a new Python application using the source code developed in the previous recipe as follows:

   ```
   $ rhc create-app myapp python-3.3 --from-code=https://github.com/
   OpenShift-Cookbook/chapter8-recipe2.git
   ```

2. Open the `hello.py` file, and update `Hello World!` to `Hello from OpenShift.`

3. To enable hot deployment, create an empty file named `hot_deploy` under the `.openshift/markers` directory. This file is called the marker file, as this does not contain any content. On the *nix machine, you can create a new file by executing the following command. On a Windows machine, you can use file explorer to create a new file.

```
$ touch .openshift/markers/hot_deploy
```

4. Add the file to the Git repository, and then commit and push changes to the application gear as shown in the following code:

```
$ git add -A .
$ git commit -am "enabled hot deployment"
$ git push
```

5. In the `git push` logs, you will see a message that cartridges are not stopped because hot deployment is enabled as follows:

**remote: Not stopping cartridge python because hot deploy is enabled**

6. Now open the application URL in your favorite web browser, and you will see the change deployed without a restart.

## How it works...

The presence of the `hot_deploy` marker file informs OpenShift that you want to do hot deployment. Before stopping and starting the application cartridges, OpenShift checks for the existence of the `hot_deploy` marker file. If the `hot_deploy` marker file exists, OpenShift will not stop the cartridges, and changes will be deployed without cartridge restart. Hot deployment is ideal for development, and I recommend that you should always use it during development.

> If you set new environment variables with hot deployment enabled or install new cartridges, you have to restart the application to allow the server to pick the new environment variables.

## See also

- The *Forcing a clean Python virtual environment* recipe
- The *Accessing an application's Python virtual environment* recipe

# Forcing a clean Python virtual environment

The first time you push your changes to the application gear, pip will download all the dependencies mentioned in `setup.py` or `requirements.txt` and populate the virtual environment with these dependencies. On every successive push, OpenShift will reuse the dependencies and will only download new dependencies mentioned in `setup.py` or `requirements.txt`. This makes the application build faster, as it does not have to download dependencies on every `git push`. There are scenarios, such as a corrupt virtual environment, where you will like to recreate the virtual environment and download all the dependencies again. In this recipe, you will learn how you can force OpenShift to recreate the virtual environment.

## Getting ready

This recipe is based on the assumption that you have read the previous recipes in this chapter. To step through this recipe, you will need the rhc command-line client installed on your machine. Please refer to the *Installing the OpenShift rhc command-line client* recipe in *Chapter 1, Getting Started with OpenShift*, for details.

## How to do it...

1. Recreate the application you developed in the *Creating and deploying Flask web applications using Python and PostgreSQL cartridges* recipe by running the following command:

   ```
   $ rhc create-app jobstore python-2.7 postgresql-9.2 --from-code
   https://github.com/OpenShift-Cookbook/chapter8-jobstore-simple.git
   ```

2. Create a marker file named `force_clean_build` in the application's `.openshift/markers` directory. On *nix machines, you can use the `touch` command as follows:

   ```
   $ cd jobstore
   $ touch .openshift/markers/force_clean_build
   ```

3. Commit the file, and push the changes to the OpenShift application gear. From now on, every `git push` will do a clean deployment. This is demonstrated using the following commands:

   ```
   $ git add .
   $ git commit -am "enabled force_clean_build"
   $ git push
   ```

## How it works...

The presence of the `force_clean_build` marker file informs OpenShift that you want to do a clean build. When you do a `git push`, OpenShift will first recreate the virtual environment, activate the environment, and finally download all the dependencies using the pip package manager. You will see the following log message in the `git push` logs:

```
remote: Force clean build enabled - cleaning dependencies
```

## See also

- ▸ The *Enabling hot deployment for Python applications* recipe
- ▸ The *Forcing a clean Python virtual environment* recipe

# Accessing an application's Python virtual environment

By now, you will be aware that every OpenShift Python application has a virtual environment associated with it. Your application will only be able to use the dependencies available in the virtual environment. In this recipe, you will learn how to access the virtual environment of your OpenShift Python application.

## Getting ready

This recipe is based on the assumption that you have read previous recipes in this chapter. To walk through this recipe, you will need the rhc command-line client installed on your machine. Please refer to the *Installing the OpenShift rhc command-line client* recipe in *Chapter 1, Getting Started with OpenShift*, for details. Also, if you want to run the application on your local machine, you will need to have Python, pip, and virtualenv installed on your machine. Please refer to the introduction section for links to installation instructions for the respective software.

## How to do it...

Perform the following steps to access the Python application virtual environment:

1. Recreate the application you developed in the *Creating and deploying Flask web applications using Python and PostgreSQL cartridges* recipe by running the following command:

   ```
   $ rhc create-app jobstore python-2.7 postgresql-9.2 --from-code
   https://github.com/OpenShift-Cookbook/chapter8-jobstore-simple.git
   ```

2. Change the directory to `jobstore`, and then SSH into the application gear by executing the `rhc ssh` command.

3. To access the virtual environment, run the following command:

```
[536fdb88e0b8cd76ee000262]\> . $VIRTUAL_ENV/bin/activate
(virtenv)[536fdb88e0b8cd76ee000262]\>
```

4. Once you are inside the virtual environment, you can manually download the new dependencies using pip. To install a command-line utility called **Yolk**, run the following command. Yolk can list packages installed within an environment.

```
(virtenv)[ 536fdb88e0b8cd76ee000262]\> pip install yolk
```

5. To list all the installed packages in this virtual environment, run the following command. Only part of the output is shown here for brevity.

```
(virtenv)[ 536fdb88e0b8cd76ee000262]\> yolk -l
Babel            - 0.9.6         - active development (/opt/rh/
python27/root/usr/lib/python2.7/site-packages)

Extractor        - 0.6           - active development (/opt/rh/
python27/root/usr/lib/python2.7/site-packages)

Flask-SQLAlchemy - 1.0           - active development (/var/lib/op
enshift/536fdb88e0b8cd76ee000262/app-root/runtime/dependencies/
python/virtenv/lib/python2.7/site-packages)
```

## How it works...

You created a new Python application in step 1 and then connected to the application gear using SSH in step 2 when you used the `rhc ssh` command. The location of the virtual environment is available as an environment variable, `$VIRTUAL_ENV`. You activated the virtual environment in step 3 so that you can use it. Finally, in step 4, you installed a package using the `pip` command manually. After installation, the package becomes available to the application.

## See also

▶ The *Enabling hot deployment for Python applications* recipe

▶ The *Forcing a clean Python virtual environment* recipe

# Using Gevent with Python applications

So far in this chapter, you have used Apache with `mod_wsgi` to run your Python applications. It is also possible to run other standalone WSGI servers, such as Gevent and Gunicorn, with OpenShift. In this recipe, you will learn how to use Gevent to run your Python applications. Gevent is a coroutine-based Python networking library that uses greenlet to provide a high-level, synchronous API on top of the libevent event loop. The source code for this repository is on GitHub at `https://github.com/OpenShift-Cookbook/chapter8-gevent-recipe`.

## Getting ready

This recipe is based on the assumption that you have read the previous recipes in this chapter. To step through this recipe, you will need the rhc command-line client installed on your machine. Please refer to the *Installing the OpenShift rhc command-line client* recipe in *Chapter 1, Getting Started with OpenShift*, for details. Also, if you want to run the application on your local machine, you will need to have Python, pip, and virtualenv installed on your machine. Please refer to the introduction section for links to installation instructions for the respective software.

## How to do it...

Perform the following steps to use Gevent's standalone WSGI server to run OpenShift Python applications:

1. Open a new command-line terminal, and run the following command to create a new Python 2.7 application:

   ```
   $ rhc app create myapp python-2.7
   ```

   If you want to create Python 2.6 or Python 3.3 applications, use Python 2.6 and Python 3.3 respectively.

2. Change the directory to `myapp`, and delete the `setup.py` and `wsgi.py` files as follows:

   ```
   $ cd myapp
   $ rm -f setup.py
   $ rm -f wsgi.py
   ```

3. Create a new virtual environment by running the following command:

   ```
   $ virtualenv venv --python=python2.7
   ```

4. Before you can work with the virtual environment, you have to activate it. To activate the virtual environment, run the following command:

   ```
   $ . venv/bin/activate
   ```

5. Once you have activated virtualenv, you can begin installing modules without affecting the system's default Python interpreter. Install the Flask module by running the following command:

   ```
   $ pip install flask
   ```

6. Create a new Python file named `hello.py` in the `myapp` directory, and populate it with the following code:

   ```
   from flask import Flask
   app = Flask(__name__)
   @app.route('/')
   ```

```
def index():
  return 'Hello World!'

if __name__ == '__main__':
  app.run()
```

7. Next, install the Gevent library, as we want to use it to run our application, as follows:

   **$ pip install gevent**

8. Create a new file named app.py, and add the following code to it:

```
import os
virtenv = os.environ['OPENSHIFT_PYTHON_DIR'] + '/virtenv/'
virtualenv = os.path.join(virtenv, 'bin/activate_this.py')
try:
    execfile(virtualenv, dict(__file__=virtualenv))
except IOError:
    pass

from gevent.wsgi import WSGIServer
from hello import app

ip   = os.environ['OPENSHIFT_PYTHON_IP']
port = int(os.environ['OPENSHIFT_PYTHON_PORT'])

http_server = WSGIServer((ip, port), app)
http_server.serve_forever()
```

9. To deploy this application on OpenShift, we have to declare all the dependencies in requirements.txt. The following command will write all of your application dependencies in requirements.txt:

   **$ pip freeze > requirements.txt**

10. The previous command will populate requirements.txt with all the application dependencies. This includes transitive dependencies as well. The requirements. txt file is shown as follows:

    **Flask==0.10.1**

    **Jinja2==2.7.2**

    **MarkupSafe==0.23**

    **Werkzeug==0.9.4**

    **gevent==1.0.1**

    **greenlet==0.4.2**

    **itsdangerous==0.24**

    **wsgiref==0.1.2**

11. Create a new file named `.gitignore` in the `myapp` directory, and add the `venv` directory to be ignored. We do not want to push the virtual environment to OpenShift, as OpenShift will create the one based on the dependencies mentioned in the `requirements.txt` file. The `.gitignore` file is shown as follows:

```
$ cat .gitignore
venv/
```

12. Now commit the code to the local repository, and then push changes to the application gear. OpenShift will install all the packages specified in `requirements.txt` and make them available to the application via the virtual environment, as follows:

```
$ git add .
$ git commit -am "using Gevent standalone WSGI server"
$ git push
```

13. Now, open the web application URL in your favorite browser to see the application in action. You will be greeted by the **Hello World** text in your browser.

## How it works...

In steps 1 through 6, you created a simple Flask web application as explained in the *Managing Python application dependencies* recipe. As we will use Gevent to run this application, you installed the Gevent library in step 7. In step 8, you created a new Python file, `app.py`. If the user does not use the default `wsgi.py` file or WSGI endpoint configured using the `OPENSHIFT_PYTHON_WSGI_APPLICATION` environment variable, OpenShift uses the server configured in the `app.py` file to serve your application. This Python file should have the name `app` and exist under the app root directory. The code in `app.py` first activates the virtual environment and then starts the Gevent WSGI server at `$OPENSHIFT_PYTHON_IP` and `$OPENSHIFT_PYTHON_PORT`.

In step 9, you used the `pip freeze` command to add all the dependencies in the `requirements.txt` file. OpenShift will download all the dependencies mentioned in this file and populate the application's virtual environment with them.

Finally, you committed the code to the local Git repository and pushed the code to the OpenShift application gear. OpenShift will use the Gevent WSGI server to run your application. You will see a line, as shown in the following command-line output, in the `git push` logs. The following line clearly tells you that OpenShift is using the server configured in `app.py`:

```
remote: Starting Python 2.7 cartridge (app.py server)
```

## There's more...

Similarly, you can use the Tornado web server to serve your Python web applications. Uninstall the Gevent and greenlet libraries, and then install the Tornado library:

```
$ pip uninstall gevent greenlet
$ pip install tornado
```

Update the `requirements.txt` file with dependencies by running the `pip freeze > requirements.txt` command.

In the `app.py` file, replace the Gevent code with the following code:

```
from tornado.wsgi import WSGIContainer
from tornado.httpserver import HTTPServer
from tornado.ioloop import IOLoop
from hello import app

http_server = HTTPServer(WSGIContainer(app))
ip   = os.environ['OPENSHIFT_PYTHON_IP']
port = int(os.environ['OPENSHIFT_PYTHON_PORT'])

http_server.listen(port, ip)
IOLoop.instance().start()
```

Now your application will use the Tornado web server.

## See also

- ▶ The *Creating your first Python application* recipe
- ▶ The *Creating and deploying Flask web applications using Python and PostgreSQL cartridges* recipe

# Installing a custom Python package

Most of the time, your application dependencies can be downloaded from PyPi using pip, but there are times when your application needs to depend on custom libraries that do not exist in the PyPi index. In this recipe, you will learn how to use custom Python packages with your OpenShift Python applications. The source code for this recipe is on GitHub at `https://github.com/OpenShift-Cookbook/chapter8-custom-package-recipe`.

## Getting ready

This recipe is based on the assumption that you have read the previous recipes in this chapter. To walk through this recipe, you will need the rhc command-line client installed on your machine. Please refer to the *Installing the OpenShift rhc command-line client* recipe in *Chapter 1, Getting Started with OpenShift*, for details. Also, if you want to run the application on your local machine, you will need to have Python, pip, and virtualenv installed on your machine. Please refer to the introduction section for links to installation instructions for the respective software.

## How to do it...

1.  Open a new command-line terminal, and run the following command to create a new Python 2.7 application:

    ```
    $ rhc create-app myapp python-2.7
    ```

    If you want to create Python 2.6 or Python 3.3 applications, use Python 2.6 and Python 3.3 respectively.

2.  Change the directory to myapp, and delete the setup.py file as follows:

    ```
    $ cd myapp
    $ rm -f setup.py
    ```

3.  Also, create a .gitignore file to ignore the virtual environment artifacts and Python-compiled files as follows:

    ```
    $ touch .gitignore
    ```

4.  Add the following lines to it:

    ```
    venv

    *.pyc
    ```

5.  Create a new virtual environment and activate it by running the following commands:

    ```
    $ virtualenv venv --python=python2.7
    $ . venv/bin/activate
    ```

6.  Once you have activated virtualenv, you can begin installing modules without affecting the system's default Python interpreter. Install the Flask module by running the following command:

    ```
    $ pip install flask
    ```

7.  Create a new directory named libs in the application root, as shown in the following code. The libs directory will be used to store your custom packages:

    ```
    $ mkdir libs
    ```

8. Now, we will create a custom package named `msgs` in the `libs` directory.
   To create a custom package, perform the following steps:

   1. Create an `msgs` directory inside the `libs` directory.

   2. Create an empty file named `__init__.py` inside the `msgs` directory.

   3. Create another file named `hello.py` inside the `msgs` directory, and place
      the following code inside it:

      ```
      def hello():
          return 'Hello World'
      ```

9. Next, create a new Python file named `myapp.py` in the `myapp` directory, and
   populate it with the following code. This simple Flask application will use the
   `msgs` package. Have a look at the following code:

   ```
   from flask import Flask
   import msgs.hello as hello
   app = Flask(__name__)
   @app.route('/')
   def index():
     return hello.hello()
   if __name__ == '__main__':
     app.run(debug=True)
   ```

10. Now, you need to update the `wsgi.py` file to load the Flask application instead of
    the default created by OpenShift. Delete all the content in the `wsgi.py` file, and
    replace it with the following code:

    ```
    #!/usr/bin/python
    import os
    virtenv = os.environ['OPENSHIFT_PYTHON_DIR'] + '/virtenv/'
    virtualenv = os.path.join(virtenv, 'bin/activate_this.py')
    try:
        execfile(virtualenv, dict(__file__=virtualenv))
    except IOError:
        pass

    from myapp import app as application
    ```

11. To deploy this application on OpenShift, we have to declare all the dependencies
    in `requirements.txt`. The following command will write all of your application
    dependencies in `requirements.txt`:

    ```
    $ pip freeze > requirements.txt
    ```

12. Now, commit the code to the local repository, and then push changes to the application gear. OpenShift will install all the packages specified in `requirements.txt` and make them available to the application via the virtual environment:

```
$ git add .
$ git commit -am "application with custom package"
$ git push
```

13. Now, open the web application URL in your favorite browser to see the application in action. You will be greeted by the **Hello World** text in your browser.

## How it works...

In the preceding steps, you learned how to use the `libs` directory to store your custom packages. The `libs` directory is an example of how OpenShift uses convention over configuration. The phrase *convention over configuration* means that if you follow certain conventions, you do not have to write the configuration code. OpenShift follows a convention that all the packages in the `libs` directory should be placed in the path so that your application can use them. In step 6, you created a custom package named `msgs` in the `libs` directory, and without any configuration, your application could access the package.

## There's more...

Now, let's suppose that you want to use the `mydeps` directory to store your custom packages. For your application to work, you have to write code in your application to add the `mydeps` directory to the system path. Adding two lines in the application's `wsgi.py` file can solve this problem. The full application source code is on GitHub at `https://github.com/OpenShift-Cookbook/chapter8-custom-package-mydeps-recipe`. Have a look at the following code:

```
import os,sys
sys.path.append(os.path.join(os.getenv("OPENSHIFT_REPO_DIR"),
"mydeps"))
```

The previous two lines will add the `mydeps` directory to the application's system path.

## See also

▶ The *Creating your first Python application* recipe
▶ The *Creating and deploying Flask web applications using Python and PostgreSQL cartridges* recipe

# Using the .htaccess file to configure Apache

By now, you will be aware that OpenShift uses Apache with `mod_wsgi` to serve your web applications. In this recipe, you will learn to use the `.htaccess` and `.htpasswd` files to configure the Apache web server for the HTTP basic authentication. The GitHub repository for this recipe is `https://github.com/OpenShift-Cookbook/chapter8-htaccess-recipe`.

## Getting ready

This recipe is based on the assumption that you have read the previous recipes in this chapter. To walk through this recipe, you will need the rhc command-line client installed on your machine. Please refer to the *Installing the OpenShift rhc command-line client* recipe in *Chapter 1, Getting Started with OpenShift*, for details.

## How to do it...

Perform the following steps to enable the HTTP basic authentication:

1. Create a new Python 2.7 application using the rhc command-line tool:

   ```
   $ rhc create-app myapp python-2.7
   ```

2. Change the directory to `myapp`, and create two files, `.htaccess` and `.htpasswd`, in the `myapp` directory. If you are using a *nix machine, you can use the `touch` command. On a Windows machine, you can use file explorer to create files. Have a look at the following commands:

   ```
   $ cd myapp
   $ touch .htaccess
   $ touch .htpasswd
   ```

3. In `.htaccess`, copy and paste the content as shown in the following code:

   ```
   AuthType Basic
   AuthName "Authentication Required"
   AuthUserFile "$OPENSHIFT_REPO_DIR/.htpasswd"
   Require valid-user
   ```

   Replace $OPENSHIFT_REPO_DIR with the $OPENSHIFT_REPO_DIR location of your application. To get the value of $OPENSHIFT_REPO_DIR, run the following command:

   ```
   $ rhc ssh --command 'echo $OPENSHIFT_REPO_DIR'
   ```

4. The `.htpasswd` file is used to store username and password credentials. To generate a new username and password, you can use the online generator at `http://www.htaccesstools.com/htpasswd-generator/`. For this recipe, the username and password combination is `admin` and `password` respectively. Place the content generated by the online tool in the `.htpasswd` file. My `.htpasswd` file looks as follows:

**admin:$apr1$EVxfKxv/$2BIOIAPHOZiyx4k52b5jT1ewdfg**

5. Commit the code, and push the changes to the application gear:

```
$ git add .
$ git commit -am "added .htaccess and .htpasswd"
$ git push
```

6. After the application is deployed, open the application URL in your favorite web browser. This time, you will be greeted by a pop up asking you to enter the username and password, as shown in the following screenshot:

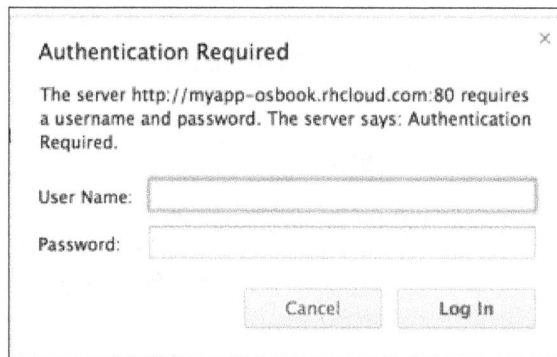

7. After entering the `admin`/`password` combination, you will be able to enter your web application.

## How it works...

This recipe is another example of the flexibility that OpenShift offers to the application developers. There are a couple of ways you can configure the Apache web server. One way to configure the Apache web server is to update the main configuration file, usually named `httpd.conf`. OpenShift does not allow users to update the `httpd.conf` file. OpenShift allows users to configure the Apache web server via the `.htaccess` file. The `.htaccess` file provides a way to make configuration changes on a per-directory basis. This file can contain one or more configuration directives. These directives will then be applied to the directory in which the `.htaccess` file exists and all its subdirectories.

In step 1, you created a new Python 2.7 application with the name myapp. Then, in step 2, you created a couple of files—.htaccess and .htpasswd—in the myapp directory. In step 3, you updated the content of the .htaccess file with the HTTP basic authentication configuration. You can learn more from the documentation at http://httpd.apache.org/docs/2.2/howto/auth.html.

Next, in step 4, you generated content for the .htpasswd file using an online .htpasswd generator. You placed the content generated by generator in the .htpasswd file and then committed all the changes in step 5. On successful deployment, you opened the application URL in the browser in step 6. You were asked to enter the admin/password username/password credentials. On entering the valid username/password combination, you were allowed to enter the application in step 7.

## See also

- The *Creating your first Python application* recipe
- The *Creating and deploying Flask web applications using Python and PostgreSQL cartridges* recipe

# 9
# OpenShift for Node.js Developers

This chapter presents a number of recipes that will help you get started with Node.js web application development on OpenShift. The specific recipes of this chapter are:

- ▶ Creating your first Node.js application
- ▶ Configuring Node supervisor options
- ▶ Managing Node.js application dependencies
- ▶ Using the use_npm marker
- ▶ Enabling hot deployment for Node.js applications
- ▶ Creating and deploying Express web applications using Node.js and MongoDB cartridges
- ▶ Working with Web Sockets
- ▶ Using CoffeeScript with OpenShift Node.js applications

# Introduction

Node.js is a server-side JavaScript platform built on top of Google's Chrome V8 JavaScript engine that developers can use to write applications. These applications can be web applications, command-line utilities, or scripts to automate tasks. Node.js is a very popular choice for web application development, as it allows web developers to use a single programming language, such as JavaScript, on both the client side and the server side. It is suitable for building highly concurrent, data-intensive, real-time web applications because of its asynchronous, event-driven, non-blocking I/O nature. Node has a small core that provides the basic building block APIs to write higher-level frameworks. The developers can then use the web frameworks to build their awesome web applications.

There are many web frameworks, such as Express (`http://expressjs.com/`), Sails.
js (`http://sailsjs.org/`), Restify (`http://mcavage.me/node-restify/`), and
Geddy (`http://geddyjs.org/`), developed by the Node community that developers can
use for their web applications. Many big tech giants, such as LinkedIn, Walmart (`http://
venturebeat.com/2012/01/24/why-walmart-is-using-node-js/`), and Yahoo,
are using Node.js for their production applications.

OpenShift provides web developers a hosting platform to deploy their Node.js web
applications. You can run applications built using any of the Node.js web frameworks, such
as Express or Geddy, on OpenShift. At the time of writing this book, OpenShift supports two
versions of Node.js—0.6 and 0.10. The following command shows the currently supported
Node.js versions:

```
$ rhc cartridges | grep node
nodejs-0.10          Node.js 0.10                            web
nodejs-0.6           Node.js 0.6                             web
```

> The Node Version 0.6 cartridge will get deprecated in the future, so
> you are advised not to use it for your web applications. This book will
> only cover Version 0.10.

The *Creating your first Node.js application* recipe will walk you through creating your first
OpenShift Node.js web application. We will look into the template application created by
OpenShift and then write a simple HTTP server using Node's HTTP module and deploy it
to OpenShift.

The Node.js web applications are very different from the traditional web applications that you
might have written so far. The web applications themselves are web servers, so you do not
need Apache or any other web server to host your web application. There are various ways to
fire up Node applications, such as using the commands `node <app script file>` and
`npm start`, `supervisor <app script file>`. OpenShift uses a Node module called
**node-supervisor** to run your application. The node-supervisor module (`https://github.
com/isaacs/node-supervisor`) runs the Node application and watches for any changes.
Once it detects changes, it restarts the application. In the *Configuring Node supervisor
options* recipe, you will learn how to customize a few supervisor options to take advantage
of the hot reloading behavior. The alternative to using supervisor is to use the `npm start`
command to run Node applications. You can configure OpenShift Node.js applications to use
`npm start` instead of `supervisor` by using a marker file. This will be covered in the *Using
the use_npm marker* recipe.

In the *Managing Node.js application dependencies* recipe, you will learn how OpenShift uses
`npm` to install and manage your application dependencies.

The example application in this chapter will be developed using the Express web framework and MongoDB database. The *Creating and deploying Express web applications using Node.js and MongoDB cartridges* recipe will walk you through all the steps required to build and deploy Express web applications on OpenShift. All the source code for this chapter is available on the OpenShift Cookbook GitHub organization (`https://github.com/OpenShift-Cookbook`).

Node.js is very popular for building real-time web applications using Web Sockets. In the *Working with Web Sockets* recipe, you will build a simple, real-time application using the Node Socket.IO library.

Instead of using JavaScript to write Node applications, developers can also use CoffeeScript to write their Node applications. CoffeeScript compiles to JavaScript and is a popular choice among developers who don't like to use JavaScript. The *Using CoffeeScript with OpenShift Node.js applications* recipe will cover this in detail.

To run the example applications that you will develop in this chapter on your local machine, you will need to install Node on your operating system. You can get the latest installer of Node.js for your operating system from the official website, `http://nodejs.org/download/`. The installer will also install npm for you. This chapter will also use the MongoDB database. You can get the latest installer of MongoDB for your operating system from their official website (`http://www.mongodb.org/downloads`).

This chapter assumes that you are comfortable with Node web development basics, OpenShift application basics, and how to work with OpenShift database cartridges. If you are not comfortable with these topics, I recommend you first read *Chapter 3*, *Creating and Managing Applications*, and *Chapter 6*, *Using MongoDB and Third-party Database Cartridges with OpenShift Applications*, before continuing with this chapter.

# Creating your first Node.js application

In this recipe, you will learn how to create your first OpenShift Node.js application using the rhc command-line tool. After understanding the template application created by OpenShift, you will write a `Hello World` Node.js application using Node's HTTP module.

## Getting ready

To complete this recipe, you will need the rhc command-line client installed on your machine. Please refer to the *Installing the OpenShift rhc command-line client* recipe in *Chapter 1*, *Getting Started with OpenShift*, for details. This application will consume one gear, so if you don't have an extra gear available for this recipe, use the `rhc delete-app <app_name> --confirm` command to delete an existing application. To run this application on your local machine, you will need Node installed on your machine. You can get the latest installer of Node.js for your operating system from the official website, `http://nodejs.org/download/`.

## How to do it...

Perform the following steps to create your first OpenShift Node.js application:

1. Open a new command-line terminal, and change the directory to a convenient location where you want to create the application. To create a Node.js 0.10 application, run the following command:

   ```
   $ rhc create-app myapp nodejs-0.10
   ```

2. Open your favorite web browser, and go to `http://myapp-{domain-name}.rhcloud.com` to view the application. Please replace `{domain-name}` with your OpenShift account domain name.

3. The template application created by OpenShift is an Express web framework application. You can use your own template application by specifying your public Git repository using the `--from-code` option. This was covered in the *Specifying your own template Git repository URL* recipe in *Chapter 3, Creating and Managing Applications*. In this recipe, you don't need the template code generated by OpenShift, so delete all the files and directories created by OpenShift except the `.openshift` directory. On the *nix machine, you can use the `rm` command to delete the files as shown in the following command. On Windows, you can use file explorer or the command-line equivalent to delete these files.

   ```
   $ cd myapp
   $ rm -rf deplist.txt index.html node_modules/ package.json server.js
   ```

4. Create a new empty file named `server.js` in the application root directory. On *nix machines, you can use the `touch` command to create a new file. On Windows machines, you can use file explorer to create the new file. Run the following command:

   ```
   $ touch server.js
   ```

   Open the file in your favorite editor, and populate it with the following code:

   ```
   var http = require('http');
   var ip = process.env.OPENSHIFT_NODEJS_IP || '127.0.0.1';
   var port = process.env.OPENSHIFT_NODEJS_PORT || 3000;
   var server = http.createServer(function(req,res){
       res.writeHead(200, {'Content-Type':'text/plain'});
       res.end('Hello World!!');
   });
   server.listen(port,ip);
   console.log('Server running at http://%s:%d',ip,port);
   ```

5.  To run the application on your local machine, run the following command:

    ```
    $ node server.js
    ```

    To see the application in action, open the `http://127.0.0.1:3000` in your favorite browser. You will see the **Hello World!!** message rendered in your browser.

6.  To deploy the application on OpenShift, commit the code to the local Git repository, and then push the changes to the application gear:

    ```
    $ git add .
    $ git commit -am "Hello World Node.js application"
    $ git push
    ```

7.  After successful deployment, open the `http://myapp-{domain-name}.rhcloud.com` in your favorite browser. The browser will render **Hello World!!**.

## How it works...

In the previous steps, you created a `Hello World` Node.js application from scratch and deployed it on OpenShift. The `Hello World` application that you wrote in the aforementioned steps is no different from the one you will write if you want to run this application on your local machine or elsewhere. There is no OpenShift-specific apart from the environment variables.

In step 1, you created an OpenShift Node.js 0.10 application using the rhc command-line tool. The `rhc create-app` command will make an HTTP POST request to the OpenShift broker. The OpenShift broker will accept the request and then initiate the application creation process. You specified that OpenShift should create a Node.js 0.10 application with `myapp` as the application name. OpenShift will use these details along with a few defaults to create the `myapp` application. The defaults include small gear size, non-scalable application, and using the current directory to clone the Git repository. OpenShift behind the scenes did the following:

▶  OpenShift created a new application gear with the Node.js cartridge.

▶  It created a private Git repository for your application and populated it with a template application. The template application that OpenShift creates is an Express web framework application.

▶  It installed a Git action hook that will build the application. During the application build phase, it will download all the dependencies mentioned in `package.json` using the `npm install` command.

▶  It created a public DNS for your application so that it is accessible from the outside world.

After successful application creation, you will have the `myapp` directory inside the current directory. You can view the application by opening the application URL in your browser as mentioned in step 2. The application creation process was explained in detail in the *Creating an OpenShift application using the rhc command-line client* recipe in *Chapter 3, Creating and Managing Applications*.

Now, let's look at the template application created by OpenShift:

```
$ cd myapp && ls -ap
.git/          README.md      index.html     package.json
.openshift/    deplist.txt    node_modules/  server.js
```

The template application has five files—`README.md`, `index.html`, `package.json`, `deplist.txt`, and `server.js`—and the `node_modules` directory apart from the `.openshift` and `.git` directories. We have already talked about `.openshift` and `.git` in the *Creating an OpenShift application using the rhc command-line client* recipe in *Chapter 3, Creating and Managing Applications*, so I will not cover them here. Let's talk about the others one by one:

- `README.md`: This is a standard Git repository markdown file where you can summarize your project. GitHub uses `README.md` to generate the HTML summary of the project.

- `index.html`: This file contains the HTML markup that you will see when you view the application in the browser. This is an HTML 5 file with Twitter Bootstrap styling.

- `package.json`: This is your Node application descriptor. This is a JSON document that contains all the information about your application, such as name, description, version, and libraries, that this application depends on. The full documentation is available at `https://www.npmjs.org/doc/json.html`.

- `deplists.txt`: This is a deprecated method to specify application dependencies in OpenShift Node.js applications. It is recommended not to use it, as this may get removed in the future. This file only exists for backward compatibility so that the application that uses it keeps running.

- `server.js`: This file houses the template Express web framework application created by OpenShift. This application exposes a couple of routes, `/` and `/asciimo`. The `/` route renders `index.html`, and the second route renders an HTML page with images. The Express application will be covered in detail in the *Creating and deploying Express web applications using Node.js and MongoDB cartridges* recipe, so we will not cover it in this recipe.

- `node_modules`: This directory houses all the application dependencies you specify in `package.json`. The `npm install` command will download all the dependencies in the `node_modules` directory.

The template application generated by OpenShift is a standard Express web application. To run this application on your local machine, you can run the following commands:

```
$ npm install
$ node server.js
```

The application will be running at `http://127.0.0.1:8080/`. The previous two commands did the following:

▸ The `npm install` command downloads all the dependencies mentioned in the `package.json` file. The template application mentions `express` as its dependency, so the `npm install` command will download Express and all its transitive dependencies in the `node_modules` directory.

▸ As mentioned in the introduction section, in Node, the server and the application are the same. So, you used the `node server.js` command to fire up the application's server. This starts the HTTP server, and you can start making requests.

The `node server.js` command is one way to fire up the application. The other alternatives to start the application are the `npm start` and `supervisor server.js` commands. The `npm start` command will run the package start script if one was provided. The start script can be mentioned in the `package.json` file:

```
"scripts":{"start":"node server.js"}
```

If the `package.json` file does not contain the start script, the `npm start` command will use the `node server.js` command as the default start script.

OpenShift, by default, does not use the `npm start` or `node <server script>` command to run your application. It uses a module called node-supervisor to run the application. You can configure OpenShift Node applications to use the `npm start` command instead of node-supervisor. This will be covered in the *Using the use_npm marker* recipe. The main advantage of using the supervisor is that it can restart the application when they crash. Also, you can use the supervisor to achieve the hot reloading behavior. It can monitor a set of directories and files and restart the application when code changes.

If you want to use node-supervisor on your local machine, you can install the node-supervisor module using the following command:

```
$ npm install supervisor -g
```

Now you can start the application using the `supervisor server.js` command. This will restart the application every time you make changes to your source code. This can be very useful during the development time, as it will save the time required to restart the application.

In step 3, you deleted the template source code generated by OpenShift so that you can write a simple HTTP server from scratch. In step 4, you created a new file named `server.js` and populated it with the `Hello World` Node.js code. The code listing in step 4 does the following:

▸ You imported the Node HTTP module using the `require()` function. This will be used to write the server.

- ▸ Then, you created two variables to hold the IP address and port. If the application runs on a local machine, OpenShift-specific environment variables will not be available. Hence, the IP and port will be `127.0.0.1` and 3000 respectively.

- ▸ Next, you created the HTTP server using the HTTP module `createServer()` function. You passed a callback that will be fired whenever a request happens. The callback function accepts two arguments—request and response—and writes `Hello World` to the response.

- ▸ Finally, you instructed the server to listen on the IP and port variables.

In step 5, you tested the `Hello World` application on the local machine by running the `node server.js` command. To deploy the application on OpenShift, you committed the code to the local Git repository and pushed the changes to the application gear in step 6.

When you push the source code to the OpenShift Node.js application Git repository, OpenShift will do the following:

- ▸ First, all the bits are pushed to the application Git repository.

- ▸ Then, if the `package.json` file is present, and this is the first time you are pushing the source code, it will download all the dependencies mentioned in `package.json`. On every subsequent push, only new dependencies that are already not present will be downloaded. All existing node modules will be cached.

- ▸ OpenShift will run the application using one of the three commands mentioned in the subsequent list. This will change when the `use_npm` marker file is present and will be covered in the *Using the use_npm marker* recipe.

    - ❑ If `package.json` is not present, OpenShift will run the `supervisor server.js` command.

    - ❑ If `package.json` is present and the name of the main file in the application is `server.js`, OpenShift will run the `supervisor server.js` command. The name of the main file is mentioned in the `package.json` main element.

    - ❑ If `package.json` is present and the name of the main file in the application is something other than `server.js` (like app.js), OpenShift will run the `supervisor app.js` command.

As you did not include `package.json`, OpenShift will run the application using the `supervisor server.js` command. Once the application is started, you can open the application URL in the browser, and you will be greeted with **HelloWorld!!** as shown in step 7.

## See also

- ▶ The *Configuring Node supervisor options* recipe
- ▶ The *Enabling hot deployment for Node.js applications* recipe
- ▶ The *Managing Node.js application dependencies* recipe

# Configuring Node supervisor options

As mentioned in the *Creating your first Node.js application* recipe, OpenShift uses the node-supervisor module to run your programs. In this recipe, you will learn how you can configure node-supervisor options. If you have the node-supervisor module installed on your machine, you can see all the supported options by running the following command. You can install node-supervisor by executing the `npm install supervisor -g` command. The help option can be viewed using the following command:

```
$ supervisor --help
```

OpenShift allows you to configure the node-supervisor watch and poll-interval options. The watch option allows you to specify a comma-delimited list of folders or JavaScript files that the supervisor watches for changes. The poll-interval option allows you to specify how often the supervisor should poll for changes.

## Getting ready

To complete this recipe, you will need the rhc command-line client installed on your machine. Please refer to the *Installing the OpenShift rhc command-line client* recipe in *Chapter 1, Getting Started with OpenShift*, for details. This application will consume one gear, so if you don't have an extra gear available for this recipe, use the `rhc delete app <app_name> --confirm` command to delete an existing application. To run this application on your local machine, you will need Node installed on your machine. You can get the latest installer of Node.js for your operating system from the official website, `http://nodejs.org/download/`.

## How to do it...

Perform the following steps to configure supervisor options:

1. If you don't already have a Node.js application running, create a new application by executing the following command. This will create the application you created in the *Creating your first Node.js application* recipe.

   ```
   $ rhc create-app myapp nodejs-0.10 --from-code https://github.com/
   OpenShift-Cookbook/chapter9-recipe1.git
   ```

2. Change the directory to `myapp`, and create two environment variables to configure the supervisor poll interval and directories to watch.

```
$ cd myapp
```

```
$ rhc env-set OPENSHIFT_NODEJS_POLL_INTERVAL=60000 OPENSHIFT_
NODEJS_WATCH=$OPENSHIFT_REPO_DIR --app myapp
```

Replace the `$OPENSHIFT_REPO_DIR` variable with the value of your application's `$OPENSHIFT_REPO_DIR` environment variable. You can get the value of `$OPENSHIFT_REPO_DIR` by running the following command:

```
$ rhc ssh --command "env |grep OPENSHIFT_REPO_DIR"
```

3. Restart the application to allow it to pick the new environment variables:

```
$ rhc restart-app --app myapp
```

## How it works...

The node-supervisor module helps OpenShift to restart Node applications when they die. This is very helpful for developers, as they do not have to restart the application themselves if applications can recover after restart. Another useful feature of node-supervisor is its support for hot reload. You can tell node-supervisor to watch directories or files, and when they change, the application will be restarted. This gives the hot reloading behavior.

In step 2, you created two environment variables that OpenShift exposes to configure the hot reloading behavior. The `OPENSHIFT_NODEJS_WATCH` environment variable allows you to specify a comma-delimited list of folders or JavaScript files that the supervisor should watch for changes. You told the supervisor to monitor the `$OPENSHIFT_REPO_DIR` variable. The `OPENSHIFT_NODEJS_POLL_INTERVAL` environment variable allows you to specify in milliseconds how often the supervisor should poll for changes. The default value for polling is 10 seconds. You told the supervisor to poll `$OPENSHIFT_REPO_DIR` every 60 seconds.

The node-supervisor hot reloading behavior is not suitable for the `git push` deployment model but can be useful if you use OpenShift SFTP support (`https://www.openshift.com/blogs/getting-started-with-sftp-and-openshift`). The reason it is not suitable for the `git push` deployment model is that you are already pushing the code to application gear, which will update the `$OPENSHIFT_REPO_DIR` variable with new code and restart the application. The preferred way to use hot deployment with `git push` is by using the `hot_deploy` marker file. This is explained in the *Enabling hot deployment for Node. js applications* recipe. To see hot reload in action, we will SSH into the application gear and change the source code as follows:

1. SSH into the OpenShift application gear using the `rhc ssh` command. Instead of SSH, you can also use the SFTP client to connect with the application gear, as mentioned in the following blog: `https://www.openshift.com/blogs/using-filezilla-and-sftp-on-windows-with-openshift`.

2.  Once connected, change the directory to the `app-root/repo` directory:

    ```
    $ cd app-root/repo
    ```

3.  Open the `server.js` file using `vim` and change `"Hello World!!"` to `"Hello OpenShift User!!"` and save the file.

4.  In the next polling cycle, the supervisor will detect the change and restart the application. You can view your change by opening the application URL in your favorite browser.

## See also

▸   The *Creating your first Node.js application* recipe

▸   The *Enabling hot deployment for Node.js applications* recipe

▸   The *Managing Node.js application dependencies* recipe

# Managing Node.js application dependencies

So far in this chapter, you didn't have to use any third-party library. The applications that you developed were simple `Hello World` applications that didn't require any third-party library to do their work. In real applications, you have to use libraries written by others. Node makes it very easy for developers to consume third-party libraries using npm. npm is the package manager for Node.js that comes bundled with Node. It is a command-line tool that allows you to publish new modules, downloads existing modules from the npm registry, and installs third-party modules. In this recipe, you will write another simple application, but that will use the Express framework. The goal of the recipe was to introduce you to the Node dependency management without getting bogged down by the application details.

## Getting ready

To complete this recipe, you will need the rhc command-line client installed on your machine. Please refer to the *Installing the OpenShift rhc command-line client* recipe in *Chapter 1, Getting Started with OpenShift*, for details. This application will consume one gear, so if you don't have an extra gear available for this recipe, use the `rhc delete app <app_name> --confirm` command to delete an existing application. To run this application on your local machine, you will need Node installed on your machine. You can get the latest installer of Node.js for your operating system from the official website (`http://nodejs.org/download/`).

## How to do it...

In this recipe, you will create a `Hello World` Express framework web application from scratch. Perform the following steps to create the application:

1. Recreate the application created in the *Creating your first Node.js application* recipe by executing the following command:

   ```
   $ rhc app create myapp nodejs-0.10 --from-code https://github.com/
   OpenShift-Cookbook/chapter9-recipe1.git
   ```

2. Create a new file in the application root directory named `package.json`. The `package.json` file is an application descriptor file that you can use to define application metadata and its dependencies.

   ```
   {
     "name": "myapp",
     "description": "My OpenShift Node.js Application",
     "version": "0.0.1"
   }
   ```

3. The application will use the Express web framework, so install the express dependency using the following command:

   ```
   $ npm install express --save
   ```

   This will download the Express framework module and its dependencies in the `node_modules` directory and populate the `package.json` file with express dependency, as shown in the following code:

   ```
   {
     "name": "myapp",
     "description": "My OpenShift Node.js Application",
     "version": "0.0.1",
     "dependencies": {
       "express": "~4.3.1"
     }
   }
   ```

4. Replace the code in `server.js` with the following code:

   ```
   var express = require('express');
   var ip = process.env.OPENSHIFT_NODEJS_IP || '127.0.0.1';
   var port = process.env.OPENSHIFT_NODEJS_PORT || 3000;
   var app = express();
   app.get('/',function(req,res){
       res.send('Hello World!!');
   });
   app.listen(port,ip);
   console.log('Server running at http://%s:%d',ip,port);
   ```

5. Add the `node_modules` directory to the `.gitignore` file. We are adding the `node_modules` directory to `.gitignore` to allow OpenShift to download all the dependencies using npm. If you don't add `node_modules` to `.gitignore`, OpenShift will not download the dependencies but use dependencies from your `node_modules` directory:

```
$ echo "node_modules/" > .gitignore
```

6. Commit the code, and push the changes to the application gear:

```
$ git add .
$ git commit -am "used express"
$ git push
```

After the application is successfully built and deployed, you will see the application running at `http://myapp-{domain-name}.rhcloud.comhttp://myapp-{domain-name}.rhcloud.com`.

## How it works...

Almost all real applications need to depend on third-party frameworks or libraries to do their work. In the following steps, you created a very simple Express web application.

In step 1, you recreated the application created in the *Creating your first Node.js application* recipe. As the example application in this recipe needs to use the Express web framework, we have to declare the dependency in `package.json`. In step 2, you created a minimalistic `package.json` file with just the name, description, and version number. Then in step 3, you ran the `npm install` command to install Express and all its transitive dependencies. All the modules will be downloaded to the `node_modules` directory. The `--save` option tells npm to update the `package.json` file with the Express dependency.

In step 4, you replaced the content of `server.js` with the Express application code. The code listing in step 4 does the following:

▸ You imported the Node Express module using the `require()` function.

▸ Then, you created two variables to hold the IP address and port. If the application runs on the local machine, OpenShift's specific environment variables will not be available; hence, the IP address and port will be `127.0.0.1` and 3000.

▸ Then, you created a new application instance by calling the `express()` function.

▸ Now you defined a new route for the root URL. In this case, an HTTP GET request to / will respond with `Hello World`.

▸ Finally, you instructed the server to bind and listen on the IP and port variables for incoming connections.

In step 5, you told Git to ignore the `node_modules` directory by adding an entry to the `.gitignore` file. The reason you did that is to allow OpenShift to download the dependencies mentioned in `package.json`. This makes your Git repository light as well. If you commit the `node_modules` directory, OpenShift will not download the dependencies and use the modules in the `node_modules` directory. You can choose either of the two options, and OpenShift will just work. There is a lot of debate on this topic in the Node community, and different people have different opinions. You can refer to the following blog for a detailed discussion on this topic: `http://www.futurealoof.com/posts/nodemodules-in-git.html`.

Finally, in step 6, you committed the code to the local Git repository and pushed the changes to the application gear. OpenShift will first download all the dependencies (and their transitive dependencies) mentioned in `package.json`, as shown in the following code snippet, and then restart the application with updated code using the supervisor `server.js` command:

```
remote: npm http GET https://registry.npmjs.org/express

remote: npm http 200 https://registry.npmjs.org/express

remote: npm info retry fetch attempt 1 at 12:45:38

remote: npm http GET https://registry.npmjs.org/express/-/express-
4.3.1.tgz

remote: npm http 200 https://registry.npmjs.org/express/-/express-
4.3.1.tgz

...
```

## There's more...

In the *Creating your first Node.js application* recipe, I mentioned that when you push the changes to the OpenShift application gear, OpenShift checks for the existence of the `package.json` file. If the `package.json` file exists, OpenShift uses the value of the main field as the primary entry point to your application. As you didn't define the main field in `package.json`, OpenShift will use `server.js` as the default entry point. Let's suppose you renamed the `server.js` to `app.js`. Then, to make this run on OpenShift, you will have to create an entry for the main field, as shown in the following code snippet:

```
{
    "name": "myapp",
    "description": "My OpenShift Node.js Application",
    "version": "0.0.1",
    "dependencies": {
        "express": "~4.3.1"
    },
    "main":"app.js"
}
```

## See also

▸ The *Creating your first Node.js application* recipe

▸ The *Using the use_npm marker* recipe

# Using the use_npm marker

OpenShift uses the node-supervisor module to run your Node apps, but you can also tell OpenShift to use the `npm start` command to run the application. In this recipe, you will learn how to do that.

## Getting ready

To complete this recipe, you will need the rhc command-line client installed on your machine. Please refer to the *Installing the OpenShift rhc command-line client* recipe in *Chapter 1, Getting Started with OpenShift*, for details. This application will consume one gear, so if you don't have an extra gear available for this recipe, use the `rhc delete app <app_name> --confirm` command to delete an existing application. To run this application on your local machine, you will need Node installed on your machine. You can get the latest installer of Node.js for your operating system from their official website (`http://nodejs.org/download/`).

## How to do it...

Perform the following steps to use the `npm start` command to run your applications:

1. Open a new command-line terminal, and recreate the application you created in the *Managing Node.js application dependencies* recipe as follows:

   ```
   $ rhc create-app myapp nodejs-0.10 --from-code https://github.com/
   OpenShift-Cookbook/chapter9-recipe3.git
   ```

2. Create a marker file named `use_npm` inside the `.openshift/markers` directory. On the *nix machine, you can use the `touch` command as shown in the following code. On Windows, you can use file explorer to create an empty file.

   ```
   $ cd myapp
   $ touch .openshift/markers/use_npm
   ```

3. Commit the code, and push the changes to the application gear:

   ```
   $ git add .
   $ git commit -am "using use_npm marker"
   $ git push
   ```

4. The `git push` logs will clearly mention that the application is started using the `npm start` command:

```
remote: *** NodeJS supervisor is disabled due to .openshift/
markers/use_npm

remote: *** Starting application using: npm start -d
```

## How it works...

In step 1, you created an Express framework web application that we created in the *Managing Node.js application dependencies* recipe. The application just has two files—`server.js` and `package.json`. The `server.js` file contains the application source code, and `package.json` contains the application metadata and its dependencies.

Then, in step 2, you created a marker file, `use_npm`. The presence of the `use_npm` marker file tells OpenShift that you want to use the `npm start` command to run the application instead of the `node-supervisor` module. The `npm start` command gives developers more flexibility to run their applications. It allows developers to specify their own start script in `package.json`, which OpenShift will use to run their application. The `package.json` is shown as follows:

```
{
  "name": "myapp",
  "description": "My OpenShift Node.js Application",
  "version": "0.0.1",
  "dependencies": {
    "express": "~4.3.1"
  }
}
```

As you can see in the previous listing, it does not mention any start script. When there is no start script in the `package.json` file, OpenShift will fall back to `node server.js` as the start script:

```
"scripts": {"start": "node server.js"}
```

This is the reason the application successfully started in step 4 after `git push`.

Now let's suppose that you want to rename `server.js` to `app.js`. If you commit the source code now and push the changes, the application will fail to start. You will see the following message in the `git push` logs:

```
remote: *** NodeJS supervisor is disabled due to .openshift/markers/use_
npm

remote: *** Starting application using: npm start -d

remote: Application 'myapp' failed to start 1
```

To make this application run again, you have to specify the start script as shown:

```
{
  "name": "myapp",
  "description": "My OpenShift Node.js Application",
  "version": "0.0.1",
  "dependencies": {
    "express": "~4.3.1"
  },
"scripts":{"start":"node app.js"}
}
```

## See also

▸ The *Creating and deploying Express web applications using Node.js and MongoDB cartridges* recipe

▸ The *Managing Node.js application dependencies* recipe

# Enabling hot deployment for Node.js applications

In this recipe, you will learn how you can enable hot deployment for Node.js applications.

## How to do it...

Perform the following steps to enable hot deployment for your application:

1. Create a new Node.js application using the source code developed in the previous recipe:

   ```
   $ rhc app create myapp nodejs-0.10 --from-code https://github.com/
   OpenShift-Cookbook/chapter9-recipe3.git
   ```

2. To enable hot deployment, create an empty file named hot_deploy under the .openshift/markers directory. This file is called the marker file, as this does not contain any content. On the *nix machine, you can use the touch command to create the file. On Windows, you can use file explorer to create a new file. If you are not in the myapp directory, first change directory to myapp. Have a look at the following commands:

   ```
   $ cd myapp
   ```

   ```
   $ touch .openshift/markers/hot_deploy
   ```

3. Add the file to the Git index, commit the file to the local Git repository, and then push changes to the application gear by typing the commands as shown:

```
$ git commit -am "enabled hot deployment"

$git push
```

4. In the `git push` logs, you will see a message that cartridges are not stopped because hot deployment is enabled:

```
remote: Not stopping cartridge node.js because hot deploy is
enabled
```

## How it works...

Every time you make a change and push it to the OpenShift application gear, OpenShift first stops your gear (that is, all cartridges), copies the source code from your application Git repo to `app-root/runtime/repo`, performs a build, prepares the artifact, and finally starts your gear (that is, all cartridges). This process takes time and does not suit rapid development and deployment. To enable rapid development and faster deployments, OpenShift supports hot deployment. Hot deployment means that you can deploy your changes without the need to restart all the application cartridges.

The presence of the `hot_deploy` marker file informs OpenShift that you want to do hot deployment. Before stopping and starting the application cartridges, OpenShift checks for the existence of the `hot_deploy` marker file. If the `hot_deploy` marker file exists, OpenShift will not stop the cartridges, and changes will be deployed without cartridges restart. Hot deployment is ideal for development, and I recommend that you always use it during development.

> If you set new environment variables with hot deployment enabled or install new cartridges, you have to restart the application to allow the server to pick the new environment variables.

## See also

▸ The *Creating and deploying Express web applications using Node.js and MongoDB cartridges* recipe

▸ The *Configuring Node supervisor options* recipe

# Creating and deploying Express web applications using Node.js and MongoDB cartridges

In this recipe, you will build a Node.js application from scratch using the Express web framework and MongoDB. I have chosen Express because it is very easy to use and is a popular web framework in the Node community. You can run any other web framework, such as Geddy, on OpenShift as well.

You will develop a job store application that will allow users to post job openings for a company. The application will be a single-page web application (http://en.wikipedia. org/wiki/Single-page_application) built using the Backbone.js (http:// backbonejs.org/) frontend. The application can do the following:

> ▸ When a user goes to the / URL of the application, the user will see a list of companies stored in the MongoDB database. Behind the scenes, the Backbone.js-based frontend will make a REST HTTP GET ('/api/v1/companies') call to fetch all the companies:

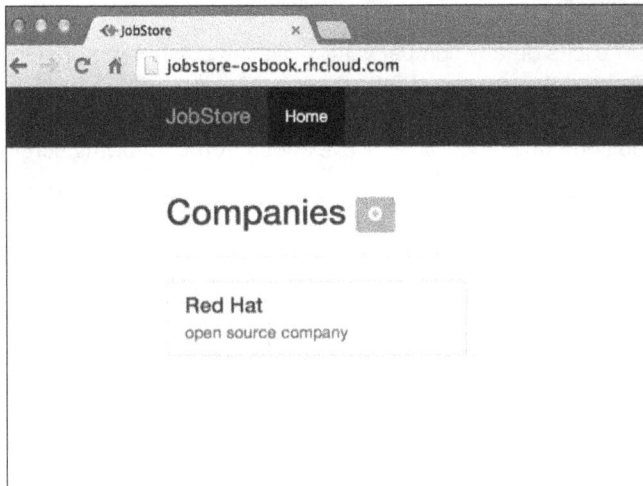

▶ Users can create a new company by visiting `http://jobstore-{domain-name}.rhcloud.com/#companies/new` or by clicking on the **+** icon. This will render a form where users can enter details about the new company, as shown in the following screenshot. When a user submits the form, the Backbone.js-based frontend will make an HTTP POST call to the REST backend and data related to a company is stored in MongoDB:

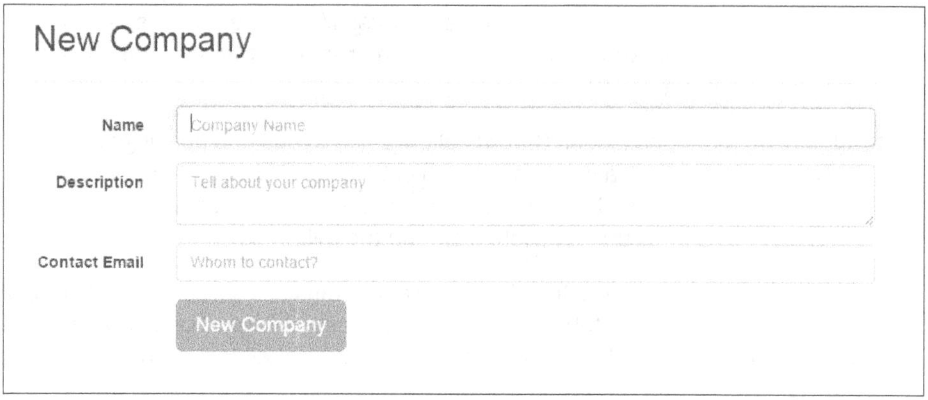

▶ When a user clicks on any company, they will see a list of job openings for that company. Behind the scenes, the Backbone.js-based frontend will make an HTTP GET (`'/api/v1/companies/company_id/jobs'`) call to fetch all the available jobs for the selected company using its ID. Have a look at the following screenshot:

► Users can post new jobs for a company by clicking on the **New Job** link. This will render a web form where users can enter their details. The Backbone.js-based frontend will make an HTTP POST call to the REST backend and data related to a job is stored in the MongoDB database:

All Jobs  ⊕ New Job

New Job

Title          Title

Description    Job description

               New Job

The source code for the application is available on GitHub at `https://github.com/OpenShift-Cookbook/chapter9-jobstore-nodejs-express`.

## Getting ready

To complete this recipe, you will need the rhc command-line client installed on your machine. Please refer to the *Installing the OpenShift rhc command-line client* recipe in *Chapter 1, Getting Started with OpenShift*, for details. This application will consume one gear, so if you don't have an extra gear available for this recipe, use the `rhc delete app <app_name> --confirm` command to delete an existing application. To run this application on your local machine, you will need Node and MongoDB installed on your machine. You can get the latest installer of Node.js for your operating system from their official website (`http://nodejs.org/download/`). You can get the latest installer of MongoDB for your operating system from their official website (`http://www.mongodb.org/downloads`).

## How to do it...

1.  Open a new command-line terminal, and navigate to a convenient location where you want to create the application. Run the command shown as follows to create the job store application:

    ```
    $ rhc create-app jobstore nodejs-0.10 mongodb-2.4
    ```

    This command will create an application named jobstore that uses Node.js and MongoDB cartridges.

2.  As the application will be built from scratch, we will delete the template source code generated by OpenShift. Change the directory to jobstore, and delete the following files and directories using the rm command on *nix machines. On Windows, you can use file explorer to delete the files and directories.

    ```
    $ cd jobstore
    ```

    ```
    $ rm -rf deplist.txt index.html node_modules/ package.json server.
    js
    ```

    Add the node_modules directory to the .gitignore file by executing the following command:

    ```
    $ echo "node_modules/" > .gitignore
    ```

3.  The Express team provides a project generator that you can use to create an Express template application. This generator will create an application skeleton using the latest Express version, that is, 4.2.0. It makes it easy for developers to get started with Express application development. You can install the express-generator package globally by running the following command:

    ```
    $ npm install -g express-generator
    ```

    > Please make sure you install express-generator Version 4.2.0 or above. This recipe was written using express-generator Version 4.2.0. You can check the version by typing the express --version command.

4.  Once the generator is installed globally, you can use the express command-line tool to generate projects anywhere on your machine. Please make sure you are in the jobstore directory, and create the project by running the following command:

    ```
    $ express --ejs . --force
    ```

5. To run this application on your local machine, you will have to first install all the dependencies using npm:

```
$ npm install
```

Now, to run the application, use the following command:

```
$ DEBUG=jobstore ./bin/www
```

You can view the application in your favorite browser by visiting `http://127.0.0.1:3000/`. The generated application exposes two routes as specified in `app.js`:

```
app.use('/', routes);
app.use('/users', users);
```

When a user makes a GET request to /, the index route callback, `routes`, is invoked. The `routes` callback is defined in `routes/index.js`. The callback renders the `index.ejs` view.

When a user makes a HTTP GET request to '/users', the users callback function is invoked. The default implementation just writes `respond with a resource` in the response body.

6. In our single-page web application, when a user makes an HTTP GET request to the application root URL, the Backbone.js-based frontend is rendered. Replace the content of `index.ejs` with `index.js` in the project's GitHub repository, `https://github.com/OpenShift-Cookbook/chapter9-jobstore-nodejs-express/blob/master/views/index.ejs`. Also, copy the css (`https://github.com/OpenShift-Cookbook/chapter9-jobstore-nodejs-express/tree/master/public/css`) and js (`https://github.com/OpenShift-Cookbook/chapter9-jobstore-nodejs-express/tree/master/public/js`) directory from the application's GitHub repository, `https://github.com/OpenShift-Cookbook/chapter9-jobstore-nodejs-express`, and place them inside the public directory.

Restart the application, and you will see the index route in action. This time it will render the application user interface.

7. The application does not need the `users.js` file in the `routes` directory, so delete it. After removing `routes/users.js`, remove its reference in the `app.js` file. You need to remove the following two lines from the `app.js` file:

```
var users = require('./routes/users');
app.use('/users', users);
```

8. Create a new file named `api.js` inside the `routes` directory. This file will house the REST backend of our application. On *nix machines, you can create a new file using the `touch` command. On Windows, you can use file explorer to create the file.

```
$ touch routes/api.js
```

9. The application will use the MongoDB database for storing data. To work with MongoDB, you need to use a third-party library. For this application, you will use the `mongojs` module. Install the module using the npm command, as shown in the following command:

```
$ npm install mongojs --save
```

10. The next step is configuring the MongoDB database so that our REST API can talk with MongoDB. Place the following code in `api.js`:

```
var db_name = process.env.OPENSHIFT_APP_NAME || "jobstore";
var connection_string = '127.0.0.1:27017/' + db_name;
// if OPENSHIFT env variables are present, use the available
connection info:
if (process.env.OPENSHIFT_MONGODB_DB_PASSWORD) {
    connection_string = process.env.OPENSHIFT_MONGODB_DB_USERNAME
+ ":" +
        process.env.OPENSHIFT_MONGODB_DB_PASSWORD + "@" +
        process.env.OPENSHIFT_MONGODB_DB_HOST + ':' +
        process.env.OPENSHIFT_MONGODB_DB_PORT + '/' +
        process.env.OPENSHIFT_APP_NAME;
}
var mongojs = require("mongojs");
var db = mongojs(connection_string, ['jobstore']);
var companies = db.collection("companies");
```

11. As mentioned in this recipe introduction, there are two company-related operations— get all companies and store a company in the MongoDB database. These will be exposed as two routes in the `app.js` file, as shown in the following commands:

```
var api = require('./routes/api');
app.get('/api/v1/companies', api.companies);
app.post('/api/v1/companies', api.saveCompany);
```

When the HTTP GET request is made to `/api/v1/companies`, the `api.companies` callback will be called. The `api.companies` callback is defined in the `api.js` route file. This callback will make a `find` call on the `companies` collection. It will find all the companies in the MongoDB database and write them to the response object. Have a look at the following commands:

```
exports.companies = function (req, res, next) {
    companies.find().sort({registeredAt: -1}, function (err,
companies) {
        if (err) {
            return next(err);
        }
        return res.json(companies);
    });
};
```

Similarly, when the HTTP POST request is made to the `/api/v1/companies` URL, the `api.saveCompany` callback will be called. The `api.saveCompany` callback is defined in the `api.js` route file. The callback will create a `company` object from the request object and then persist the `company` object in the MongoDB database:

```
exports.saveCompany = function (req, res, next) {
    var company = {
        "name": req.body.name,
        "description": req.body.description,
        "registeredAt": new Date(),
        "contactEmail": req.body.contactEmail,
        "jobs": []
    };
    companies.save(company, function (err, saved) {
        if (err) {
            return next(err);
        }
        console.log(saved);
        res.json(saved);
    })
};
```

12. Next, you will write REST endpoints to store and list the jobs data. There are two REST endpoints related to jobs—listing all jobs for a company and saving a job for a company. These will be exposed as two routes in `app.js`. Have a look at the following code:

```
app.get('/api/v1/companies/:companyId/jobs', api.jobsForCompany);
app.post('/api/v1/companies/:companyId/jobs', api.
postJobForCompany);
```

When the HTTP GET request is made to `/api/v1/companies/:companyId/jobs`, the `jobsForCompany` callback will be called. This callback will find the company corresponding to `companyId` and then return the jobs embedded in the array:

```
exports.jobsForCompany = function (req, res, next) {
    var companyId = req.param('companyId');
    companies.findOne({"_id": mongojs.ObjectId(companyId)},
function (err, company) {
        if (err) {
            return next(err);
        }
        return res.json(company.jobs);
    });

};
```

When a user makes the HTTP POST request to `/api/v1/companies/:companyId/jobs`, the `postJobForCompany` callback function will be called. This callback will be defined in the `api.js` routes file. This route will update the company document with the embedded job document. Finally, it will return the updated company document:

```javascript
exports.postJobForCompany = function (req, res, next) {
    var companyId = req.param('companyId');
    var job = {
        "title": req.body.title,
        "description": req.body.description
    }

    companies.update({"_id": mongojs.ObjectId(companyId)}, {$push:
{"jobs": job}}, function (err, result) {
        if (err) {
            return next(err);
        }
        return companies.findOne({"_id": mongojs.
ObjectId(companyId)}, function (err, company) {
            if (err) {
                return next(err);
            }

            return res.json(company);
        })
    })
};
```

13. To test the application on your local machine, start the MongoDB database server, and then restart the Node application.

14. To make this application run on OpenShift, you have to update the `bin/www` script:

```javascript
#!/usr/bin/env node
var debug = require('debug')('jobstore');
var app = require('../app');
var ipaddress = process.env.OPENSHIFT_NODEJS_IP || "127.0.0.1";
var port = process.env.OPENSHIFT_NODEJS_PORT || 3000;
app.set('port', port);
app.set('ipaddress', ipaddress);
var server = app.listen(app.get('port'), app.get('ipaddress'),
function() {
  debug('JobStore application running at http://%s:%d ',app.
get('ipaddress'), app.get('port'));
});
```

This code sets the correct IP address and port values so that the application can work on OpenShift.

15. Add the `node_modules` directory to the `.gitignore` file as follows:

    ```
    $ echo "node_modules/" > .gitignore
    ```

16. Update the `package.json` main field value. This is required, because, otherwise, OpenShift will look for the `server.js` file. As this application does not have a `server.js` file, the application will not start. This was explained in the *Creating your first Node.js application* recipe:

    ```
    "main":"./bin/www",
    ```

17. Add the changes to the Git index, commit the code to the local Git repository, and then finally push the changes to the application gear:

    ```
    $ git add .
    $ git commit -am "jobstore app"
    $ git push
    ```

18. After a successful build, changes will be deployed, and your application will be available at `http://jobstore-{domain-name}.rhcloud.com`.

## How it works...

Let's now understand what we did in the previous steps. In step 3, you installed the **express-generator** module. In the previous version of Express, express-generator package was part of the Express module itself. Now, in the latest versions, you will have to install express-generator separately. This recipe was written using 4.2.0. This module is installed globally using the `-g` option to run the Express executable from any directory.

Next, in step 4, you generated the project inside the `jobstore` directory using the `express . --ejs --force` command. The command instructs Express to create the template in the current directory. The `--ejs` option tells Express to configure the app with the `ejs` template engine. Express supports almost all the template engines built for Node, but express-generator only supports `hogan`, `jade`, and `ejs`. The `--force` option instructs Express to forcefully create the project template inside a non-empty directory. If you don't use the `--force` option, the generator will ask you for confirmation, as shown in the following code:

**destination is not empty, continue?**

The `express` command generates a folder structure suitable for the Express web development as follows:

```
$ ls -p
app.js      bin/      package.json      public/      routes/      views/
```

The `package.json` file is an application descriptor file based on CommonJS (`http://wiki.commonjs.org/wiki/CommonJS`). It contains application metadata and its dependencies. The `npm install` command parses the dependencies mentioned in `package.json` and installs them in the `node_modules` directory.

The `app.js` file configures the Express framework along with Connect middleware components. The application server startup boilerplate is defined inside the `bin/www` script. This is a Node script that creates an Express web server and binds it to a 3000 port number. To run the application, you can use either the `./bin/www` or `npm start` command.

The Express command creates three other subdirectories apart from `bin`—`public`, `routes`, and `views`. The `public` directory houses all the static resources of the application. The `app.js` file configures the Express application to use the `public` directory for static files:

```
app.use(express.static(path.join(__dirname, 'public')));
```

In step 6, you copied the `css` and `js` directories from the project's GitHub repository.

The `routes` directory has two files—`index.js` and `users.js`. Both these files are used by `app.js`. These files define callbacks that will be invoked when the user makes requests to the `http://jobstore-{domain-name}.rhcloud.com` and `http://jobstore-{domain-name}.rhcloud.com/users` URLs.

The `views` directory holds the template files that will be shown to the user. In step 6, you updated `index.ejs` with the one from the project's GitHub repository. As mentioned before, the view of the application is built using Backbone.js and will not be covered as it is outside the scope of this book.

From steps 7 through step 12, you defined the REST backend for the application. The application exposes a REST call backed by the MongoDB database, which is consumed by the Backbone.js frontend. You created a new file named `api.js` to define all the API callbacks. You installed the `mongojs` package so that you can work with the MongoDB database. You defined four methods in `api.js`—`companies`, `saveCompany`, `jobsForCompany`, and `postJobForCompany`. All the methods work on the MongoDB database asynchronously and write the database result to the response object.

In `app.js`, you defined four routes for the REST endpoints. The callbacks are defined in `api.js` as follows:

```
app.get('/api/v1/companies', api.companies);
app.post('/api/v1/companies', api.saveCompany)
app.get('/api/v1/companies/:companyId/jobs', api.jobsForCompany);
app.post('/api/v1/companies/:companyId/jobs', api.postJobForCompany);
```

After writing the backend logic, you updated the `bin/www` script so that it can bind and listen to the correct IP address and port when running on OpenShift.

Finally, you committed the code and pushed the changes to the application gear. This will download all the dependencies mentioned in the `node_modules` directory and then restart the application with the updated code.

## See also

▶  The *Creating your first Node.js application* recipe

▶  The *Enabling hot deployment for Node.js applications* recipe

▶  The *Working with Web Sockets* recipe

# Working with Web Sockets

HTTP was designed to be half-duplex, which means it allows transmission of data in just one direction at a time. This makes it unsuitable for building real-time applications that need an open, persistent connection always. To overcome this limitation of HTTP, developers have created some workarounds or hacks. Some of these workarounds are polling, long polling, and streaming.

Web Sockets provide an asynchronous, bidirectional, full-duplex messaging implementation over a single TCP connection. In this recipe, you will learn how you can use Socket.IO and Express to create a simple echo application. The application simply reverses the message and echoes it back to the user browser.

## Getting ready

To complete this recipe, you will need the rhc command-line client installed on your machine. Please refer to the *Installing the OpenShift rhc command-line client* recipe in *Chapter 1, Getting Started with OpenShift*, for details. This application will consume one gear, so if you don't have an extra gear available for this recipe, use the `rhc delete app <app_name> --confirm` command to delete an existing application. To run this application on your local machine, you will need Node installed on your machine. You can get the latest installer of Node.js for your operating system from their official website (`http://nodejs.org/download/`).

## How to do it...

Perform the following steps to create an application that uses Web Sockets:

1.  Open a new command-line terminal, and navigate to a convenient location where you want to create the application. Run the following command to create the application:

    ```
    $ rhc create-app reverseecho nodejs-0.10
    ```

2. Change the directory to `reverseecho`, and delete the template application source code:

```
$ cd reverseecho
$ rm -rf deplist.txt index.html node_modules/ package.json server.
js
```

Add the `node_modules` directory to the `.gitignore` file by executing the following command:

```
$ echo "node_modules/" > .gitignore
```

3. Create a `package.json` file:

```
{
    "name": "reverse-echo",
    "version": "0.0.1",
    "private": true,
    "main": "server.js"
}
```

4. Install the `express` and `socket.io` modules as follows:

```
$ npm install express -save
$ npm install socket.io --save
```

5. Create a new file named `server.js` in the app root directory and populate it with the following code:

```
var express = require("express");
var app = express();
var server = require('http').createServer(app);
var ip = process.env.OPENSHIFT_NODEJS_IP || '127.0.0.1';
var port = process.env.OPENSHIFT_NODEJS_PORT || 3000;
server.listen(port,ip);
var io = require('socket.io').listen(server);

app.get('/',function(req,res){
    res.sendfile(__dirname+'/index.html');
});
console.log('App running at http://%s:%d',ip,port);
io.sockets.on('connection', function (socket) {

    // when the client emits 'sendchat', this listens and executes
    socket.on('message', function (data) {
        io.sockets.emit('rev-message', data.split("").reverse().
join(""));
    });
});
```

In this code, you first created the Express server application instance. Then, you imported the Socket.IO library and started the Socket.IO server, providing it with the already-created Express server so that it can share the same TCP/IP address and port. You defined a couple of event listeners using the `io.sockets.on()` function. The `io.sockets.on()` function takes two arguments—the event name and a callback function. The event name can be any string, such as `'connection'` and `'message'`. The callback function defines work to perform when an event is received.

6. Create `index.html` in the `app` root directory, and populate it with the following code. This page has one textbox where the user can enter any text and submit it to the server by pressing a button. The data is transferred to the server using Web Sockets.

```html
<html>
<head>
    <title>ReverseEcho</title>
application    <meta name="viewport" content="width=device-width,
initial-scale=1.0">
    <link href="//cdnjs.cloudflare.com/ajax/libs/twitter-
bootstrap/3.1.1/css/bootstrap.css" rel="stylesheet">
    <style type="text/css">
      body {
        padding-top:60px;
        padding-bottom: 60px;
      }
    </style>
</head>
<body>
<div class="container">
    <div class="row">
        <div class="col-md-6">
            <input type="text" class="form-control" rows="3"
id="message" placeholder="Write a message">
            <input type="button" id="echobutton" value="Reverse Echo" />
        </div>
        <div class="col-md-6">
            <p id="result"></p>
        </div>
    </div>
</div>

<script src="/socket.io/socket.io.js"></script>
<script src="https://ajax.googleapis.com/ajax/libs/jquery/1.6.4/
jquery.min.js"></script>
<script>
```

```
            var wsUrl;
            if(window.location.host == '127.0.0.1:3000'){
                wsUrl = window.location.protocol + "//" + window.
location.host;
            }else{
                if (window.location.protocol == 'http:') {
                wsUrl = 'ws://' + window.location.host + ':8000/';
                } else {
                wsUrl = 'wss://' + window.location.host + ':8443/';
                }
            }
            console.log('WebSockets Url : ' + wsUrl);
            var socket = io.connect(wsUrl);
            socket.on('connect', function(){
                console.log('User connected');
            });
            socket.on('rev-message', function (data) {
                    $('#result').text(data);
            });
            $(function(){
                    $('#echobutton').click( function() {
                            var message = $('#message').val();
                            $('#message').val('');
                            socket.emit('message', message);
                    });
            });

    </script>
    </body>
    </html>
```

This JavaScript code in the `index.html` file opens a Web Socket connection with the backend Node server deployed on OpenShift. In OpenShift, Web Sockets are not available over standard 80 and 443 ports because of the reasons outlined in the official OpenShift blog, `https://www.openshift.com/blogs/paas-websockets`, so you will have to use port numbers 8000 and 8443.

7. Add the code to the Git index, commit the code to the local Git repository, and then finally push the changes to the application gear by executing the following commands:

```
$ git add .
$ git commit -am "OpenShift Node Web Socket application"
$ git push
```

8. After the code is deployed, you can see the application running at `http://reverseecho-{domain-name}.rhcloud.com`. If you type `OpenShift` and click on the **Reverse Echo** button, you will see **tfihSnepO** as the result. This is shown in the following screenshot:

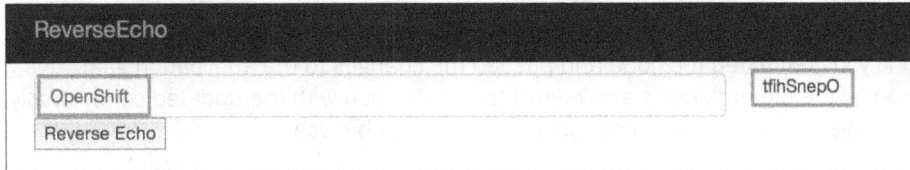

## How it works...

In the previous steps, you built an echo server that will reverse the message sent by the user and send it back to the user. To build this application, you installed two modules —Socket. IO and Express as covered in step 3. Socket.IO provides an API abstraction over the Web Sockets and other transports for the Node.js and client-side JavaScript. It will fall back to other alternatives transparently if Web Sockets is not implemented in a web browser while keeping the same API.

The code listing shown in step 4 does the following:

▶ It first imports the Express library using the `require()` function and then creates the server using the Express application object.

▶ Then, it imports the Socket.IO library and starts the Socket.IO server using the `listen()` function.

▶ Next, you defined a route for the root URL, which will render `index.html` (created in the next step).

▶ Lastly, you added event handlers for connection and message events. On the connection event, you will write a message in the server logs. On the message event, you will reverse the message and emit the `rev-message` event. The client will listen for the `rev-message` event and will render the user interface.

In the listing shown in step 5, you created an `index.html` file using Twitter Bootstrap styling. The script tag does the following:

▶ On page load, you connected with the Web Socket backend using the backend Web Socket URL. In OpenShift, Web Sockets are not available over standard 80 and 443 ports because of the reasons outlined in this blog, so you will have to use port numbers 8000 and 8443. You constructed the correct URL and then connected with Socket.IO backend.

- ▶ You added listeners for the `connect` and `rev-message` events.

- ▶ When the `rev-message` event is received, you write the message in `results div`.

- ▶ You added a jQuery event listener, which will emit the message event when the button is pressed. This message will be received by the Socket.IO server backend, and that will emit the `rev-message` event.

In step 7, you committed the code and pushed the changes to the application gear. This will download all the dependencies and restart the application with the updated code. Finally, in step 8, you tested the reverse echo functionality in your browser.

## See also

- ▶ The *Creating and deploying Express web applications using Node.js and MongoDB cartridges* recipe

- ▶ The *Creating your first Node.js application* recipe

# Using CoffeeScript with OpenShift Node.js applications

In the last recipe of this chapter, you will learn how to use CoffeeScript with OpenShift Node.js applications. You will develop an Express web application in CoffeeScript and deploy it to OpenShift.

## Getting ready

To complete this recipe, you will need the rhc command-line client installed on your machine. Please refer to the *Installing the OpenShift rhc command-line client* recipe in *Chapter 1, Getting Started with OpenShift*, for details. This application will consume one gear, so if you don't have an extra gear available for this recipe, use the `rhc delete app <app_name> --confirm` command to delete an existing application. To run this application on your local machine, you will need Node installed on your machine. You can get the latest installer of Node.js for your operating system from their official website (`http://nodejs.org/download/`).

## How to do it...

Perform the following steps to create a CoffeeScript Express application:

1. Open a new command-line terminal, and navigate to a convenient location where you want to create the application. Run the following command to create the application:

```
$ rhc create-app myapp nodejs-0.10
```

2. Change the directory to `myapp`, and delete the template application source code.

   ```
   $ cd myapp
   $ rm -rf deplist.txt index.html node_modules/ package.json server.js
   ```

   Add the `node_modules` directory to the `.gitignore` file by executing the following command:

   ```
   $ echo "node_modules/" > .gitignore
   ```

3. Create a `package.json` file to store your application metadata and dependencies as follows:

   ```
   {
       "name": "myapp",
       "version": "0.0.1"
   }
   ```

4. Install CoffeeScript and Express modules using npm as follows:

   ```
   $ npm install express coffee-script --save
   ```

5. Create a new file, `app.coffee`, and place the following contents in it. This is the `Hello World` Express web application written in CoffeeScript:

   ```
   express = require('express')
   app = express()
   ip = process.env.OPENSHIFT_NODEJS_IP || '127.0.0.1'
   port = process.env.OPENSHIFT_NODEJS_PORT || 3000
   # App Routes
   app.get '/', (request, response) ->
     response.send 'Hello World!!'

   # Listen
   app.listen port,ip
   console.log "Express server listening on port http://%s:%d",
   ip,port
   ```

6. Create the `use_npm` marker file to tell OpenShift that you want to use the `npm start` command to run the application:

   ```
   $ touch .openshift/markers/use_npm
   ```

7. Update the `package.json` file with the start script:

   ```
   {
       "name": "myapp",
       "description": "My OpenShift Node.js Application",
       "version": "0.0.1",
       "dependencies": {
   ```

```
        "express": "~4.3.1",
        "coffee-script": "~1.7.1"
    },
    "scripts":{"start":"~/app-root/runtime/repo/node_modules/.bin/
coffee app.coffee"}
}
```

This start script makes use of the `coffee` executable in the `node_modules .bin` directory. The `node_modules` directory is available inside the `$OPENSHIFT_REPO_DIR` directory.

8. Add the code to the Git index, commit the code to the local Git repository, and then finally push the changes to the application gear by executing the following commands:

```
$ git add .
$ git commit -am "OpenShift Node CoffeeScript application"
$ git push
```

## How it works...

CoffeeScript is a programming language that transcompiles to JavaScript. The Python programming language inspires the CoffeeScript syntax. As a result, the code written using CoffeeScript tends to be clean and readable inspires its syntax. Many developers that do not like JavaScript syntax prefer to use CoffeeScript to build their Node applications. From steps 1 through 5, you built a `Hello World` Express web application in CoffeeScript. To run the CoffeeScript code, you will need `coffee` executables from the `coffee-script` package. The `coffee` executable is inside the `node_modules/.bin` directory.

To run CoffeeScript applications on the local machine, you can install the `coffee-script` module globally using the `npm install coffee-script -g` command. This will install the `coffee` executable globally, allowing you to run the `coffee` command anywhere on your machine. This does not work with OpenShift. If you push the code after step 5, the supervisor will fail to start the application, as it will not be able to find the `coffee` executable. The `use_npm` marker can solve this problem. As explained in the *Using the use_npm marker* recipe, with the `use_npm` marker, you can specify your own start script. OpenShift will use the start script in `package.json` to run your application. In step 7, you defined the start script that will use the `coffee` executable from the `$OPENSHIFT_REPO_DIR/node_modules/.bin` directory to run the application.

## See also

- The *Creating and deploying Express web applications using Node.js and MongoDB cartridges* recipe
- The *Creating your first Node.js application* recipe

# 10
# Continuous Integration for OpenShift Applications

This chapter will help you to add continuous integration to your OpenShift applications using the Jenkins cartridge. The specific recipes of this chapter are as follows:

- ▶ Adding Jenkins CI to your application
- ▶ Increasing the slave idle timeout
- ▶ Installing Jenkins plugins
- ▶ Using Jenkins to build projects hosted on GitHub
- ▶ Creating a Jenkins workflow for your OpenShift applications
- ▶ Upgrading Jenkins to the latest version

## Introduction

In this chapter, you will learn how to add **Continuous Integration** (**CI**) support to your OpenShift applications. CI is an **Extreme Programming** (**XP**) practice in which a tool monitors your version control system, such as Git or SVN, for code changes. Whenever it detects a change, it builds the project and runs its test cases. If the build fails for some reason, the tool will notify the development team about the failure via e-mail or other communication channels so that they can fix the build failure immediately. CI tools can do much more beyond building and testing the application. They can also keep track of the code quality over a period of time, run functional tests, perform automatic deployment, apply database migrations, and perform a lot of other tasks. This helps us to discover defects early in the software development cycle, improves code quality, and automates deployment.

OpenShift supports Jenkins as its CI tool of choice. Jenkins (`http://jenkins-ci.org/`) is the most dominant and popular CI server in the market today. It is an open source project written in the Java programming language. Jenkins is feature rich and extensible through plugins. There are more than 600 Jenkins plugins made by an active community at your disposal, which can cover everything from version control system, build tools, code quality metrics, build notifiers, and much more.

The *Adding Jenkins CI to your application* recipe will help you to add Jenkins to your existing OpenShift application. We will use a Java application to showcase OpenShift Jenkins integration. This chapter discusses Jenkins in the context of Java applications. Nevertheless, even if you are using any other web cartridge supported by OpenShift, this chapter will give you a good understanding on how to add the OpenShift Jenkins CI support to your application.

OpenShift uses the Jenkins master/slave topology (`https://wiki.jenkins-ci.org/display/JENKINS/Distributed+builds`) to distribute build jobs among different slaves. This ensures you get a scalable Jenkins environment for your OpenShift applications. Also, the Jenkins master will create different types of slaves to build different OpenShift application types. The type of slave depends on the application type. For example, to build a JBoss EAP application, the Jenkins master will create a slave that has a JBoss EAP cartridge installed. By default, a slave will die after 15 minutes of inactivity. The *Increasing the slave idle timeout* recipe will cover how you can increase the idle timeout for slaves.

Plugins make Jenkins extensible and allow you to extend it to meet your needs. In the *Installing Jenkins plugins* recipe, you will learn how to install Jenkins plugins. You can view the full list of Jenkins plugins at `https://wiki.jenkins-ci.org/display/JENKINS/Plugins`.

You can use Jenkins not only to build applications hosted on OpenShift but also to build projects hosted elsewhere. The *Using Jenkins to build projects hosted on GitHub* recipe will cover how you can build projects hosted on GitHub.

The *Creating a Jenkins workflow for your OpenShift applications* recipe will show how you can customize the default build created by OpenShift for your needs. In this recipe, you will create a Jenkins workflow, including three Jenkins jobs. The first Jenkins job will poll a Git repository for changes, the second job will run code coverage over the application source code, and the third will deploy the application to OpenShift.

The Jenkins version supported by OpenShift is not the latest version. In the *Upgrading Jenkins to the latest version* recipe, you will upgrade Jenkins to the latest version. The advantage of using the latest version is that some of the plugins do not work with the Jenkins version supported by OpenShift.

Jenkins is not the only CI server you can use to build and deploy OpenShift applications. You can also use a hosted CI server, such as Travis CI, to build and deploy an OpenShift application. The OpenShift Travis CI integration is not covered in this chapter, but you can refer to my blog for more information on this topic at `https://www.openshift.com/blogs/how-to-build-and-deploy-openshift-java-projects-using-travis-ci`.

# Adding Jenkins CI to your application

Adding Jenkins to your application is a two-step process. You have to first create the Jenkins server application and then add the Jenkins client cartridge to your application. In this recipe, you will learn how to add Jenkins CI to an existing OpenShift application. After adding Jenkins to your application, each Git push to your OpenShift application Git repository will initiate a Jenkins job that will build the project and then deploy it to OpenShift.

## Getting ready

To complete this recipe, you will need three available gears. One gear will be used by the application, and Jenkins will consume the remaining two gears. This chapter will use the application created in *Chapter 7, OpenShift for Java Developers*. If you don't have this application running, then recreate the application using the following command:

```
$ rhc app create jobstore jbosseap postgresql-9.2 --from-code
https://github.com/OpenShift-Cookbook/chapter7-jobstore-javaee6.git
```

## How to do it...

Perform the following steps to add Jenkins to your application:

1. Before you can add the Jenkins cartridge to your application, you have to create the Jenkins server application:

   ```
   $ rhc create-app jenkins jenkins
   ```

2. After the preceding command is executed, the Jenkins server will be available at `http://jenkins-{domain-name}.rhcloud.com`. Please replace `{domain-name}` with your OpenShift account domain name.

3. Make note of the username and password that the OpenShift `rhc` command-line client presented to you in the application creation logs. These are used to log in to the Jenkins web console. This is shown in the following command-line output:

   ```
   Creating application 'jenkins' ... done

      Jenkins created successfully.  Please make note of these
   credentials:

      User: admin

      Password: xxxxxx

   Note:  You can change your password at: https://jenkins-
   {domain-name}.rhcloud.com/me/configure
   ```

4. Log in to Jenkins at `https://jenkins-{domain-name}.rhcloud.com/me/configure` using the credentials you got in step 1. I recommend that you change the Jenkins password to something that you can easily remember. To change the password, enter your new password in the **Password** section, and click on the **Save** button:

| | |
|---|---|
| Your name | Jenkins Admin |
| Description | |

**API Token**

Show API Token...

**Credentials**

Add Credentials ▼

**E-mail**

| E-mail address | changeme@changeme.com |
|---|---|
| | Your e-mail address, like joe.chin@sun.com |

**My Views**

| Default View | All |
|---|---|
| | The view selected by default when navigating to the users private views |

**Password**

| Password: | ......................... |
|---|---|
| Confirm Password: | ......................... |

**SSH Public Keys**

| SSH Public Keys | |
|---|---|

**Setting for search**

| Case-sensitivity | ⬜ Insensitive search tool |
|---|---|

Save   Apply

5. After saving your new password, log out and log in again using the new password. You will be presented with the Jenkins dashboard as shown in the following screenshot:

**Jenkins**

search    admin | log out

Jenkins

ENABLE AUTO REFRESH

add description

- New Job
- People
- Build History
- Manage Jenkins
- My Views

Welcome to Jenkins! Please create new jobs to get started.

**Build Queue**

No builds in the queue.

**Build Executor Status**

Help us localize this page    Page generated: May 28, 2014 4:05:14 AM    REST API    Jenkins ver. 1.509.1

6. Now that you have created the Jenkins server application, you can add the Jenkins cartridge to the `jobstore` application. To add the cartridge, run the following command:

   ```
   $ rhc add-cartridge jenkins --app jobstore
   ```

7. Go to the Jenkins dashboard at `https://jenkins-{domain-name}.rhcloud.com/`, and you will see a new job configured for the `jobstore` application, as shown in the following screenshot:

8. Click on the **jobstore-build** link (`https://jenkins-{domain-name}.rhcloud.com/job/jobstore-build/`) to view the Jenkins job details.

9. To initiate a new build, you can either click on the **Build Now** link on the left-hand side or make a change to the project source, commit it, and then push the change to the application Git repository. Let's make a small change to our application source code. Change the title in the `src/main/webapp/index.html` location from `<title>JobStore</title>` to `<title>JobStore with Jenkins</title>`:

   ```
   $ git commit -am "updated title"
   $ git push
   ```

10. The `git push` logs will show that Jenkins is building the project as follows:

    ```
    remote: Executing Jenkins build.

    remote: You can track your build at https://jenkins-
    xxxx.rhcloud.com/job/jobstore-build

    remote:

    remote: Waiting for build to
    schedule................................Done

    remote: Waiting for job to
    complete...............................
    ```

11. You can view the build logs in the Jenkins web console by clicking on the **Console Output** option as shown in the following screenshot:

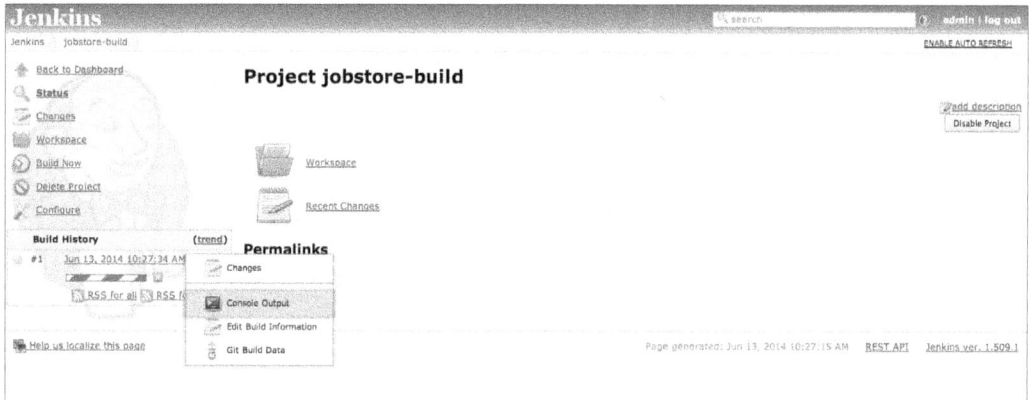

12. After the job is completed, you will see the build status under **Build History**. The successful builds are shown in blue and failed builds are shown in red.

13. You can verify that your changes are applied by opening the application URL in your favorite browser (`http://jobstore-{domain-name}.rhcloud.com`). You will see that the title has been updated to **Jobstore with Jenkins**.

## How it works...

One of the powerful features of Jenkins is its ability to distribute builds over multiple machines. Jenkins uses the master/slave architecture to manage distributed builds. In the master/slave architecture, there is a Jenkins server whose job is to schedule jobs, dispatch builds to the slave for the actual execution, monitor the slave health, and record and present build results. The slave runs the actual build and shares job results with the master.

OpenShift uses the Jenkins master/slave architecture to build your applications. You can only have one Jenkins master for an OpenShift domain, and all the applications under that domain will use the Jenkins master for application builds. The Jenkins master, depending on the Jenkins job configuration for that application, will create a slave that will build the application. Every OpenShift Jenkins installation has the OpenShift Jenkins plugin installed. This plugin makes it possible for Jenkins to talk with your OpenShift account and create slaves on your behalf. The Jenkins slaves are nothing more than OpenShift gears.

In step 1, you created the Jenkins master application. You can use the master instance to execute jobs directly but, most of the time in the master/slave architecture, slaves are used to build the projects. The Jenkins master created by OpenShift is configured not to run any jobs by setting the number of executors configuration to 0. The number of executors lets you define the number of concurrent jobs an instance can run. As the number of executors for the master instance is set to 0, you can't use it to build any project. You can set the number of executors to a number greater than 0 by updating the **# of executors** system configuration value in the Jenkins configuration screen (`https://jenkins-{domain-name}.rhcloud.com/configure`), as shown in the following screenshot. In the *Using Jenkins to build projects hosted on GitHub* recipe, you will use the Jenkins master to build the project. Have a look at the following screenshot:

Once you have created the Jenkins master application, you can add the Jenkins client to the `jobstore` application. If you try to add the Jenkins client to an application before creating the Jenkins master, you will get an error message in the `rhc add-cartridge` command logs.

In step 5, you added the Jenkins client cartridge to the `jobstore` application. The Jenkins client cartridge creates a new Jenkins job for the `jobstore` project. In Jenkins, a job defines what needs to be done. You can view the job configuration by opening `https://jenkins-{domain}.rhcloud.com/job/jobstore-build/configure` in your favorite browser.

The job configuration can be divided into three sections: builder configuration, source code management configuration, and build configuration.

▶ **Builder configuration**: The configuration values shown in the following screenshot will be used to create a slave. The configuration says that it needs a builder slave with a small gear size of type `redhat-jbosseap-6`. This means the slave gear will have a JBoss EAP 6 cartridge installed. It also defines a timeout for which the Jenkins master will wait for the slave to come online. The default builder timeout is 5 minutes or 300000 milliseconds. The **Restrict where this project can be run** configuration defines that this project will only be built on the slave with the label `jobstore-build`. As you might have probably noticed, the name of the label is the same as the name of the job. The OpenShift Jenkins plugin uses the label name to read the job configuration and creates a slave using the builder configuration of the job. So, if you change the name of the label from `jobstore-build` to `jobstore-os-build`, then the Jenkins plugin will not be able to find the associated job configuration, and the job will not be executed.

▶ **Git configuration**: The next important configuration is the Git version control configuration. This configuration specifies the application Git repository URL. The Jenkins job will clone this Git repository using the specified Git repository URL and build this project. The following screenshot shows the Git configuration:

▶ **Build configuration**: This is the most important part of our job configuration. It defines what needs to be done. The job configuration is shown in the following screenshot. The configuration does the following:

1. It downloads the contents from the actual application to the builder application using Git and `rsync`.

2. If the `force_clean_build` marker is not present, then it also copies the content of the `$OPENSHIFT_BUILD_DEPENDENCIES_DIR` and `$OPENSHIFT_DEPENDENCIES_DIR` directories from the actual application to the builder application. When the `force_clean_build` marker is present, then the dependencies are downloaded again on the builder application, and the build will take more time to finish.

3. Then, it builds the application using whatever build commands the cartridge uses. For Java applications, it will use the `mvn clean install -Popenshift -DskipTests` command.

4. After the build finishes successfully, it stops the application gear.

5. Then Jenkins copies the new content from the builder application to the actual application using `rsync`.

6. Finally, it starts the application. Have a look at the following screenshot:

```
Execute shell

Command  source $OPENSHIFT_CARTRIDGE_SDK_BASH

         alias rsync="rsync --delete-after -az -e '$GIT_SSH'"

         upstream_ssh="539b4d8b500446a3c60003ac@jobstore-${OPENSHIFT_NAMESPACE}.rhcloud.com"

         # remove previous metadata, if any
         rm -f $OPENSHIFT_HOMEDIR/app-deployments/current/metadata.json

         if ! marker_present "force_clean_build"; then
           # don't fail if these rsyncs fail
           set +e
           rsync $upstream_ssh:'$OPENSHIFT_BUILD_DEPENDENCIES_DIR' $OPENSHIFT_BUILD_DEPENDENCIES_DIR
           rsync $upstream_ssh:'$OPENSHIFT_DEPENDENCIES_DIR' $OPENSHIFT_DEPENDENCIES_DIR
           set -e
         fi

         # Build/update libs and run user pre_build and build
         gear build

         # Run tests here

         # Deploy new build

         # Stop app
         $GIT_SSH $upstream_ssh "gear stop --conditional --exclude-web-proxy --git-ref $GIT_COMMIT"

         deployment_dir=`$GIT_SSH $upstream_ssh 'gear create-deployment-dir'`

         # Push content back to application
         rsync $OPENSHIFT_HOMEDIR/app-deployments/current/metadata.json $upstream_ssh:app-deployments/$deployment_dir/metadata.json
         rsync --exclude .git $WORKSPACE/ $upstream_ssh:app-root/runtime/repo/
         rsync $OPENSHIFT_BUILD_DEPENDENCIES_DIR $upstream_ssh:app-root/runtime/build-dependencies/
         rsync $OPENSHIFT_DEPENDENCIES_DIR $upstream_ssh:app-root/runtime/dependencies/

         # Configure / start app
         $GIT_SSH $upstream_ssh "gear remotedeploy --deployment-datetime $deployment_dir"


         See the list of available environment variables

                                                                         Delete
```

If you don't have Jenkins enabled in your application, then the code is built on the same gear on which the application is running. When you push changes to your application gear, OpenShift first stops your application, builds the application, deploys the artifact, and finally starts the application.

In step 8, after adding the Jenkins cartridge to the `jobstore` application, you made a change to the source code and pushed changes to the application gear. This time, rather than building the project on the application gear, the Jenkins server launches a slave and initiates the build. The process is explained in detail in the following steps:

1. The user makes a change and pushes the changes to the application gear using the `git push` command.

2. After receiving the bits, a Git action hook is called that notifies the Jenkins server.

3. The Jenkins server creates a dedicated Jenkins slave (builder) to build this project. You can see the new gear created by Jenkins using the `rhc apps` command:

```
jobstorebldr @ http://jobstorebldr-xxxx.rhcloud.com/ (uuid:
539b660ce0b8cdeba00000e1)
-----------------------------------------------------------------
----------------------
Domain:     xxxx
Created:    2:28 AM
Gears:      1 (defaults to small)
Git URL:    ssh://539b660ce0b8cdeba00000e1@jobstorebldr-
xxxx.rhcloud.com/~/git/jobstorebldr.git/
SSH:        539b660ce0b8cdeba00000e1@jobstorebldr-
xxxx.rhcloud.com
Deployment: auto (on git push)


jbosseap-6 (JBoss Enterprise Application Platform 6)
----------------------------------------------------
Gears: 1 small
```

4. Jenkins runs the build using the steps mentioned in the build configuration section. After a successful build, the build artifact is copied to the application gear using the `rsync` tool, as mentioned in the build configuration.

5. Jenkins starts the application after a successful build and then archives the build artifact that you can use later.

6. After 15 minutes of idle time, the Jenkins builder is destroyed and will no longer show up in the `rhc apps` command-line output. The build artifacts, however, will still exist in Jenkins and can be viewed there.

Using Jenkins with your OpenShift application has the following advantages:

- **No application downtime in case of build failure**: Without Jenkins' support, OpenShift runs the build on the same gear on which your application is running. It first stops all the cartridges on the application gear, runs the build, and finally deploys the successful build artifact. In the event of build failure, the build artifact will not be deployed and your application will have downtime. With CI enabled for your application, OpenShift stops the application only after the build finishes successfully. This avoids downtime due to build failures.

- **More resources to build your project**: As the Jenkins builders run on separate gears, they have additional resources, such as memory and storage, to run your application build.

- **Store previous builds**: Jenkins can store your previous successful build artifacts for you. You can use these build artifacts if you want to roll back to a previous version.

- **Jenkins plugins**: Jenkins has a strong and active community that has built a variety of plugins to perform various common tasks. You can use these plugins to automate various tasks of your application. Throughout this chapter, you will install various Jenkins plugins to do various tasks.

You can view the logs of your Jenkins server using the following command:

```
$ rhc tail --app jenkins
```

## There's more...

You can also enable Jenkins support at application creation time using the `--enable-jenkins` option as shown in the following command:

```
$ rhc create-app jobstore jbosseap postgresql-9.2 --from-code
https://github.com/OpenShift-Cookbook/chapter7-jobstore-javaee6.git -
-enable-jenkins
```

The preceding command will create the Jenkins server application and add the Jenkins client to the application. If the Jenkins server application already exists, then it only adds the `jenkins` client cartridge to the application.

## See also

- The *Increasing the slave idle timeout* recipe
- The *Installing Jenkins plugins* recipe
- The *Creating a Jenkins workflow for your OpenShift applications* recipe

# Increasing the slave idle timeout

The Jenkins master creates slaves to build the project. These slaves remain alive only for 15 minutes after building the project, that is, they will be reused only if the next build request is received within 15 minutes of finishing the first build. If they don't receive the build request in 15 minutes after building the project, then the Jenkins master will kill the slave instance. The next build request will again create a new slave and build the application on it. Slave creation is a time-consuming process and is not ideal during the development cycle, when you expect quick feedback from your CI server.

In this recipe, you will learn how to increase the slave idle timeout so that you can reuse the slave for a longer time and get quick feedback from the CI server.

## Getting ready

This recipe assumes that you already have a Jenkins-enabled application, as discussed in the *Adding Jenkins CI to your application* recipe.

## How to do it...

Perform the following steps:

1. Log in to your Jenkins dashboard, and then go to the Jenkins configuration page at `https://jenkins-{domain-name}.rhcloud.com/configure`.

2. Under the **Cloud** configuration section, there is a **Slave Idle Time to Live** configuration as shown in the following screenshot. The default configuration is 15 minutes.

3. Update the **Slave Idle Time To Live** value to 60 minutes, and save the configuration by clicking on the **Save** button.

# How it works...

The Jenkins master created by OpenShift comes bundled with a few plugins that Jenkins needs to work effectively. You can see all the installed plugins by navigating to **Plugin Manager** | **Installed** as shown in the following screenshot:

The plugin that makes it possible for Jenkins to talk with your OpenShift account is **OpenShift Origin Jenkins Cloud Plugin**. This plugin is responsible for managing the slave gears that build your application.

Most of the Jenkins plugins have global configuration and job-level configuration. Global configuration applies to all the Jenkins jobs, whereas the job-level configuration applies only to a particular Jenkins job. You can view the Jenkins global configuration by navigating to the **Configure System** screen at `https://jenkins-{domain-name}.rhcloud.com/configure`. Many plugins that you will install will also need to be configured here. Jenkins dynamically adds new fields when you install the plugins.

The default screen contains a number of sections to configure either a general, system-wide parameter or various plugin configurations. The OpenShift Jenkins plugin adds the **OpenShift Cloud** subsection under the **Cloud** section. This configuration is used to talk with your OpenShift account and create slaves required to build your application.

In the preceding steps, you increased the slave idle timeout to 60 minutes in the OpenShift **Cloud** configuration section. This is the maximum slave idle timeout that you can assign to the slave. The next slave that Jenkins will create will use this configuration and will be alive for 60 minutes after building the project.

## See also

▸ The *Adding Jenkins CI to your application* recipe

▸ The *Installing Jenkins plugins* recipe

▸ The *Creating a Jenkins workflow for your OpenShift applications* recipe

# Installing Jenkins plugins

The extensible architecture of Jenkins makes it very powerful. There are third-party plugins that enable you to add extra features to your Jenkins instance. These features enable you to work with different SCM tools, such as Git, to generate code quality and code coverage reports, or to automate other manual tasks, such as database schema migration, and so on. In this recipe, you will learn how you can install the Green Balls plugin (`https://wiki.jenkins-ci.org/display/JENKINS/Green+Balls`) to your OpenShift Jenkins instance. The Green Balls plugin makes Jenkins use green balls instead of blue balls for successful builds.

## Getting ready

This recipe assumes you already have a Jenkins-enabled application, as discussed in the *Adding Jenkins CI to your application* recipe.

## How to do it...

Perform the following steps to install a plugin:

1. Log in to your OpenShift Jenkins dashboard and go to the **Manage Jenkins** screen at `https://jenkins-{domain-name}.rhcloud.com/manage`. The **Manage Jenkins** screen is a central place where you can configure all the aspects of the Jenkins system configuration.

2. Next, click on **Manage Plugins** to work with Jenkins plugins. You can install, remove, or update plugins through the **Manage Plugins** screen. Have a look at the following screenshot:

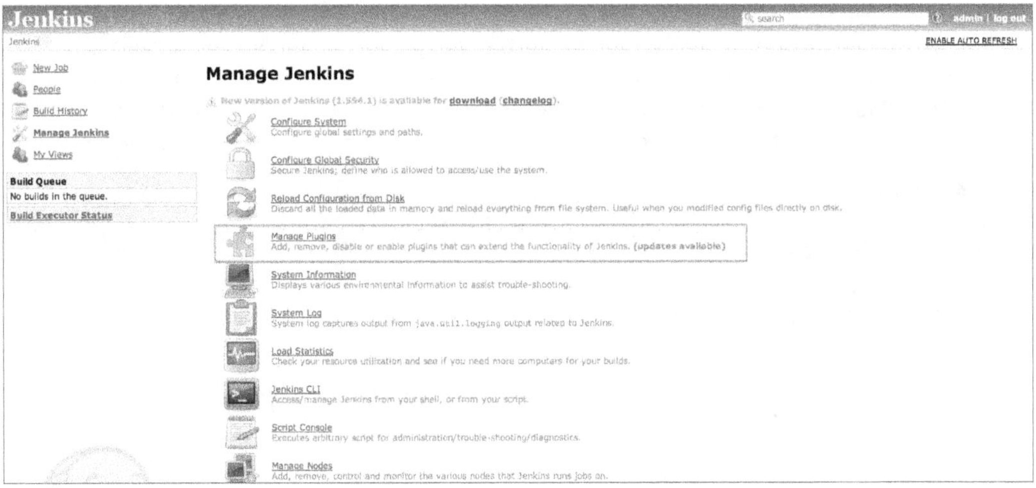

3. The **Manage Plugins** screen is divided into four tabs: **Updates**, **Available**, **Installed**, and **Advanced**, as shown in the following screenshot:

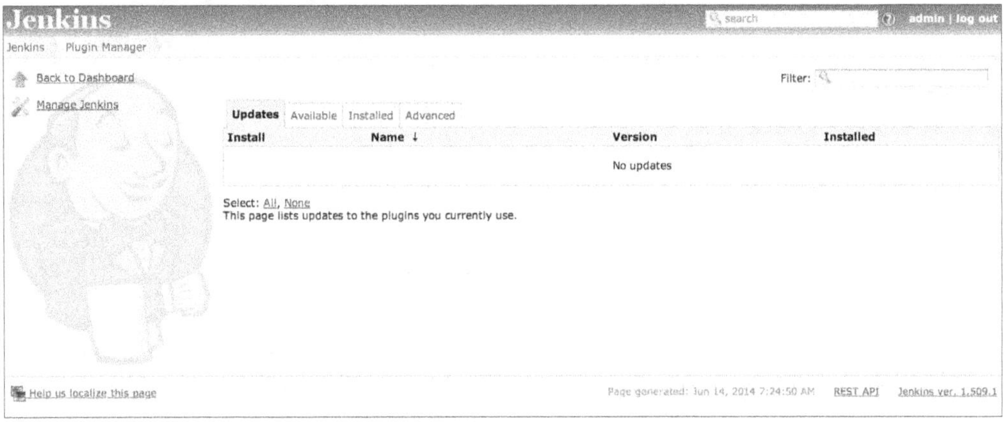

The **Updates** tab shows all the installed plugins that have updates, the **Available** tab shows all the plugins that you can install on your Jenkins instance, the **Installed** tab shows all the plugins that are already installed on your Jenkins instance, and the **Advanced** tab allows you to manually install the plugin or force Jenkins to check for updates.

4.  All the Jenkins plugins available in the Jenkins plugin registry are shown in the **Available** tab. If you click on the **Available** tab, you will find that the list is empty. To enable Jenkins to show plugins under the **Available** tab, navigate to **Manage Plugins | Advanced**, and click on the **Check Now** button, as shown in the following screenshot, to forcefully check for new updates:

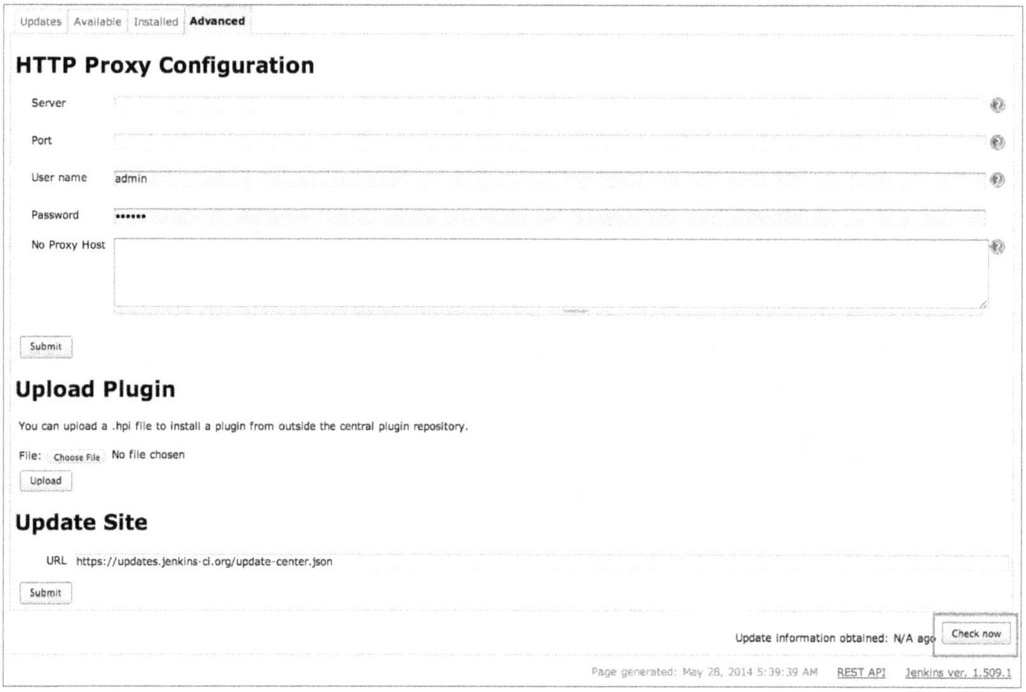

5.  Once done, you will see a list of plugins available under the **Available** tab.

6.  To install the Green Balls plugin, filter the available plugins, and then click on **Install without restart**. Have a look at the following screenshot:

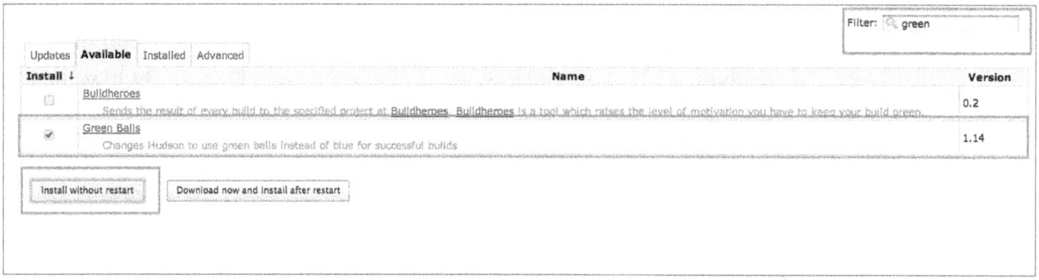

7. After the plugin is installed, you will see the Green Balls plugin in action. Please clean your browser cache if you still see blue balls.

## How it works...

In the preceding steps, you installed the Green Balls plugin to your OpenShift Jenkins instance. The Green Balls plugin does what it says: it makes successful builds display as green balls instead of the default blue balls.

There are a couple of ways to install plugins to your Jenkins instance. You can either use the automatic method or the manual method. In the preceding steps, you used the automatic method to install the plugins. The automatic method works for plugins that are listed in the Jenkins central plugins registry available at `http://updates.jenkins-ci.org/download/plugins/`. The plugins that are not available in the central plugin registry need to be installed manually. To install a plugin manually, navigate to **Manage Jenkins | Manage Plugins | Advance**. In the **Advanced** tab, there is a section called **Upload Plugin** that you can use to upload your plugin. Click on the **Choose File** button, select the plugin from your local machine, and then click on the **Upload** button to upload the plugin:

## Upload Plugin

You can upload a .hpi file to install a plugin from outside the central plugin repository.

File: Choose File No file chosen

Upload

The manually installed plugins are not installed until you restart Jenkins. So, once the plugin is uploaded, restart Jenkins by going to `https://jenkins-{domain-name}.rhcloud.com/safeRestart`. This will restart Jenkins after the current builds have been completed and will install your plugin.

## See also

- ▸ The *Adding Jenkins CI to your application* recipe
- ▸ The *Using Jenkins to build projects hosted on GitHub* recipe
- ▸ The *Creating a Jenkins workflow for your OpenShift applications* recipe

# Using Jenkins to build projects hosted on GitHub

You can use the OpenShift Jenkins instance to build your non-OpenShift projects as well. This recipe will use a Maven-based project publicly hosted on GitHub at `https://github.com/OpenShift-Cookbook/chapter10-demo-app`. The goal of this recipe is to build the project whenever you push code to the GitHub repository and send an e-mail in case the build status changes, that is, the build fails or recovers from a build failure. This is the first step an organization takes when they try to introduce CI.

## Getting ready

This recipe assumes that you already have a Jenkins-enabled application, as discussed in the *Adding Jenkins CI to your application* recipe.

## How to do it...

Perform the following steps to learn how to build projects hosted on GitHub:

1. In this recipe, we will use the Jenkins master to build the project. Go to `https://jenkins-{domain-name}.rhcloud.com/configure`, and update the **# of executors** property to 1. Any number greater than 0 will allow the master to run build jobs. Also, change the **Usage** field value to **Leave this machine for tied jobs only**. This configuration will make sure that the master instance is only used for the job explicitly configured to run on the master. Later in the job configuration, you will configure a job to run only on the master. Click on the **Save** button to save the new values:

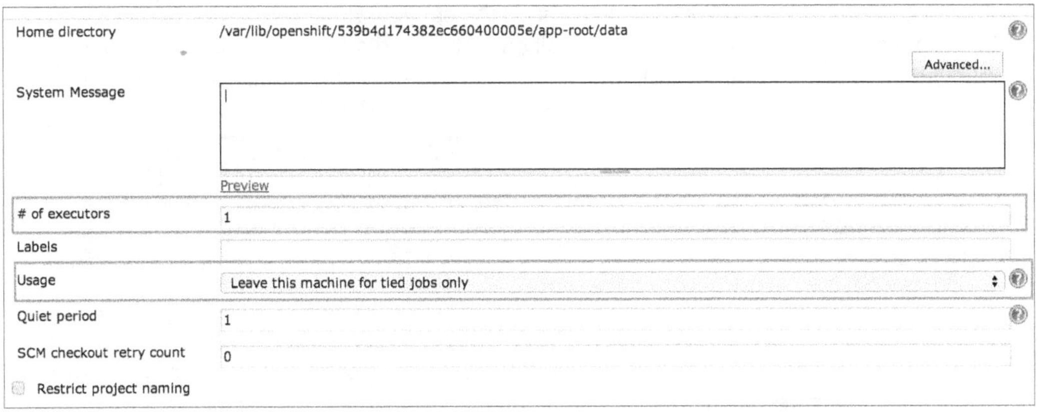

| Home directory | /var/lib/openshift/539b4d174382ec660400005e/app-root/data | |
| System Message | | |
| | Preview | |
| # of executors | 1 | |
| Labels | | |
| Usage | Leave this machine for tied jobs only | |
| Quiet period | 1 | |
| SCM checkout retry count | 0 | |
| ☐ Restrict project naming | | |

2. One of the goals of this recipe is to send e-mails when the project becomes unstable. To allow Jenkins to send an e-mail, you have to provide e-mail settings in the **E-mail Notification** section under the Jenkins **Configure System** screen. Click on the **Advanced** tab to see all the configuration options. The configuration shown in the following screenshot uses Gmail to send e-mails. Gmail is shown just for demonstration here. Google might send you an e-mail stating that someone is hacking your account, as your account is accessed from a different location than it is usually used. Ideally, you should use your organization SMTP server configuration.

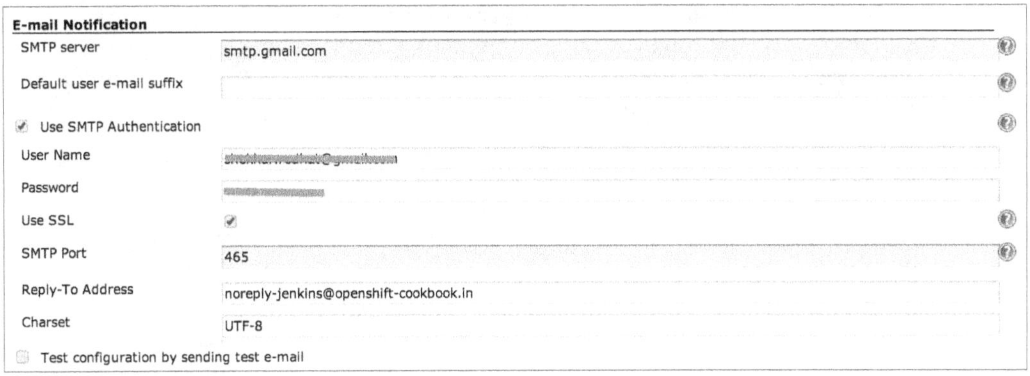

**E-mail Notification**

| SMTP server | smtp.gmail.com | |
| Default user e-mail suffix | | |
| ☑ Use SMTP Authentication | | |
| User Name | shubheenvedhab@gmail.com | |
| Password | ●●●●●●●●●●●●●● | |
| Use SSL | ☑ | |
| SMTP Port | 465 | |
| Reply-To Address | noreply-jenkins@openshift-cookbook.in | |
| Charset | UTF-8 | |
| ☐ Test configuration by sending test e-mail | | |

3. You can also send a test e-mail to check the configuration. Check the **Test configuration by sending a test e-mail** checkbox and providing it with the e-mail address you want to send an e-mail to. You will receive an e-mail like the one shown in the following screenshot:

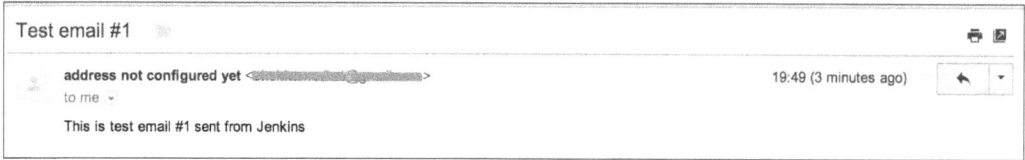

4. One thing that you will find annoying in the preceding screenshot is that the address is not configured yet in the from section of the e-mail. You can configure it to something else by updating the value of the **System Admin e-mail address** property from **address not configured yet** to something user friendly, as shown in the following screenshot. After making this change, the notification e-mails from Jenkins will be sent with this address in the from header.

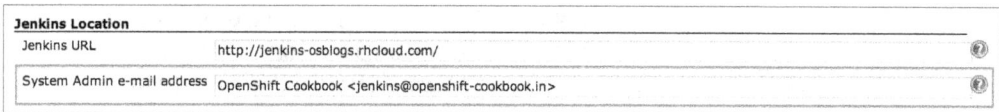

5. Fork the GitHub repository (`https://github.com/OpenShift-Cookbook/chapter10-demo-app`) by clicking on the **Fork** button. You need to log in to GitHub with a valid account before you can fork this repository. You have to fork this repository so that you can push your changes to the repository.

6. Go to your Jenkins dashboard, and click on **New Job**. Have a look at the following screenshot:

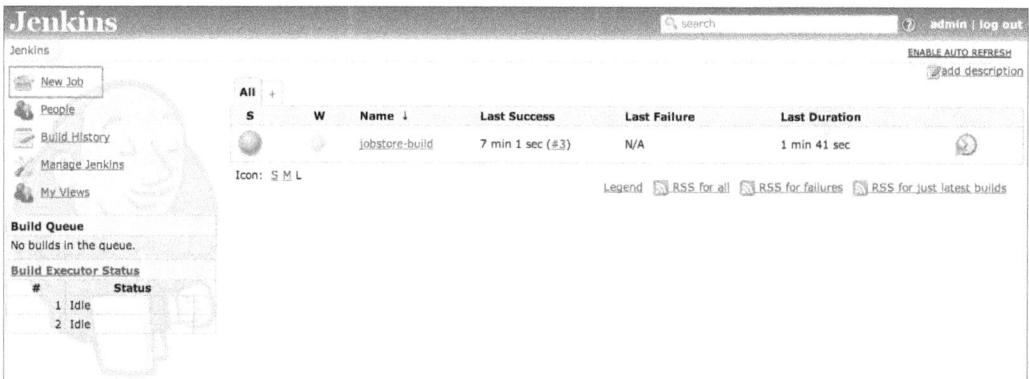

7. Select the **Build a free-style software project** build type, and give it a name, `chapter10-github-recipe-build`, as shown in the following screenshot. Click on **OK** to create the job.

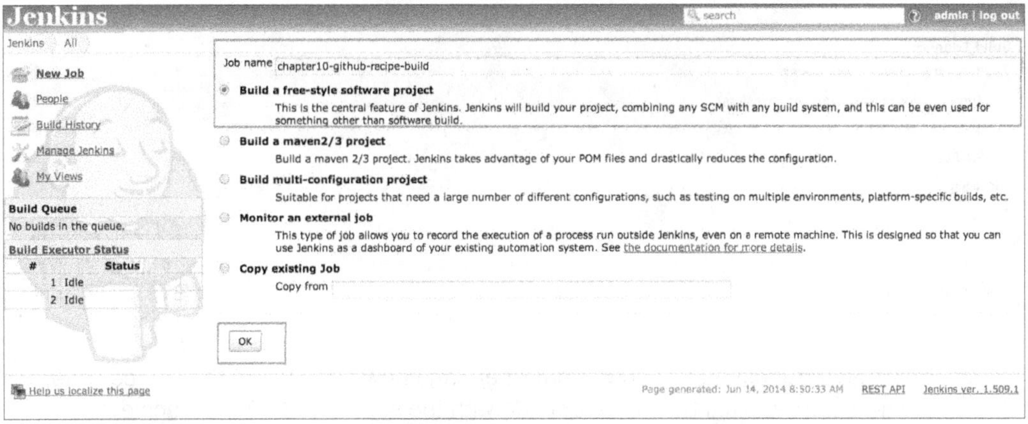

8. Next, you will be shown the job configuration page where you can configure this job. The first configuration that you will update is under the **Source Code Management** section. As the project is hosted on GitHub, enter the URL of the GitHub repository that you want to build. The GitHub repository URL will be `https://github.com/<username>/chapter10-demo-app.git`. The username corresponds to your GitHub username. The following screenshot shows the **Source Code Management** section:

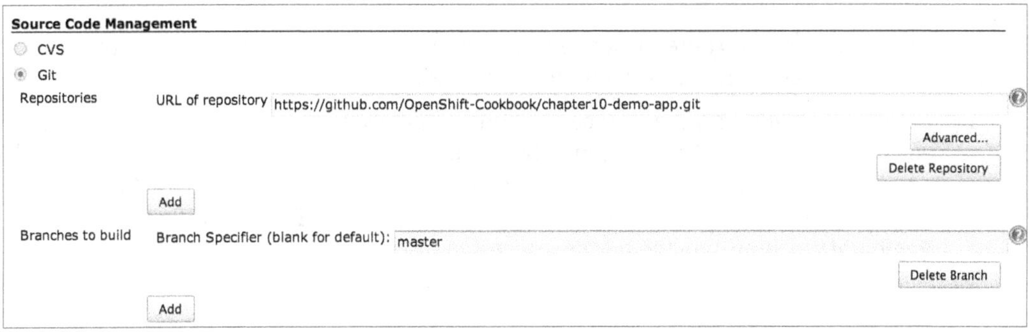

9. Next, you have to configure when this build should get triggered. This is configured under the **Build Triggers** section. In the configuration shown in the following screenshot, you told Jenkins to poll SCM every minute. It uses the same syntax as `crontab` on Unix/Linux.

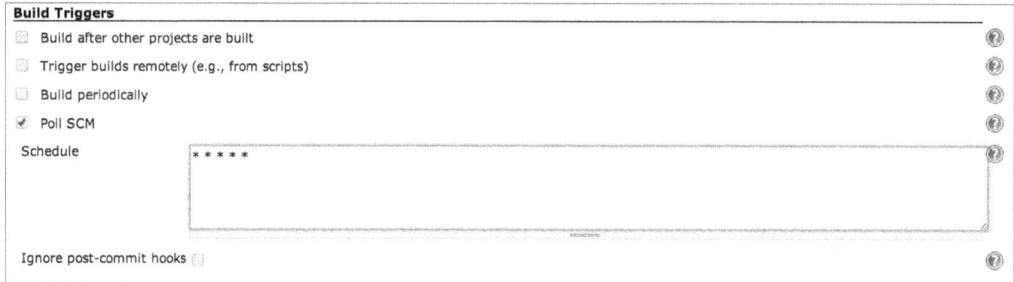

**Build Triggers**

☐ Build after other projects are built

☐ Trigger builds remotely (e.g., from scripts)

☐ Build periodically

☑ Poll SCM

Schedule
```
* * * * *
```

Ignore post-commit hooks ☐

10. Now that the Jenkins job knows from where and how often to get the source code, the next step is to tell the job what to do with the source code. This is achieved by defining the build steps. A job can have one or more build steps. To add a new build step, click on the **Add build step** dropdown, and select **Execute shell**, as shown in the following screenshot:

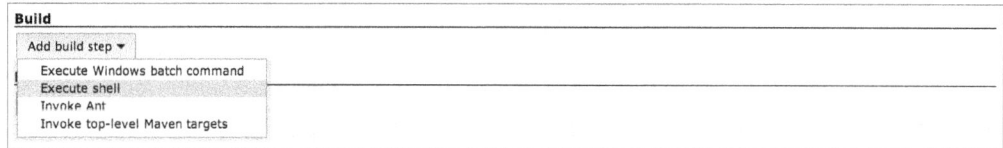

**Build**

Add build step ▼

Execute Windows batch command
Execute shell
Invoke Ant
Invoke top-level Maven targets

11. This will render a text area where you can enter the command you want to run. Enter the `mvn clean install` command in the text area.

12. The next configuration that you can optionally specify in your job is what to do after building your project. This is defined by creating one or more post-build actions. Let's add an action that will send an e-mail when the build becomes unstable. Click on the **Add post-build action** drop-down list, and then select **E-mail notification**. In the **Recipients** textbox, provide a whitespace-separated list of e-mail IDs that you want to send an e-mail to in the event of a build failure, as shown in the following screenshot:

**Post-build Actions**

☐ **E-mail Notification**

Recipients `shekhargulati84@gmail.com`

Whitespace-separated list of recipient addresses. May reference build parameters like $PARAM. E-mail will be sent when a build fails, becomes unstable or returns to stable.

☑ Send e-mail for every unstable build

☐ Send separate e-mails to individuals who broke the build

[ Delete ]

[ Add post-build action ▼ ]

13. The last configuration left before you can save this job is to configure it to run on the master node. This is done by checking the **Restrict where this project can be run** checkbox and then giving it the name of the node that should be used to build the project, as shown in the following screenshot:

☑ Restrict where this project can be run

Label Expression    `master`

**Advanced Project Options**

[ Advanced... ]

14. Now, save the configuration by clicking on the **Save** button.

15. To test the new Jenkins job, first clone the project on your local machine. To clone the project, use the following command. Please replace the username with your GitHub account username.

```
$ git clone git@github.com:<username>/chapter10-demo-app.git
```

16. To test whether the job is working correctly, let's change one of the test cases so that it fails. Update the `MessageRepositoryTest` assertion from `assertEquals(1, messages.size());` to `assertEquals(2, messages.size());`.

17. Commit the code, and push the changes to your GitHub repository:

```
$ git commit -am "added test failure"
$ git push
```

18. Jenkins will pick the change and start a new build. The build will fail, and you will receive an e-mail with the job logs.

19. Now, let's fix the build failure by reverting the change from `assertEquals(2, messages.size());` to `assertEquals(1, messages.size());`. Then run the following commands:

```
$ git commit -am "fixed test failure"
$ git push
```

20. Again, Jenkins will pick the change and start a new build. This time, you will receive an e-mail saying that the build is back to normal, as shown in the following screenshot:

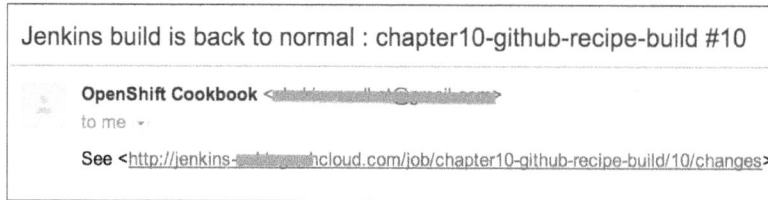

Jenkins build is back to normal : chapter10-github-recipe-build #10

**OpenShift Cookbook** <~~~~~~~~~@~~~~~>
to me ▾

See <http://jenkins-~~~~~~cloud.com/job/chapter10-github-recipe-build/10/changes>

## How it works...

You created a freestyle Jenkins job that will poll Jenkins every minute and, if it detects a new commit, it will build the project. In step 1, you updated the Jenkins master configuration so that it can run build jobs. By default, the Jenkins master is not configured to run any builds. Setting the number of executors to 1 in the Jenkins system configuration enables the Jenkins master to run builds. The number of executors lets you define how many concurrent builds a Jenkins instance can perform.

E-mail is one of the most popular ways of communication. In step 2, you configured Jenkins to send an e-mail using the Gmail SMTP settings. You can send 99 e-mails per day using the Gmail SMTP server, which is fine for most individual projects, but for your organization projects, you should use your organization SMTP server.

This recipe requires you to have your own Git repository that will be polled by Jenkins. This is required so that you can push changes to your Git repository, as you can't push changes to the Git repository of another person unless you are added as a collaborator. You forked the repository in step 3 so that you have your own copy of this repository that you can work with.

In step 4, you created a new Jenkins job that will be used to build the project you forked in step 3. You used a freestyle build job, as it is the most flexible build option that you can use to build any type of project.

From steps 5 through step 9, you configured the job so that Jenkins polls the Git repository every minute and uses the Jenkins master to build the project. After saving the job in step 10, you will see your new job listed in the Jenkins dashboard. Jenkins will automatically run the build for the first time, as it does not have any history for this job. After running the job for the first time, Jenkins will wait for the changes in your Git repository before it starts another build.

Once the job was configured, you tested the Jenkins job in steps 11 through 15 by making a change to your local repository and pushing the change to GitHub. Jenkins will poll the Git repository in the next one minute, detect the change, and start the build.

▶  The *Creating a Jenkins workflow for your OpenShift applications* recipe

# Creating a Jenkins workflow for your OpenShift applications

In this recipe, you will create a Jenkins workflow that you could use to build and deploy applications on OpenShift.

## Getting ready

This recipe will cover all the steps from the start to make sure you have all the three gears available.

## How to do it...

Perform the following steps to create a Jenkins workflow for your OpenShift applications:

1.  Create a new Jenkins server application by running the following command. This was covered in detail in the *Adding Jenkins CI to your application* recipe.

    ```
    $ rhc create-app jenkins jenkins
    ```

2.  Create an OpenShift Apache Tomcat 7 application that will be used to deploy the project. The project will be created with the `--no-git` option, as we do not want to clone the repository, because the code will be hosted on GitHub. The `--enable-jenkins` option will create a new Jenkins job that will build and deploy the application on OpenShift:

    ```
    $ rhc create-app forumapp tomcat-7 postgresql-9 --enable-
    jenkins --no-git
    ```

3.  Log in to your Jenkins dashboard, and you will see the **forumapp-build** job listed on the dashboard.

4.  Create a new Jenkins job with the name `forumapp-github-build` by following the steps mentioned in the *Using Jenkins to build projects hosted on GitHub* recipe. Once the job is created, any change pushed to your GitHub repository will result in a Jenkins build.

5.  Next, install the Jenkins Cobertura plugin by following the instructions mentioned in the *Installing Jenkins plugins* recipe.

6. Once the plugin is installed, create another job with the name `forumapp-quality-build`. But, rather than creating a job from the start, you can use the `forumapp-github-build` job as a template. After entering the details, click on **OK**:

Job name [forumapp-quality-build]

○ **Build a free-style software project**
This is the central feature of Jenkins. Jenkins will build your project, combining any SCM with any build system, and this can be even used for something other than software build.

○ **Build a maven2/3 project**
Build a maven 2/3 project. Jenkins takes advantage of your POM files and drastically reduces the configuration.

○ **Build multi-configuration project**
Suitable for projects that need a large number of different configurations, such as testing on multiple environments, platform-specific builds, etc.

○ **Monitor an external job**
This type of job allows you to record the execution of a process run outside Jenkins, even on a remote machine. This is designed so that you can use Jenkins as a dashboard of your existing automation system. See the documentation for more details.

◉ **Copy existing Job**
Copy from  forumapp-github-build

[ OK ]

7. You will be directed to the `forumapp-quality-build` job configuration page. Update the following configuration values to suit this job:

   1. Change the **Restrict this project can be run** value from `master` to `forumapp-build`.

   2. Uncheck **Poll SCM** under the **Build Triggers** section.

   3. Change the **Execute Shell** command from `mvn clean install` to `mvn clean package -Pquality`.

8. Now, you need to add two post-build actions to `forumapp-quality-build`, first to kick the `forumapp-build` job that will deploy the application to OpenShift and, second, publish the Cobertura code coverage report. Add the post-build action to trigger `forumapp-build` when the build succeeds. To add the Cobertura code coverage post-build action, click on the **Add post-build action hook** option, select **Publish Cobertura Coverage Report**, and provide `**/target/site/cobertura/coverage.xml` for the **Cobertura xml report pattern** field.

9. After updating the `forumapp-quality-build` job configuration, click on the **Save** button.

10. One of the responsibilities of `forumapp-github-build` is to start the `forumapp-quality-build` job after it has been completed successfully. Update the `forumapp-github-build` job configuration by adding a post-build action. Add the **Build other projects** post-build action to build `forumapp-github-build` when the build is successful. Click on the **Save** button after adding the post-build action:

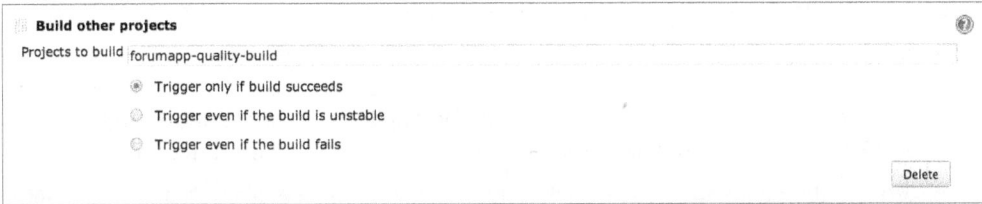

11. Now that you have configured the `forumapp-github-build` and `forumapp-quality-build` jobs, you need to update the `forumapp-build` job configuration to pull the code from the GitHub repository and deploy the latest code to OpenShift. Go to `https://jenkins-{domain-name}.rhcloud.com/job/forumapp-build/configure`, and add a new **Execute Shell** build step. This build step will first add a Git remote to the GitHub repository and then pull code from the GitHub repository. This is shown in the following commands:

```
$ git remote add upstream -m master
https://github.com/<username>/chapter10-demo-app.git

$ git pull -s recursive -X theirs upstream master
```

12. Please replace the username with your GitHub account username. Also, make sure that the order of the build action hooks is the same as the order shown in the following screenshot:

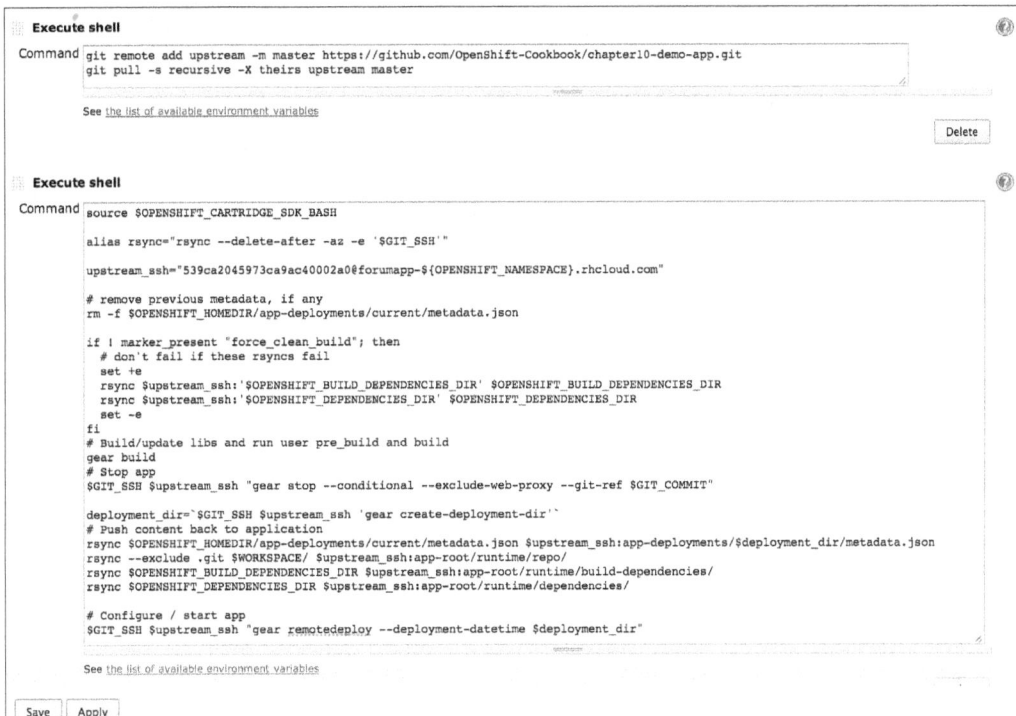

13. Click on the **Save** button to save the configuration.

14. Now, to test whether all our jobs are configured properly, go to the Jenkins dashboard and manually start the `forumapp-github-build` job. Instead of manually starting the job, you could also make a change to the application source and push the change to the GitHub repository. Jenkins will detect the change and start the build process.

15. After all the builds are successfully completed, you will see all the builds in a healthy state on the Jenkins dashboard, as shown in the following screenshot:

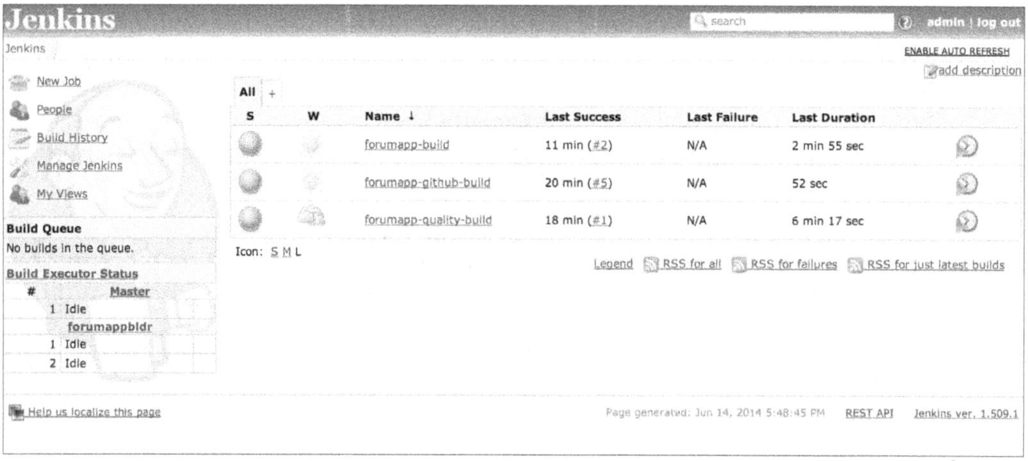

16. To view the code coverage of your project, go to the **forumapp-quality-build** page, and click on **Coverage Report** to see the code coverage of your project:

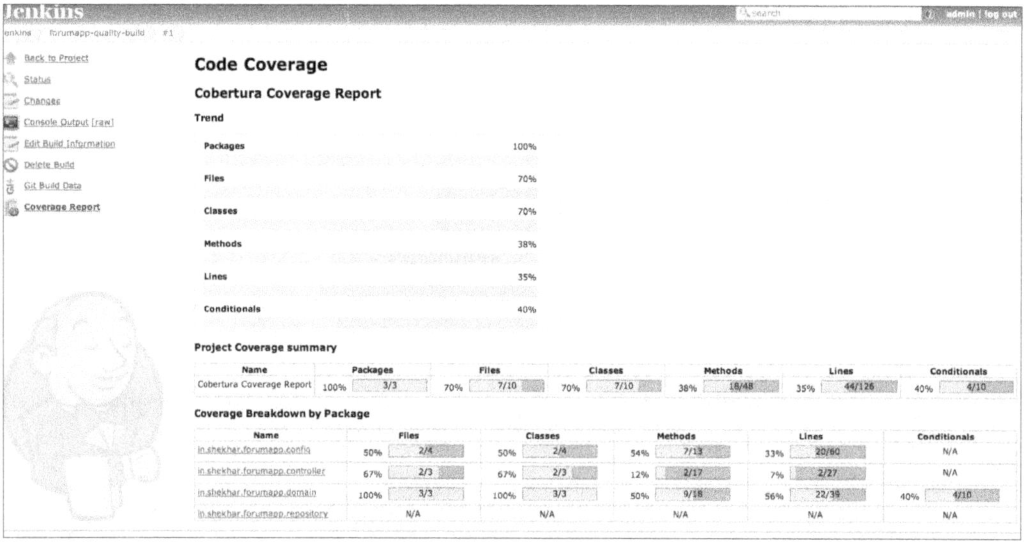

## How it works...

In the preceding steps, you created a simple workflow with three Jenkins jobs, each responsible for a specific task. The first job polls the GitHub repository at a specified interval for code changes and then builds the project when the changes are found. This job builds the project and runs its unit tests. It used the Jenkins master to build the project. The advantage of using Jenkins for light jobs like this is that you don't have to wait for the slave creation. You should only use the master for jobs that are light in nature; otherwise, the Jenkins master might go down.

The first build, if successful, starts the quality job that runs the code coverage over the application code. This build uses Cobertura (`http://cobertura.github.io/cobertura/`) to identify the parts of the Java application that lack test coverage. The quality build was configured to execute the `mvn clean install -Pquality` command. This command will run the Maven Cobertura plugin. The Maven plugin will generate both HTML and XML reports. The XML report is used by Jenkins to parse the coverage results. The quality build will use the Jenkins slave instead of the master, as a quality build usually tends to be memory- and CPU-intensive, and you will not like the master going down because of one job.

On successful completion of the quality build, the third Jenkins job will deploy the application to OpenShift. This job will also use the Jenkins slave.

## See also

▶ The *Upgrading Jenkins to the latest version* recipe

# Upgrading Jenkins to the latest version

The Jenkins application created by OpenShift runs an old version of Jenkins. At the time of this writing, the Jenkins application created by OpenShift runs the 1.509.1 Version. This version is quite old, and some Jenkins plugins do not work with this version. In this recipe, you will learn how to upgrade Jenkins to the latest version. The latest version of Jenkins at the time of this writing is 1.567.

> This recipe is experimental, and I don't recommend that people use it for their production Jenkins instances. The aim of this recipe is to show that it is feasible to upgrade the Jenkins version. This might result in build data loss or a break in the Jenkins instance. So, use this recipe in your test environments first.

## Getting ready

This recipe assumes you already have a Jenkins-enabled application, as discussed in the *Adding Jenkins CI to your application* recipe.

## How to do it...

Perform the following steps to upgrade the Jenkins version:

1. Open a new command-line terminal, and SSH into your Jenkins application by running the following command:

   ```
   $ rhc ssh --app jenkins
   ```

2. Create a new directory called `jenkins-latest-version` inside `$OPENSHIFT_DATA_DIR`, and download the latest Jenkins WAR file using `wget` by running the following command:

   ```
   cd $OPENSHIFT_DATA_DIR && mkdir jenkins-latest-version && cd
   jenkins-latest-version && wget http://mirrors.jenkins-
   ci.org/war/latest/jenkins.war
   ```

3. Exit the SSH session by typing the `exit` command.

4. Create two environment variables by running the following command. Please replace `$OPENSHIFT_DATA_DIR` with your Jenkins application's `$OPENSHIFT_DATA_DIR` environment variable value:

   ```
   rhc env-set JENKINS_WAR_PATH=$OPENSHIFT_DATA_DIR/jenkins-
   latest-version/jenkins.war JENKINS_JAR_CACHE_PATH="~/app-
   root/data/.jenkins/cache/jars" --app jenkins
   ```

5. Go to the Jenkins plugin manager, and uninstall the OpenShift Jenkins plugin. Restart Jenkins after uninstalling the plugin for the changes to take effect. You can restart Jenkins by going to the `https://jenkins-{domain-name}.rhcloud.com/safeRestart` URL.

6. After the Jenkins restart, you will see the latest version of Jenkins running, as shown in the following screenshot:

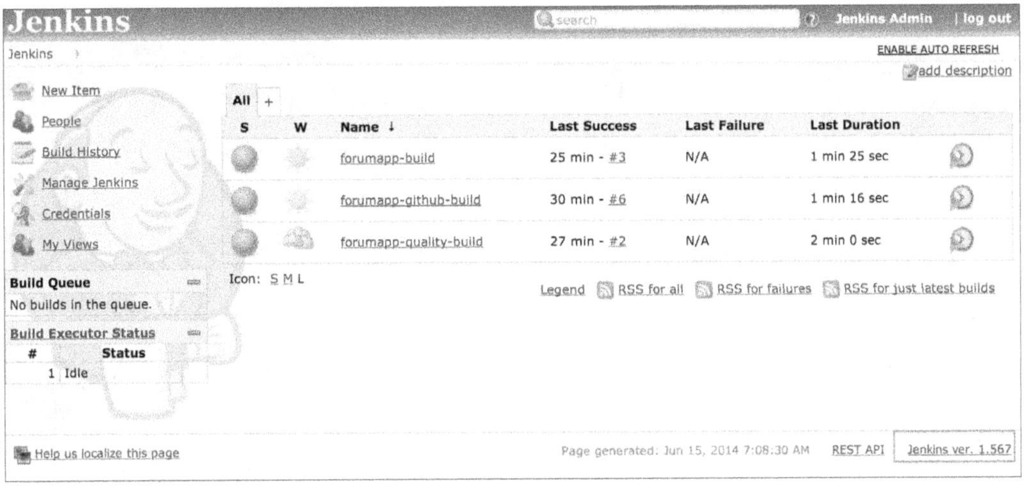

7. The default OpenShift plugin installed with the Jenkins installation does not work with the latest version of Jenkins. You have to build the latest OpenShift Jenkins plugin from source. The source code is available on GitHub at `https://github.com/openshift/jenkins-cloud-plugin`. I have packaged the latest version and made it available at `https://github.com/OpenShift-Cookbook/chapter10-openshift-jenkins-plugin`. Download the latest plugin from `https://github.com/OpenShift-Cookbook/chapter10-openshift-jenkins-plugin/raw/master/openshift.hpi` to a convenient location on your machine.

8. Install the plugin manually by going to the plugin manager **Advanced** tab and uploading the plugin.

9. Restart Jenkins so that the plugin gets installed.

10. Go to the Jenkins system configuration, add a new OpenShift cloud, and click on **Save**. Have a look at the following screenshot:

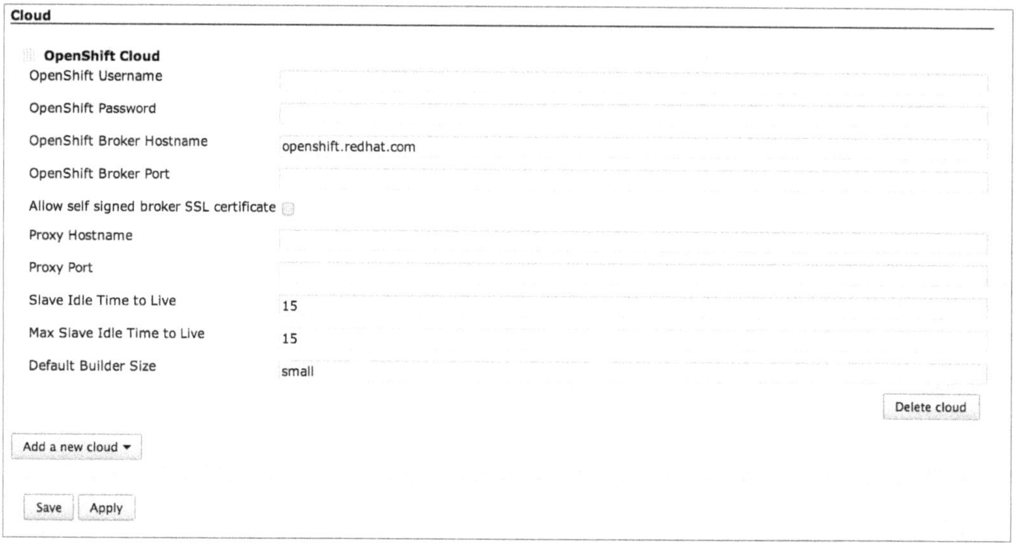

11. Go to **Plugin Manager** (`https://jenkins-{domain-name}.rhcloud.com/pluginManager/`), and update all the installed plugins.

12. Finally, to test whether all of your existing jobs are working fine, start an existing job manually. If you followed the last recipe, then you will already have three Jenkins jobs listed on the Jenkins dashboard.

## How it works...

The OpenShift Jenkins cartridge allows a user to upgrade the Jenkins version by defining an environment variable, `JENKINS_WAR_PATH`. If this environment variable were used, then the OpenShift Jenkins cartridge will use the Jenkins `war` file located at this path. From step 1 through step 4, you first downloaded the latest version of Jenkins WAR and then created the `JENKINS_WAR_PATH` environment variable.

You also created another environment variable called `JENKINS_JAR_CACHE_PATH`. This is required with Jenkins Version 1.540 or higher. The reason you need to set this environment variable is that if you don't set this environment variable, then Jenkins will try to cache the plugin in the user home directory at `~/.jenkins/cache/jars`. In OpenShift, you can only write to the `$OPENSHIFT_DATA_DIR` directory. This environment variable makes sure that JARs are cached in a writable directory; otherwise, your build will fail.

After setting the environment variables, you restarted Jenkins so that the new environment variables are picked up by Jenkins. You will now see the latest Jenkins version running.

## See also

> ▸ The *Adding Jenkins CI to your application* recipe

# 11

# Logging and Scaling Your OpenShift Applications

The specific recipes of this chapter are as follows:

- ▶ Viewing application logs
- ▶ Working with JBoss application logs
- ▶ Enabling JBoss access logs
- ▶ Working with Tomcat application logs
- ▶ Working with Python application logs
- ▶ Creating scalable applications
- ▶ Configuring a different health check URL for HAProxy
- ▶ Configuring HAProxy to use a different balance algorithm
- ▶ Creating scalable apps from nonscalable apps
- ▶ Enabling manual scaling with marker files

## Introduction

This chapter consists of recipes that will help you to work with the application logs and create scalable applications. The logging recipes will help you to access your application logs and debug any problems you might encounter while running your applications. You will learn how OpenShift uses a component called logshifter to store all application- and cartridge-specific logs in OPENSHIFT_LOG_DIR. This chapter will go into application logging in detail and cover various aspects of logging the JBoss, Tomcat, and Python applications. The logging concepts covered in this chapter will help you work with any web cartridge logs.

The *Viewing application logs* recipe will give you a general introduction to application logging, with the PHP web cartridge as an example. You will learn how to access application logs using the rhc command-line tool, and understand the log format used by Apache-based cartridges. Next, you will learn how to access JBoss application logs in the *Working with JBoss application logs* and *Enabling JBoss access logs* recipes. The *Working with Python application logs* recipe will cover how to effectively work with Python application logs.

The second section of this chapter will discuss application scaling in detail. You will learn how to create autoscalable applications in the *Creating scalable applications* recipe. Autoscaling is not always desired, and at times you need manual control over application scaling. In the *Enabling manual scaling with marker files* recipe, you will learn how to disable autoscaling and manually scale OpenShift applications using the rhc command-line tool.

# Viewing application logs

Logs are important data generated by your application that can help you understand user heuristics, monitor application performance, and debug problems. They are the first place you look when something goes wrong in your application. OpenShift uses a service called logshifter, which collects logs from all the different pieces of your application and makes them accessible at a single location. These logs can then be fed to your favorite log management solution, such as Splunk, to gain more useful insights. In this recipe, you will learn how easily you can view all the logs of your application using a single command. This recipe covers logging in a cartridge-agnostic manner. The language-specific aspects of logging will be covered later in this chapter.

## Getting ready

To complete this recipe, you will need rhc installed on your machine. Also, we will make use of the OpenShift application created in the *Creating an OpenShift application using the rhc command-line client* recipe in *Chapter 3*, *Creating and Managing Applications*.

To recreate the application, run the following command:

```
$ rhc create-app myapp php-5.4
```

## How to do it...

To view the logfiles of your application, perform the following steps:

1.  Open a command-line terminal and run the following command, either from within the application directory or by passing the application name using the --app option. Have a look at the following command:

    ```
    $ rhc tail
    ```

2. You can also use the app name, as shown in the following command:

   ```
   $ rhc tail --app myapp
   ```

3. Open your favorite browser and go to `http://myapp-{domain-name}.rhcloud.com`. You will notice new logs being tailed on your command-line terminal. A small snippet of logs is shown in the following command-line output:

   ```
   117.212.42.145 - - [22/Jun/2014:15:28:03 -0400] "GET /
   HTTP/1.1" 200 39627 "-" "Mozilla/5.0 (Macintosh; Intel Mac OS
   X 10_8_5) AppleWebKit/537.36 (KHTML, like Gecko)
   Chrome/35.0.1916.153 Safari/537.36"
   ```

## How it works...

Every OpenShift application uses one or more cartridges to do its work. Each cartridge is configured to log messages to `stdout` or `stderr`. An OpenShift service called `logshifter` captures all the messages sent to `stdout` as well as `stderr` and logs them properly. In OpenShift Online, all the messages captured by `logshifter` are written to the `$OPENSHIFT_LOGS_DIR` directory. You can SSH into your application gear using the `rhc ssh` command and look into the `$OPENSHIFT_LOGS_DIR` directory, as follows:

```
[myapp-{domain-name}.rhcloud.com logs]\> cd $OPENSHIFT_LOG_DIR
[myapp-{domain-name}.rhcloud.com logs]\> ls
php.log
```

As you can see in the preceding command line, the `$OPENSHIFT_LOGS_DIR` directory contains one logfile called `php.log`. All the application and Apache logs (both access and error) will be written to this logfile. The name of the logfile depends on the tag name passed to `logshifter` during the cartridge startup. For example, the `php` cartridge is started using the `nohup /usr/sbin/httpd $HTTPD_CMD_CONF -D FOREGROUND |& /usr/bin/logshifter -tag php &` command. This command ensures that the Apache logs are piped to the `logshifter` service and uses `php` as the tag name. The tag name serves two purposes: first, it identifies the program that generated the log message, and second, it is used as the name of the logfile.

In step 1, you ran the `rhc tail` command; this command opened an SSH tunnel behind the scenes and ran the `tail -f */log*/*` command on your application gear. The `-f` option allows a file to be monitored continuously. As new lines are added to the logfile, `tail` will update the display. The `rhc tail` command will tail all the logs in your application gear's `$OPENSHIFT_LOG_DIR` directory, as shown in step 2. The sample output is shown in the following command. All the Apache-based cartridges (PHP, Python, Perl, and Ruby) will have similar output in the logs. Have a look at the following command output:

```
117.212.42.145 - - [22/Jun/2014:15:28:03 -0400] "GET / HTTP/1.1" 200
39627 "-" "Mozilla/5.0 (Macintosh; Intel Mac OS X 10_8_5)
AppleWebKit/537.36 (KHTML, like Gecko) Chrome/35.0.1916.153
Safari/537.36"
```

At first glance, the output might look a bit cryptic; on closer inspection, it is no different from most application logs. The log follows Apache Combined Log Format (`https://httpd.apache.org/docs/trunk/logs.html#combined`). The format used is `"%{X-Forwarded-For}i %l %u %t \"%r\" %>s %b \"%{Referer}i\" \"%{User-Agent}i\""`. Let's look at all these options one by one:

▶ `%{X-Forwarded-For}i`: This is the HTTP request `X-Forwarded-For` header. It contains the IP address of the original client. In the log line shown in the preceding command, it corresponds to `117.212.42.145`.

▶ `%l`: This is the user identity determined by `identd`. This will return `-` when the value is not present. In the log line shown in the preceding command, the value is `-`.

▶ `%u`: This is the remote user determined by HTTP authentication. This will return `-` when the value is not present. In the log line shown in the preceding command, the value is `-`.

▶ `%t`: This is the time when the HTTP request is received. In the log line shown in the preceding command, the value is `[22/Jun/2014:15:28:03 -0400]`.

▶ `\"%r\"`: This is the first line of the HTTP request. In the log line shown in the preceding command, the value is `GET / HTTP/1.1`.

▶ `%>s`: This is the HTTP status code. In the log line shown in the preceding command, the value is `200`, which means the request was successful.

▶ `%b`: This is the response from the server in bytes. In the log line shown in the preceding section, the value is `39627`.

▶ `\"%{Referer}i\"`: This is the referrer URL that is linked to this URL. In the log line shown in the preceding section, the value is `-`, which means it was not present.

▶ `\"%{User-Agent}i\"`: This is the user agent taken from the HTTP request header. In the log line shown in the preceding section, the value is `Mozilla/5.0 (Macintosh; Intel Mac OS X 10_8_5) AppleWebKit/537.36 (KHTML, like Gecko) Chrome/35.0.1916.153 Safari/537.36`.

As mentioned in the preceding section, `logshifter` will write one logfile per cartridge. So, if you add the MySQL cartridge to your application, then `logshifter` will create another logfile with the name `mysql.log` and write all the MySQL-specific logs to it. The `rhc tail` command will tail all the files present inside `$OPENSHIFT_LOG_DIR`. Make sure to run the `tail` command again so it can read the new logfile:

```
==> app-root/logs/php.log <==

117.212.42.145 - - [22/Jun/2014:17:18:09 -0400] "GET / HTTP/1.1" 200
39627 "-" "Mozilla/5.0 (Macintosh; Intel Mac OS X 10_8_5)
AppleWebKit/537.36 (KHTML, like Gecko) Chrome/35.0.1916.153
Safari/537.36"

==> app-root/logs/mysql.log <==
```

```
140622 17:17:31 [Note] Event Scheduler: Loaded 0 events
140622 17:17:31 [Note] /opt/rh/mysql55/root/usr/libexec/mysqld: ready
for connections.
```

The `mysql.log` logfile will contain all the MySQL logs. If you want to tail only a specific cartridge log, then you can use the `-f` or `--files` option of the `rhc tail` command, as shown in the following command. This will tail only the `mysql.log` file.

```
$ rhc tail --files app-root/logs/mysql.log
```

You can view all the `rhc tail` command options by looking at its help, as shown in the following command:

```
$ rhc tail --help
```

Another responsibility `logshifter` performs is rolling logfiles based on the file size when they reach a configurable threshold. It also allows you to retain a configurable number of rolled files before removing the oldest prior to the next roll. You can configure the file size and the number of rolled files using the `LOGSHIFTER_$TAG_MAX_FILESIZE` and `LOGSHIFTER_$TAG_MAX_FILES` environment variables, where `$TAG` is replaced by an uppercase string equal to the value of the `-tag` argument. The default values used by `logshifter` are `10M` (M for megabytes) for file size and `10` for the number of rolled files. Let's suppose you want to configure values as `20M` for file size and `5` for the number of rolled files. To configure these new values, you have to first use the `rhc env` command to set new environment variables and then restart the application, as shown in the following command:

```
$ rhc env-set LOGSHIFTER_PHP_MAX_FILES=5
LOGSHIFTER_PHP_MAX_FILESIZE=20M && rhc restart-app
```

You can specify the file size in kilobytes (for example, `100K`), megabytes (for example, `20M`), gigabytes (for example, `10G`), or terabytes (for example, `2T`). The value of `0` for the file size will effectively disable the file rolling.

## There's more...

You can also ask the `rhc tail` command to output the last n lines using `--opts` or `-o`. To output the last 100 lines, run the following command:

```
$ rhc tail --opts "-n 100"
```

You can pass other `tail` command options, as well, using the `--opts` option.

## See also

▸ The *Creating an OpenShift application using the rhc command-line client* recipe in Chapter 3, *Creating and Managing Applications*

▸ The *Working with JBoss application logs* recipe

▸ The *Working with Tomcat application logs* recipe

▸ The *Working with Python application logs* recipe

# Working with JBoss application logs

As mentioned in the *Viewing application logs* recipe, logs are important data generated by your applications. This recipe will cover in detail how you can work with logs in OpenShift's JBoss cartridge applications. This recipe will start with viewing logs of an existing JBoss application, and then you will add application-specific logging using the SLF4J library. This recipe assumes you have already read the *Viewing application logs* recipe.

## Getting ready

This recipe will use the application created in the *Creating and deploying Java EE 6 applications using the JBoss EAP and PostgreSQL 9.2 cartridges* recipe in Chapter 7, *OpenShift for Java Developers*. You can recreate the application using the following command:

```
$ rhc create-app jobstore jbosseap postgresql-9.2 --from-code
https://github.com/OpenShift-Cookbook/chapter7-jobstore-javaee6.git
```

## How to do it...

Perform the following steps:

1. You can view the JBoss cartridge logs by running the following command:

   ```
   $ rhc tail --files */log*/jbosseap.log --app jobstore
   ```

2. You used the `--files` option to restrict the `rhc tail` command to only show JBoss-specific logs; otherwise, it will show all the logs in the $OPENSHIFT_LOG_DIR directory. This will print logs, as shown in the following command:

   ```
   ==> app-root/logs/jbosseap.log <==

   2014/06/28 13:05:59,844 INFO  [org.jboss.web] (ServerService
   Thread Pool -- 65) JBAS018210: Register web context:

   2014/06/28 13:06:00,153 INFO  [org.jboss.as.server]
   (ServerService Thread Pool -- 36) JBAS018559: Deployed
   "ROOT.war" (runtime-name : "ROOT.war")
   ```

3. Open the application URL at `http://jobstore-{domain-name}.rhcloud.com` in your favorite browser, and you will see Hibernate-specific logs in your terminal. When you go to the application root, then an HTTP GET request is made to fetch all the companies in the database. The following query is the SQL statement that Hibernate executes to get data from the database:

```
2014/06/28 13:42:50,423 INFO [stdout] (http-
127.13.169.1/127.13.169.1:8080-1) Hibernate: select
company0_.id as col_0_0_, company0_.name as col_1_0_,
company0_.description as col_2_0_ from Company company0_
```

4. OpenShift's JBoss cartridge is configured to log all the `INFO` and preceding messages to the console. As mentioned in the *Viewing application logs* recipe, any message written to `stdout` will be picked by `logshifter` and written to a logfile. For the JBoss EAP cartridge, the logfile name is `jbosseap.log`, and for the JBoss AS 7 cartridge, the logfile name will be `jbossas.log`. You can update the logging configuration to show all the `DEBUG` and preceding messages by updating the logging subsystem in the `standalone.xml` file inside the `.openshift/config` directory with the following code:

```
<subsystem xmlns="urn:jboss:domain:logging:1.3">
  <console-handler name="CONSOLE">
    <level name="DEBUG" />
    <formatter>
      <pattern-formatter
        pattern="%d{yyyy/MM/dd HH:mm:ss,SSS} %-5p [%c] (%t)
%s%E%n" />
    </formatter>
  </console-handler>
  <logger category="com.arjuna">
    <level name="WARN" />
  </logger>
  <logger category="org.apache.tomcat.util.modeler">
    <level name="WARN" />
  </logger>
  <logger category="sun.rmi">
    <level name="WARN" />
  </logger>
  <logger category="jacorb">
    <level name="WARN" />
  </logger>
  <logger category="jacorb.config">
    <level name="ERROR" />
  </logger>
  <root-logger>
```

```
      <level name="DEBUG" />
      <handlers>
        <handler name="CONSOLE" />
      </handlers>
    </root-logger>
</subsystem>
```

5. Commit the changes in your local Git repository, and then push them to the OpenShift application gear. OpenShift will now use the updated `standalone.xml` file, and you will see the `DEBUG` logs in the output of the `rhc tail` command.

6. As the application is not logging anything, the output of the `rhc tail` command either shows the application server logs or the logs of the different libraries used by your application. You can use any of the Java logging libraries to add application-specific logs. In this recipe, you will use `SLF4J` with `java.util.logging` binding to log the application logs, but you can use any other `SLF4J` binding, such as `log4j` or `logback`, as well. Open the Maven `pom.xml` file, and add the following dependencies to it:

```
<dependency>
    <groupId>org.slf4j</groupId>
    <artifactId>slf4j-api</artifactId>
    <version>1.7.7</version>
</dependency>
<dependency>
    <groupId>org.slf4j</groupId>
    <artifactId>slf4j-jdk14</artifactId>
    <version>1.7.7</version>
</dependency>
```

7. Open the `CompanyResource.java` file inside the `org.osbook.jobstore.rest` package in an editor, and add a couple of statements to import the `SLF4J` classes, as shown in the following code:

```
import org.slf4j.Logger;
import org.slf4j.LoggerFactory;
```

8. After adding the `import` statements, update the `createNewCompany()` and `showAll()` methods in `CompanyResource.java` with log messages, as shown in the following code:

```
private Logger logger =
LoggerFactory.getLogger(CompanyResource.class);
@Inject
private CompanyService companyService;

@POST
@Consumes(MediaType.APPLICATION_JSON)
```

```java
public Response createNewCompany(@Valid Company company) {
    logger.debug("inside createNewCompany().. creating new
company {}" , company);
    Company existingCompanyWithName =
companyService.findByName(company.getName());
    if (existingCompanyWithName != null) {
        logger.debug("Company with name {} already exists : {}"
, company.getName(), existingCompanyWithName);
        return Response.status(Status.NOT_ACCEPTABLE)
                .entity(String.format("Company already exists
with name: %s",company.getName())).build();
    }
    company = companyService.save(company);
    logger.info("Created new company {}" , company);
    return
Response.status(Status.CREATED).entity(company).build();
}


@GET
@Produces(MediaType.APPLICATION_JSON)
public List<Company> showAll() {
    List<Company> companies = companyService.findAll();
    logger.info("Found {} companies" , companies.size());
    return companies;
}
```

9. Revert the changes you made to the `standalone.xml` file in step 3 to view only
   the INFO messages. Change the `root-logger` level to INFO, as shown in the
   following code:

```xml
<root-logger>
  <level name="INFO" />
  <handlers>
    <handler name="CONSOLE" />
  </handlers>
</root-logger>
```

10. Commit the changes to the local Git repository, and then push them to the application
    gear using the `git push` command.

11. After the changes are deployed, make another request to the web application,
    and this time you will see your application logs in the `rhc tail` command output,
    as follows:

```
2014/06/28 14:24:50,959 INFO
[org.osbook.jobstore.rest.CompanyResource] (http-
127.13.169.1/127.13.169.1:8080-1) Found 1 companies
```

12. If you try to create a new company, then you see that only the INFO messages are getting logged. This is because the logging configuration in the standalone.xml file is configured to only log INFO and preceding messages to the console.

13. To view the debug messages of your application, you have to update the standalone.xml logging subsystem configuration with the one shown in the following code:

```
<subsystem xmlns="urn:jboss:domain:logging:1.3">
  <console-handler name="CONSOLE">
    <level name="DEBUG" />
    <formatter>
      <pattern-formatter
        pattern="%d{yyyy/MM/dd HH:mm:ss,SSS} %-5p [%c] (%t)
%s%E%n" />
    </formatter>
  </console-handler>
  <logger category="com.arjuna">
    <level name="WARN" />
  </logger>
  <logger category="org.apache.tomcat.util.modeler">
    <level name="WARN" />
  </logger>
  <logger category="sun.rmi">
    <level name="WARN" />
  </logger>
  <logger category="jacorb">
    <level name="WARN" />
  </logger>
  <logger category="jacorb.config">
    <level name="ERROR" />
  </logger>
  <logger category="org.osbook.jobstore">
    <level name="DEBUG"></level>
  </logger>
  <root-logger>
    <level name="INFO" />
    <handlers>
      <handler name="CONSOLE" />
    </handlers>
  </root-logger>
</subsystem>
```

14. Now, you will also see the application-specific DEBUG logs in the output of the rhc tail command:

```
2014/06/28 14:40:22,410 DEBUG
[org.osbook.jobstore.rest.CompanyResource] (http-
/127.13.169.1:8080-1) inside createNewCompany().. creating new
company
```

## How it works...

In the preceding steps, you learned how you can view the logs of a JBoss application and add application-specific logging using the SLF4J library. In step 1, you ran the rhc tail command to view all the JBoss-specific logs. All the JBoss EAP-specific logs are written to the jbosseap.log file. This file contains both the JBoss server.log and boot.log content. As discussed in the *Viewing application logs* recipe, logshifter will collect all the logs written to stdout or stderr and write them to the cartridge-specific logfile. Logging the subsystem configuration in the standalone.xml configuration file controls the logging in JBoss cartridges. The standalone.xml file is present inside the .openshift/config directory, and you can override it to meet your needs. The logging subsystem consists of three parts: one or more handler configurations, such as console-handle or file-handler, one or more loggers to define a logger category, such as com.arjuna shown in the next code, and a root-logger declaration. You can read more about the JBoss logging configuration in the official documentation at https://docs.jboss.org/author/display/AS71/ Logging+Configuration. Have a look at the following code:

```
<subsystem xmlns="urn:jboss:domain:logging:1.3">
  <console-handler name="CONSOLE">
    <level name="DEBUG" />
    <formatter>
      <pattern-formatter
        pattern="%d{yyyy/MM/dd HH:mm:ss,SSS} %-5p [%c] (%t)
%s%E%n" />
    </formatter>
  </console-handler>
  <logger category="com.arjuna">
    <level name="WARN" />
  </logger>
  <root-logger>
    <level name="DEBUG" />
    <handlers>
      <handler name="CONSOLE" />
    </handlers>
  </root-logger>
</subsystem>
```

In step 3, you updated the `root-logger` level to `DEBUG`. This enables the JBoss server to generate `DEBUG` and preceding-level logs.

From step 5 through step 11, you first added the application logs using the `SLF4J` library and then updated `standalone.xml` logger subsystem configuration to allow JBoss to log the application `DEBUG` and preceding messages. This was done by adding an application-specific `logger category` at the `DEBUG` level. Have a look at the following code:

```
<logger category="org.osbook.jobstore">
  <level name="DEBUG"></level>
</logger>
```

## There's more...

After reading through this recipe, you might be wondering if there is a way to update the logging configuration at runtime. Yes, you can do so using the JBoss admin console. To use the JBoss admin console, first run the `rhc port-forward` command, as follows:

**$ rhc port-forward --app jobstore**

Then, go to the admin console at `http://127.0.0.1:9990/`. Navigate to **Configuration | Core | Logging**, as shown in the following screenshot:

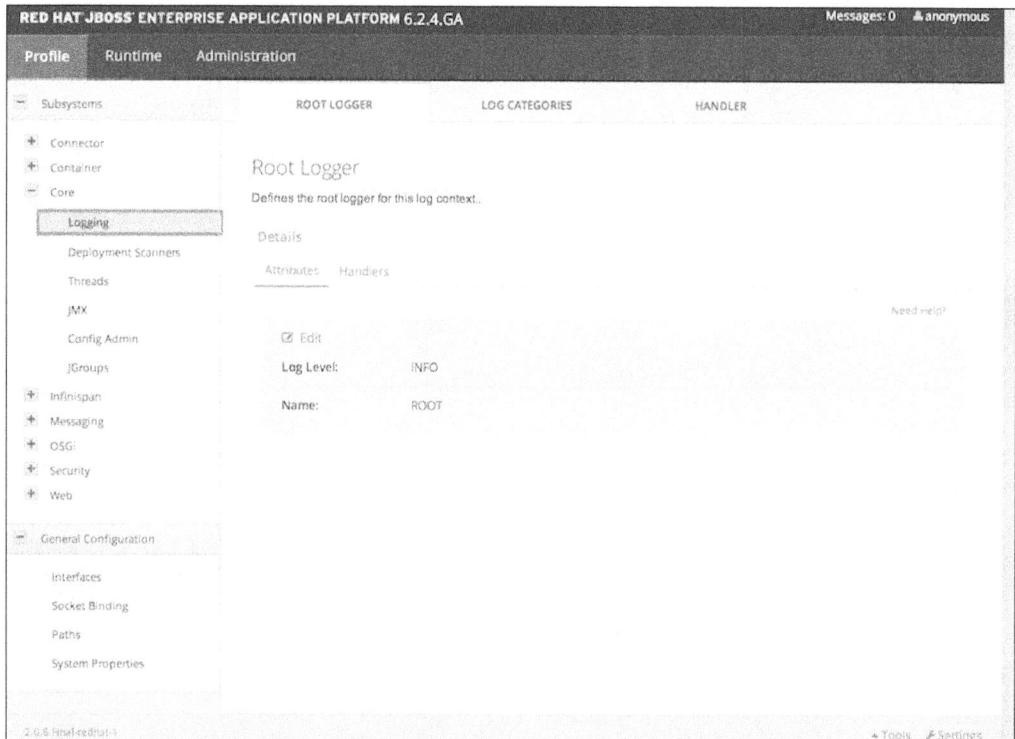

Now, go to **LOG CATEGORIES**, and you will see a category for `org.osbook.jobstore`, as shown in the following screenshot:

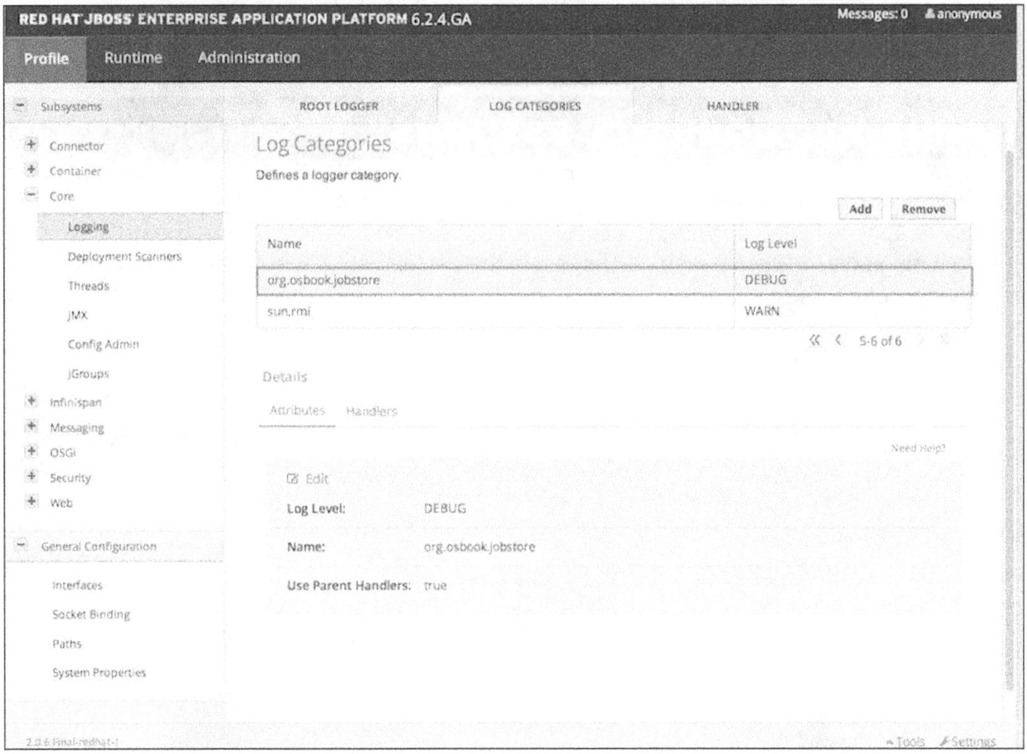

Change the **Log Level** value to **INFO**, and click on the **Save** button:

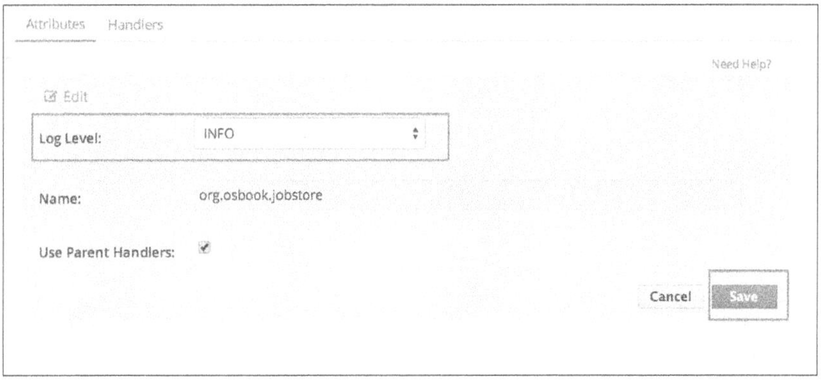

Now, if you try to create a new company, you will not see the DEBUG messages. You will only see the INFO and preceding messages.

## See also

- ▸ The *Viewing application logs* recipe
- ▸ The *Enabling JBoss access logs* recipe

# Enabling JBoss access logs

Access logs are very useful when you want to see a list of all the requests processed by a server. For Apache-based cartridges, access logs are enabled by default, but you will have to enable it manually in JBoss-based cartridges. In this recipe, you will learn how to enable the access logs for JBoss cartridges.

## Getting ready

This recipe will pick up where we left off in the *Working with JBoss application logs* recipe.

## How to do it...

Perform the following steps to enable the access logs:

1. Open the `standalone.xml` file inside the `.openshift/config` directory in your favorite editor.

2. Update the `urn:jboss:domain:web:1.5` subsystem with the one shown in the following code:

```
<subsystem xmlns="urn:jboss:domain:web:1.5"
  default-virtual-server="default-host" native="false">
  <connector name="http" protocol="HTTP/1.1" scheme="http"
    socket-binding="http" />
  <virtual-server name="default-host" enable-welcome-
root="false">
    <alias name="localhost" />
    <access-log pattern="%a %t %H %p %U %s %S %T"
rotate="true">
      <directory path="app-root/logs/" relative-
to="user.home" />
    </access-log>
  </virtual-server>
  <valve name="remoteipvalve" module="org.jboss.as.web"
    class-name="org.apache.catalina.valves.RemoteIpValve">
    <param param-name="protocolHeader" param-value="x-
forwarded-proto" />
  </valve>
</subsystem>
```

3. Commit the changes to the local Git repository, and then push them to the application gear using the `git push` command.

4. Run the `rhc tail` command again, and you will see the access logs in the `tail` command output, as follows:

```
==> app-root/logs/access_log.2014-06-28 <==
106.211.32.170 [28/Jun/2014:15:43:28 -0400] HTTP/1.1 80
/api/v1/companies 200 - 5.409
```

## How it works...

An access log stores all the user requests for individual resources. These include requests to fetch HTML files, JavaScript files, CSS files, REST calls, and so on. The data stored in this file can then be analyzed by another application to get meaningful information out of it. An access log can help you with following:

▶ It can help to calculate the number of unique visitors to your website.

▶ It can help to calculate the number of successful and failed requests. The requests with the 2XX code are considered successful, and the requests with 4xx and 5xx are considered errors.

▶ It can help basic performance analysis. Each access log line contains the time taken to process the request.

▶ It can help to analyze your web application usage pattern in terms of the time of the day, the day of the week, and so on.

In the preceding steps, you updated the `urn:jboss:domain:web:1.5` subsystem configuration to enable the access logs. Adding the following two lines to the configuration enables the access logs:

```
<access-log pattern="%a %t %H %p %U %s %S %T" rotate="true">
<directory path="app-root/logs/" relative-to="user.home" />
```

The `access-log` element enables the access logs, and the `directory` element is used to specify the directory that should be used to generate the logs. The preceding `directory` element configures JBoss to write the access logs to `$OPENSHIFT_LOG_DIR` as it looks for the `app-root/logs` directory relative to the user home. The `app-root/logs` directory relative to the user home is `$OPENSHIFT_LOG_DIR`. We have used this value so that the `rhc tail` command can read this file along with other JBoss logs. The `access-log` element takes one mandatory attribute called `pattern`. The `pattern` element defines the logs format. The following pattern codes are supported:

▶ `%a`: Remote IP address

▶ `%A`: Local IP address

▶ `%b`: Bytes sent, excluding HTTP headers, or - if zero

▸ `%B`: Bytes sent, excluding HTTP headers

▸ `%h`: Remote hostname (or IP address if `resolveHosts` is `false`)

▸ `%H`: Request protocol

▸ `%l`: Remote logical username from `identd` (always returns `-`)

▸ `%m`: Request method (GET, POST, and so on)

▸ `%p`: Local port on which this request was received

▸ `%q`: Query string (prepended with a `?` if it exists)

▸ `%r`: First line of the request (method and request URI)

▸ `%s`: HTTP status code of the response

▸ `%S`: User session ID

▸ `%t`: Date and time in Common Log Format

▸ `%u`: Remote user that was authenticated (if any), else -

▸ `%U`: Requested URL path

▸ `%v`: Local server name

▸ `%D`: Time taken to process the request in milliseconds

▸ `%T`: Time taken to process the request in seconds

▸ `%I`: Current request thread name (can compare later with stacktraces)

## See also

▸ The *Working with JBoss application logs* recipe

▸ The *Viewing application logs* recipe

# Working with Tomcat application logs

In this recipe, you will learn how to work with logs in Tomcat cartridges. You will start with tailing the logs of an existing Tomcat application, and then you will learn how to add application-specific logging using the `SLF4J` library.

## Getting ready

This recipe will use the application created in the *Creating and Deploying Spring Applications using the Tomcat 7 cartridge* recipe in *Chapter 7, OpenShift for Java Developers*. You can recreate the application using the following command:

```
$ rhc create-app jobstore tomcat-7 mysql-5.5 --from-code
https://github.com/OpenShift-Cookbook/chapter7-jobstore-spring.git --
timeout 180
```

## How to do it...

Perform the following steps:

1. You can view the logs of a Tomcat application using the `rhc tail` command. Tomcat logs are written to a file named `jbossews.log` inside the `$OPENSHIFT_LOG_DIR` directory:

   ```
   $ rhc tail --files */log*/jbossews.log --app jobstore
   ```

2. The `jbossews.log` file will contain logs of both Tomcat-specific and application-specific logs, as shown in the following output:

   ```
   INFO: Starting ProtocolHandler ["http-bio-127.5.249.129-8080"]

   Jun 29, 2014 5:03:01 AM org.apache.catalina.startup.Catalina
   start

   INFO: Server startup in 22062 ms
   ```

3. Before you can add application-specific logging, you will have to add the following dependencies to your Maven `pom.xml` file. In this recipe, you will use `SLF4J` along with `logback` binding to add application logging:

   ```
   <dependency>
     <groupId>org.slf4j</groupId>
     <artifactId>slf4j-api</artifactId>
     <version>1.7.7</version>
   </dependency>
   <dependency>
     <groupId>ch.qos.logback</groupId>
     <artifactId>logback-classic</artifactId>
     <version>1.0.13</version>
   </dependency>
   ```

4. Open the `CompanyResource.java` file inside the `org.osbook.jobstore.rest` package in an editor, and add a couple of statements to import the `SLF4J` classes, as shown in the following code:

   ```
   import org.slf4j.Logger;
   import org.slf4j.LoggerFactory;
   ```

5. Now, update the `CompanyResource` Java class under the `org.jobstore.rest` package to add application-specific logging, as follows:

   ```
   private Logger logger =
   LoggerFactory.getLogger(CompanyResource.class);

   @RequestMapping(method = RequestMethod.POST, consumes =
   MediaType.APPLICATION_JSON_VALUE, produces =
   MediaType.APPLICATION_JSON_VALUE)
   ```

```java
public ResponseEntity<Company>
createNewCompany(@RequestBody Company company) {
  logger.debug("inside createNewCompany().. creating new
company {}" , company);
  Company existingCompany =
companyRepository.findByName(company.getName());
  if(existingCompany != null){
    logger.debug("Company with name {} already exists : {}"
, company.getName(), existingCompany);
    return new ResponseEntity<>(HttpStatus.NOT_ACCEPTABLE);
  }
  company = companyRepository.save(company);
  logger.info("Created new company {}" , company);
  return new ResponseEntity<>(company,HttpStatus.CREATED);
}


@RequestMapping(method=RequestMethod.GET, produces =
MediaType.APPLICATION_JSON_VALUE)
public @ResponseBody List<Company> showAll(){
  List<Company> companies = companyRepository.findAll();
  logger.info("Found {} companies" , companies.size());
  return companies;
}
```

6. Commit the changes to the local Git repository, and then push them to the application gear using the `git push` command.

7. After the application restarts, you will start seeing various log messages. A short snippet is shown in the following output:

   ```
   05:43:00.182 [http-bio-127.5.249.129-8080-exec-6] INFO
   org.jobstore.rest.CompanyResource - Created new company
   Company [id=1, name=Red Hat, description=open source company,
   contactEmail=contact@redhat.com]
   ```

   ```
   05:43:00.245 [http-bio-127.5.249.129-8080-exec-6] DEBUG
   o.s.w.s.m.m.a.HttpEntityMethodProcessor - Written [Company
   [id=1, name=Red Hat, description=open source company,
   contactEmail=contact@redhat.com]] as "application/json" using
   [org.springframework.http.converter.json.MappingJackson2HttpMe
   ssageConverter@1d300d2]
   ```

8. You can use the `logback` configuration file to enable the logging of specific packages. Create a new file with the name `logback.xml` inside the `src/main/resources` directory, and add the following contents to it:

   ```xml
   <?xml version="1.0" encoding="UTF-8"?>
   <configuration>
   ```

```
        <appender name="console" class="ch.qos.logback.core.
ConsoleAppender">
                <encoder>
                        <pattern>%d %5p %C:%4L - %m%n</pattern>
                </encoder>
        </appender>
        <logger name="org.jobstore" level="debug" />
        <root level="WARN">
                <appender-ref ref="console" />
        </root>
</configuration>
```

9. Commit the changes to the local Git repository, and push them to the application gear using the `git push` command. After the app restarts, you will only see the application-specific `DEBUG` and preceding messages. Have a look at the following commands:

```
INFO: Server startup in 49113 ms

2014-06-29 06:07:27,817  INFO
org.jobstore.rest.CompanyResource:  45 - Found 1 companies

2014-06-29 06:07:38,513 DEBUG
org.jobstore.rest.CompanyResource:  31 - inside
createNewCompany().. creating new company Company [id=null,
name=test, description=test, contactEmail=test@test.com]

2014-06-29 06:07:38,752  INFO
org.jobstore.rest.CompanyResource:  38 - Created new company
Company [id=2, name=test, description=test,
contactEmail=test@test.com]
```

## How it works...

In the preceding steps, you learned how to view the logs of a Tomcat application and add application-specific logging using the SLF4J library. In step 1, you ran the `rhc tail` command to view all the Tomcat-specific logs. All the Tomcat-specific logs are written to the `jbossews.log` file. As discussed in the *Viewing application logs* recipe, `logshifter` will collect all the logs written to `stdout` or `stderr` and write them to the cartridge-specific logfile.

From step 2 through step 5, you added log statements to the `CompanyResource.java` file using the SLF4J library. The SLF4J library underneath uses the Logback library that has a default log level of `DEBUG`. This means if you don't specify any Logback configuration, then all the `DEBUG` and preceding messages will be logged to `jbossews.log`.

Logback can be configured using the `logback.xml` file. In step 6, you created a `logback.xml` file and added configuration to only the log application DEBUG messages. All other messages will be logged at WARN level. Then, finally, in step 7, you committed the changes and pushed them to the application gear.

## There's more...

You can enable the access logs for the Tomcat cartridge by performing the following steps:

1. Open the Tomcat `server.xml` configuration file inside the `.openshift/config` directory in your favorite editor.

2. Add the `AccessLogValve` configuration to the `server.xml` file's `Host` element:

    ```
    <Valve
    className="org.apache.catalina.valves.AccessLogValve"
    directory="${user.home}/app-root/logs"
    prefix="localhost_access_log." suffix=".txt" pattern="%h %l
    %u %t &quot;%r&quot; %s %b"/>
    ```

3. Commit the changes to the local Git repository, and push them to the application gear using the `git push` command.

4. Run the `rhc tail` command again, and this time, you will see the access logs, as well:

    ```
    ==> app-root/logs/localhost_access_log.2014-06-29.txt <==

    127.5.249.129 - - [29/Jun/2014:07:18:57 -0400] "POST
    /api/v1/companies HTTP/1.1" 201 133

    127.5.249.129 - - [29/Jun/2014:07:18:58 -0400] "GET
    /api/v1/companies HTTP/1.1" 200 344
    ```

## See also

▶ The *Viewing application logs* recipe

▶ The *Working with JBoss application logs* recipe

▶ The *Enabling JBoss access logs* recipe

# Working with Python application logs

In this recipe, you will learn how to add view and logging to your Python applications. As discussed in *Chapter 8, OpenShift for Python Developers*, OpenShift Python applications use Apache with `mod_wsgi`.

## Getting ready

This recipe will use the application created in the *Creating and deploying Flask web applications using Python and PostgreSQL cartridges* recipe in *Chapter 8, OpenShift for Python Developers*. You can recreate the application using the following command:

```
$ rhc create-app jobstore python-2.7 postgresql-9.2 --from-code
https://github.com/OpenShift-Cookbook/chapter8-jobstore-python-
flask.git
```

## How to do it...

Perform the following steps:

1. Open a new command-line terminal, and navigate to the directory where you have created the Python application.

2. To view the logs of a Python application, run the following command:

   ```
   $ rhc tail --files */log*/python.log
   ```

3. By visiting the application URL, you will see the following logs in the `rhc tail` command output when you make a request to the application:

   ```
   117.207.184.93 - - [29/Jun/2014:14:50:09 -0400] "GET
   /api/v1/companies HTTP/1.1" 200 17 "http://jobstore-
   osbook.rhcloud.com/" "Mozilla/5.0 (Macintosh; Intel Mac OS X
   10_8_5) AppleWebKit/537.36 (KHTML, like Gecko)
   Chrome/35.0.1916.153 Safari/537.36"
   ```

4. Open the `jobstore.py` file inside the application directory, and add the following lines just above the `index()` function. The following lines import the `logging` module and then create a new `logger` object with the `INFO` log level. This logger will be used in the next step for logging.

   ```
   import logging
   logging.basicConfig(level=logging.INFO)
   logger = logging.getLogger(__name__)
   ```

5. Next, update the `index()` function with a log statement, as shown in the following code:

   ```
   @app.route('/')
   def index():
   logger.info('inside index()...')
   return render_template('index.html')
   ```

6.  Commit the change to the local Git repository, and then push the changes to the application gear. After the app has started successfully, visit the application URL and you will see the log message you added to `jobstore.py`, as follows:

    ```
    [Sun Jun 29 14:56:08 2014] [error] INFO:jobstore:inside
    index()...
    ```

7.  There are times when you will prefer to use a different file to store your application logs. This can be done using `TimedRotatingFileHandler`. Open `jobstore.py` in the application root directory and replace the logging lines added in step 3 with the ones shown in the following code:

    ```
    import logging
    import logging.handlers
    logger = logging.getLogger(__name__)
    logger.setLevel(logging.DEBUG)
    formatter = logging.Formatter('%(asctime)s - %(name)s -
    %(levelname)s - %(message)s')
    log_location = os.environ.get('OPENSHIFT_LOG_DIR') if
    os.environ.get('OPENSHIFT_LOG_DIR') else '/tmp/'
    log_filename = log_location + 'jobstore.log'
    handler =
    logging.handlers.TimedRotatingFileHandler(log_filename,when
    ='midnight',backupCount=5)
    handler.setFormatter(formatter)
    logger.addHandler(handler)
    ```

8.  Commit the change, and push the changes to the application gear. After the app restarts, you will see a new file, `jobstore.log`, with all the application-specific logs, as shown in the following command lines. You will have to run the `rhc tail` command so that the `tail` command can find the new file, as follows:

    ```
    ==> app-root/logs/jobstore.log <==
    2014-06-29 15:25:34,158 - jobstore - INFO - inside index()...
    ```

## How it works...

Python application logs are logged in the `python.log` file inside `$OPENSHIFT_LOG_DIR`. This file will contain both Apache access logs and error logs, as well as any application-specific logs. The log follows Apache Combined Log Format discussed in the *Viewing application logs* recipe.

To add application-level logging, you used the Python standard logging module in step 3. After pushing these changes to the application gear, you will start seeing your application-specific log messages. You will only see the log messages with the level `INFO` or above. This is because you have configured the default logging level to `logging.INFO`.

OpenShift, by default, will log all the messages written to `stdout` or `stderr` to the `python.log` file. If you want to use a different logfile for application-specific logs, then you can use `TimedRotaingFileHandler` to log messages to the `jobstore.log` file inside `$OPENSHIFT_LOG_DIR`, as shown in step 5. In step 6, you pushed the changes to the OpenShift application gear, and after running the `rhc tail` command again, you will start seeing messages written to `jobstore.log` in the output.

## See also

▸  The *Viewing application logs* recipe

# Creating scalable applications

As your application becomes popular and more users start using it, you will have to scale your application to meet the increased usage. Application scaling can be done in either of the following two ways: vertical scaling (or scaling up) and horizontal scaling (scaling out). Vertical scaling is about adding more power to a single machine, that is, faster CPU, more RAM and SSD, and so on. Vertical scalability has a limit and the cost increases exponentially. Horizontal scaling, on the other hand, is about handling more requests and load by adding more machines.

With most PaaS solutions such as OpenShift, you will soon hit the vertical scaling limit. Currently, in OpenShift, you can't get a bigger gear size than 2 GB of RAM space (that is, large gear), so it is recommended that you design your application for horizontal scalability. There are many good books, such as *Scalability Rules, Martin L. Abbott and Michael T. Fisher, Addison-Wesley Professional*, written on this subject, and you can refer to them for more information. I have also written an article on best practices to create scalable web applications (`https://www.openshift.com/blogs/best-practices-for-horizontal-application-scaling`) that you can refer to, as well.

In this recipe, you will learn how to create scalable applications in OpenShift.

## Getting ready

To complete this recipe, you will need `rhc` installed on your machine. This recipe will require all three available gears, so please make sure to delete any existing applications.

## How to do it...

To create a scalable application, perform the following steps:

1.  Open a command-line terminal and change the directory to a convenient location where you want to create the application.

2. Next, execute the following command to create the scalable application:

```
$ rhc create-app jobstore jbosseap postgresql-9 --scaling --
from-code https://github.com/OpenShift-Cookbook/chapter7-
jobstore-javaee6.git
```

## How it works...

The `rhc create-app` command used in the preceding steps instructs OpenShift to create an application named `jobstore` with the JBoss EAP and PostgreSQL 9.2 cartridges. The `--scaling` option tells OpenShift to create a horizontally scalable application instead of a nonscalable application. The `--from-code` option tells OpenShift to use the specified Git repository as the reference application. You can also use `-s` instead of `--scaling`. The `-s` option is a shorthand notation of the `--scaling` option.

This command will create two OpenShift gears. The HAProxy load balancer and JBoss EAP application server will share the first gear, and the PostgreSQL database will use the second gear. The gear that has the HAProxy cartridge installed is called the `main` gear. All the commands that work against a gear will apply to this gear. For example, when you run the `rhc ssh` command, you will be logged in to the HAProxy gear. Similarly, the `rhc tail` command will tail the logs in the `app-root/logs` directory of this gear.

HAProxy is a software-based load balancer that sits in front of your web application and accepts all the incoming requests. It then parses the HTTP request and, depending on its configuration, will route the incoming request to a backend. The backend here means one or more JBoss EAP instances. OpenShift helps you scale your application by adding new application instances (in our example, JBoss EAP instances) as the number of concurrent HTTP connections reaches a threshold. The current threshold is 16 concurrent HTTP connections. This behavior is called autoscaling, as OpenShift manages the application scaling without any user intervention. You can also configure your application to use manual scaling, which will give you more control over application scaling. This will be covered in the *Enable manual scaling with marker files* recipe.

OpenShift currently does not support database scaling. You can use services such as Amazon RDS (covered in the *Using an Amazon RDS MySQL DB instance with OpenShift* recipe in *Chapter 4*, *Using MySQL with OpenShift Applications*), Enterprise DB PostgreSQL Cloud Database (covered in the *Using EnterpriseDB PostgreSQL cloud database with OpenShift* recipe in *Chapter 5*, *Using PostgreSQL with OpenShift Applications*), or MongoLab (covered in the *Using MongoLab MongoDB-as-a-Service with OpenShift* recipe in *Chapter 6*, *Using MongoDB and Third-party Database Cartridges with OpenShift Applications*) to get database scaling.

Every OpenShift scalable application has a daemon running called `haproxy_ctld`. This daemon controls the autoscaling behavior by polling the HAProxy Unix socket status port every five seconds to collect the basic HAProxy statistics. By default, it is configured to use the HTTP concurrent connection of autoscaling, but users can customize it to autoscale applications based on other factors such as CPU usage, as well (`https://www.openshift.com/blogs/customizing-autoscale-functionality-in-openshift`).

The daemon checks the current concurrent HTTP connections, and if the number of concurrent connections is more than 90 percent of the allocated, that is, 16, then it fires the scale-up event. When a scale-up event happens, the daemon will make an HTTP request to the OpenShift broker to add a new gear to the application. The broker will spin up a new gear with the same configuration as the existing application gear, attach the new gear with HAProxy, use the `rsync` command to copy the contents of the `~/app-root/repo` directory on the main gear to the new gear, and finally start the new gear. From now on, HAProxy will start sending requests to both the gears based on the configured algorithm. By default, OpenShift uses sticky sessions along with the least connection balance algorithm to make sure that the request from a user ends up on the same gear always, and the server with the least connection gets the request from the new client. Users can override the default HAProxy configuration according to their needs. We will cover that later in this chapter.

Applications will scale down when your application web traffic falls below 50 percent of the allocated HTTP connections for several minutes. Then, the new gear will be removed, and it will also be removed from the HAProxy configuration.

An OpenShift application developer can see the HAProxy stats on the HAProxy status page. This page is located at `http://jobstore-{domain-name}.rhcloud.com/haproxy-status`, as shown in the following screenshot:

The HAProxy status page is divided into two sections: **stats** and **express**. The **stats** section is configured to listen to all the requests made to the HAProxy status page. Every time you refresh the `http://jobstore-domainname.rhcloud.com/haproxy-status page` page, the total number of sessions under the **Sessions** tab will increment. This is shown under the **Total** column. The **Cur** column is the number of users currently accessing the status page. The **Max** column is the maximum number of concurrent users. All these numbers are calculated since HAProxy was started; if you restart HAProxy, the stats will reset.

The **express** section is more interesting from the application point of view. The **local-gear** row corresponds to the requests handled by JBoss EAP. The total number of sessions handled by the application is shown in the **Total** column. The **Cur** column is the number of users currently accessing the application. The **Max** column is the maximum number of concurrent users. All these figures pertain to the time period since HAProxy was started; if you restart HAProxy, the stats will reset. In the preceding screenshot, we can see that **local-gear** has handled seven requests, one at a time. When the application scales, it will add more rows for the new gears.

## There's more...

You can define the minimum and maximum values for application scaling. By default, a scalable application will consume at least one gear and, at peak traffic, can consume all the gears in your OpenShift account. You can set the minimum and maximum values using the `rhc scale-cartridge` command, as shown in the following command:

```
$ rhc scale-cartridge <web cartridge> --app <app_name> --min <minimum
gears> --max <maximum gear>
```

Let's take the following example:

```
$ rhc scale-cartridge jbosseap --app jobstore --min 2 --max 4
```

The preceding command will make sure that the `jobstore` application will at least have two instances of the JBoss EAP cartridge, and at maximum, four instances.

## See also

- The *Configuring a different health check URL for HAProxy* recipe
- The *Configuring HAProxy to use a different balance algorithm* recipe
- The *Enabling manual scaling with marker files* recipe

# Configuring a different health check URL for HAProxy

In this recipe, you will learn how to update the HAProxy configuration file to configure a different heath check URL.

## Getting ready

To complete this recipe, you will need `rhc` installed on your machine. This recipe will utilize the application created in the *Creating scalable applications* recipe.

## How to do it...

Perform the following steps:

1. Open a command-line terminal and navigate to the application directory created in the *Creating scalable applications* recipe.

2. SSH into the main application gear using the `rhc ssh` command, as follows:

   ```
   $ rhc ssh --app jobstore
   ```

3. Change the directory to the `haproxy` configuration directory, as follows:

   ```
   $ cd haproxy/conf
   ```

4. Now, open the `haproxy.cfg` file using VIM, and remove the following content:

   ```
   option httpchk GET /
   ```

   In its place, insert the following content:

   ```
   option httpchk GET /api/v1/ping
   ```

5. Finally, restart the HAProxy cartridge from your local machine using the `rhc` command-line client:

   ```
   $ rhc restart-cartridge --cartridge haproxy --app jobstore
   ```

## How it works...

HAProxy performs periodic health checks to determine the health of the application gears. The default configuration pings the root URL / every two seconds. If HAProxy receives an HTTP code other than `2xx` or `3xx`, then it considers it a server failure, and your application will give a `Service Unavailable` error. One scenario where you will see this behavior is when you use OpenShift to host your REST backend at a nonroot URL, such as `/api/v1/`. In the preceding steps, you updated the `haproxy.cfg` file to use a different health check URL.

## See also

► The *Configuring HAProxy to use a different balance algorithm* recipe
► The *Enabling manual scaling with marker files* recipe

# Configuring HAProxy to use a different balance algorithm

The HAProxy load balancer can work with several load-balancing algorithms. The configuration used by HAProxy in OpenShift applications uses the **leastconn** load-balancing algorithm. This algorithm is useful when you have long-lived connections, but is not recommended for short connections. For short connections, as in the case of our application, it is more suitable to use the **roundrobin** algorithm.

In this recipe, you will learn how to configure HAProxy to use the **roundrobin balance** algorithm instead of the leastconn algorithm.

## Getting ready

To complete this recipe, you will need `rhc` installed on your machine. This recipe will utilize the application created in the *Creating scalable applications* recipe.

## How to do it...

Perform the following steps to configure HAProxy to use the roundrobin balance algorithm:

1.  Open a command-line terminal and navigate to the application directory created in the *Creating scalable applications* recipe.

2.  Scale the JBoss EAP cartridge to use two JBoss EAP instances by running the following command:

    ```
    $ rhc scale-cartridge --min 2 --cartridge jbosseap-6
    ```

3.  SSH into the main application gear using the `rhc ssh` command, as follows:

    ```
    $ rhc ssh --app jobstore
    ```

4.  Once you are inside the application gear, change the directory to the `haproxy/conf` directory, as follows:

    ```
    $ cd haproxy/conf
    ```

5.  It is always a good idea to make a backup of the configuration files before making any changes to them. Use the `copy` command to create a copy of the `haproxy.cfg` file in $OPENSHIFT_DATA_DIR, as follows:

    ```
    $ cp haproxy.cfg $OPENSHIFT_DATA_DIR
    ```

6. Now, open the `haproxy.cfg` file using VIM, and update the section under `balance leastconn` to the following code:

```
balance roundrobin
      server gear-2 host2:port2 check fall 2 rise 3 inter
2000 weight 1
      server local-gear host1:port1 check fall 2 rise 3 inter
2000 weight 1
```

7. Replace `gear-2` with your application's second gear name. Also, replace `host1` and `host2` and `port1` and `port2` with the gear 1 and gear 2 host and port values. You can get the values from the copy of `haproxy.cfg` saved in step 5.

8. You can ask HAProxy to reload the configuration by running the following command:

   ```
   $ rhc reload-cartridge --cartridge haproxy
   ```

9. Run Apache Benchmark to see the new configuration in action, as follows:

   ```
   $ ab -n 1000 -c 20 http://jobstore-{domain-
   name}.rhcloud.com/api/v1/companies
   ```

10. In the preceding test, `ab` will make a total of `1000` requests with `20` concurrent requests at a time. As we are using the roundrobin algorithm, both the gears should handle 500 requests each. You can verify the number of requests by looking at the following HAProxy status page (screenshot):

| express | | | | | | | | | | | |
|---|---|---|---|---|---|---|---|---|---|---|---|
| | Queue | | | Session rate | | | Sessions | | | | |
| | Cur | Max | Limit | Cur | Max | Limit | Cur | Max | Limit | Total | LbTot |
| Frontend | | | | 0 | 172 | - | 0 | 28 | 128 | 1 000 | |
| gear-53d31f4f5004468f52000060-osbook | 0 | 0 | - | 0 | 86 | | 0 | 20 | - | 500 | 500 |
| local-gear | 0 | 0 | - | 0 | 86 | | 0 | 18 | - | 500 | 500 |
| Backend | 0 | 0 | | 0 | 172 | | 0 | 20 | 128 | 1 000 | 1 000 |

## How it works...

HAProxy supports various load-balance algorithms. The algorithm you choose will determine which backend server will be used to serve the request. The default load-balance algorithm used by OpenShift's scalable applications is leastconn. This algorithm selects the server with the least number of active connections. HAProxy is also configured to use persistent cookies to achieve sticky session behavior. Session stickiness ensures that a user request is served from the same gear that served their first request.

In the preceding steps, you overrode the default configuration to use the roundrobin algorithm. The algorithm to use can be set using the `balance` parameter. The roundrobin algorithm selects servers in turn to make sure requests are balanced fairly. You can assign weights to the servers to manipulate how frequently a server is selected compared to others. In step 6, you used `roundrobin` as the value of the balance parameter and assigned a weight of `1` to both the servers. Because we gave both servers the same weight, both will serve an equal number of requests. Then, you asked HAProxy to reload the configuration using the `rhc reload-cartridge` command in step 7.

In step 8, you ran a load test on the application using Apache Benchmark, to see if your changes were working as expected. Because both servers had a weight of `1`, they both handled 500 requests each.

Now, let's update the HAProxy configuration to use different weights for different servers. Update the `haproxy.cfg` roundrobin section with the following code:

```
balance roundrobin
    server gear-2 host2:port2 check fall 2 rise 3 inter 2000
weight 1
    server local-gear host1:port1 check fall 2 rise 3 inter 2000
weight 2
```

Again, reload the configuration by running the `rhc reload-cartridge` command, and then run the Apache Benchmark test performed in step 8. Because `gear-2` has a weight of 1 and `gear-1` has a weight of 2, gear 1 will serve twice as many requests as gear 2. You can verify that by looking at the following HAProxy status page (screenshot):

| express | | | | | | | | | | | |
| --- | --- | --- | --- | --- | --- | --- | --- | --- | --- | --- | --- |
| | Queue | | | Session rate | | | Sessions | | | | |
| | Cur | Max | Limit | Cur | Max | Limit | Cur | Max | Limit | Total | LbTot |
| Frontend | | | | 0 | 172 | - | 0 | 35 | 128 | 1 000 | |
| gear-53d31f4f5004468f52000060-osbook | 0 | 0 | - | 0 | 57 | | 0 | 20 | - | 333 | 333 |
| local-gear | 0 | 0 | - | 0 | 114 | | 0 | 15 | - | 667 | 667 |
| Backend | 0 | 0 | | 0 | 171 | | 0 | 20 | 128 | 1 000 | 1 000 |

## See also

▸ The *Configuring a different health check URL for HAProxy* recipe

▸ The *Enabling manual scaling with marker files* recipe

# Creating scalable apps from nonscalable apps

OpenShift currently does not support the conversion of an existing nonscalable application to a scalable application. In this recipe, you will learn how to create a new scalable application using an existing nonscalable application.

## Getting ready

To complete this recipe, you will need `rhc` installed on your machine. This recipe will require all three available gears, so please make sure to delete any existing applications.

## How to do it...

Perform the following steps to covert a nonscalable application to a scalable application:

1. Open a new command-line terminal and navigate to a convenient location where you want to create the application.

2. Create a nonscalable application with JBoss EAP 6 using the following command:

   ```
   $ rhc create-app jobstore jbosseap postgresql-9.2 --from-code
   https://github.com/OpenShift-Cookbook/chapter7-jobstore-
   javaee6.git
   ```

3. To create a scalable application using the application created in step 2, run the following command:

   ```
   $ rhc create-app jobstorescalable --from-app jobstore --
   scaling
   ```

## How it works...

Using another application as a template, you can create a new application using the `--from-app` option. When you specify the `--from-app` option, OpenShift will use the template application configuration to create the new application. The configuration includes existing cartridges, storage configuration, gear sizes, scaling configuration, deployment configuration, and so on.

In the preceding steps, you created a scalable application from a nonscalable application. Because you want to create a scalable application, you have to provide the `--scaling` option; otherwise, a nonscalable application will be created. You can also specify different gear sizes using the `--gear-size` option:

```
$ rhc create-app jobstorescalable --from-app jobstore --scaling --
gear-size large
```

Apart from `--scaling` and `--gear-size`, you can also provide the `--env`, `--no-git`, and `--enable-jenkins` options.

The `--from-app` option makes use of application snapshots to transfer the template application data and Git repository. It first takes the `jobstore` application snapshot, transfers it to the `jobstorescalable` application, and then restores it. This can be seen in the application creation logs as shown in the following command line:

```
Setting deployment configuration ... done
Pulling down a snapshot of application 'jobstore' to
/var/folders/9s/kp39j6zj1wg90n4jwshtdykh0000gn/T/jobstore_temp_clone.
tar.gz

...

done
Restoring from snapshot
/var/folders/9s/kp39j6zj1wg90n4jwshtdykh0000gn/T/jobstore_temp_clone.
tar.gz to application

'jobstorescalable' ...

done
```

> The cartridge data is not transferred when you create an application using `--from-app`, but any data stored in `$OPENSHIFT_DATA_DIR` is transferred to the new application.

## See also

▸ The *Creating scalable applications* recipe
▸ The *Enabling manual scaling with marker files* recipe

# Enabling manual scaling with marker files

In this recipe, you will learn how you can disable autoscaling and add gears manually to a scalable application using the `rhc` command-line tool.

## Getting ready

To complete this recipe, you will need `rhc` installed on your machine. This recipe will utilize the application created in the *Creating scalable applications* recipe.

## How to do it...

Perform the following steps to manually add a new gear to a scalable application:

1. Open a command-line terminal and navigate to the application directory created in the *Creating scalable applications* recipe.

2. Create a new marker file with the name `disable_auto_scaling` in the `.openshift/marker` directory inside your application director. On Mac and Linux machines, you can use the following command:

   ```
   $ touch .openshift/markers/disable_auto_scaling
   ```

3. On Windows machines, you can create a new file using the **File** menu.

4. Commit the file to the local Git repository, and push the changes to the OpenShift application gear Git repository using the following commands:

   ```
   $ git add .
   $ git commit -am "disabled auto scaling"
   $ git push
   ```

5. Restart the HAProxy cartridge so that it does not run the `haproxy_ctld` process. The `haproxy_ctld` process is responsible for publishing scale-up and scale-down events. Have a look at the following command:

   ```
   $ rhc cartridge-restart haproxy
   ```

6. Now, to add a new gear to your application, you can use the following command:

   ```
   $ rhc scale-up-app --app jobstore
   ```

7. To remove a gear from your application, you can use the following command:

   ```
   $ rhc scale-down-app --app jobstore
   ```

## How it works...

OpenShift scalable applications are by default autoscalable in nature, which means they can add or remove web cartridge gears based on the number of concurrent users. While autoscaling is useful in most cases, there are times when you will prefer to control the scaling behavior yourself. You will enable manual scaling in situations where you can anticipate web traffic on your application well in advance. Examples are a holiday season or a promotion, where you know in advance that you can expect more visitors to your applications. For such situations, you can enable manual scaling to have a bunch of gears available to serve the web traffic.

OpenShift allows users to manually add or remove gears using the `rhc scale-up-app` or `rhc scale-down-app` commands. These commands add or remove one gear at a time. Under the covers, these commands use the OpenShift REST API to publish scale-up and scale-down events to the broker. OpenShift Broker consumes these requests and acts accordingly. After running the `rhc scale-up-app` command in step 5, you should see that the `jobstore` application is consuming three gears. You can also see the new gear in the HAProxy status page:

```
$ rhc show-app --app jobstore
jobstore @ http://jobstore-osbook.rhcloud.com/ (uuid:
53d405dd4382ec661c001842)
-------------------------------------------------------------------------
------
  Domain:        osbook
  Created:       1:17 AM
  Gears:         3 (defaults to small)
```

## There's more...

As mentioned in the preceding section, the `rhc scale-up-app` or `scale-down-app` commands use the REST API to add or remove a gear. So, if you don't want to use OpenShift tooling to perform manual scaling, then you can call the REST API yourself to add or remove gears from the application.

To scale up using `curl`, you can run the following command:

```
curl -k -X POST
https://openshift.redhat.com/broker/rest/domains/{domain_name}
/applications/{app_name}/events --user
"openshift_login:openshift_login_password" --data
"event=scale-up"
```

Replace `domain_name`, `app_name`, `openshift_login`, and `openshift_login_password` with their respective values.

To scale down using `curl`, you can run the wfollowing command:

```
curl -k -X POST
https://openshift.redhat.com/broker/rest/domains/{domain_name}/applic
ations/{app_name}/events --user
"openshift_login:openshift_login_password" --data "event=scale-down"
```

## See also

- ▶ The *Creating scalable applications* recipe
- ▶ The *Enabling manual scaling with marker files* recipe

# Running OpenShift on a Virtual Machine

OpenShift Origin is the free and open source flavor of OpenShift PaaS. It is the upstream project to both OpenShift Online and Enterprise. You will learn how to run OpenShift Origin in a **Virtual Machine** (**VM**) running on your machine. This will help you work with OpenShift even when you are not connected to the Internet. You can use the OpenShift Origin VM as your development environment to test your changes, and then when you are ready for deployment, you can push the source code to OpenShift Online. To use the OpenShift Origin VM as your development environment, run the `rhc setup --server` command. The `--server` option should point to the OpenShift Origin VM broker. You can refer to the *Specifying a different OpenShift server hostname* recipe in *Chapter 1, Getting Started with OpenShift*, for more details.

To prepare yourself, you will need to have VirtualBox installed on your machine. If you do not have it installed, please download it from the official website at `https://www.virtualbox.org/`. Also, install the 7-Zip software for your operating system, which you can download from its official website at `http://www.7-zip.org/download.html`.

Perform the following steps to run OpenShift on a VM:

1. Download the OpenShift Origin Version 3 VM image. The VM is over 2 GB in size. You can run the following command:

   ```
   $ wget https://mirror.openshift.com/pub/origin-
   server/release/3/images/openshift-origin.zip -secure-
   protocol=SSLv3
   ```

2. Windows users can download either via the browser, or they can first download the `wget` software for Windows at `http://gnuwin32.sourceforge.net/packages/wget.htm`, and then use it to download the OpenShift Origin VM.

3. The advantage of using `wget` is that you can resume the partial download using the `-c` option. This will help if you are at a location where the Internet connection is not stable, so you can resume the download using the following command:

```
$ wget -c  https://mirror.openshift.com/pub/origin-
server/release/3/images/openshift-origin.zip --secure-
protocol=SSLv3
```

4. Next, unpack the zip archive using the 7-Zip file archiver:

```
$ 7z x openshift-origin.zip
```

5. Typing in this command will result in three additional files, as shown in the next command:

```
$ ls -1t
```

These are `OpenShift Origin Release 3.vmx`, `OpenShift Origin Release 3.vbox`, and `origin-rel3.vmdk`.

6. Start the VirtualBox manager, and click on the **New** button. Have a look at the following screenshot:

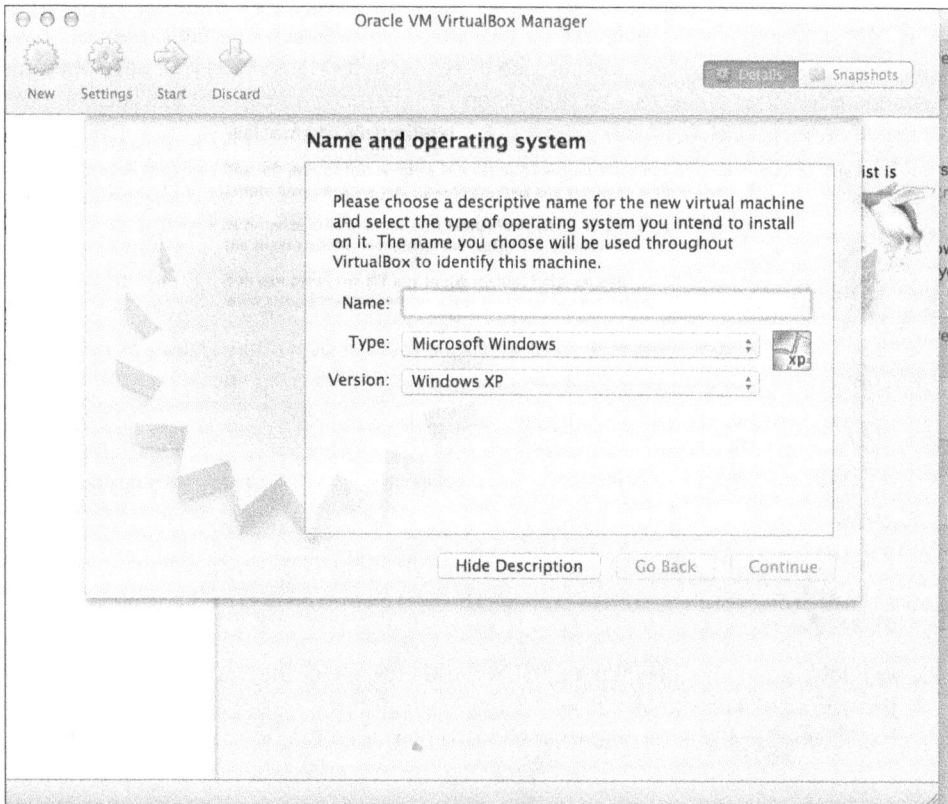

7. Change the details required for the OpenShift Origin VM. You can keep whatever name you like, but you have to use **Type** as **Linux** and **Version** as **Fedora (64 bit)**. Have a look at the following screenshot:

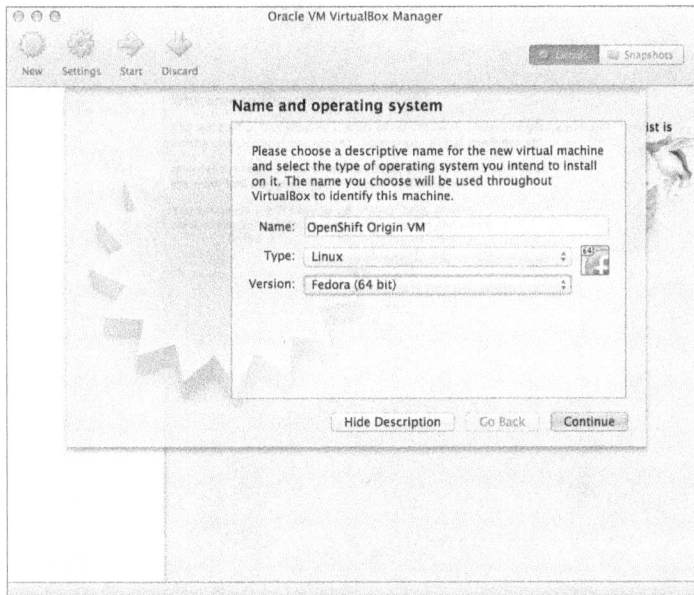

8. Next, set the memory size to 1 GB, as this will give the VM a reasonable amount of memory to work well with. Have a look at the following screenshot:

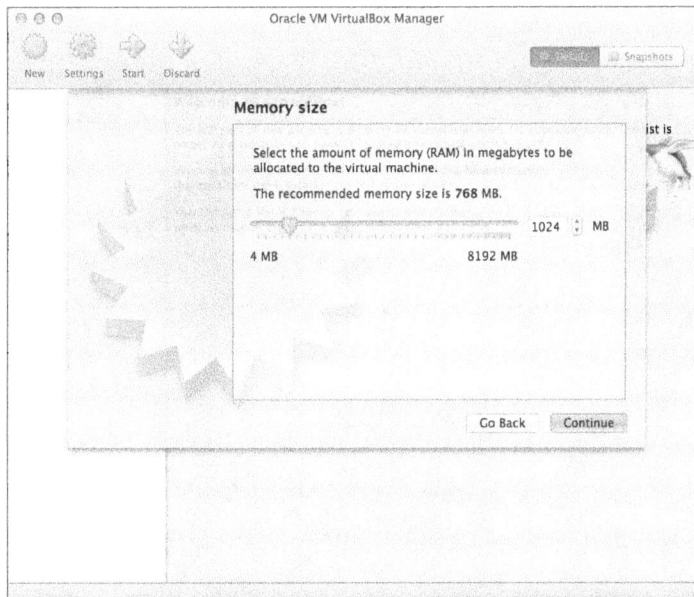

9. Next, you will add a virtual hard drive to the new machine. Please select the **Use an existing virtual hard drive file** option, and click on the **Choose a virtual hard drive file upload** button. Have a look at the following screenshot:

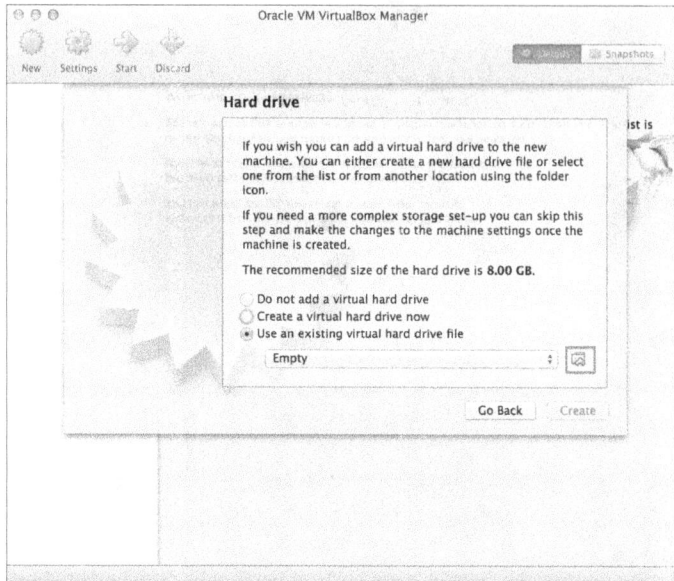

10. VirtualBox will present a file selection dialog. Browse to find the `origin-rel3.vmdk` file, and select it. Click on the button labeled **Open**. Have a look at the following screenshot:

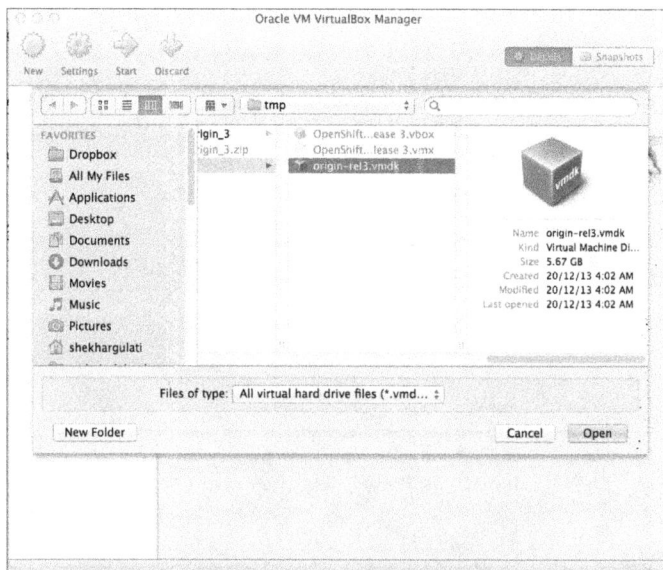

11. After selecting the file, click on **Create** to create a new VM. You will see a new VM in the virtual manager display. Have a look at the following screenshot:

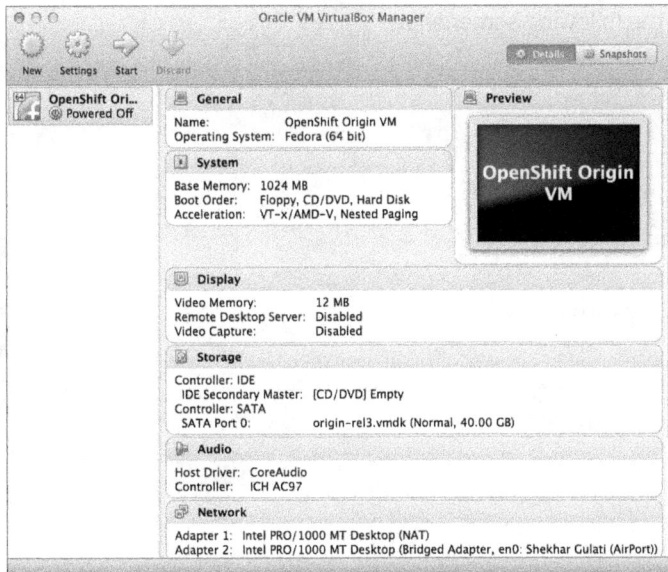

12. Next, you will set up a bridged network adapter, which will allow you to work with the OpenShift Origin VM from your local machine. Select the VM, and right-click on it. Then, click on the **Settings** icon:

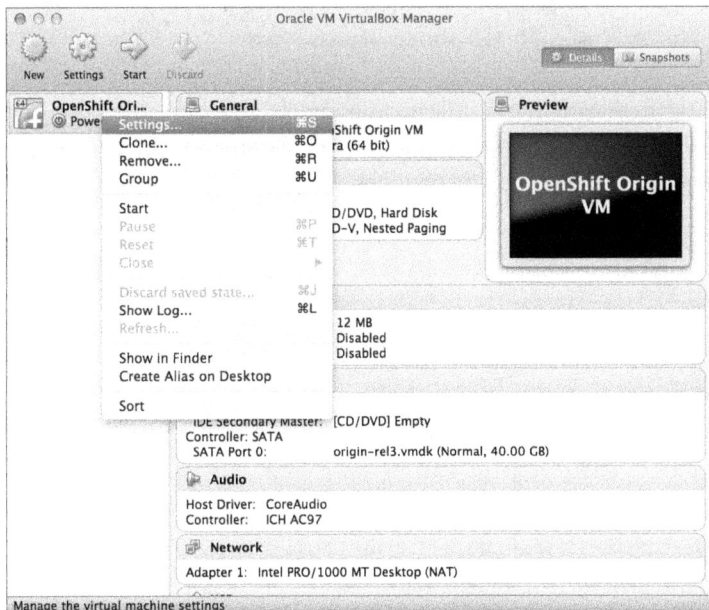

13. Navigate to the **Network** settings, and select **Adapter 2**. Check the **Enable Network Adapter** checkbox, and then set the **Attached to** drop-down menu to **Bridged Adapter**. Finally, set the name to the network adapter you want to bridge. Have a look at the following screenshot:

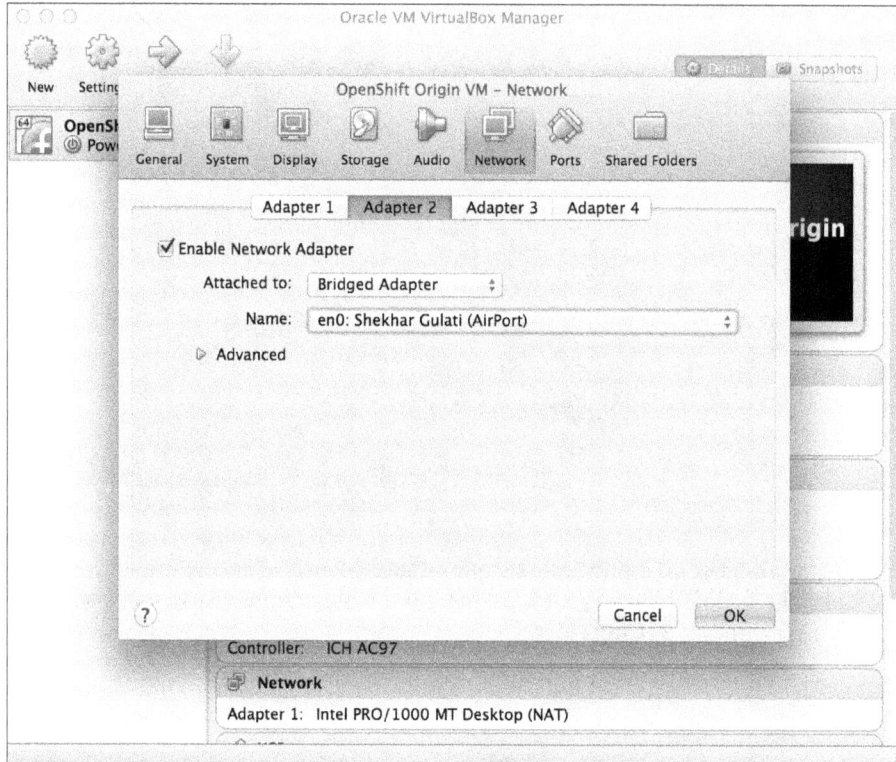

Each system may have different names for their physical network adaptors. Click on **OK** after making the preceding changes.

14. Start the VM by clicking on the **Start** button. Have a look at the following screenshot:

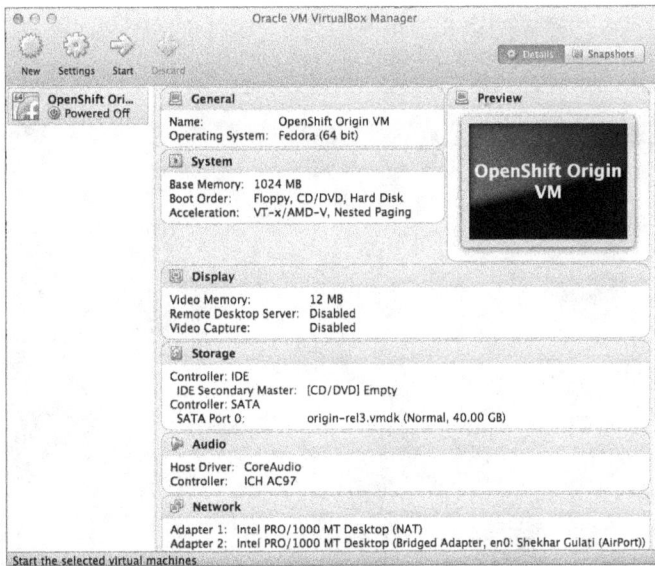

15. When the VM has finished booting, it will present you with a tutorial that will help you understand how to work with the OpenShift Origin VM, as shown in the following screenshot:

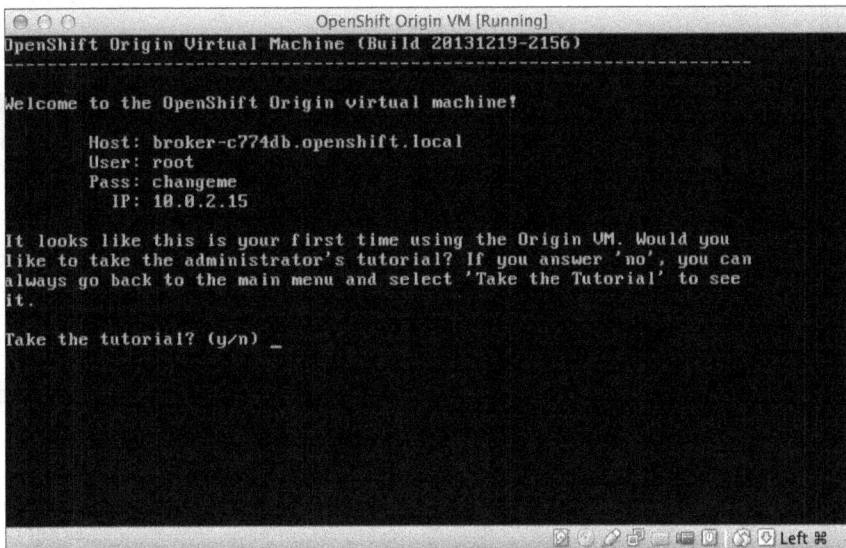

After you enter `yes`, the tutorial will walk you through the features of the OpenShift Origin VM from an administrator's perspective.

16. After finishing the admin tutorial, you will be shown a menu where you can select options to interact with the OpenShift Origin VM. Choose the second option to connect with the web console. You will be shown the web console details, as shown in the following screenshot:

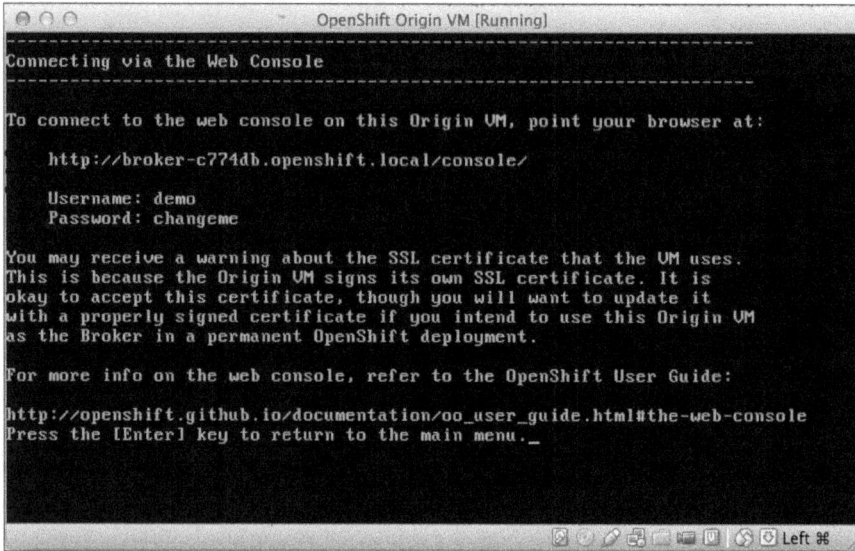

17. Copy the URL and paste it into your browser. The default username/password combination is demo/changeme. Have a look at the following screenshot:

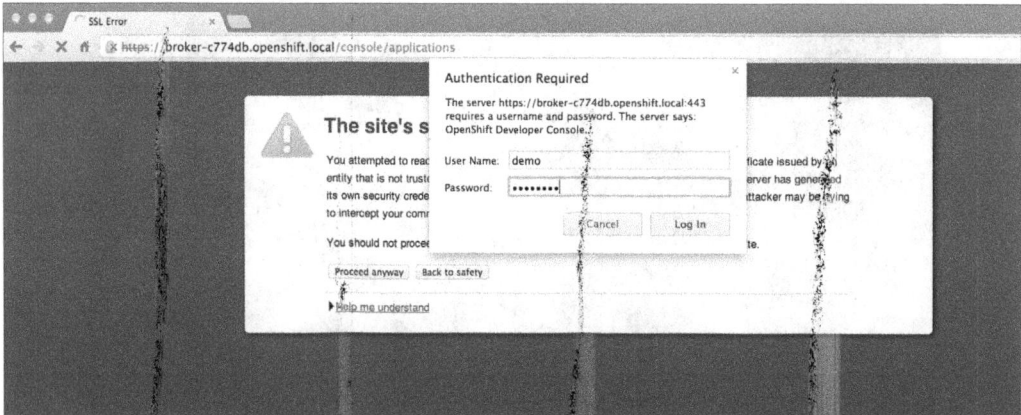

Log in to the web console using the default username and password. You will be directed to the application creation page. You can create the WordPress application by following the steps mentioned in the *Creating a WordPress application using the web console* recipe in *Chapter 1, Getting Started with OpenShift*.

# Index

## O

OpenJDK 6
 switching to 224, 225
OpenShift
 about 8, 68
 Amazon RDS MySQL DB instance,
  using with 134-140
 components 10
 EnterpriseDB PostgreSQL Cloud Database,
  using with 162-164
 MongoLab MongoDB-as-a-Service, using
  with 183-187
 reference, for sign-up page 11, 12
 reference link, for application settings web
  page 13
 reference link, for applications web page 15
 reference link, for domain web page 49
 reference link, for quickstarts 17
 running, on VM 397-404
OpenShift account
 reference link, for settings web page 24
 setting up, rhc used 36, 37
OpenShift application psql shell
 configuring, .psqlrc configuration file
  used 157-159
OpenShift applications
 downloadable cartridges, using with 83, 84
 Jenkins workflow, creating for 353-357
OpenShift blog
 URL 324
OPENSHIFT_DATA_DIR environment
  variable 91
OpenShift domains
 creating, web console used 12-14
OpenShift Enterprise 9
OpenShift Java applications
 developing, Eclipse used 233-245
OpenShift Node.js applications
 CoffeeScript, using with 326-328
OpenShift Online
 about 9
 reference link, for account settings
  web page 12
 reference link, for login page 12

OpenShift Online account
 creating 11, 12
OpenShift Online pricing
 reference link 9, 12
OpenShift Origin 9, 397
OpenShift PaaS 397
OpenShift server hostname
 specifying 41, 42
OpenShift SFTP support
 URL 302
OpenShift Travis CI integration
 URL, for blog 330
OpenShift web console
 PostgreSQL database, adding from 148, 149

## P

pam_namespace 69
pattern codes
 %a 377
 %A 377
 %b 377
 %B 378
 %D 378
 %h 378
 %H 378
 %I 378
 %l 378
 %m 378
 %p 378
 %q 378
 %r 378
 %s 378
 %S 378
 %t 378
 %T 378
 %u 378
 %U 378
 %v 378
pgAdmin
 URL, for downloading 152
 used, for connecting PostgreSQL
  cartridge 152-155
phpMyAdmin
 about 120
 URL 120

## Thank you for buying
# OpenShift Cookbook

## About Packt Publishing

Packt, pronounced 'packed', published its first book "*Mastering phpMyAdmin for Effective MySQL Management*" in April 2004 and subsequently continued to specialize in publishing highly focused books on specific technologies and solutions.

Our books and publications share the experiences of your fellow IT professionals in adapting and customizing today's systems, applications, and frameworks. Our solution based books give you the knowledge and power to customize the software and technologies you're using to get the job done. Packt books are more specific and less general than the IT books you have seen in the past. Our unique business model allows us to bring you more focused information, giving you more of what you need to know, and less of what you don't.

Packt is a modern, yet unique publishing company, which focuses on producing quality, cutting-edge books for communities of developers, administrators, and newbies alike. For more information, please visit our website: www.packtpub.com.

## About Packt Open Source

In 2010, Packt launched two new brands, Packt Open Source and Packt Enterprise, in order to continue its focus on specialization. This book is part of the Packt Open Source brand, home to books published on software built around Open Source licenses, and offering information to anybody from advanced developers to budding web designers. The Open Source brand also runs Packt's Open Source Royalty Scheme, by which Packt gives a royalty to each Open Source project about whose software a book is sold.

## Writing for Packt

We welcome all inquiries from people who are interested in authoring. Book proposals should be sent to author@packtpub.com. If your book idea is still at an early stage and you would like to discuss it first before writing a formal book proposal, contact us; one of our commissioning editors will get in touch with you.

We're not just looking for published authors; if you have strong technical skills but no writing experience, our experienced editors can help you develop a writing career, or simply get some additional reward for your expertise.

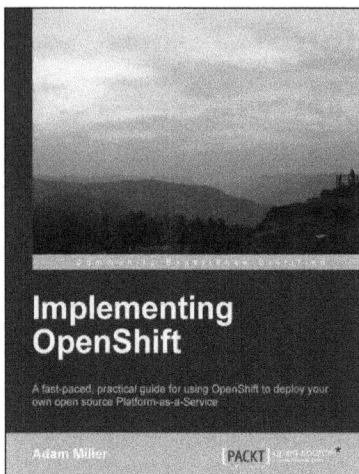

## Implementing OpenShift

ISBN: 978-1-78216-472-2          Paperback: 116 pages

A fast-paced, practical guide for using OpenShift to deploy your own open source Platform-as-a-Service

1. Discover what the cloud is, tear through the marketing jargon, and go right to the tech.

2. Understand what makes an open source Platform-as-a-Service work by learning about OpenShift architecture.

3. Deploy your own OpenShift Platform-as-a-Service cloud using DevOps orchestration and configuration management.

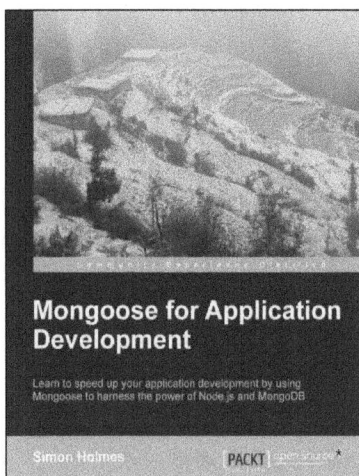

## Mongoose for Application Development

ISBN: 978-1-78216-819-5          Paperback: 142 pages

Learn to speed up your application development by using Mongoose to harness the power of Node.js and MongoDB

1. Rapid application development with Mongoose on the Node.js stack.

2. Use Mongoose to give structure and manageability to MongoDB data.

3. Practical examples on how to use Mongoose for CRUD operations.

4. Provides a number of helpful tips and takes away the complexity of everyday MongoDB operations.

Please check **www.PacktPub.com** for information on our titles

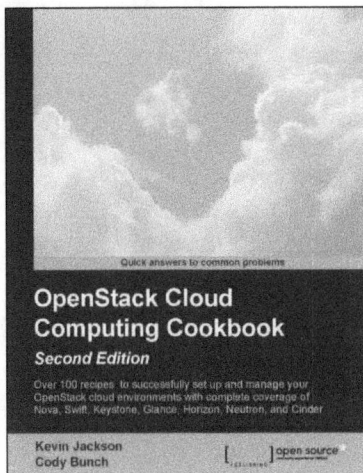

## OpenStack Cloud Computing Cookbook
### Second Edition

ISBN: 978-1-78216-758-7          Paperback: 396 pages

Over 100 recipes to successfully set up and manage your OpenStack cloud environments with complete coverage of Nova, Swift, Keystone, Glance, Horizon, Neutron, and Cinder

1.  Updated for OpenStack Grizzly.

2.  Learn how to install, configure, and manage all of the OpenStack core projects including new topics such as block storage and software defined networking.

3.  Learn how to build your Private Cloud utilizing DevOps and Continuous Integration tools and techniques.

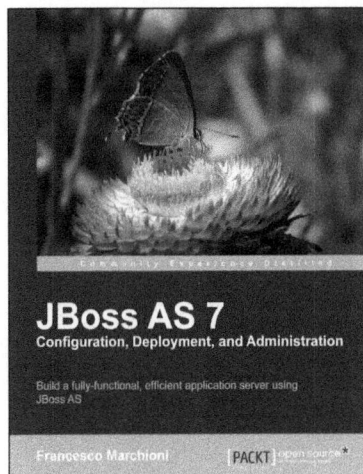

## JBoss AS 7
## Configuration, Deployment, and Administration

ISBN: 978-1-84951-678-5          Paperback: 380 pages

Build a fully-functional, efficient application server using JBoss AS

1.  Covers all JBoss AS 7 administration topics in a concise, practical, and understandable manner, along with detailed explanations and lots of screenshots.

2.  Uncover the advanced features of JBoss AS, including High Availability and clustering, integration with other frameworks, and creating complex AS domain configurations.

3.  Discover the new features of JBoss AS 7, which has made quite a departure from previous versions.

Please check **www.PacktPub.com** for information on our titles

www.ingramcontent.com/pod-product-compliance
Lightning Source LLC
Chambersburg PA
CBHW080140220326
41598CB00032B/5124